주한미군지위협정(SOFA)

서명 및 발효 9

주한미군지위협정(SOFA)

서명 및 발효 9

한국학술정보

| 머리말

미국은 오래전부터 우리나라 외교에 있어서 가장 긴밀하고 실질적인 우호 · 협력관계를 맺어 온 나라다. 6 · 25전쟁 정전 협정이 체결된 후 북한의 재침을 막기 위한 대책으로서 1953년 11월 한미 상호방위조약이 체결되었다. 이는 미군이 한국에 주둔하는 법적 근거였고, 그렇게 주둔하게 된 미군의 시설, 구역, 사업, 용역, 출입국, 통관과 관세, 재판권 등 포괄적인 법적 지위를 규정하는 것이 바로 주한미군지위협정(SOFA)이다. 그러나 이와 관련한 협상은 계속된 난항을 겪으며 한미 상호방위조약이 체결로부터 10년이 훌쩍 넘은 1967년이 돼서야 정식 발효에 이를 수 있었다. 그럼에도 당시 미군 범죄에 대한 한국의 재판권은 심한 제약을 받았으며, 1980년대 후반 민주화 운동과 함께 미군 범죄 문제가 사회적 이슈로 떠오르자 협정을 개정해야 한다는 목소리가 커지게 되었다. 이에 1991년 2월 주한미군지위협정 1차 개정이 진행되었고, 이후에도 여러 사건이 발생하며 2001년 4월 2차 개정이 진행되어 현재에 이르고 있다.

본 총서는 외교부에서 작성하여 최근 공개한 주한미군지위협정(SOFA) 관련 자료를 담고 있다. 1953년 한미 상호방위조약 체결 이후부터 1967년 발효가 이뤄지기까지의 자료와 더불어, 이후 한미 합동위원회을 비롯해 민 · 형사재판권, 시설, 노무, 교통 등 각 분과위원회의 회의록과 운영 자료, 한국인 고용인 문제와 관련한 자료, 기타 관련 분쟁 자료 등을 포함해 총 42권으로 구성되었다. 전체 분량은 약 2만 2천여 쪽에 이른다.

2024년 3월

한국학술정보(주)

| 일러두기

· 본 총서에 실린 자료는 2022년 4월과 2023년 4월에 각각 공개한 외교문서 4,827권, 76만 여 쪽 가운데 일부를 발췌한 것이다.

· 각 권의 제목과 순서는 공개된 원본을 최대한 반영하였으나, 주제에 따라 일부는 적절히 변경하였다.

· 원본 자료는 A4 판형에 맞게 축소하거나 원본 비율을 유지한 채 A4 페이지 안에 삽입하였다. 또한 현재 시점에선 공개되지 않아 '공란'이란 표기만 있는 페이지 역시 그대로 실었다.

· 외교부가 공개한 문서 각 권의 첫 페이지에는 '정리 보존 문서 목록'이란 이름으로 기록물 종류, 일자, 명칭, 간단한 내용 등의 정보가 수록되어 있으며, 이를 기준으로 0001번부터 번호가 매겨져 있다. 이는 삭제하지 않고 총서에 그대로 수록하였다.

· 보고서 내용에 관한 더 자세한 정보가 필요하다면, 외교부가 온라인상에 제공하는 『대한민국 외교사료요약집』 1991년과 1992년 자료를 참조할 수 있다.

| 차례

정/리/보/존/문/서/목/록					
기록물종류	문서-일반공문서철	등록번호	922 9595	등록일자	2006-07-27
분류번호	741.12	국가코드	US	주제	
문서철명	한.미국 간의 상호방위조약 제4조에 의한 시설과 구역 및 한국에서의 미국군대의 지위에 관한 협정 (SOFA) 전59권. 1966.7.9 서울에서 서명 : 1967.2.9 발효 (조약 232호) *원본				
생산과	미주과/조약과	생산년도	1952 - 1967	보존기간	영구
담당과(그룹)	조약	조약	서가번호	--	
참조분류					
권차명	V.24 실무교섭회의, 제57-62차, 1964.7-8월				
내용목차	1. 제57차 회의, 7.8 (p.2~19) 2. 제58차 회의, 7.16 (p.20~45) 3. 제59차 회의, 7.28 (p.46~) 4. 제60차 회의, 8.7 (p.~169) 5. 제61차 회의, 8.14 (p.170~206) 6. 제62차 회의, 8.28 (p.207~256) * 일지 : 1953.8.7 이승만 대통령-Dulles 미국 국무장관 공동성명 - 상호방위조약 발효 후 군대지위협정 교섭 약속 1954.12.2 정부, 주한 UN군의 관세업무협정 체결 제의 1955.1월, 5월 미국, 제의 거절 1955.4.28 정부, 군대지위협정 제의 (한국측 초안 제시) 1957.9.10 Hurter 미국 국무차관 방한 시 각서 수교 (한국측 제의 수락 요구) 1957.11.13, 26 정부, 개별 협정의 단계적 체결 제의 1958.9.18 Dawling 주한미국대사, 형사재판관할권 협정 제외 조건으로 행정협정 체결 의사 전달 1960.3.10 정부, 토지, 시설협정의 우선적 체결 강력 요구 1961.4.10 장면 국무총리-McConaughy 주한미국대사 공동성명으로 교섭 개시 합의 1961.4.15, 4.25 제1, 2차 한.미국 교섭회의 (서울) 1962.3.12 정부, 교섭 재개 촉구 공한 송부 1962.5.14 Burger 주한미국대사, 최규하 장관 면담 시 형사재판관할권 문제 제기 않는 조건으로 교섭 재개 통고 1962.9.6 한.미국 간 공동성명 발표 (9월 중 교섭 재개 합의) 1962.9.20~ 1965.6.7 제1-81차 실무 교섭회의 (서울) 1966.7.8 제82차 실무 교섭회의 (서울) 1966.7.9 서명 1967.2.9 발효 (조약 232호)					

마/이/크/로/필/름/사/항				
촬영연도	*롤 번호	화일 번호	후레임 번호	보관함 번호
2006-11-22	I-06-0069	01	1-256	

0001

1. 제57차 회의, 7.8

0002

기 안 용 지

관리번호 1482

자체통제		기안처	미주과 이근팔	전화번호	근거서류접수일자
	과장	국장	차관	장관	
관계관 서명					
기안년월일	1964. 7. 11.	시행년월일		보존년한	정서기장
분류기호	외구미 722.2—	전체통제		종결	
경유 수신 참조	대통령 참조: 비서실장 국무총리 참조: 비서실장			발신	장관
제목	제 57 차 주둔군지위협정 체결 교섭 실무자회의 개최 보고				

1964. 7. 8. 하오 3시 부터 동 4시 까지 외무부 제 1 회의실에서 개최된 제 57 차 주둔군지위협정 체결 교섭 실무자 회의에서 토의된 내용을 별첨과 같이 보고합니다.

유 첨: 제 57 차주둔군지위협정 체결 교섭실무자회의 보고서

끝.

발 No. 327 1964. 7. 15 외무부

보통문서로 재분류(1966.12.31.)

1966, 12. 31 예고문에 의거 일반문서로 재분류됨

승인서식 1—1—3 (11 00900 03) (195mm×265mm16절지)

0003

제 57 차

한.미 간 주둔군지위협정 체결 교섭실무자회의

보 고 서

1. 일 시: 1964 년 7 월 8 일 하오 3 시 부터 동 4 시 까지.

2. 장 소: 외무부 제 1 회의실

3. 토의사항:

가. 관세업무

(1) 양측은 군사화물이라함은 미군대에 탁송되는 무기 및 장비 뿐만 않이라 비세출자금기관 앞으로 송부되는 화물까지 포함하며 비세출자금기관 앞으로 송부되는 화물에 관한 정보는 정규적으로 한국당국에 제공되어야 한다는 점에 합의를 보았으며 이에 관련하여 다음과 같은 2 개의 양해사항을 채택하였다.

(가) 제공될 정보는 적하목록 및 기타 선적서류를 포함한다.

(나) 정규적으로 제공되는 정보에 추가하여 합동위원회를 통하여 요구하면 기타 필요한 정보가 제공되어야 한다.

(2) 양측은 또한 휴가목적을 제외하고 공무로 한국을 출입국하는 미군대구성원에 대하여서는 세관검사를 면제하는데 합의하였다.

(3) 공적우편물에 대한 세관검사의 면제문제는 이미 제 41 차 회의에서 합의된 바 있는데 미측대표의 요청에 의하여 다음과 같은 양해사항을 가록에 추가하기로 하였다.

(가) 공적우편 표식이 없는 제 1 종 서신우편물에 대하여서도 한국정부는 관계 현행법령에 따라 세관검사를 면제한다.

(나) 공적문서라 ~~및 소포라~~ 함은 공적으로 이서된 또는 미군 기관으로 탁송되는 문서 및 소포를 포함한다.

(4) 기타 양측은 미군대구성원 군속 및 그들의 가족이 입국 후 6 개월 이내에 그들의 개인용품과 가재도구를 반입함에 있어서 적당한 수량으로 한정할 것에 합의하고 다음과 같은 양해사항을 유보하였다.

(가) 적당한 수량 여부 결정의 제 1 차적 책임이 미군당국에 있으나 한국당국~~은~~이 필요하다고 인정하는 때에는 합동위원회에서 토의할 수 있는 기회가 부여되어야 한다.

0004

64-3-41

64-3-23(2)　　미.문 110-4 (2)

0005

(5) 이상으로 관세조항에서는 비세출자금기관 사용자의 범위가 결정됨에 따라 자동적으로 결정될 미군 commissary 에 관한 문제를 제외한 모든 문제에 합의를 보았다.

4. 군계약자

(1) 양측은 군계약자 소유 차량 및 그 고용자 또는 그들의 가족의 사유차량에 대하여서는 차량관계 세금을 면제하는 대신 운전면허 및 차량등록에 관한 법령을 준수할 것과 그에 따른 각종 수수료를 납부한다는 원칙에 합의를 보았다.
양측은 또한 이들에게 적용될 운전면허 및 차량등록에 관한 수수료는 일반 한국인에게 적용되는 것과 동일할 것과 이들의 언어상의 장애에 대하여 응분의 고려가 되어야 한다는 점에 양해를 보았다.

(2) 군계약자에 대한 형사재판관할권 행사문제는 형사재판관할권에 관한 조항의 토의가 끝날 때까지 보류하기로 하였으며 이상으로 기타 군계약자에 관한 문제는 모두 합의를 보게 되었다.

4. 기타 사항: 차기 회의 일자: 1964 년 7 월 16 일 하오 3 시부터. 끝.

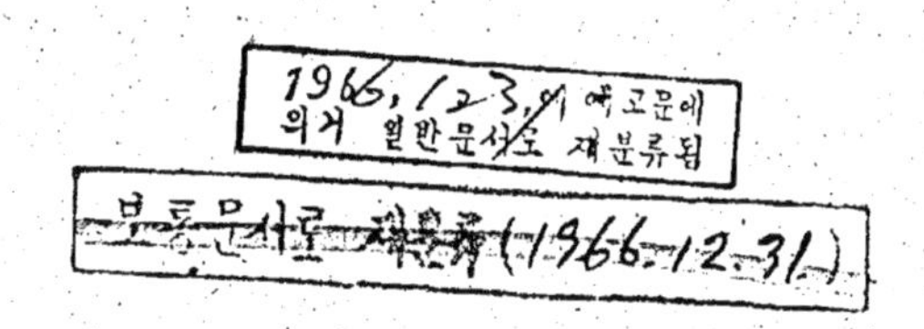
1966, 12.3, 예고문에 의거 일반문서로 재분류됨
보통문서로 재분류(1966.12.31.)

0006

64-) -62

CONFIDENTIAL

STATUS OF FORCES NEGOTIATIONS: 57th Meeting

SUBJECTS: 1. Customs
2. Invited Contractors

PLACE: Ministry of Foreign Affairs

DATE: July 8, 1964

PARTICIPANTS:

Republic of Korea

CHANG Sang-mun
KU Chung-hoe
Colonel KIM Won-kil, ROKA
Major YI Kae-hun, ROKA
CHO Chung-hun
YI Kae-chol
YI Kun-pal (Interpreter)
HWANG Yong-chae
HUH, Hyung Koo

United States

Philip C. Habib
Brig. General G.G. O'Connor, USA
Colonel Howard Smigelow, USA
Captain John ~~Wayne~~ Wayne, USN
Colonel Kenneth C. Crawford, USA
~~[illegible]~~ Benjamin A. Fleck
Robert A. Kinney
Lt. Colonel Charles Wright, USA
Robert A. Lewis

0008

Customs

1. Mr. Chang opened the meeting by referring to previous discussions of the Customs Article. He recalled that with regard to Agreed Minute #3, the negotiators had already agreed on language that would provide for the furnishing by the U.S. armed forces on a routine basis of pertinent information on cargo consigned to non-appropriated fund organizations. He recalled that at the 56th meeting the Korean negotiators had offered to accept the revision of Agreed Minute #3 tabled by the U.S. negotiators at the 55th meeting if the U.S. negotiators would agree to include two understandings in the negotiating record. In reply, the U.S. negotiators had counterproposed the following understanding:

"With respect to Agreed Minute #3, in addition to the information provided on a routine basis, other pertinent information will be provided on request through the Joint Committee."

2. Mr. Chang stated that informal conversations had been held subsequent to the 56th meeting and had been fruitful, in the opinion of the Korean negotiators. The Korean negotiators were now prepared to agree to the revision of Agreed Minute #3 tabled by the U.S. negotiators, provided the U.S. negotiators would agree to include the following two understandings in the negotiating record:

a. Pertinent information shall include cargo manifests and shipping documents;

b. In addition to information provided on a routine basis, other pertinent information will be provided on request through the Joint Committee.

Mr. Chang noted that if the U.S. negotiators would agree to these understandings full agreement would be reached on [redacted] Agreed Minute #3.

3. Mr. Habib replied that the U.S. negotiators agreed to the inclusion of the proposed understandings in the negotiated record and that full agreement [redacted]

had been reached on Agreed Minute #3.

4. Mr. Habib suggested that the negotiators clear up the remaining points of difference in this article. He recalled that at the 41st meeting, the Korean negotiators had tabled a proposed revision of Paragraph 5(a), with the purpose of distinguishing between members of the U.S. armed forces entering or leaving the Republic of Korea on orders and those travelling for recreational purposes. The U.S. negotiators agreed with the principle proposed by the Korean negotiators but wished to suggest alternative language which was simpler and more precise than that of the Korean revision. Mr. Habib then tabled the following language:

> "(a) Members of the United States armed forces under orders, other than leave orders, entering or leaving the Republic of Korea;"

5. Mr. Chang asked whether travel for rest and recreation ("R and R") was included in the term "leave orders". Upon being assured by Mr. Habib that this was the case, Mr. Chang stated that the Korean negotiators agreed to the revised wording proposed by the U.S. negotiators.

6. Mr. Habib stated that the U.S. negotiators wished to clarify certain aspects of Paragraph 5(b). In that subparagraph, the negotiators had agreed to exempt First Class letter mail under official postal seal from customs examination. During discussions of this subparagraph, the Korean negotiators had stated on several occasions that the Korean authorities had no interest in inspecting First Class letter mail. In view of those statements, and in view of the fact that there might be occasions when First Class letter mail might enter the ROK lacking the official postal seal, the U.S. negotiators would like the Korean negotiators to reaffirm their previous statements that the ROKG has no intention of inspecting First Class letter mail even when it is not under official postal seal. Mr. Habib pointed out that it was the intention of the U.S. authorities that such mail should always enter the ROK under official seal but that if this was not always the case, it would still be clearly identifiable as First

Class mail.

7. Mr. Chang replied that even if First Class letter mail entering the ROK through military post offices was not under official postal seal, in accordance with the relevant ROK laws and regulations, the ROKG would not inspect such mail.

8. Mr. Habib said that the U.S. negotiators also wished to clarify the term "official documents". This term included documents and parcels bearing an official endorsement or addressed to a military organization. Mr. Chang asked whether the term included documents and parcels addressed to individuals in their official capacity. Mr. Habib explained that mail addressed to a military organization included that addressed either to the organization itself or to "The Commanding Officer" of the organization. Personal mail addressed to individual officers by name would not fall within this definition. Mr. Chang replied that the Korean negotiators agreed with this interpretation of the term "official documents".

9. Mr. Habib then recalled that the Korean negotiators had proposed the insertion in Agreed Minute #2 of the phrase "reasonable quantities of" following the word "duty". The U.S. negotiators agreed to that revision but wished to clear up any ambiguity that might exist. It was the understanding of the U.S. negotiators that the U.S. armed forces will be responsible for determining what constitutes "reasonable quantities". If the Korean authorities have any doubts or questions, they can always raise the matter in the Joint Committee.

10. Mr. Chang expressed appreciation for the agreement of the U.S. negotiators to this revision of Agreed Minute #2. The Korean negotiators agreed that the primary responsibility for determining what constitutes "reasonable quantities" would rest with the U.S. military authorities. But they also believed that the Korean authorities should have the opportunity to discuss the question whenever they thought it necessary. Since the spirit of the U.S. negotia-

tors reflected a mood of cooperation, the Korean negotiators were sure that any difficulty which might arise with regard to this Agreed Minute would be satisfactorily resolved by the Joint Committee.

11. Mr. Habib expressed agreement and reiterated that the right of the Korean authorities to raise the matter in the Joint Committee was unquestioned. He commented that full agreement had now been reached on the Customs Article, with the exception of Agreed Minute #7. He asked whether the Korean negotiators had any views to express regarding this Agreed Minute.

12. Mr. Chang replied that Agreed Minute #7 was closely related to the provisions of the article dealing with non-appropriated fund organizations. The Korean negotiators believed that final agreement on the latter article would mean automatic agreement on this Agreed Minute.

13. Mr. Habib agreed and remarked that full agreement had now been reached on the text of the Customs Article.

Invited Contractors

14. Turning to the Invited Contractors Article, Mr. Chang stated that the Korean negotiators had considered the position stated previously by the U.S. negotiators regarding the payment of taxes on vehicles. The Korean negotiators were now prepared to waive all taxes on vehicles, including those privately owned by contractors and their employees, provided the contractors and their employees would respect and obey the laws and regulations relating to registration of vehicles and issuance of driving permits. Therefore, the Korean negotiators were willing to withdraw their proposed Agreed Minute #3 if the U.S. negotiators would withdraw their proposed subparagraph (i) of Paragraph 3.

15. Mr. Habib replied that the U.S. negotiators would agree to the deletion of subparagraph (i), provided that the Korean negotiators would state for the ne-

0012

gotiating record that the registration fees and drivers' permit regulations will be the same for contractors and their employees as for Korean nationals, with due allowance for language problems. The U.S. negotiators considered this to be a reasonable request. All that they were asking for was a statement by the Korean negotiators that there would be no discrimination against the contractors and their employees.

16. Mr. Chang stated that the Korean negotiators wished to outline the following procedures which would be followed with regard to the contractors and their employees:

a. Driving Permits - Anyone holding a valid driving permit issued by a foreign government or subdivision thereof would be required to take a simple test on local traffic regulations and pay a fee of Won 770. This would be handled, if the driver is located in Seoul, by the Traffic Section of the Seoul City Municipal Police Bureau;

b. Registration - Upon presentation of an appropriate certificate regarding the exemption from vehicle tax, the owner of a vehicle would be required to pay registration fees totalling Won 4,355, broken down as follows:

Registration -	W 1000
Inspection -	3060
License Plates	295
	W 4355

17. Mr. Habib asked whether the above-outlined procedures and fees were identical with those applied to Korean citizens. Mr. Chang replied affirmatively. Mr. Habib said it was the understanding of the U.S. negotiators that these procedures applied only to vehicles owned by the contractors or by their employees and did not apply to U.S.Government-owned vehicles used by the contractors. Mr. Chang replied that this was the understanding of the Korean negotiators also. Complete agreement was thereupon reached on the text of the Invited Contractors Article, with the exception of Paragraph 8. It was agreed that further discussion of Paragraph 8 would

be held after agreement had been reached on the Criminal Jurisdiction Article.

18. The next meeting was scheduled for July 16 at 3:00 p.m.

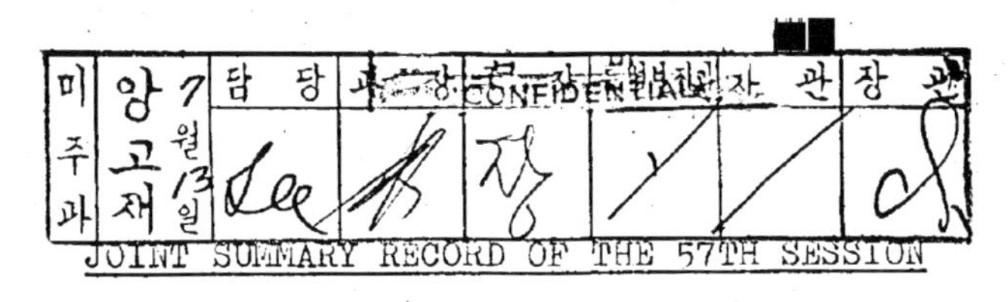

CONFIDENTIAL

JOINT SUMMARY RECORD OF THE 57TH SESSION

1. Time and Place: 3:00 - 4:00 P.M. July 8, 1964 at the Foreign Ministry's Conference Room (No.1)

2. Attendants:

ROK Side

Mr. Chang, Sang Moon	Director European and American Affairs Bureau
Mr. Koo, Choong Whay	Chief, America Section Ministry of Foreign Affairs
Mr. Cho, Choong Hoon	Chief Customs Section Ministry of Finance
Mr. Hur, Hyong Koo	Chief Prosecutors Section Ministry of Justice
Col. Kim, Won Kil	Chief Military Affairs Section Ministry of National Defense
Maj. Lee, Kye Hoon	Military Affairs Section Ministry of National Defense
Mr. Ahn, Yun Gi	3rd Secretary Ministry of Foreign Affairs
Mr. Lee, Keun Pal (Rapporteur and Interpreter)	3rd Secretary Ministry of Foreign Affairs
Mr. Hwang, Young Jae	3rd Secretary Ministry of Foreign Affairs

U.S. Side:

Mr. Philip C. Habib	Counselor American Embassy
Brig. Gen. G.G. O'Connor	Deputy Chief of Staff 8th U.S. Army
Col. Howard Smigelow	Deputy Chief of Staff 8th U.S. Army
Capt. John Wayne	Assistant Chief of Staff USN/K
Col. Kenneth C. Crawford	Staff Judge Advocate 8th U.S. Army

0015

Mr. Benjamin A. Fleck (Rapporteur and Press Officer)	First Secretary American Embassy
Mr. Robert A. Kinney	J-5 8th U.S. Army
Lt. Col. Charles Wright	Staff Judge Advocate's Office 8th U.S. Army
Mr. Robert A. Lewis	2nd Secretary American Embassy
Mr. Edward Hurwitz	2nd Secretary American Embassy

Customs

1. Mr. Chang opened the meeting by referring to previous discussions of the Customs Article. He recalled that with regard to Agreed Minute #3, the negotiators had already agreed on language that would provide for the furnishing by the U.S. armed forces on a routine basis of pertinent information on cargo consigned to non-appropriated fund organizations. He recalled that at the 56th meeting the Korean negotiators had offered to accept the revision of Agreed Minute #3 tabled by the U.S. negotiators at the 55th meeting if the U.S. negotiators would agree to include two understandings in the negotiating record. In reply, the U.S. negotiators had counterproposed the following understanding:

> "With respect to Agreed Minute #3, in addition to the information provided on a routine basis, other pertinent information will be provided on request through the Joint Committee."

2. Mr. Chang stated that informal conversations had been held subsequent to the 56th meeting and had been fruitful, in the opinion of the Korean negotiators. The Korean negotiators were now prepared to agree to the revision of Agreed Minute #3 tabled by the U.S. negotiators, provided the U.S. negotiators would agree to include the following two understandings in the negotiating record:

0016

a. Pertinent information shall include cargo manifests and shipping documents;

b. In addition to information provided on a routine basis, other pertinent information will be provided on request through the Joint Committee.

Mr. Chang noted that if the U.S. negotiators would agree to these understandings full agreement would be reached on Agreed Minute #3.

3. Mr. Habib replied that the U.S. negotiators agreed to the inclusion of the proposed understandings in the negotiated record and that full agreement had been reached on Agreed Minute #3.

4. Mr. Habib suggested that the negotiators clear up the remaining points of difference in this article. He recalled that at the 41st meeting, the Korean negotiators had tabled a proposed revision of Paragraph 5(a), with the purpose of distinguishing between members of the U.S. armed forces entering or leaving the Republic of Korea on orders and those travelling for recreational purposes. The U.S. negotiators agreed with the principle proposed by the Korean negotiators but wished to suggest alternative language which was simpler and more precise than that of the Korean revision. Mr. Habib then tabled the following language:

> "(a) Members of the United States armed forces under orders, other than leave orders, entering or leaving the Republic of Korea;"

5. Mr. Chang asked whether travel for rest and recreation ("R and R") was included in the term "leave orders". Upon being assured by Mr. Habib that this was the case, Mr. Chang stated that the Korean negotiators agreed to the revised wording proposed by the U.S. negotiators.

0017

6. Mr. Habib stated that the U.S. negotiators wished to clarify certain aspects of Paragraph 5(b). In that subparagraph, the negotiators had agreed to exempt First Class letter mail under official postal seal from customs examination. During discussions of this subparagraph, the Korean negotiators had stated on several occasions that the Korean authorities had no interest in inspecting First Class letter mail. In view of those statements, and in view of the fact that there might be occasions when First Class letter mail might enter the ROK lacking the official postal seal, the U.S. negotiators would like the Korean negotiators to reaffirm their previous statements that the ROKG has no intention of inspecting First Class letter mail even when it is not under official postal seal. Mr. Habib pointed out that it was the intention of the U.S. authorities that such mail should always enter the ROK under official seal but that if this was not always the case, it would still be clearly identifiable as First Class mail.

7. Mr. Chang replied that even if First Class letter mail entering the ROK through military post offices was not under official postal seal, the ROKG would not inspect such mail, in accordance with the relevant ROK laws and regulations.

8. Mr. Habib said that the U.S. negotiators also wished to clarify the term "official documents". This term included documents and parcles bearing an official endorsement or addressed to a military organization. Mr. Chang asked whether the term included documents and parcels addressed to individuals in their official capacity. Mr. Habib explained that mail addressed to a military organization included that addressed either to the organization itself or to "The Commanding Officer" of the organization. Personal mail

0018

addressed to individual officers by name would not fall within this definition. Mr. Chang replied that the Korean negotiators agreed with this interpretation of the term "official documents".

9. Mr. Habib then recalled that the Korean negotiators had proposed the insertion in Agreed Minute #2 of the phrase "reasonable quantities of" following the word "duty". The U.S. negotiators agreed to that revision but wished to clear up any ambiguity that might exist. It was the understanding of the U.S. negotiators that the U.S. armed forces will be responsible for determining what constitutes "reasonable quantities". If the Korean authorities have any doubts or questions, they can always raise the matter in the Joint Committee.

10. Mr. Chang expressed appreciation for the agreement of the U.S. negotiators to this revision of Agreed Minute #2. The Korean negotiators agreed that the primary responsibility for determining what constitutes "reasonable quantities" would rest with the U.S. military authorities. But they also believed that the Korean authorities should have the opportunity to discuss the question whenever they thought it necessary. Since the spirit of the U.S. negotiators reflected a mood of cooperation, the Korean negotiators were sure that any difficulty which might arise with regard to this Agreed Minute would be satisfactorily resolved by the Joint Committee.

11. Mr. Habib expressed agreement and reiterated that the right of the Korean authorities to raise the matter in the Joint Committee was unquestioned. He commented that full agreement had now been reached on the Customs Article, with the exception of Agreed Minute #7. He asked whether the Korean negotiators had any views to express regarding this Agreed Minute.

0019

12. Mr. Chang replied that Agreed Minute #7 was closely related to the provisions of the article dealing with non-appropriated fund organizations. The Korean negotiators believed that final agreement on the latter article would mean automatic agreement on this Agreed Minute.

13. Mr. Habib agreed and remarked that full agreement had now been reached on the text of the Customs Article.

Invited Contractors

14. Turning to the Invited Contractors Article, Mr. Chang stated that the Korean negotiators had considered the position stated previously by the U.S. negotiators regarding the payment of taxes on vehicles. The Korean negotiators were now prepared to waive all taxes on vehicles, including those privately owned by contractors and their employees, provided the contractors and their employees would respect and obey the laws and regulations relating to registration of vehicles and issuance of driving permits. Therefore, the Korean negotiators were willing to withdraw their proposed Agreed Minute #3 if the U.S. negotiators would withdraw their proposed subparagraph (i) of Paragraph 3.

15. Mr. Habib replied that the U.S. negotiators would agree to the deletion of subparagraph (i), provided that the Korean negotiators would state for the negotiating record that the registration fees and drivers' permit regulations will be the same for contractors and their employees as for Korean nationals, with due allowance for language problems. The U.S. negotiators considered this to be a reasonable request. All that they were asking for was a statement by the Korean negotiators that there would be no discrimination against the contractors and their employees.

0020

16. Mr. Chang stated that the Korean negotiators wished to outline the following procedures which would be followed with regard to the contractors and their employees:

a. Driving Permits - Anyone holding a valid driving permit issued by a foreign government or subdivision thereof would be required to take a simple test on local traffic regulations and pay a fee of Won 770. This would be handled, if the driver is located in Seoul, by the Traffic Section of the Seoul City Municipal Police Bureau;

b. Registration - Upon presentation of an appropriate certificate regarding the exemption from vehicle tax the owner of a vehicle would be required to pay registration fees totalling Won 4,355, broken down as follows:

Registration -	W 1000
Inspection -	3060
License Plates	295
	W 4355

17. Mr. Habib asked whether the above-outlined procedures and fees were identical with those applied to Korean citizens. Mr. Chang replied affirmatively. Mr. Habib said it was the understanding of the U.S. negotiators that these procedures applied only to vehicles owned by the contractors or by their employees and did not apply to U.S. Government-owned vehicles used by the contractors. Mr. Chang replied that this was the understanding of the Korean negotiators also. Complete agreement was thereupon reached on the text of the Invited Contractors Article, with the exception of Paragraph 8. It was agreed that further discussion of Paragraph 8 would be held after agreement had been reached on the Criminal Jurisdiction Article.

18. The next meeting was scheduled for July 16 at 3:00 p.m.

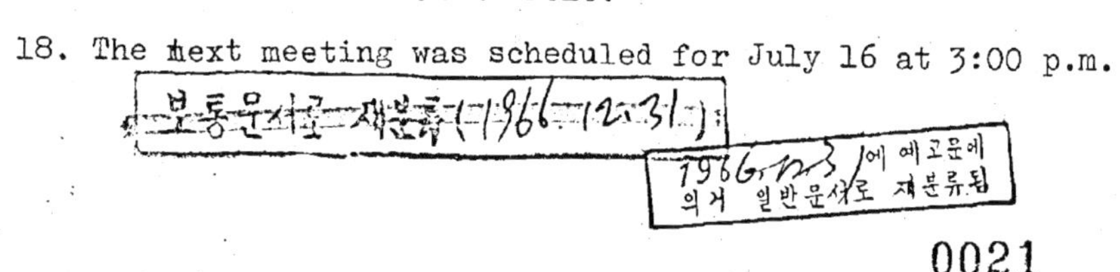

2. 제58차 회의, 7.16

0022

SOFA (Foreigner's Commissary) 회의

1. 일시: 1964. 7. 10. 15:00 P.M.

2. 장소: 외무부 제1회의실

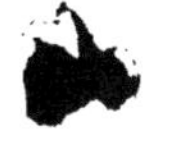

참석자:

교통부 관광국 업무과장	양한식 담당 김남중	3-7464
관광공사 업무과장		
특정외래품판매소장	정혜택	4-3841
재무부 세관국 관세과장	조충훈	72-0011~0019
상공부 상역국 상무과장	남제영 대리 서정욱	74-2671
외무부 의전과장	박상두 담당 강성구	
외무부 미주과장		

0023

기 안 용 지

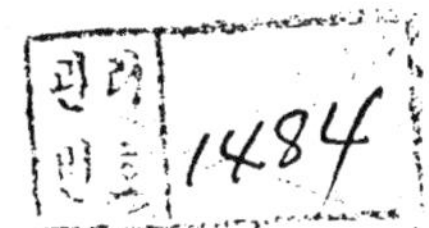

자체 통제		기안처	미주과 이근팔	전화번호	근거서류접수일자
	과장	국장	차관	장관	
관계관 서명					
기안 년월일	1964. 7. 21.	시행 년월일		보존 년한	정서기장
분류 기호	외구미 722.2-	전체 통제	종결		
경유 수신 참조	대통령 : 참조: 비서실장 국무총리 : 참조: 비서실장 사본: 법무부장관			발신	장관
제목	제 58 차 주둔군지위협정 체결 교섭 실무자회의 개최 보고				

1964. 7. 16. 하오 3 시부터 동 5 시 10 분 까지 외무부 제 1 회의실에서 개최된 제 58 차 주둔군지위협정 체결 교섭 실무자회의에서 토의된 내용을 별첨과 같이 보고합니다.

유 첨: 제 58 차 주둔군지위협정 체결 교섭실무자회의 보고서. 1 부. 끝.

사본 배부처: 법무부장관.

보통문서로 재분류(1966. 12. 31.)

1966. 12. 31 에 예고문에 의거 일반문서로 재분류됨

승인서식 1—1—3 (11 00900—03) (195mm×265mm16절지)

0024

제 58 차

한·미 간 주둔군지위협정 체결 교섭실무자회의

보 고 서

1. 일 시: 1964 년 7 월 16 일 하오 3 시 부터 5 시 10 분 까지.

2. 장 소: 외무부 제 1 회의실

3. 토의사항:

가. 비세출자금기관

(1) 우리측은 비세출자금기관의 사용자의 범위 중 미군이 보급을 담당하고 있는 중립국휴전감시위원단 ~~및 유엔군 ... 직원~~을 제외하고 UNCURK, UNTAB 주한미대사관직원을 제외한 주한외교단원 전원, Scandinavian Medical Mission, International Lutheran Mission, American-Korean Foundation, United Nations Children's Fund, F.A.O. 등 제기관 및 개인의 비세출자금기관 사용을 배제할 것을 제안하였다.

나. 형사재판관할권

(1) 우리측은 미군당국의 관할권에 복하는 자의 범위를 "미군법에 복하는 모든 자"로 할 것을 주장한데 대하여 미측은 (가) 주한 미군관계 민간인 범법자를 재판하기 위하여 한국내에 군법회의 이외에 일반법원을 설치하지는 않을 것이며 (나) 장차 미국회가 미군관계 민간인 범법자를 미국에 이송하여 재판할 수 있는 법률을 제정할 가능성이 있음으로 미국안 대로 "미군대구성원, 군속, 및 그들의 가족"으로 할 것을 계속 주장하였다.

(2) 우리측은 어떤 경우에 있어서나 미군관계 범법자를 군법회의에 회부하지 않을 것을 미측에 보장하는 대신 한국의 관할권 행사 기관을 "대한민국당국"으로 할 것을 제안한데 대하여 미측은 한국측이 그와 같은 보장을 하는 이상 미국안 대로 "대한민국민사당국"으로 할 것을 주장하는 취지와 동일하다고 하여 계속 그대로 주장하였다.

(3) 우리측이 미군법무관이 발행한 공무집행중 범죄 여부에 관한 증명서에 충분한 증명력을 인정하되 반증이 있는 경우 합동위원회에서 심의

0025

64-3-(5)

64-3-24 (2) 미국.문 110-3 (2)

0026

결정하기를 원하며 만일 합동위원회에서 해결을 보지 못할 때에는 한국법원이 결정하기를 원하는데 반하여 미측은 (가) 미군 발행 증명서는 미측이 수정하지 않는 한 확정적이며 (나) 한국측이 이의를 제의하는 것은 무방하나 신속한 재판 진행을 방해하여서는 안 된다는 조건을 제시하고 한국측이 상기 조건을 수락하는 경우 우리 대안을 검토하여 볼 용의가 있다고 제안하였다.

(4) 우리측은 피의자의 신병 구금 및 제일차적관할권의 포기에 관하여 미측의 주장을 참작하는 대신 미측이 전투지역의 개념을 삭제할 것을 주장한데 대하여 미측은 우리측이 미측의 제일차적관할권의 포기에 관한 주장을 수락하면 전투지역의 개념 및 한국군인이 범하면 군법회의에 회부될 범죄에 관련된 미군인은 미군법회의에 회부하여야 한다는 주장을 철회할 용의가 있음을 제안하였다.

(5) 한국측은 미군이 재판전 피의자의 신병을 구금하고 있는 경우에는 사법절차가 끝나고 신병 인도를 한국당국이 요청할 때 까지 미군이 계속 구금할 것이며 특별한 경우 한국당국이 신병 인도를 요청하면 미측은 호의적인 고려를 할 것을 요구한데 대하여 미측은 원안대로 계속 주장하였으며 한국의 안전에 관한 범죄에 관련된 미군범법자는 한국당국이 신병을 구금할 것을 요구한데 대하여 미측은 (가) 한국의 신병 구금은 양국의 합의를 요하며 (나) 한국의 구금시설은 미국의 수준으로 보아 적당하여야 한다는 양해사항을 한국측이 수락하면 받을 수 있다고 제안하였다.

(6) 미측은 피의자의 권리중 (가) 영문으로 된 재판의 축어적 보고서를 받을 권리 및 (나) 상소의 권리중 "형을 선고받는 경우 법원으로부터 상소의 권리와 상소할 기간을 고지받는다"는 초안 규정의 삭제를 제의하였다.

4. 기타 사항: 차기 회의 일자: 1964 년 7 월 24 일 하오 3 시. 끝.

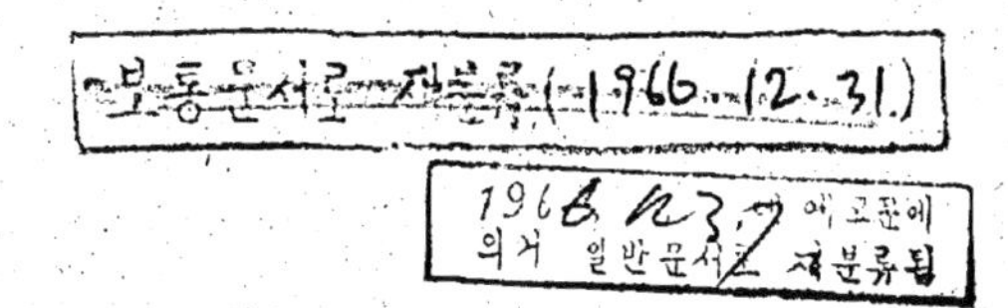

0027

64-3 -64

0028

CONFIDENTIAL

STATUS OF FORCES NEGOTIATIONS: 58th Meeting

SUBJECTS: 1. Non-Appropriated Fund Organizations
2. Criminal Jurisdiction

PLACE: Ministry of Foreign Affairs

DATE: July 16, 1964

PARTICIPANTS:

Republic of Korea	United States
CHANG Sang-mun	Philip C. Habib
KU Chung-hoe	Brig. General G.G. O'Connor, USA
Colonel KIM Won-kil, ROKA	Colonel Howard Smigelow, USA
Major YI Kae-hun, ROKA	Captain John Wayne, USN
CHO Chung-hun	Colonel Kenneth C. Crawford, USA
HO Hyung-ku	Frank R. LaMacchia
YI Kae-chol	Benjamin A. Fleck
YI Kun-pal (Interpreter)	Robert A. Kinney
HWANG Yong-chae	Lt. Colonel Charles Wright, USA
	Robert A. Lewis
PAK Sang-yong (Observer)	David Y.C. Lee (Interpreter)
	Daniel A. O'Donohue (Observer)

0029

1. Mr. Chang opened the meeting by introducing Mr. Pak Sang-yong, who was attending as an Observer. Mr. Habib in turn introduced Mr. David Y.C. Lee, and Mr. Daniel A. O'Donohue, who were attending as Interpreter and Observer, respectively, for the U.S. negotiators.

Non-Appropriated Fund Organizations

2. Taking up the Non-Appropriated Funds Organizations Article, Mr. Chang remarked that the only remaining point at issue was the question of what persons and organizations should be entitled to use the NAFO facilities. He said the Korean negotiators had carefully studied the text of the Agreed Minute proposed by the U.S. negotiators. Inasmuch as the Status of Forces Agreement was concerned with the U.S. armed forces, the Korean negotiators believed that persons and organizations not connected in any way with the U.S. armed forces or the U.S. Government could not be appropriately included in the terms of the Agreement. Therefore, they believed that item (f) of the U.S. draft was not an appropriate subject for discussion at the negotiating table. They proposed the deletion of item (f). At the 36th negotiating meeting, the U.S. negotiators had indicated that the deletion of this item might cause problems. Nevertheless, the Korean negotiators continued to believe that it should be deleted.

3. Mr. Habib replied that the Korean negotiators were taking a position that would, in effect, prevent the U.S. armed forces or the ROK Government from exercising in the future any flexibility with regard to this subject. The U.S. negotiators had made it clear that the provisions of item (f) would be applied to persons and organizations only with the express consent of the ROK Government.

4. Mr. Habib stated that elimination of item (f) would create problems with regard to three organizations: the United Nations Commission for the Unification and Rehabilitation of Korea (UNCURK); the Swiss and Swedish members of the Neutral Nations Supervisory Commission (NNSC); and the United

0030

Nations Memorial Cemetery in Korea (UNMCK). He pointed out that if there were no clause in the Agreement providing for the extension of NAFO facilities to these organizations, the U.S. armed forces would be unable to extend such facilities, even if they or the ROK Government wanted to do so.

5. Mr. Habib stated that the Swiss and Swedish members of the NNSC, given their function in terms of the Armistice Agreement, have a direct relationship with the U.S. armed forces. Both the U.S. Government and the ROK Government have a substantial interest in them and the U.S. armed forces provide them with logistical support at ~~xxxxxxxxxxxxxx~~ Pan Mun Jom.

6. Mr. Habib pointed out that the members of UNCURK view ~~that~~ their organization as being the political arm of the United Nations in Korea, even as the United Nations Command is the military arm. They have already expressed to members of the U.S. negotiating team their concern over the possibility that the SOFA might not provide for the continued extension of NAFO facilities to them. In reply, they have been told that the matter will be considered during the negotiations. The extension of NAFO facilities to UNCURK is a burden to the U.S. armed forces. Nevertheless, the U.S. negotiators believe that it is desirable to continue to do so, in view of the need to maintain harmonious relations with ~~xxxx~~ that organization. It is in the interest, not only of the U.S. authorities but also of the ROK Government, to remain on good terms with UNCURK. The U.S. negotiators believed that there was no difference of opinion on this question between the negotiating teams but that they were faced with a mutual problem, for which a satisfactory solution must be found.

7. Mr. Chang remarked that at previous meetings, the U.S. negotiators had already indicated that under item (f) would be included, in addition to UNCURK, the United Nations Technical Assistance Board (UNTAB), the Scandinavian Medical Mission, the American-Korean Foundation, and members of the Diplomatic Corps. Now, the U.S. negotiators were suggesting the addition of NNSC personnel and UNMCK personnel. The Korean negotiators still desired the deletion of ~~xxxx~~ item (f) but they found the arguments of

0031

the U.S. negotiators with regard to NNSC ~~and UNMCK~~ personnel to be reasonable. Therefore, they proposed the deletion of item (f) and the inclusion of NNSC ~~and UNMCK~~ personnel under item (b). ~~He emphasized that the Korean negotiators were not proposing the inclusion of UNCURK personnel under item (b). If NAFO privileges were extended to UNCURK personnel, members of other UN agencies in the ROK would demand similar treatment and there would be a chain reaction.~~

~~8. The Korean negotiators stated that their final position on this question was that NNSC and UNMCK personnel should be included in item (b), that item (f) should be deleted, and that UNCURK personnel should not be covered by any of the provisions of the proposed Agreed Minute.~~

Criminal Jurisdiction

8 ~~9~~. Turning to the Criminal Jurisdiction Article, Mr. Habib stated that the U.S. negotiators would make a paragraph by paragraph reply to the proposals made by the Korean negotiators at the 52nd meeting.

9 ~~10~~. Mr. Habib recalled that the Korean negotiators had proposed the substitution in Paragraph 1(a) of the Korean draft of the phrase "all persons subject to the military law of the United States" for the phrase "the members of the United States armed forces and the civilian components". They had also expressed concern over the possibility that the language in the U.S draft ~~unless this change was made, the paragraph~~ would permit the exercise in Korea of judicial power by some U.S. authority other than military authorities. The U.S. negotiators wished to give a categorical assurance that the U.S. Government has no intention to establish civil courts which could exercise jurisdiction in the Republic of Korea. There is no intention that U.S.

authorities

0032

other than military authorities will exercise jurisdiction in Korea over U.S. ~~xxxxxxxx~~ personnel. At the same time, however, the U.S. negotiators would like to call attention to the possibility that legislation may be passed eventually in the United States which would provide that accused U.S. civilians abroad could be returned to the United States for trial. Paragraph 1(a) of the U.S. draft had been drafted specifically so as not to preclude this possibility. The U.S. ~~nxggtxx~~ negotiators, therefore, believed the U.S. draft preferable to the proposed change in the Korean draft, since it would not preclude the applicability of any legislation which might be passed to bridge the present "jurisdiction gap" over U.S. civilians abroad.

10. ~~11~~. Mr. Habib recalled that at the 52nd meeting, the Korean negotiators had stated that the ROK Government would not exercise jurisdiction over U.S. military personnel by military tribunal under any circumstances. They had also given the same assurance with regard to the civilian component. The U.S. negotiators welcomed these assurances. They wished to point out again that the language of Paragraph 1(b) of the U.S. draft plainly sets forth the ROK Government's intention, since it states that ~~the~~ "the civil authorities of the Republic of Korea shall have the right to exercise...". The U.S. draft of this subparagraph contained the phrase "the right to exercise", which was not contained in the Korean draft. On restudying the subparagraph, the U.S. negotiators had found the Korean phraseology to be clear and acceptable and agreed to the deletion of the phrase "the right to exercise". The only remaining difference in language in the two drafts of the subparagraph, therefore, was the inclusion of the word "civil" in the U.S. draft. Since the Korean negotiators had already given the assurances just referred to, they should be able to agree to the inclusion of this word.

11. ~~12~~. Turning to the subject of the Duty Certificate, Mr. Habib recalled that at the 47th meeting, the Korean negotiators had proposed

that the definition of official duty based on that contained in the U.S. Army, Far East, circular of January 1956 be read into the Agreed Joint Summary. At the 49th meeting, the U.S. negotiators had agreed to this proposal, provided the Korean negotiators would agree to Agreed Minute #2 Re Paragraph 3(a) of the U.S. draft. Instead of agreeing to this package proposal of the U.S. negotiators, the Korean negotiators at the 52nd meeting had proposed an alternative Agreed Minute Re Paragraph 3(a)(ii). Before commenting on this Korean counter-proposal, the U.S. negotiators wished to seek clarification of the Korean position and, at the same time, wished to make the U.S. position regarding duty certificates quite clear.

12. Mr. Habib stated that in the view of the U.S. negotiators, the duty certificate would be definitive unless it is modified by the U.S. authorities, either as a result of a request by the ROK authorities for modification or otherwise. There was no intention to foreclose requests by the Korean authorities for reconsideration of duty certificates in specific cases where there is a justifiable basis for questioning the correctness of the certificate. What is important, in the view of the U.S. negotiators, is that the certificate will be conclusive unless modification is agreed upon. This is not made clear in the Korean draft. A second matter of concern to the U.S. negotiators is that the accused should not be deprived of his entitlement to a prompt and speedy trial as a result of protracted reconsideration of the duty certificate. If agreement to modification were not reached within a specified time, the U.S. authorities would expect the duty certificate to be conclusive for that case, although discussions could continue concerning the propriety of issuing a duty certificate under similar circumstances in a future case.

13. The U.S. negotiators had been instructed to inform the Korean negotiators, Mr. Habib continued, that the U.S. Government was concerned lest modification of the U.S. position on duty certificates was being sought by the Korean negotiators as a means of acquiring jurisdiction in cases involving action taken

0034

by sentries to protect U.S. property. In the absence of special circumstances, such cases would be certified as official duty. The U.S. authorities would be willing to reconsider the duty certificate in such a case, if requested to do so by the Korean authorities. However, the duty certificate would be definitive unless it were modified as a result of the reconsideration. Mr. Habib made it clear that the U.S. negotiators were not responding to the revised draft of the Agreed Minute tabled by the Korean negotiators and, before doing so, wished to clarify the views of the Korean negotiators on the points he had mentioned.

14 ~~15~~. Mr. Chang replied that whereas the U.S. draft provides that the duty certificate shall be "conclusive" (Agreed Minute #2 Re Paragraph 3(a)), the Korean draft uses the word "sufficient"(revised Agreed Minute Re Paragraph 3(a)(ii)). The Korean draft provides for specific procedures to be followed if the Korean authorities raise an objection to a duty certificate, while the U.S. draft does not outline any procedure. The Korean negotiators, therefore, preferred the Korean draft.

15 ~~16~~. Mr. Habib stated that the U.S. negotiators wished to make it clear that a Korean appeal regarding a duty certificate would not alter the conclusive nature of the certificate unless the U.S. authorities agreed to modify the certificate after reconsideration. He asked what procedure the Korean negotiators had in mind.

16 ~~17~~. Mr. Chang reviewed the position stated by the U.S. negotiators. They held that once the duty certificate were issued, it would remain valid unless modified by the U.S. authorities after considering objections raised by the Korean authorities. According to the U.S. position, there were two possibilities: the duty certificate would either be conclusive or it would be modified by the U.S. authorities. Mr. Chang stated that this was contrary to the position set forth in the revised draft tabled by the Korean negotiators. They had in mind that if the

0035

Korean authorities objected to a duty certificate, agreement would then be reached by the Joint Committee, not unilaterally by the U.S. authorities. The Korean negotiators also believed that the Joint Committee must be allowed sufficient time to reach a decision. There might be cases in which the validity of the duty certificates would be ambiguous; therefore it would take some time for both sides to reach agreement. For these reasons, the Korean negotiators could not agree to the two points made by the U.S. negotiators.

17. ~~18.~~ In reply to Mr. Habib's request for clarification of the concept of "sufficient time", Mr. Chang stated that "appropriate time" might be a better phrase. The Korean negotiators believed that agreement could be reached on a certain number of days as a time limit for Joint Committee consideration of duty certificate cases.

18. ~~19.~~ Referring to the Korean revised draft, Mr. Habib asked who would determine that "the contrary is proved" or that a decision had been reached. Mr. Chang replied that the Korean draft provided that the Korean authorities could base an objection to a duty certificate on the belief of the chief prosecutor that there was proof contrary to the certificate. Mr. Chang added that the third paragraph of the Korean revised draft of the Agreed Minute Re Paragraph 3(a)(ii) provided for referral of the case to the Korean courts if the Joint Committee were unable to reach agreement regarding modification of a duty certificate to which the Korean authorities had objected.

19. ~~20.~~ Moving on to another portion of the Article, Mr. Habib recalled that the Korean negotiators had previously indicated that they did not wish to accept the concept of the combat zone, as contained in Agreed Minute #1 Re Paragraph 1(b) of the U.S. draft. They had expressed the hope that a workable arrangement could be agreed upon to satisfy the U.S. concern over assuring the combat readiness of U.S. troops without resort to the concept of a combat zone. The Korean negotiators had

0036

also requested deletion from the U.S. draft of Agreed Minute #1 Re Paragraph 3(a), which would give the U.S. authorities primary right to exercise jurisdiction over court martial offenses. Having carefully studied the Korean requests, the U.S. negotiators were prepared to make a significant counter-proposal in an effort to reach full agreement on the waiver question. The U.S. negotiators would agree to the deletion of the two Agreed Minutes just mentioned if the Korean negotiators would accept the Agreed Minute Re Paragraph 3 of the U.S. draft. This would be a substantial concession by the U.S. negotiators.

20 ~~21~~. Regarding the subject of pre-trial custody, Mr. Habib recalled that at the 52nd meeting, the Korean negotiators had tabled a revised draft of Paragraph 5(d) and a new Paragraph 5(e). The U.S. negotiators believed the revised version of Paragraph 5(d) to be an improvement over the original language but they still considered Paragraph 5(c) of the U.S. draft to be preferable. Transfer of an accused to Korean custody is adequately covered by the last sentence of the latter paragraph. The U.S. negotiators had studied the proposed new Paragraph 5(e), regarding Korean custody of offenders against the security of the Republic of Korea. The U.S. armed forces in Korea are there to help protect and preserve the security of the ROK and will continue to do everything possible to carry out that mission. Therefore, the U.S. negotiators were prepared to agree the inclusion of the new ROK paragraph 5(e), i.e. to Korean custody in security cases if the Korean negotiators would agree to the following two understandings:

a. There must be mutual U.S.-ROK agreement as to the circumstances in which such custody is appropriate;

b. Korean confinement facilities must be adequate by U.S. standards.

21, ~~22~~. With regard to the question of trial safeguards, Mr. Habib recalled that the Korean negotiators had indicated general agreement with Paragraph 9 and related Agreed Minutes of the U.S. draft but had raised some question regarding several of the trial safeguards enumerated in the Agreed Minute Re Paragraph 9. In order to be responsive to the ROK views and to facilitate early agreement on this subject, the U.S. negotiators proposed the following changes in the Agreed Minute Re Paragraph 9 of the U.S. draft:

a. Deletion of subparagraph (a);

b. In subparagraph (b), deletion of all language after the words "shall have the right to appeal a conviction or sentence".

22 ~~23~~. Mr. Chang stated that the Korean negotiators appreciated the extensive response which the U.S. negotiators had made to the Korean proposals. However, the U.S. position did not fully meet the Korean requirements. The Korean negotiators were disappointed but would consider the U.S. position and would respond at the next meeting.

23 ~~24~~. The next meeting was tentatively scheduled for July 24 at 3:00 p.m.

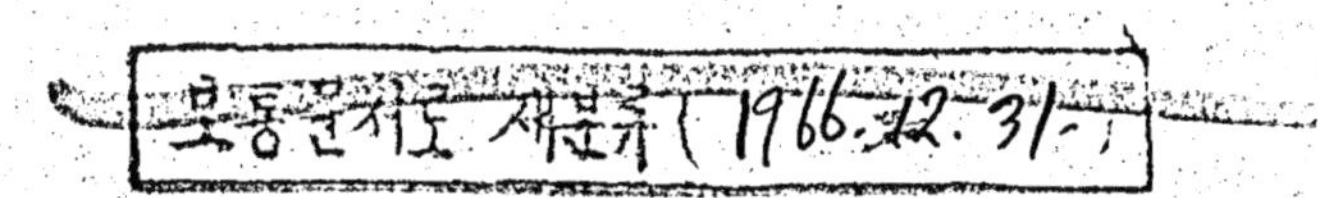

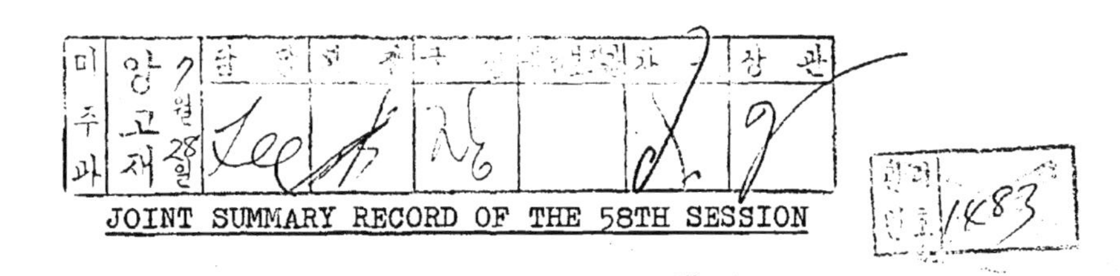

JOINT SUMMARY RECORD OF THE 58TH SESSION

1. Time and Place: 3:00 - 5:10 P.M. July 16, 1964 at the Foreign Ministry's Conference Room (No.1)

2. Attendants:

ROK Side:

Mr. Chang, Sang Moon	Director European and American Affairs Bureau
Mr. Koo, Choong Whay	Chief, America Section Ministry of Foreign Affairs
Mr. Cho, Choong Hoon	Chief Customs Section Ministry of Finance
Mr. Hur, Hyong Koo	Chief Prosecutors Section Ministry of Justice
Col. Kim, Won Kil	Chief Military Affairs Section Ministry of National Defense
Maj. Lee, Kye Hoon	Military Affairs Section Ministry of National Defense
Mr. Park, Sang Yong	3rd Secretary Ministry of Foreign Affairs
Mr. Ahn, Yun Gi	3rd Secretary Ministry of Foreign Affairs
Mr. Lee, Kae Chul	3rd Secretary Ministry of Foreign Affairs
Mr. Lee, Keun Pal (Rapporteur and Interpreter)	3rd Secretary Ministry of Foreign Affairs
Mr. Hwang, Young Jae	3rd Secretary Ministry of Foreign Affairs

U.S. Side:

Mr. Philip C. Habib	Counselor American Embassy
Brig. Gen. G.G. O'Connor	Deputy Chief of Staff 8th U.S. Army
Col. Howard Smigelow	Deputy Chief of Staff 8th U.S. Army

0039

Capt. John Wayne	Assistant Chief of Staff USN/K
Col. Kenneth C. Crawford	Staff Judge Advocate 8th U.S. Army
Mr. Frank R. La Macchia	First Secretary American Embassy
Mr. Benjamin A. Fleck (Rapporteur and Press Officer)	First Secretary American Embassy
Mr. Robert A. Kinney	J-5 8th U.S. Army
Lt. Col. Charles Wright	Staff Judge Advocate's Office 8th U.S. Army
Mr. Robert A. Lewis	2nd Secretary American Embassy
Mr. David Y. C. Lee (Interpreter)	2nd Secretary American Embassy
Mr. Daniel A. O'Donohue	2nd Secretary American Embassy

1. Mr. Chang opened the meeting by introducing Mr. Park Sang-yong, who was attending as an Observer. Mr. Habib in turn introduced Mr. David Y.C. Lee, and Mr. Daniel A. O'Donohue, who were attending as Interpreter and Observer, respectively, for the U.S. negotiators.

Non-Appropriated Fund Organizations

2. Taking up the Non-Appropriated Funds Organizations Article, Mr. Chang remarked that the only remaining point at issue was the question of what persons and organizations should be entitled to use the NAFO facilities. He said the Korean negotiators had carefully studied the text of the Agreed Minute proposed by the U.S. negotiators. Inasmuch as the Status of Forces Agreement was concerned with the U.S. armed forces, the Korean negotiators believed that persons and organizations not connected in any way with the U.S. armed forces or the U.S. Government could not be appropriately included in the terms of the Agreement. Therefore, they believed that item (f) of the U.S. draft was not an appropriate

0040

subject for discussion at the negotiating table. They proposed the deletion of item (f). At the 36th negotiating meeting, the U.S. negotiators had indicated that the deletioh of this item might cause problems. Nevertheless, the Korean negotiators continued to believe that it should be deleted.

3. Mr. Habib replied that the Korean negotiators were taking a position that would, in effect, prevent the U.S. armed forces or the ROK Government from exercising in the future any flexibility with regard to this subject. The U.S. negotiators had made it clear that the provisions of item (f) would be applied to persons and organizations only with the express consent of the ROK Government.

4. Mr. Habib stated that elimination of item (f) would create problems with regard to three organizations: the United Nations Commission for the Unification and Rehabilitation of Korea (UNCURK); the Swiss and Swedish members of the Neutral Nations Supervisory Commission (NNSC); and the United Nations Memorial Cemetery in Korea (UNMCK). He pointed out that if there were no clause in the Agreement providing for the extension of NAFO facilities to these organizations, the U.S. armed forces would be unable to extend such facilities, even if they or the ROK Government wanted to do so.

5. Mr. Habib stated that the Swiss and Swedish members of the NNSC, given their function in terms of the Armistice Agreement, have a direct relationship with the U.S. armed forces. Both the U.S. Government and the ROK Government have a substantial interest in them and the U.S. armed forces provide them with logistical support at Pan Mun Jom.

0041

6. Mr. Habib pointed out that the members of UNCURK view their organization as being the political arm of the United Nations in Korea, even as the United Natinns Command is the military arm. They have already expressed to members of the U.S. negotiating team their concern over the possibility that the SOFA might not provide for the continued extension of NAFO facilities to them. In reply, they have been told that the matter will be considered during the negotiations. The extension of NAFO facilities to UNCURK is a burden to the U.S. armed forces. Nevertheless, the U.S. negotiators believe that it is desirable to continue to do so, in view of the need to maintain harmonious relations with that organization. It is in the interest, not only of the U.S. authorities but also of the ROK Government, to remain on good terms with UNCURK. The U.S. negotiators believed that there was no difference of opinion on this question between the negotiating teams but that they were faced with a mutual problem, for which a satisfactory solution must be found.

7. Mr. Chang remarked that at previous meetings, the U.S. negotiators had already indicated that under item (f) would be included, in addition to UNCURK, the United Nations Technical Assistance Board (UNTAB), the Scandinavian Medical Mission, the American-Korean Foundation, and members of the Diplomatic Corps. Now, the U.S. negotiators were suggesting the addition of NNSC personnel and UNMCK personnel. The Korean negotiators still desired the deletion of item (f) but they found the arguments of the U.S. negotiators with regard to NNSC personnel to be reasonable. Therefore, they proposed the deletion of item (f) and the inclusion of NNSC personnel under item (b).

0042

Criminal Jurisdiction

8. Turning to the Criminal Jurisdiction Article, Mr. Habib stated that the U.S. negotiators would make a paragraph by paragraph reply to the proposals made by the Korean negotiators at the 52nd meeting.

9. Mr. Habib recalled that the Korean negotiators had proposed the substitution in Paragraph 1(a) of the Korean draft of the phrase "all persons subject to the military law of the United States" for the phrase "the members of the United States armed forces and the civilian components". They had also expressed concern over the possibility that the language in the U.S. draft would permit the exercise in Korea of judicial power by some U.S. authority other than military authorities. The U.S. negotiators wished to give a categorical assurance that the U.S. Government has no intention to establish civil courts which could exercise jurisdiction in the Republic of Korea. There is no intention that U.S. other than military authorities will exercise jurisdiction in Korea over U.S. personnel. At the same time, however, the U.S. negotiators would like to call attention to the possibility that legislation may be passed eventually in the United States which would provide that accused U.S. civilians abroad could be returned to the United States for trial. Paragraph 1(a) of the U.S. draft had been drafted specifically so as not to preclude this possibility. The U.S. negotiators, therefore, believed the U.S. draft preferable to the proposed change in the Korean draft, since it would not preclude the applicability of any legislation which might be passed to bridge the present "jurisdiction gap" over U.S. civilians abroad.

10. Mr. Habib recalled that at the 52nd meeting, the Korean negotiators had stated that the ROK Government would not exercise jurisdiction over U.S. military personnel by military tribunal under any circumstances. They had also given the same assurance with regard to the civilian component. The U.S. negotiators welcomed these assurances. They wished to point out again that the language of Paragraph 1(b) of the U.S. draft plainly sets forth the ROK Government's intention, since it states that "the civil authorities of the Republic of Korea shall have the right to exercise ...". The U.S. draft of this subparagraph contained the phrase "the right to exercise", which was not contained in the Korean draft. On restudying the subparagraph, the U.S. negotiators had found the Korean phraseology to be clear and acceptable and agreed to the deletion of the phrase "the right to exercise". The only remaining difference in language in the two drafts of the subparagraph, therefore, was the inclusion of the word "civil" in the U.S. draft. Since the Korean negotiators had already given the assurances just referred to, they should be able to agree to the inclusion of this word.

11. Turning to the subject of the Duty Certificate, Mr. Habib recalled that at the 47th meeting, the Korean negotiators had proposed that the definition of official duty based on that contained in the U.S. Army, Far East, circular of January 1956 be read into the Agreed Joint Summary. At the 49th meeting, the U.S. negotiators had agreed to this proposal, provided the Korean negotiators would agree to Agreed Minute #2 Re Paragraph 3(a) of the U.S. draft. Instead of agreeing to this package proposal of the U.S. negotiators, the Korean negotiators at the 52nd meeting had proposed an alternative Agreed Minute Re Paragraph

0044

3(a) (ii). Before commenting on this Korean counter-proposal, the U.S. negotiators wished to seek clarification of the Korean position and, at the same time, wished to make the U.S. position regarding duty certificates quite clear.

12. Mr. Habib stated that in the view of the U.S. negotiators, the duty certificate would be definitive unless it is modified by the U.S. authorities, either as a result of a request by the ROK authorities for modification or otherwise. There was no intention to foreclose requests by the Korean authorities for reconsideration of duty certificates in specific cases where there is a justifiable basis for questioning the correctness of the certificate. What is important, in the view of the U.S. negotiators, is that the certificate will be conclusive unless modification is agreed upon. This is not made clear in the Korean draft. A second matter of concern to the U.S. negotiators is that the accused should not be deprived of his entitlement to a prompt and speedy trial as a result of protracted reconsideration of the duty certificate. If agreement to modification were not reached within a specified time, the U.S. authorities would expect the duty certificate to be conclusive for that case, although discussions could continue concerning the propriety of issuing a duty certificate under similar circumstances in a future case.

13. The U.S. negotiators had been instructed to inform the Korean negotiators, Mr. Habib continued, that the U.S. Government was concerned lest modification of the U.S. position on duty certificates was being sought by the Korean negotiators as a means of acquiring jurisdiction in cases involving action taken by sentries to protect U.S. property.

0045

In the absence of special circumstances, such cases would be certified as official duty. The U.S. authorities would be willing to reconsider the duty certificate in such a case, if requested to do so by the Korean authorities. However, the duty certificate would be definitive unless it were modified as a result of the reconsideration. Mr. Habib made it clear that the U.S. negotiators were not responding to the revised draft of the Agreed Minute tabled by the Korean negotiators and, before doing so, wished to clarify the views of the Korean negotiators on the points he had mentioned.

14. Mr. Chang replied that whereas the U.S. draft provides that the duty certificate shall be "conclusive" (Agreed Minute #2 Re Paragraph 3(a)), the Korean draft uses the word "sufficient" (revised Agreed Minute Re Paragraph 3(a) (ii)). The Korean draft provides for specific procedures to be followed if the Korean authorities raise an objection to a duty certificate, while the U.S. draft does not outline any procedure. The Korean negotiators, therefore, preferred the Korean draft.

15. Mr. Habib stated that the U.S. negotiators wished to make it clear that a Korean appeal regarding a duty certificate would not alter the conclusive nature of the certificate unless the U.S. authorities agreed to modify the certificate after reconsideration. He asked what procedure the Korean negotiators had in mind.

16. Mr. Chang reviewed the position stated by the U.S. negotiators. They held that once the duty certificate were issued, it would remain valid unless modified by the U.S. authorities after considering objections raised by the Korean authorities. According to the U.S. position,

0046

there were two possibilities: the duty certificate would either be conclusive or it would be modified by the U.S. authorities. Mr. Chang stated that this was contrary to the position set forth in the revised draft tabled by the Korean negotiators. They had in mind that if the Korean authorities objected to a duty certificate, agreement would then be reached by the Joint Committee, not unilaterally by the U.S. authorities. The Korean negotiators also believed that the Joint Committee must be allowed sufficient time to reach a decision. There might be cases in which the validity of the duty certificates would be ambiguous; therefore it would take some time for both sides to reach agreement. For these reasons, the Korean negotiators could not agree to the two points made by the U.S. negotiators.

17. In reply to Mr. Habib's request for clarification of the concept of "sufficient time", Mr. Chang stated that "appropriate time" might be a better phrase. The Korean negotiators believed that agreement could be reached on a certain number of days as a time limit for Joint Committee consideration of duty certificate cases.

18. Referring to the Korean revised draft, Mr. Habib asked who would determine that "the contrary is proved" or that a decision had been reached. Mr. Chang replied that the Korean draft provided that the Korean authorities could base an objection to a duty certificate on the belief of the chief prosecutor that there was proof contrary to the certificate. Mr. Chang added that the third paragraph of the Korean revised draft of the Agreed Minute Re Paragraph 3(a) (ii) provided for referral of the case to the Korean courts if the Joint Committee were unable to reach agreement regarding modification of a duty certificate to which the Korean authorities had objected.

0047

19. Moving on to another portion of the Article, Mr. Habib recalled that the Korean negotiators had previously indicated that they did not wish to accept the concept of the combat zone, as contained in Agreed Minute #1 Re Paragraph 1(b) of the U.S. draft. They had expressed the hope that a workable arrangement could be agreed upon to satisfy the U.S. concern over assuring the combat readiness of U.S. troops without resort to the concept of a combat zone. The Korean negotiators had also requested deletion from the U.S. draft of Agreed Minute #1 Re Paragraph 3(a), which would give the U.S. authorities primary right to exercise jurisdiction over court martial offenses. Having carefully studied the Korean requests, the U.S. negotiators were prepared to make a significant counter-proposal in an effort to reach full agreement on the waiver question. The U.S. negotiators would agree to the deletion of the two Agreed Minutes just mentioned if the Korean negotiators would accept the Agreed Minute Re Paragraph 3 of the U.S. draft. This would be a substantial concession by the U.S. negotiators.

20. Regarding the subject of pre-trial custody, Mr. Habib recalled that at the 52nd meeting, the Korean negotiators had tabled a revised draft of Paragraph 5(d) and a new Paragraph 5(e). The U.S. negotiators believed the revised version of Paragraph 5(d) to be an improvement over the original language but they still considered Paragraph 5(c) of the U.S. draft to be preferable. Transfer of an accused to Korean custody is adequately covered by the last sentence of the latter paragraph. The U.S. negotiators had studied the proposed new Paragraph 5(e), regarding Korean custody of offenders against the security of the Republic of Korea.

0048

The U.S. armed forces in Korea are there to help protect and preserve the security of the ROK and will continue to do everything possible to carry out that mission. Therefore, the U.S. negotiators were prepared to agree to inclusion of the new ROK paragraph 5(e), e.i. to Korean custody in security cases if the Korean negotiators would agree to the following two understandings:

a. There must be mutual U.S.-ROK agreement as to the circumstances in which such custody is appropriate;

b. Korean confinement facilities must be adequate by U.S. standards.

21. With regard to the question of trial safeguards, Mr. Habib recalled that the Korean negotiators had indicated general agreement with Paragraph 9 and related Agreed Minutes of the U.S. draft but had raised some question regarding several of the trial safeguards enumerated in the Agreed Minute Re Paragraph 9. In order to be responsive to the ROK views and to facilitate early agreement on this subject, the U.S. negotiators proposed the following changes in the Agreed Minute Re Paragraph 9 of the U.S. draft:

a. Deletion of subparagraph (a);

b. In subparagraph (b), deletion of all language after the words "shall have the right to appeal a conviction or sentence".

22. Mr. Chang stated that the Korean negotiators appreciated the extensive response which the U.S. negotiators had made to the Korean proposals. However, the U.S. position did not fully meet the Korean requirements. The Korean negotiators were disappointed but would consider the U.S. position and would respond at the next meeting.

23. The next meeting was tentatively scheduled for July 28 at 3:00 p.m.

0049

3. 제59차 회의, 7.28

0050

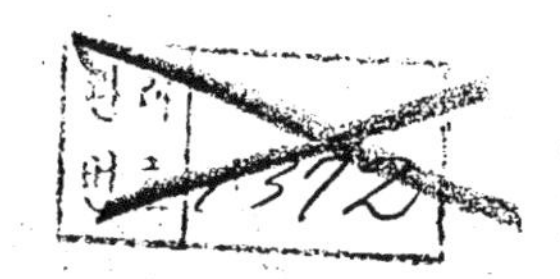

기 안 용 지

자체 통제		기안처	미주과 이근팔	전화번호	근거서류접수일자
	과장	국장	차관	장관	
관계관 서명					
기안 년월일	1964.7.27.	시행 년월일		보존 년한	정서 기장
분류 기호	외구미722.2—	전체 통제		종결	
경유 수신 참조	건 의			발신	
제목	제 59 차 주둔군지위협정 체결 교섭실무자회의에 임할 우리측 입장				

1964. 7. 28.일 개최될 제 59 차 주둔군지위협정 체결 교섭 한.미 간 실무자회의에서는 형사재판관할권에 관한 조항을 토의하도록 예정하고 있는바 이에 관하여 우리측 실무자는 7.25.일 회합을 갖고 우리측이 취할 입장을 별첨과 같이 결정하였아오니 재가하여 주시기 바랍니다.

유 첨: 제 59 차 주둔군지위협정 체결 교섭 실무자회의에 임할 우리측 입장. 끝.

보통문서로 재분류(1966.12.31.)

1966.12.31.에 예고문에 의거 일반문서로 재분류됨

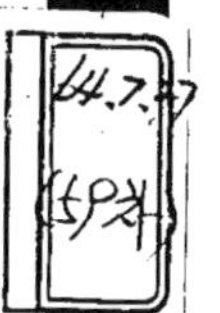

승인서식 1-1-3 (11-00900-03) (195mm×265mm16절지)

0051

제 59 차 주둔군지위협정 체결 교섭 실무자 회의에 임할 우리측 입장

1. 관할권의 인적적용범위 및 미측의 행사기관

미측은 58차 회의에서 (1) 주한미군에 동반하는 가족을 재판하기 위하여 한국내에 미국의 일반법원을 설치하지는 않을 것이며 (2) 미국회에서 입법이 통과되어 가족을 본국으로 이송 재판할수 있는 가능성을 고려하여 우리측 제안인 "미군법에 복하는 모든자"의 용어 보다 미측원안대로 "미군대구성원 군속 및 가족"으로 할것을 주장하였는바 우리측은 인적적용범위와 관할권의 행사기관과는 구별하여 논의하여야 할것으로 생각된다.

가. 인적적용범위

(1) 우리측은 우리측의 원안인 "미군대구성원 및 군속"을 대체하기 위하여 "미군법에 복하는 모든자"로 할것을 제안한바 있는데 우리안의 용어는 합리적이며 가족이 포함될수도 있는 여지를 유보한 것인만큼, 가족이 미군법에 복할 것인가 아닌가는 전적으로 미국의 국내문제인 것으로 본다.

나. 행사기관

(1) 미측은 미측의 행사기관을 "미국당국"이라고 주장하고 있으나, 우리는 주한미군의 지위를 규정코서 교섭을 진행하고 있다는 사실을 명백히 하고저 한다. 따라서 주한미군당국이외의 어떤 기타 기관의 관할권 행사를 생각할수 없다.

(2) 미측은 장차 협의를 받는 가족을 본국으로 이송하여 재판할수 있도록 미국회에서 법률이 개정될 가능성을 고려하고 있다고 하였다. 그러나, 우리는 1956년이래 미대심원에서 가족이 미군법에 복하느냐에 관하여 내린 판결의 변천 과정을 흥미있게 살펴보았다. 따라서 미측이

0052

미 연방 심원의 오 1956 년 판결은 1960 년도에 번복한 사실을 상기할때 하물며 막연한 장차의 입법을 근거로 협정을 체결하고저 함은 부당하다.
우리는 장차 만일 미국국회에서 그러한 입법이 성립한다면 그때 협정의 개정을 논의할수 있다고 본다.

(3) 근대 사법제도의 원칙은 피의자를 범죄지 또는 범죄지에서 가까운 곳에서 재판함으로서 일반이 재판의 내용을 방청할수 있는 또는 알수있어야 한다는 것을 요구하고 있다. 따라서 피의자를 미본국으로 이송한다는 것은 이정신에 위배되는 것이다.

(4) 국제법상, 대한민국은 영토주권에 의하여 원칙적으로 국내에 거주하는 모든국민과 일반외국인에 대하여 광범위한 관할권을 행사하게 되며, 주둔군당국은 한국이 인정한 범위내에서 제한적인 관할권만을 행사할수 있는 것이다. 우리는 위에 열거한 이유에 비추어 미측이 관할권의 행사기관을 미국당국으로 할것을 조장하는 것을 수락할수 없다.

2. <u>한국민사당국 (1 (b) 항)</u>

미측은 1 (b) 항에 "한국민사당국" 이라고 한것은 한국정부는 여하한 경우에도 미군을 한국군사재판에 회부하지 않겠다는 보장에 관한 한국정부의 의도를 시사하는 것이라 말하였다.

그러나 미측은 한국측의 의도를 잘못 이해한것 같다. 한국측은 미측이 "민사"라는 말을 삭제하여야 한다는 바로 그명확한 조건하에 그보장을 하였던 것이다. 이보장은 미군인이 한국군사재판에 회부될 가능성에 관한 미측의 염려에 대하여 미측은 입장을 충족시켜주려는 의도에서 행하여 진것이다.

한국측이 미측의 요구를 만족시켜 주기 위하여 그러한 확실한 보장을 한것이므로 한국측으로서는 왜 미측에서 아직도 "민사"라는 말을 포함할것을 주장하고 있는지 그이유를 알수가 없다.

0053

만일 한국측이 미측초안과 같은 그러한 선례에 없는 말을 수락한다면, 이는 틀림없이 한국정부나 한국 국민에 대하여 대단히 난처한 문제를 이르킬 것이다. 한국국민의 감정이나 국회의 분위기로 보아 그들이 한국의 주권을 침해할 가능성이 있는 내용을 수락하는데 대하여 참을수는 없을 것이다.

우리는 그러한 곤란한 문제를 야기시키는 것은 한미양측에서 모다 의도하는바가 아님을 확신하다.

3. 공무집행중 범죄

미측은 지난번 회의에서 Official duty certificate 에 관하여 다음 두가지 사항을 제시하였다.

가. 증명서는 수정에 관하여 합의되지 않는한 최종적이다.

나. 피고는 증명서에 관한 재심이 지연되는 탓으로 신속한 재판을 받을 그의 권리를 박탈당해서는 안된다.

한국대표는 미국측 설명을 검토한 결과, 미국의 Agreed Minute Re Par. 3 (a) 조항과 전술한 미국측 제안은 서로 gap 가 있다고 본다. 즉,

(1) 미측의 제안에 의하면 Certificate issued by or on behalf of the commanding officer ... shall be conclusive for the purpose of determining primary jurisdiction 으로 되어 있다. 그러나 귀측의 지난번 회의에서의 제의에 의하면 unless modification is agreed upon either through request of the Korean authorities or otherwise 라고 말하고 있다. 그렇다면 이는 오히려 한국측에서 제출한 대안이 미측의 제안설명에 접근한 것으로 생각한다. 한국의 입장으로서는 지휘관을 대신하여 군법무관이 발행한 증명서는 반증이 없는한 그것으로서 충분하다고 인정하고, 반증이 있으면 합동위원회에서도 재고할수 있도록 되어 있다.

0054

(2) 신속한 재판을 받을 권리를 박탈당한다는 이유로, 미국측은 재판이 시간이 걸릴것을 염려하고 있으나, 우리가 보기에는 쌍방의 합의를 통하여 이에 대한 해결이 있어야 할줄로 안다. 따라서 이문제에 관한 반증이 있을때는 합동위원회에 회부할수 있는 길이 있어야 할것이다.

문제는 이증명서에 관한 조항을 해결하는데 있어서 미국측이 한국측에 의한 반증이 있던 없던 그증명서는 확정적이라고 함은 일방적으로 이문제를 해결코저 하는 것이니 이와같은 미측의 태도는 우리측으로서는 받아드릴수 없는 것이다. 어떠한 **Mechanism** 을 택하던 우리로서는 이증명서의 수정여부에 관한 문제를 해결함에 있어 쌍방의 합의로서 해결지우는 방도를 발견해야 할것이다.

4. 전투지역의 개념 및 제 1 차관할권의 포기

가. 미측대표는 제 58 차 회의에서 만일 한국측이 제 1 차 관할권의 포기에 관한 미측안의 합의의사록 제 3 항의 규정을 수락한다면 미국측은 전투지역의 개념 및 한국군이 범하면 한국군법회의에 회부될 그러한 범죄에 관련된 미군은 미군법회의에 회부한다는 미측안 합의의사록 제 3 항의 규정을 철회할 용의가 있다고 제안하는 동시에 이제안은 미측으로서는 상당한 양보를 하는 것이라고 말한바 있다.

한국측은 미측이 그러한 뜻있는 제의를 한데 대하여 감사하는 동시에 그러한 제안은 미측이 전투지역의 개념을 철회하려는 용의가 있다는 것을 시사한 것으로 본다.

~~그러한 제안이 우리측이 제 1 차 관할권에 관한 미측안을 수락하는 것을 조건으로 하고 있지만 그러한 제안을 우선 환영하는 바이다.~~ 그러나, 우리는 미측이 전투지역의 개념을 철회한다 할지라도

0055

미측은 제일차관할권에 관한 규정을 유보함으로서 관할권을 전적으로 행사하려는 미측의 최종적 목적을 달성하게 될것으로 본다.

나. 우리는 한국당국이 접수국 당국으로서 특히 중요하다고 인정하는 경우를 제외하고 관할권을 포기할것인가의 여부를 결정할수 있는 재량권이 있어야 한다고 보는 바이다.

그러나 우리는 일본이 미·일간의 간결한 협정문 하에서 관할권을 포기하는 정도로 관대히 포기할 용의는 가지고 있다.

우리측은 다음과 같은 점에 감하여 미측제안을 수락할수 없다:

(1) 미측안에 의하면 한국당국은 우선 전적으로 포기하고 특정한 경우 포기된 관할권을 회복하기 위하여 합동위원회의 협의를 구하게 되어 있다.

(2) 또한 미측안은 한국당국의 포기는 모든 목적을 위하여 무조건이고도 최종적이며 한국당국은 물론 국민으로 하여금 형사소송의 진행을 금하게 되어 있다. 그러나, 미측이 포기라는 단순한 사실 때문에 국민으로 하여금 정부당국의 포기로 인하여 영향을 받을수 없는 민사소송의 제기를 봉쇄하고 있을뿐만 아니라, ~~재판안하는 경우에도~~ 한국정부당국 이 ~~으로 하여금~~ 포기한 사건에 대하여 미측이 재판하지 않하였을 경우에도 한국측이 무조건 간여할수 없게 하고 있는 ~~형사소송을 진행할수 없게하고 있는~~ 것은 극히 부당하다고 믿는 바이다. 그것은 포기가 최종적이라는 것은 미군당국이 관할권을 행사하여야 한다는 것을 조건으로 하는것이기 때문이다.

다. 우리는 서로 상대방의 신의를 믿고 교섭에 임하고 있는 것이다. 만약한국측의 이러한 가정이 옳다면 미측도 협조적 정신을 발휘하여 미측초안에 내포되고 있는 모든 불신을 ~~불식~~ 제기 시키기를 바란다. 만약에

0056

그래도 미측이 한국측의 의도를 의심한다면 우리측은 미측이 원하는 바에 따라 양해사항을 합의의사록에 유보할 용의도 있다. 그러나, 미측에 나타난바와 같은 지나치게 강경한 문구는 수락할수 없다. 따라서 미측이 우리측의 포기에 관한 대안을 재고하기를 바란다.

5. <u>재판전 피의자의 신병구금</u>

재판전 피의자의 신병구금에 관하여 미측은 제5차 회의에서 우리측의 5(d)항의 대안은 원안보다 진전된 것이지만 미측초안의 5(c)항이 좋다고 말하고 안전에 관한 피의자의 구금에 관한 한국측 대안 5(e)항을 수락할 용의를 표명하였다.

가. 재판전 피의자의 신병이 미측수중에 있을 때에 관한 우리측 대안의 내용은 미측초안과 거의 동일하다. 그러나 우리측은 한국당국이 특수한 경우에 신병인도를 미측에 요구할때에 미측의 호의적 고려를 보장할수 있는 규정을 유보하고저 한다.

나. 우리는 미측이 안전에 관한 피의자의 신병구금에 관한 우리측 대안을 수락할 용의를 표명한데 대하여 감사를 드리는 바이다. 동시에 우리는 미측이 제시한 2개의 양해사항에 대하여:

(1) 신병구금에 합의를 요한다는 첫째 양해사항에 대하여서는 ~~양측의 합의가 없으면~~ 국가안전에 관한 피의자를(의) 구금 여부는 한국당국만이 결정해야 될것이다 ~~못할 가능성이 있으므로 삭제할것을 주장한다.~~

(2) 우리는 한국의 구금 시설은 미국수준에 의하여 적당하여야 한다는 미측의 양해사항을 기록에 남길것을 수락하는 바이다.

다. 피의자의 신병이 한국당국에 있을때에는 특수한 경우를 제외하고는 거의 모두 미측에 이양할 용의가 있으며 특수한 경우에 한국당국이 신병을 구금할

0057

때에도 그필요성 유무에 관하여서는 합동위원회에 회부하여 미측의 양해를 구할 용의가 있다.

6. 피의자의 권리

가. 지난번 회의에서 미측은 피의자의 권리중 부과적 권리인 (1) 영문으로된 재판의 축어적 보고서를 받을 권리와 (2) 상소의 권리중 "형을 선고받는 경우 법원으로 부터 상소의 권리와 상소할 기간을 고지 받는다"는 초안 규정의 삭제를 제의한데 대하여 감사를 드리는 바이며, 이러한 협조적 정신으로 기타 부문에 관하여서도 우리측 (이 50차 회의에서 제시한) 입장을 참작하여 주기를 바란다.

1966. 12. 31. 에 예고문에 의거 일반문서로 재분류됨

0058

1. The provision of Re paragraph 9(l) of the Korean draft in the agreed minutes guarantees to all persons on trial in the Korean court not only those rights enumerated in paragraph 9 of the main text tabled by the United States negotiators, but also such other rights as are provided under the Constitution and laws of the Republic of Korea. Therefore, the Korean negotiators, with the view to eliminating the unnecessary and duplicate enumeration, propose the deletion of the following trial safeguards and rights enumerated in the Re paragraph 9 of the U.S. agreed minutes: the first sentence of Re paragraph 9(a), the latter part of the second subparagraph of Re paragraph 9(b), Re paragraph 9(c) and (d), Re paragraph 9(f), the preamble of Re paragraph 9, additional right of subparagraph (b), (c), (d), (g), (h), (j) and the entire provisions except the second and third provisions of subparagraph (l) of the Re paragraph 9.

2. The following provisions are either objectionable or questionable from the view point of relevant laws and regulations currently in effect and our views and counter-proposals on these provisions were presented.

(1) Re paragraph 9(a)

With respect to a military tribunal provided in the second sentence of paragraph 9(a), the Korean negotiators would like to withhold their views until such time as the matter would be taken up in connection with text Para. (2) at a subsequent meeting.

(2) Re paragraph 9(b)

The Korean negotiators propose to delete the sentence with respect to the right to be informed a reasonable time prior to trial of the nature of the evidence that is to be used against the accused since there is no counterpart

0059

provision in the Korean code of criminal procedures and it is contrary to the spirit of the existing Law. However, in accordance with the provisions of article 291, 292, 293, 296 and 307 of the Korean Code of Criminal Procedure, during the proceedings of a trial, the nature of the evidence is informed to the accused.

(3) Re Paragraph 9(e)

If the United States negotiators delete the word "confidentially" from the draft, the Korean negotiators will have no objection to the right to legal representation. The present Korean system requires to put the accused under surveillance of the competent officer during the interview. However, such presence of an officer shall not in any way interfere with the right of a counsel to communicate freely with the accused.

(4) Re Paragraph 9(g)

1) The Korean negotiators guarantee that a representative of the Government, a counsel, an interpreter, and the accused himself are all given the right to be present at all of the judicial proceedings. Therefore, it is entirely within the scope of discretion on the part of such a representative whether or not to exercise the already granted right. The Korean negotiators deem it extremely unfair that the absence of a representative of his own accord nullifies the statements of the accused, whereas the absence of a representative and the admissibility of statements as valid evidence are different matters. The Korean negotiators, therefore, propose to delete the sentence "and no statement of the accused taken in the absence of such a representative shall be admissible as evidence in support of the guilt of the accused."

0060

2) Subparagraph 2 of Re paragraph 9 of the Korean draft regarding a public trial should be included as an additional sentence to Re paragraph 9(g) of the U.S. draft so that the provision of Re paragraph 9(g) may not prejudice the provisions of article 105 of the Constitution and article 53 of Court Organization Law. While the provisions guarantee that trials and decisions of the courts shall be open to the public, they also provide that trials may be closed to the public by a court decision when there is a possibility that open trials may disturb the public safety and order or be harmful to decent customs.

(5) Additional right (a)

Korean negotiators are prepared to accept the U.S. draft with the understanding that U.S. side would bear the expenses incurred in accordance with the provision of Article 56-2 of the Korean Code of Criminal Procedure.

(6) Additional right (e)

The Korean negotiators propose the deletion of the subparagraph with respect to the right that the accused shall not be subject to a heavier penalty than the one that was applicable at the time the alleged criminal offense was committed, the Korean negotiators have no objection to it, however, regarding the latter part of subparagraph (e), it would be contrary to the spirit of judicial appeal system, if a prosecutor, defeder of public interests, were not permitted to appeal to a higher court when he considers the amount of punishment or the judgement of factsare not proper. Consequently, a heavier penalty may be imposed by a higher court when appeal of a prosecutor is granted. Therefore, the Korean negotiators propose the U.S. draft be replaced by the following:

0061

"shall not be subject to a heavier penalty than the one that was applicable at the time the alleged criminal offense was committed or was adjudged by the court of the first instance as the original sentence when an appeal of a case is made by or on behalf of the accused."

(7) Additional right (f)

The Korean negotiators wish to hear the clarification of the meaning of the phraseology "requirement of proof."

(8) Additional right (i)

Korean negotiators interpret U.S. draft as impling merely that U.S. offenders should not be subject to punishment other than the decision of judicial court. If the interpretation is correct, and concurred by U.S. side the Korean side may further consider the U.S. draft.

(9) Additional right (k)

With respect to the provision of subparagraph (k), the Korean negotiators propose the following alternative draft:

"shall be entitled to request the postponement of his presence at a trial if he is physically or mentally unfit to stand trial and participate in his defense;"

The U.S. version does not preclude a possibility of abuses of such right as provided in U.S. draft by the accused. Furthermore, the Korean negotiators deem it proper for the court to give consideration to the request of the accused and approve the postponement of trial. The above proposal is also compatible with the provision of article 306 of the Korean Code of Criminal Procedure regarding the suspension of procedure of public trial on the basis of mental or physical unfitness.

0062

(10) Additional right (1)

1) Regarding the right provided in the second provision of subparagraph (1), the Korean negotiators propose the deletion of the word "improper" from the U.S. draft to avoid the ambiguity of the meaning of the word.

2) With respect to the right provided in the third provision of subparagraph (1), the Korean negotiators propose the deletion of the provision for the reasons explained in the clause of additional right (e). Article 361 and 383 of the Korean Code of Criminal Procedure enumerate reasons of appeal to an appellate or the Supreme court respectively.

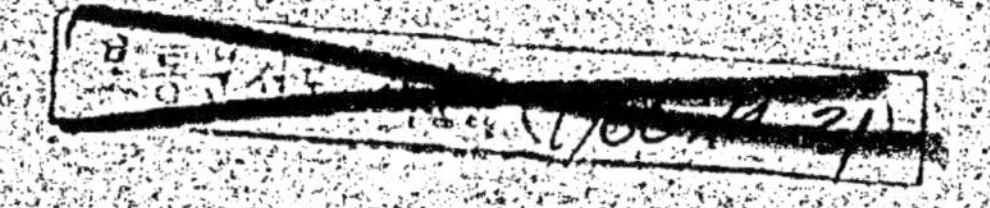

0063

Since the drafts on the subject of Criminal Jurisdiction were exchanged at the 42nd meeting, the positions of both sides have become quite clear through a number of meetings over three months. During the period, the both sides have had considerable time to study on each others' positions as well as their major concerns. We believe past sessions have been productive in this sense.

However, we still face a wide gap between the two positions and the Korean negotiators believe it is a high time for both side to endeavor in order to narrow down the differences which exist between the two drafts readjust their positions based in the spirit of friendly understanding and mutual cooperation.

On our part, we have carefully studied and reviewed the concerns and difficulties of U.S. side as indicated through the meetings and have decided to make voluntary concession in order to accommodate the U.S. side's desire as far as we can go. As you will notice, the new proposal which the Korean negotiators are going to table at today's meeting is indeed a great concession. We sincerely hope that the U.S. negotiators would give due consideration on our new proposals and would convey your views at a later meeting.

Now I would like to explain our new proposals item by item. First, in paragraph 1(a) of our draft, we offer to replace the phrase "the members of the United States armed forces and the civilian components" with new phrase reading "all persons subject to the military law of the United States."

Our new proposal may not sound to you a very much new idea. However, by proposing this phrase, we are prepared to recognize the jurisdiction of U.S. military authorities in Korea over the dependents to the extent they are subject to U.S. military law. Whether the dependents are covered by the uniform code of military justice is a internal matter on your side.

0064

With regard to "authorities of the United States," to exercise criminal jurisdiction in Korea, we have designated the U.S. military authorities as sole authorities to exercise criminal jurisdiction since it is inconceivable for us that authorities other than U.S. military authorities would exercise jurisdiction within theRRepublic of Korea.

The chief U.S. negotiator stated at the 46th session that this is a matter of internal concern for the U.S. and that the language had been made broad enough to provide for any possible exercise of jurisdiction by U.S. authority. However, we are in the opinion that it is not the internal concern soly for the U.S. We believe the authorities of the United States, whether they be military authorities or other than military authorities, to exercise criminal jurisdiction have to be mutually agreed upon. We have serious concern over the statement which implies the possibility of U.S. authorities in Korea other than military authorities exercising judicial power in Korea.

As for the authorities of the Republic of Korea to exercise criminal jurisdiction, we understand your intention of limiting our authorities to civil side is motivated from apprehention that the U.S. military personnel might be tried by the Korean court-martial. We are prepared to assure you that we would not exercise the jurisdiction over U.S. military personnel by military tribunal under any circumstances. Accordingly we propose to record this assurance in the joint minute and we believe you would accept our version. We are sure that our new proposal will certainly meet your requirements.

Turning to the so-called "combat zone", basically, our position of not recognizing the concept of combat zone remains

0065

as before. We understand that the U.S. side's primary objective to establish combat zone is to ensure combat readiness of the U.S. troops by having exclusive criminal jurisdiction in that area. Our view is that a workable arrangements in the custody clause and waiver clause could be agreed upon to satisfy your concern without resorting to the concept of combat zone. Accordingly, we would suggest revision on our draft on the two respective clauses on the condition that the U.S. side will withdraw the concept of combat zone.

0066

~~the condition that the U.S. side will withdraw the concept of combat zone.~~

With respect to paragraphs 3(c) of our draft concerning the problem of waiver of primary right to exercise jurisdiction, we offer to add the following paragraph as first paragraph "the authorities of the Republic of Korea will, upon the notification of individual cases falling under the waiver provided in Article ___ paragraph 3(c) from the military authorities of the United States, waive its primary right to exercise jurisdiction under Article ____ except where they determine that it is of particular importance that jurisdiction be exercised by the authorities of the Republic of Korea."

Further, we propose to add the words "In addition to the foregoing provisions" before the second paragraph which has been placed as the first paragraph in our original draft. We are also prepared to consider the U.S. paragraph "To facilitate the expeditious disposal of offenses of minor importance, arrangements may be made between United States authorities and the competent authorities of the Republic of Korea to dispense with hotification"

As you may notice in our proposal, we are greatly binding ourselves by this paragraph, because under this clause we have to waive most of the cases by simple notification from the U.S. side. Under this clause, our ground for retaining primary right despite the waiver request is extremely limited due to the key phrase "particular importance". We would like to recall that at the previous meeting your side stated that the U.S. intention is to obtain maximum waiver. We believe that our new proposal would effectively meet your device.

0067

As to the procedure for mutual waiver, we would prefer to settle the detailed arrangements through Joint Committee. However, in accordance with the principle set forth above, we could conceive the following detailed procedures for future reference. "When the Korean authorities hold the view that by reason of special circumstances in a specific case, major interests of the Korean administration of justice make imperative the exercise of the Korean jurisdiction, it will notify the military authorities of the United States of that opinion within a reasonable period. In case an understanding cannot be reached in discussion between both sides, the U.S. military authorities will seek agreement of the Joint Committee within fifteen days from the date of receipt of such notification.

If the U.S. authorities do not reply within fifteen days, the request for waiver will be deemed to have recalled." We have mentioned the above procedures as an example. We would propose that the final procedures would be negotiated at the Joint Committee.

With respect to the provisions of the paragraph 5(d) of the Korean draft regarding the pre-trial custody of the accused, we wish to propose the following revision and the additional paragraph 5(e):

"Paragraph 5(d) An accused member of the United States Armed Forces or civilian component over whom the Republic of Korea is to exercise jurisdiction will, if he is in the hand of the United States, be under the custody of the United States during all judicial proceedings and until custody is requested by the authorities of the Republic of Korea.

0068

The military authorities of the United States may transfer custody to the Korean authorities at any time and shall give sympathetic consideration to any request for the transfer of custody which may be made by the Korean authorities in specific cases.

Paragraph 5(e) In respect of offenses solely against the security of the Republic of Korea provided in Paragraph 2(c), custody shall remain with the authorities of the Republic of Korea."

We with a view to sufficing the desires of the U.S. negotiators to the maximum extent, generally accepting the context of the U.S. draft, proposed to provide some additional provisions to faciliate expeditious investigation and trial on the part of the authorities of the Republic of Korea.

With respect to the provisions regarding the custody in the hands of the Republic of Korea, we are assuring you that custody be turned over in the hands of the United States unless there is any specific reason and if there arise the question as the existence of adequate cause and necessity to retain such accused they will be determined at the Joint Committee.

With respect to pre-trial custody of the security offenses, we would like to emphasize that it remains as their firm position that the custody of such offender should rest with the authorities of the Republic of Korea since it is possible that a offender of the security offenses against the Republic of Korea, taking advantage of their custody in the hands the authorities other than Korea may disclose information to others, accordingly the Korean negotiators find no reason the military authorities of the United States should take in custody of such offender.

0069

The Korean negotiators would like to delete from the provision of paragraph 3(a) (ii) of the Korean draft the sentence "provided that such act or omission is directly related to the duty. The question as to whether offenses were committed in the performance of official duty shall be decided by a competent district public prosecutor of the Republic of Korea. In case the offender's commanding officer finds otherwise, he may appeal from the prosecutor's decision to the Ministry of Justice within ten days from the receipt of the decision of the prosecutor, and the decision of the Minister of Justice shall be final." and propose the following alternative draft as agreed minute re Paragraph 3(a) (ii). If the U.S. negotiators accept the proposed alternative draft, the Korean negotiators would give favorable consideration to the U.S. proposal made at the previous meeting to record in the Joint Summary the definition of official duty modified after the FEAF version of 1956:

Re Paragraph 3(a) (ii)

"Where a member of the United States armed forces or civilian component is charged with an offense, a certificate issued by a staff judge advocate on behalf of his commanding officer stating that the alleged offense, if committed by him, arose out of an act or omission done in the performance of official duty, shall be sufficient evidence of the fact for the purpose of determining primary jurisdiction, unless the contrary is proved.

If the chief prosecutor of the Republic of Korea considers that there is proof contrary to the certificate of official duty, he will refer the matter to the Joint Committee for decision.

0070

The above statements shall not be interpreted to prejudice in any way Article 308 of the Korean Code of Criminal Procedure."

The Korean negotiators propose the alternative draft to meet the desires expressed by the United States negotiators with respect to the issuance of a duty certificate for determining primary jurisdiction over offenses arising out of an act done in the performance of official duty.

1. However, the Korean negotiators, taking into account the highly legal affairs involved, deem it proper that a staff judge advocate should exercise the right to make such determination on behalf of the commanding officer of divisional level.

2. With respect to the validity of a duty certificate, the Korean draft provided that a certificate shall be sufficient evidence of the fact for the purpose of determining primary jurisdictioh, unless the contrary is proved, whereas the U.S. draft provides that it shall be conclusive. The Korean negotiators believe that the Korean authorities should be accorded the opportunity to express their views as to the validity of a certificate in the event they find evidence contrary to the certificate.

3. The Korean draft provided the Joint Committee as the reviewing system of disputes to work out a mutually acceptable solution.

4. The Korean negotiators reserved to the court the power to make determination of fact by referring to Article 308 of the Korean Code of Criminal Procedure.

0071

With respect to martial law clause, we have already mentioned our intention of giving assurance that the U.S. military personnel would not be subject to the Korean court-martial. As we understand your major interest in this clause is not to subject U.S. military personnel to our military tribunal which would be established under martial law, we believe that with this assurance your major requirement is satisfied and we hope your side would withdraw the provisions with regard to martial law.

With regard to the exclusive jurisdiction, at the previous meeting, your side stated that you would study the legal aspects of the problem involved. We are still awaiting U.S. response in this regard.

0072

Re Paragraph 3(a) (ii)

Where a member of the United States armed forces or civilian component is charged with an offense, a certificate issued by a staff judge advocate on behalf of his commanding officer stating that the alleged offense, if committed by him, arose out of an act or omission done in the performance of official duty, shall be sufficient evidence of the fact for the purpose of determining primary jurisdiction, unless the contrary is proved.

If the chief prosecutor of the Republic of Korea considers that there is proof contrary to the certificate of official duty, he will refer the matter to the Joint Committee for decision.

The above statements shall not be interpreted to prejudice in any way Article 308 of the Korean Code of Criminal Procedure.

0073

Paragraph 5(d)

An accused member of the United States Armed Forces or civilian component over whom the Republic of Korea is to exercise jurisdiction will, if he is in the hand of the United States, be under the custody of the United States during all judicial proceedings and until custody is requested by the authorities of the Republic of Korea.

The military authorities of the United States may transfer custody to the Korean authorities at any time and shall give sympathetic consideration to any request for the transfer of custody which may be made by the Korean authorities in specific cases.

Paragraph 5(e)

In respect of offenses solely against the security of the Republic of Korea provided in Paragraph 2(c), custody shall remain with the authorities of the Republic of Korea.

0074

Agreed Minute

Re Paragraph 3(c)

The authorities of the Republic of Korea will, upon the notification of individual cases falling under the waiver provided in Article ____ paragraph 3(c) from the military authorities of the United States, waive its primary right to exercise jurisdiction under Article ____ except where they determine that it is of particular importance that jurisdiction be exercised by the authorities of the Republic of Korea.

0075

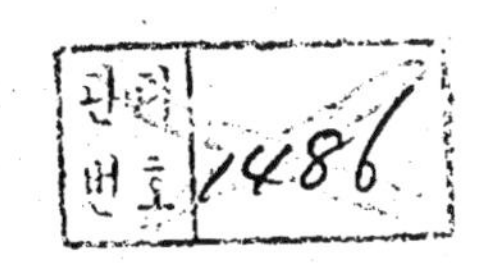

기 안 용 지

자체 통제		기안처	미주과 이근	전화번호	근거서류접수일자

과장	국장	차관	장관

관계관 서명	

기안 년월일	1964. 7. 30.	시행 년월일	83	보존 년한		정서	기장
분류 기호	외구미 722.2—	전체 통제	종결				

경유 수신 참조	대통령, 참조: 비서실장 국무총리, 참조: 비서실장 사본: 법무부장관	발신	장관

제목	제 59 차 주둔군지위협정 체결 교섭 실무자회의 개최 보고

1964. 7. 28. 하오 3 시 부터 동 4 시 45 분 까지 외무부 제 1 회의실에서 개최된 제 59 차 주둔군지위협정 체결 교섭 실무자회의에서 토의된 내용을 별첨과 같이 보고합니다.

유 첨: 제 59 차 주둔군지위협정 체결 교섭실무자회의 보고서. 1 부. 끝.

보통문서로 재분류(1966.12.31.)

1966.12.31 에 예고문에 의거 일반문서로 재분류됨

1964. 8. 3 외무부

승인서식 1—1—3 (11 00900—03) (195mm×265mm16절지)

0076

제 59 차

한.미 간 주둔군지위협정 체결 교섭실무자회의

보 고 서

1. 일 시: 1964 년 7 월 28 일 하오 3 시 부터 동 4 시 45 분 까지.

2. 장 소: 외무부 제 1 회의실

3. 토의사항:

형사재판관할권

가. 관할권의 인적범위 및 미측의 행사기관

(1) 우리측은 관할권의 인적적용범위를 "미군법에 복하는 모든 자"로 할 것을 계속 주장하고 협정은 장차 일어날 모든 사항에 대처하기 위하여 융통성이 있어야 한다는 원칙에는 반대하지 않으나 미측이 주장한 바와 같이 장차의 입법사항과 같은 불확실한 요소는 협정 체결 교섭에 영향을 미칠 수 없는 것이며 1960 년도에 미대심원은 가족이 평화시 미군법에 복하지 않는다고 판결한바 있으나 장차 그 판결이 번복될 가능성도 예상할 수 있음을 지적하고

(2) 미측이 피의자인 민간인을 본국으로 이송하여 재판하려는데 대하여서는 범죄지에서 가까운 장소에서 재판해야 한다는 현대재판제도의 정신에 위배되는 것이며 머욱이 일 주권국가 내에서 범한 범죄에 관하여 타 주권국가로 이송 재판한다는 것은 주권 침해의 문제를 야기함으로 미측 주장은 수락할 수 없다고 우리측 태도를 밝혔다.

나. 한국의 관할권 행사기관

(1) 미측이 한국의 관할권 행사기관을 "대한민국 민사당국"으로 할 것을 주장한 것은 한국정부가 여하한 경우에도 미군을 한국의 군사재판에 회부하지 않을 것이라는 언질을 미측에 준 의도를 시사한 것이라고 말한데 대하여 우리는 미군이 군법재판에 회부되기를 원치 않는 미측의 요구를 충족시키기 위하여 그러한 보장을 한 것이며

(2) 우리측이 만일 미측이 주장하는 바와 같이 관할권의 행사기관을 "대한민국 민사당국"이라는 선례에도 없는 제한적 용어를 수락한다면 우리 나라 국민감정이나 국회가 용인하지는 않을 것이라고 설명하고 우리측 제안을 수락할 것을 요구하였다.

0077

64-3-65

61-3-25 (3) 미3·문 110-2(3)

0078

다. 공무 집행중 범죄

(1) 미측은 제 58 차 회의에서 우리측 공무 집행중 범죄에 관한 제안을 검토하는 조건으로 (가) 증명서는 수정에 합의되지 않는한 최종적이며 (나) 피의자는 증명서에 관한 재심이 지연되는 탓으로 신속한 재판을 받을 권리를 박탈당하여서는 않된다는 양해사항을 우리측이 수락할 것을 요구하였으나

(2) 우리측은 미군이 발행한 증명서의 증명력에 대하여 반증이 제시된 이상 미측 주장대로 일방적으로 결정되어서는 아니되며 일단 합동위원회에 회부하여 쌍방의 합의로서 해결지우는 방도를 발견해야 할 것이라고 주장하였다.

라. 전투지역의 개념 및 제 일차관할권의 포기

(1) 미측은 우리측이 제일차관할권의 포기에 관한 미측 제안을 수락한다면 그대신 전투지역의 개념 및 한국군인이 범하면 한국군법재판에 회부될 그러한 범죄를 범한 미군인은 미군법재판에 회부한다는 규정을 삭제할 용의가 있음을 밝힌데 대하여 우리는 그러한 미측의 제안이 조건부이긴 하지만 미측이 전투지역의 개념을 삭제할 용의를 표명한데 대하여 환영의 뜻을 표하고 그러나

(2) 설사 미측이 전투지역의 개념을 철회한다 하여도 제일차관할권의 포기에 관한 규정 만으로도 미측은 한국당국으로 부터 관할권의 전면적 포기를 획득하려는 그들의 목적을 달성할 수 있을 것임을 지적하였다. 즉 미측 초안에 의하면

(가) 한국당국은 미측으로부터의 포기 통고를 받으면 자동적으로 포기하게 되어 있으며

(나) 특별한 경우 한국당국이 포기를 철회하려면 합동위원회의 합의를 얻어야 하며

(다) 일단 포기한 범죄는 모든 목적을 위하여 확정적이고도 최종적일 것을 요구하고 있음으로 수락할 수 없다고 말하고

(3) 우리는 일본이 미.일간 협정 하에서 관할권을 포기하는 정도로 관대하게 포기할 용의가 있지만 원칙적으로 접수국으로서 관할권을 포기할 것인가의 여부를 스스로 결정할 수 있는 재량권을 갖기를 요구하였다.

0079

64-3-66

64-3-25 [illegible] 110-2

0080

마. 재판전 피의자의 신병 구금

(1) 우리측은 재판전 피의자의 신병이 미측 수중에 있을 때에 관한 우리측 대안의 내용은 미측 초안과 동일한 것이며 다만 특수한 경우에 한국당국이 미측에 신병인도를 요청할 때에 미측의 호의적 고려를 보장받을 수 있기를 희망하고 있음을 밝히고

(2) 미측이 한국의 국가안전에 관한 피의자의 신병 구금에 관한 우리측 대안을 수락하는 조건으로 제시한 2 개의 양해사항 중

(가) 신병구금에 합의를 요한다는데 대하여서는 우리는 그러한 피의자의 신병구금의 필요성 여부에 관하여 미측과 상의하지 않는다는 것은 아니지만 한국의 국가 안전에 관한 범죄에 관한 한 한국당국 만이 신병 구금의 정당성 여부를 결정할 유일하고도 최종적인 권리를 보유하여야 한다고 보며

(3) (나) 한국의 구금시설이 미국 수준에 의하여 적당하여야 한다는데 대하여서는 동의함을 표명하였다.

바. 피의자의 권리

미측이 58 차 회의에서 피의자의 권리중 (가) 영문으로 된 재판의 축어적 기록을 받을 권리와 (나) 상소의 권리중 "형의 선고를 받는 경우 법원으로 부터 상소의 권리와 상소할 기간을 고지 받는다"는 초안규정을 삭제한데 대하여 사의를 표하고 우리측이 제 50 차 회의에서 이의를 제시한 기타 부분에 대하여서도 참작할 것을 미측에 촉구하였다.

사. 미측 반향

미측은 상기와 같은 우리측 입장에 대하여 수락할 수 없다는 의견을 제시하고 이를 검토하여 다음 기회에 답변할 것이라고 말하였다.

4. 기타 사항: 차기 회의 일자: 1964 년 8 월 7 일 하오 3 시 부터. 끝.

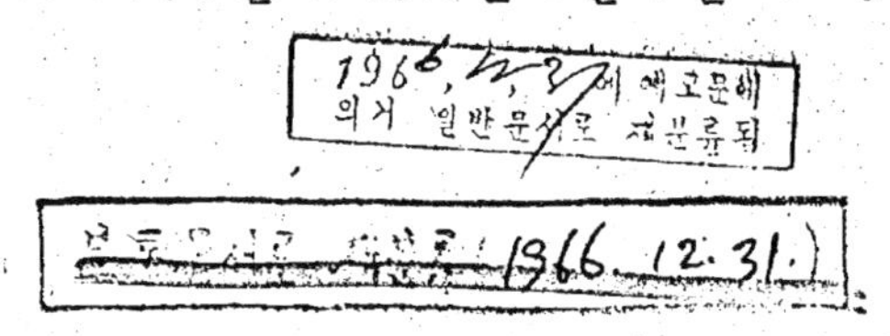

64-3-69

CONFIDENTIAL

STATUS OF FORCES NEGOTIATIONS: 59th Meeting

SUBJECT: Criminal Jurisdiction

PLACE: Ministry of Foreign Affairs

DATE: July 28, 1964

PARTICIPANTS:

Republic of Korea	United States
CHANG Sang-mun	Philip C. Habib
KU Chung-hoe	Brig. General G.G. O'Connor, nUSA
Major YI Kae-hun, ROKA	Colonel Howard Smigelow, USA
HWANG Yong-chae	Captain John Wayne, USN
YI Kun-pal (Interpreter)	Colonel Kenneth C. Crawford, USA
	~~Benjamin A. Fleck~~ Frank R. LaMacchia
	~~Robert A.~~ Benjamin A. Fleck
	Robert A. Kinney
	Major Alton H. Harvey, USA
	Kenneth Campen (Interpreter)
	Daniel A. O'Donohue (Observer)

0083

~~SOFA NEGOTIATIONS~~

1. Mr. Habib opened the meeting by introducing Major Harvey, who was replacing Lt. Colonel Wright as a member of the U. S. negotiating team. Mr. Chang welcomed Major Harvey to the negotiations.

Criminal Jurisdiction

2. Taking up the criminal jurisdiction article, Mr. Chang stated that at the previous session the Korean negotiators had expressed their initial disappointment at the response made by the U. S. negotiators to the proposals tabled by the Korean negotiators at the 50th and 52nd meetings. The Korean negotiators, after studying the U. S. position, would like to make a point by point comment on the U. S. response to their proposals.

3. Mr. Chang then made the following statement:

4. "a. All persons subject to the military law of the U. S., Para 1(a)

"With respect to our proposal to substitute the phrase 'all persons subject to the military law of the United States' for the phrase 'the members of the U. S. armed forces and the civilian components,' the U. S. side gave an assurance that the U. S. Government has no intention to establish civil courts which could exercise jurisdiction in the Republic of Korea. At the same time, the U. S. negotiators stated their preference for the language in their draft to the Korean proposal, on the grounds that legislation may be passed eventually in the U. S. which would provide that any accused U. S. civilian abroad could be taken to the U. S. for trial.

5. "We have no objection to the principle that the SOFA language should be flexible enough to accommodate all future eventualities. However,

0084

it is inconceivable that such an uncertain eventuality as the legislation referred to by the U.S. negotiators should affect in any way our Status of Forces negotiations. Furthermore, decisions of the Supreme Court of the United States on the matter have been subject to reversal since 1956. Therefore, we can think not only of the possibility over which the U.S. negotiators are concerned but also of the possibility that the U.S. Supreme Court may eventually reverse its decision of 1960 so that civilian offenders may be tried by U.S. Court Martial overseas.

6. "Moreover, in our view, the proposed idea of taking the accused civilians back to the U.S. for trial is neither consonant with the established principle of judicial proceedings nor acceptable to any sovereign nation hosting foreign troops. We believe the contemporary principle and practice of trial in any given country demand that the trial should be held at the place where the offense is committed or at least at a place reasonably distant from the site of the crime. We also believe that if an accused who committed an offense in the territory of one sovereign country is brought to another sovereign country for trial there would arise a serious question as to infringement of sovereignty."

7. "b. The Civil Authorities of the Republic of Korea, Para. 1(b)

"Regarding the provision of Paragraph 1(b), the United States negotiators stated that the language of paragraph 1(b) of the U.S. draft, 'the civil authorities of the Republic of Korea', sets forth the Korean Government's intention as expressed in assurances given by the Korean negotiators that the Korean Government will not exercise jurisdiction over U.S. military personnel by military tribunal under any circumstances.

0085

8. "The assurance was intended to meet the requirement of the U. S. negotiators, who have expressed their concern over the possibility of subjecting their military personnel to Korean military tribunal and claimed that in no other SOFA has it been agreed to include any provision envisaging such a possibility.

9. "In as much as such a significant assurance was given to your side, we have naturally expected that you would no longer insist on retaining the word 'civil'. Since this word 'civil' cannot be found in other SOFAs we wonder what was your understanding or arrangement with other countries in agreeing to the provision without the word 'civil'.

10. "If the Korean negotiators would accept such unprecedented wording as appeared in the U. S. draft, this would undoubtedly cause very delicate problems in the Korean Government as well as with the Korean people. Neither the sentiment of the Korean people nor the atmosphere of the National Assembly would tolerate acceptance of such a version.

11. "c. Regarding the official duty certificate, the U. S. side stated at the last session the following two points:

(1) The certificate will be conclusive unless modification is agreed upon;

(2) The accused should not be deprived of his entitlement to a prompt and speedy trial as a result of protracted reconsideration of the duty certificate.

12. "The Korean negotiators should like to concentrate on the first point alone at this meeting. The Korean negotiators have studied the U. S. statement, and we have

0086

found that the statement indicates an improvement over the U. S. Agreed Minute re Paragraph 3(a).

13. "The provision of the U. S. Agreed Minute re Paragraph 3(a) reads as follows: 'A certificate issued by or on behalf of his commanding officer etc... shall be conclusive for the purpose of determining primary jurisdiction.' However, the statement the U. S. negotiators made at the last session tells that unless modification is agreed upon either through request of the Korean authorities or otherwise, the certificate will be conclusive. The indication of possible modification is an improvement from our point of view.

14. "At this point, the Korean negotiators believe that the position taken by the United States side in its explanation comes much closer to the alternative proposal submitted by the Korean side.

15. "In our view, any question relating to the certificate could definitely be solved by mutual consultation. Therefore, if there is proof contrary to the certificate, the Matter should be handed over to the Joint Committee for reconsideration.

16. "The point is that the attitude taken by United States side towards the certificate is unilateral, using such word as 'conclusive', indicating that any question raised to the effect of the certificate by the Korean side could be totally disregarded, unless the question is favorably considered. Under these circumstances, we are compelled to state that the U. S. proposal is not acceptable to the Korean side. Whatever mechanism we may choose, we must find a method which would provide means for mutual consultation for solving any problem relating to the validity of the official duty certificate.

0087

17. "d. The Concept of the Combat Zone and the Waiver of the Primary Jurisdiction

"At the previous session, the United States negotiators proposed that if the Korean negotiators would accept the Agreed Minute Re Paragraph 3 of the United States draft with respect to the waiver of primary jurisdiction, the U.S. side would delete the clause on the combat zone of Agreed Minute #1, Re Paragraph 1(b) and Agreed Minute #1, Re Paragraph 3(a). At the same time, the U.S. negotiators added that this proposal was a substantial concession by the U.S. side.

18. "The Korean negotiators appreciate the significant suggestion made by the U.S. side. We take the suggestion as an indication on the U.S. part to accommodate our concern over the proposed concept of the combat zone. Although the indication was conditioned upon the acceptance by the Korean side of the provision of the Agreed Minute Re Paragraph 3 of the U.S. draft, we welcome the qualified responsiveness of the U.S. side.

19. "However, to our regret, we cannot view the U.S. proposal as a significant concession even if the U.S. negotiators would, as indicated, withdraw the concept of the combat zone. The U.S. negotiators would accomplish their ultimate purpose of obtaining total waiver from the Korean authorities by retaining the provisions of the Agreed Minute Re Paragraph 3 of the U.S. draft. Let's review the U.S. draft of the waiver clause, which amounts to what we call 'total waiver'.

20. "According to the provisions of U.S. draft:

(a) The Korean authorities have to waive automatically their primary jurisdiction upon the receipt of notice from U.S. side, dispensing with the request for waiver.

(b) We are also required, as the next step, to seek agreement of the

0088

Joint Committee afterwards to recall the waiver for any particular case.

"(c) Furthermore, the draft provides that the waiver thus granted by the Korean authorities shall be unconditional and final for all purposes and shall bar both the authorities and the nationals of the Republic of Korea from instituting criminal procedures. It is extremely unfair that the United States side, by the mere fact of waiver granted by the Korean Government, intends to bar not only Korean nationals from initiating appropriate remedial actions, but also the authorities of the Korean Government from instituting criminal procedures even in a case where the U.S. has not tried the waivered case.

21. "In this regard, we are unable to find any international precedents similar to the U.S. draft in any other SOFA.

22. "We are willing to assure you that we would be ready to waive the primary jurisdiction as generously as Japan does under the very simple provision in the U.S. -- Japan SOFA. However, as a principle, we believe that the Korean authorities, as the authorities of the receiving state, should have the right to determine at their discretion whether or not to waive primary jurisdiction.

23. "e. Pre-trial Custody, Paragraph 5(d) and 5(e)

"Regarding the subject of pre-trial custody, the U.S. chief negotiator stated that the revised draft of Paragraph 5(d) is an improvement over the original language but they still believed Paragraph 5(c) of the U.S. draft to be preferable. At the same time he stated that the U.S. side was prepared to agree to the revised Paragraph 5(e) of the Korean draft regarding custody in security offenses.

24. "With respect to pre-trial custody in the hands of the U.S., the revised

0089

Korean version of Paragraph 5(d) is almost identical with the language of the U. S. draft and fully reflects the views of the U. S. side. However, the Korean negotiators believe that we should reserve the language which would guarantee the U. S. side's sympathetic consideration to any request for the transfer of custody which may be made by the Korean authorities in specific cases.

25. "With respect to Korean custody in security offenses, the Korean negotiators appreciate the acceptance by the U. S. side of the revised proposal made by the Korean side. However, we have noted that the acceptance by the U. S. side is conditioned upon the acceptance by the Korean negotiators of the two understandings: (a) mutual agreement, and (b) standard of faciliities.

"(a) The first proposed understanding is not acceptable to the Korean negotiators, since we believe that in security offenses, the Korean authorities should be the only and final authorities to determine whether or not such custody is appropriate. This does not necessarily mean that we would not consult with U. S. authorities as to the necessity of such custody. But, as a matter of principle, we believe ~~agreement~~ agreement with U. S. side is not necessary in a security case.

"(b) Regarding the second question, the Korean negotiators are prepared to accept the proposed understanding.

26. "With respect to custody in the hands of the Korean authorities, the Korean negotiators assure you that most cases in the hands of the Korean authorities would be transferred to the U. S. authorities except in specific cases where there is adequate reason to retain such custody. Even in such cases, if there arises any question as to the existence of adequate cause and necessity to retain the accused, the matter will be referred to the Joint Committee for review.

0090

27. "f. Trial Safe Guards

"The Korean negotiators appreciate the proposal by the U.S. negotiators of the following changes in the Agreed Minute Re Paragraph 9 of the U.S. draft:

a) Deletion of subparagraph (a);

b) In subparagraph (b), deletion of all language after the words 'shall have the right to appeal a conviction or sentence.'

28. "The Korean negotiators request that the U.S. negotiators would display the same cooperative spirit and take into consideration other outstanding issues regarding trial safe guards on which the Korean negotiators made their views clear at the 50th session."

0091

29. Mr. Habib stated that the U.S. negotiators would reserve until the next meeting a detailed reply to the remarks just made by the Korean Chief Negotiator. However, the U.S. negotiators would like to make some general observations regarding the positions stated by Mr. Chang.

30. Mr. Habib said the U.S. negotiators do not accept the principle that phraseology appearing in other status of forces agreements is definitive with regard to the Korean SOFA. The U.S. negotiators regarded precedents as useful, but not binding. In addition to the precedents found in the language of other agreements, the negotiators also had to take into account a body of experience. This experience included awareness of the way in which other status of forces agreements were actually working and accumulated knowledge of conditions in Korea. The task at hand was the negotiation of a status of forces agreement for Korea, not for Japan or any other country.

31. Mr. Habib noted that the statement made by the Korean negotiators was simply a repetition of views which they had stated previously and did not appear to take into account the expressed views of the U.S. negotiators on certain key issues. The U.S. negotiators would make detailed comments at the next meeting. Before doing so, they wished to ask a few questions in order to clarify certain points.

32. Regarding Paragraph 1(a), Mr. Habib noted that the Korean negotiators had expressed the wish to retain the phrase "all persons subject to the military law of the United States", despite the assurance given by the U.S. negotiators that no U.S. courts would be established in Korea and despite the desire of the U.S. negotiators to retain flexibility in case legislation should be passed in the future which would establish jurisdiction over U.S. civilians abroad. The objections of the Korean negotiators were apparently based on: (a) a feeling that the passage of such legislation was inconceivable, and (b) the possibility of a reversal of the 1960 Supreme Court decision. In stating these objections, the Korean negotiators were attempting

0098

to exercise the right of review of U.S. legislation, which was certainly not relevant to the question at hand. The Korean negotiators were seeking to differentiate between military personnel and civilians in the application of U.S. law. If U.S. law is to apply, it should apply equally to military personnel and civilians, who are in Korea for the accomplishment of the same mission under the provisions of the Mutual Security Treaty. The U.S. negotiators were concerned that the application of rights under the SOFA should not be discriminatory between the military personnel and the civilians who were in Korea under identical conditions and for the same purpose. Mr. Habib asked what the attitude of the Korean negotiators would be if the Supreme Court decision of 1960 had not been made.

33. Regarding Paragraph 1(b), Mr. Habib stated that the position of the U.S. negotiators that jurisdiction over the U.S. armed forces by the host government should be limited to the civil authorities of that government was a firm U.S. position in every country in which a SOFA is in force. The U.S. negotiators wanted to have it stated explicitly in the SOFA with the ROK. If the Korean negotiators were willing to give the assurances that they had given in this respect, why were they unwilling to spell the assurances out in the Agreement? The absence of the phrase "civil authorities" from other agreements is no reason why it should not be included in this Agreement. The experience of the past two years had clearly shown that the ROK Government does not hesitate to resort to military courts to try civil crimes. The Korean negotiators had argued that it would be difficult to explain this provision to the public and to the National Assembly. Why could the National Assembly not be told simply that the U.S. authorities were unwilling to pass jurisdiction from U.S. military courts to Korean military courts. The U.S. negotiators believed that such an explanation would be palatable and acceptable to the National Assembly. They believed the Korean objections to this provision to be shallow and urged the Korean negotiators to reconsider.

0093

34. With regard to the question of the duty certificate, Mr. Habib reminded the

Korean negotiators that the U.S. negotiators had not responded specifically to the proposed revision of the Agreed Minute Re Paragraph 3(a)(ii) of the Korean draft. Now that the U.S. negotiators had received further explanation of what the Korean negotiators had in mind, they would respond in detail to this proposed revision at the next meeting.

35. With regard to the waiver provision, Mr. Habib said the Korean negotiators appeared to be concerned over the question of automaticity. The concern of the U.S. negotiators was to obtain the maximum possible degree of waiver. The implication of the remarks made by the Korean Chief Negotiator was that the Korean authorities did no desire to try all cases that may arise and that only in special circumstances would they wish to try a case. The U.S. draft does not preclude this and provides the means whereby the Korean authorities could recall their waiver.

36. With regard to pre-trial custody, Mr. Habib noted that the Korean negotiators had made no concessions to meet what the U.S. negotiators consider to be a serious problem. With respect to this subject, also, the U.S. negotiators based their position on experience. The U.S. draft was clear. It provided that defendants in the custody of the U.S. authorities would be produced promptly at the request of the Korean authorities. The U.S. negotiators did not understand the Korean desire to retain custody, except in the case of security cases, with regard to which the U.S. negotiators had made a concession. The U.S. negotiators had also pointed out that the final sentence of Paragraph 5(c) of the U.S. draft was related to this question and would permit the Korean authorities to take custody when requested to do so. In view of the assurances already given by the U.S. negotiators, the Korean authorities could exercise jurisdiction just as effectively if the U.S. military authorities retain custody.

37. Mr. Habib noted that the U.S. negotiators had considered the views of the Korean negotiators regarding trial safeguards and had given their reply. They believed

0094

there was no reason to withdraw elementary safeguards which are generally accepted as necessary under U.S. law, and, in most cases, under ROK law. The trial safeguards listed in the U.S. draft were not onerous and did not detract from the exercise of jurisdiction by the Korean authorities. The objections of the Korean negotiators appeared to rest on narrow legalistic bases. A lack of safeguards for ROK citizens was no argument for the omission of those safeguards from an international agreement. More important criteria for judging these provisions included the questions whether the provisions were onerous, unfair, or lacking precedents. The U.S. negotiators believed them to be not onerous, quite fair, and supported by sound precedents.

38. Mr. Habib asked whether the Korean negotiators wished to make any further comments to assist the U.S. negotiators in their consideration of the Korean position.

39. Mr. Chang replied that a wide gap separated the positions of the two sides. Perhaps the explanation given by the Korean negotiators had not been extensive enough or the U.S. negotiators had misunderstood the Korean position. The question of trial safeguards presented delicate problems. He proposed that this subject be taken up in informal discussions between the legal members of the negotiating teams.

40. Mr. Habib replied that the U.S. negotiators believed that more rapid progress could be made by discussing this question in the negotiating meetings. At the next meeting, the U.S. negotiators would be prepared to hold a point by point discussion of this subject.

41. Mr. Habib remarked that obviously a gap did exist between the two positions. The Korean negotiators were proposing that the U.S. negotiators go all the way toward meeting the Korean position. Such a course would not meet the U.S. requirements.

42. Mr. Chang replied that the Korean negotiators did not expect the U.S. negotiators to come all the way to meet the Korean position. Each side should consider the position of the other. The Korean negotiators believed that international precedents were important. They suggested that standard language be agreed to wherever

possible.

43. Mr. Habib replied that standard language ~~[illegible]~~ should not be used if standard conditions did not exist. The language had to be modified to suit specific situations existing in the country. He suggested that both sides think about these problems.

44. The next meeting was scheduled for August 7 at 3:00 p.m.

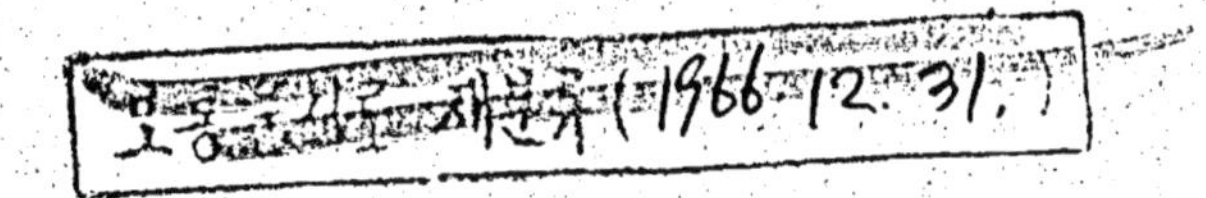

1966.12.31 에 예고문에 의거 일반문서로 재분류됨

0096

Chang
Ku
Maj Lee
[illegible]
Yi Kunpal
Park Won Chul
Park Sang Yong
Hun Hyung Koo
An Yonki

1. Mr. Habib opened the meeting by introducing Major Harvey, who was replacing Lt. Colonel Wright as a member of the U.S. negotiating team. Mr. Chang welcomed Major Harvey to the negotiations.

Criminal Jurisdiction

2. Taking up the criminal jurisdiction article, Mr. Chang stated that at the previous session the Korean negotiators had expressed their initial disappointment at the response made by the U.S. negotiators to the proposals tabled by the Korean negotiators at the 50th and 52nd meetings. The Korean negotiators, after studying the U.S. position, would like to make a point by point comment on the U.S. response to their proposals.

3. Mr. Chang then made the following statement:

4. "a. All persons subject to the military law of the U.S., Para 1(a)

"With respect to our proposal to substitute the phrase 'all persons subject to the military law of the United States' for the phrase 'the members of the U.S. armed forces and the civilian components,' the U.S. side gave an assurance that the U.S. Government has no intention to establish civil courts which could exercise jurisdiction in the Republic of Korea. At the same time, the U.S.

0097

negotiators ~~stated~~ indicated their preference for the language in their draft to the Korean proposal, on the grounds that legislation may be passed eventually in the U.S. which would provide that any accused U.S. civilian abroad could be taken to the U.S. for trial.

5. "We have no objection to the principle that the SOFA language should be flexible enough to accommodate all ~~future~~ eventualities foreseen in the near future. However, it is inconceivable that such an uncertain eventuality as the legislation referred to by the U.S. negotiators should affect in any way our Status of Forces negotiations. Furthermore, decisions of the Supreme Court of the United States on the matter have been subject to reversal since 1956. Therefore, we can think not only of the possibility over which the U.S. negotiators are concerned but also of the possibility that the U.S. Supreme Court may eventually reverse its decision of 1960 so that civilian offenders may be tried by U.S. Court Martial overseas.

6. "Moreover, in our view, the proposed idea of taking the accused civilians back to the U.S. for trial is neither consonant with the established principle of judicial proceedings nor acceptable to any sovereign nation hosting foreign troops. We believe the contemporary principle and practice of trial in any given country demand that the

0098

trial should be held at the place where the offense is committed or at least at a place reasonably distant from the site of the crime. We also believe that if an accused who committed an offense in the territory of one sovereign country is brought to another sovereign country for trial there would arise a serious question as to possible infringement of sovereignty."

7. "b. The civil Authorities of the Republic of Korea, Para. 1(b)

"Regarding the provision of Paragraph 1(b), the United States negotiators stated that the language of paragraph 1(b) of the U.S. draft, 'the civil authorities of the Republic of Korea', sets forth the Korean Government's intention as expressed in assurances given by the Korean negotiators that the Korean Government will not exercise jurisdiction over U.S. military personnel by military tribunal under any circumstances.

8. "The assurance was intended to meet the requirement of the U.S. negotiators, who have expressed their concern over the possibility of subjecting their military personnel to Korean military tribunal ~~and claimed that in no other SOFA has it been agreed to include any provision envisaging such a possibility.~~

0099

9. "Inasmuch as such a significant assurance was given to your side, we have naturally expected that you would no longer insist on retaining the word 'civil'. Since this word 'civil' cannot be found in other SOFAs we wonder what were your understandings or arrangements with other countries in agreeing to the provision without the word 'civil'.

10. "If the Korean negotiators would accept such unprecedented wording as appeared in the U.S. draft, this would undoubtedly cause very delicate problems in the Korean Government as well as with the Korean people. Neither the sentiment of the Korean people nor the atmosphere of the National Assembly would tolerate acceptance of such a version."

11. "e. Official Duty Certificate (Agreed Minutes Re para 3(a)(ii))

11. "e. Regarding the official duty certificate, the U.S. side stated at the last session the following two points:

(1) The certificate will be conclusive unless modification is agreed upon;

(2) The accused should not be deprived of his entitlement to a prompt and speedy trial as a result of protracted reconsideration of the duty certificate.

12. "The Korean negotiators should like to concentrate on the first point alone at this meeting. The Korean

0100

#3.

~~However, the Korean negotiators believe that the U.S. position as explained by the U.S. negotiators at the last session still ~~pose a~~ indicates fundamental difference with the alternative Korean proposal ~~submitted by the Korea side~~ in one respect, namely: unilateral conclusiveness of the certificate issued by the U.S. side.~~

14. In our view, any possible controversy over the duty certificate, though we do not expect to encounter many of them, should be solved by mutual consultation and to ~~the~~ mutual satisfaction ~~and agreement~~. Therefore, if ~~there arises a~~ a controversy arises over the certificate, the matter should be handed over to the Joint Committee for reconsideration. Whatever way we may take to solve this problem of duty certificate, we must find a mechanism under which mutual consultation and agreement are provided for resolution of controversy over the validity of the official duty certificate.

0101

negotiators have studied the U.S. statement, and we have found that the statement indicates an improvement over the U.S. Agreed Minute re Paragraph 3(a).

13. "The provision of the U.S. Agreed Minute re Paragraph 3(a) reads as follows: 'A certificate issued by or on behalf of his commanding officer etc... shall be conclusive for the purpose of determining primary jurisdiction.' However, ~~the statement~~ the U.S. negotiators ~~made~~ at the last session ~~tells~~ stated that unless modification is agreed upon either through request of the Korean authorities or otherwise, the certificate will be conclusive. The indication of possible modification at the request of the Korean authorities is an improvement from our point of view.

14. "At this point, the Korean negotiators believe that the position taken by the United States side in its explanation comes much closer to the alternative proposal submitted by the Korean side.

15. "In our view, any question relating to the certificate could definitely be solved by mutual consultation. Therefore, if there is proof contrary to the certificate, the matter should be handed over to the Joint Committee for reconsideration.

16. "The point is that the attitude taken by United States side towards the certificate is unilateral, using such word as 'conclusive', indicating that any question

3

0102

raised to the effect of the certificate by the Korean side could be totally disregarded, unless the question is favorably considered. Under these circumstances, we are compelled to state that the U.S. proposal is not acceptable to the Korean side. Whatever mechanism we may choose, we must find a method which would provide means for mutual consultation for solving any problem relating to the validity of the official duty certificate.

15. "d. The Concept of the Combat Zone and the Waiver of the Primary Jurisdiction

"At the previous session, the United States negotiators proposed that if the Korean negotiators would accept the Agreed Minute Re Paragraph 3 of the United States draft with respect to the waiver of primary jurisdiction, the U.S. side would delete the clause on the combat zone of Agreed Minute #1, Re Paragraph 1(b) and Agreed Minute #1, Re Paragraph 3(a). At the same time, the U.S. negotiators added that this proposal was a substantial concession by the U.S. side.

16. "The Korean negotiators appreciate the significant suggestion made by the U.S. side. We take the suggestion as an indication on the U.S. part to accommodate our concern

0103

#4

You have to note that the recall of waiver which has automatically been made by the Korean side is not granted by the U.S. side on the same automatic basis. In other words, while the Korean waiver is automatic, U.S. grant of recall is conditioned upon approval by the Joint Committee.

0104

over the proposed concept of the combat zone. Although the ~~indication~~ suggestion was conditioned upon the acceptance by the Korean side of the provision of the Agreed Minute Re Paragraph 3 of the U.S. draft, we welcome the qualified responsiveness of the U.S. side.

19. "However, to our regret, we cannot view the U.S. proposal as a significant concession as the U.S. negotiators have claimed. Even if the U.S. negotiators ~~would, as indicated,~~ withdraw the concept of the combat zone, the U.S. negotiators would accomplish their ultimate purpose of obtaining total waiver from the Korean authorities by retaining the provisions of the Agreed Minute Re Paragraph 3 of the U.S. draft. ~~Let's~~ A quick review of the U.S. draft of the waiver clause would show clearly that the contents of the clause ~~[illegible]~~ amounts to what we call 'total waiver'.

18. "According to the provisions of U.S. draft:

(a) The Korean authorities have to waive automatically their primary jurisdiction upon the receipt of notice from the U.S. side, ~~dispensing with~~ instead of the request for waiver.

(b) ~~[illegible]~~ The Korean authorities are also required ~~as the next step~~ to seek agreement of the Joint Committee ~~afterwards~~ in case they desire to recall the waiver for any particular case.

4

(c) Furthermore, the U.S. draft provides that the waiver thus granted by the Korean authorities shall be unconditional

0105

#5. 1991 후72

This right can not be replaced by the automatic waiver clause which the U.S. side seeks. We should like to reiterate our position that whatever the final agreement we may reach on this subject, the agreement has to retain the language and mechanism that would provide for the principle of self-determination by the Korean auth. on waiver of primary jurisdiction.

0106

and final for all purposes and shall bar both the authorities and the nationals of the Republic of Korea from instituting criminal procedures. It is extremely unfair that the United States side, by the mere fact of waiver granted by the Korean authorities, intends to bar not only Korean nationals from initiating appropriate remedial actions, but also to prevent the authorities of the Korean Government from instituting criminal procedures even in a case where the U.S. has not tried the waivered case.

18. In this regard, we are unable to find any international precedents similar to the U.S. draft in any other SOFA.

19. "We are willing to assure you that we are prepared to waive the primary jurisdiction as generously as any NATO party does under the very simple provision in NATO SOFA. However, as a matter of principle, we believe that the Korean authorities, as the authorities of the receiving state, should have the right to determine whether or not to waive primary jurisdiction.

20. "e. Pre-trial Custody, Paragraph 5(d) and 5(e)

"Regarding the subject of pre-trial custody, the U.S. chief negotiator stated that the revised draft of

Paragraph 5(d) is an improvement over the original language but they still believed Paragraph 5(c) of the U.S. draft to be preferable. At the same time he stated that the U.S. side was prepared to agree to the revised Paragraph 5(e) of the Korean draft regarding custody in security offenses.

21. "With respect to pre-trial custody in the hands of the U.S., the revised Korean version of Paragraph 5(d) is almost identical with the language of the U.S. draft and fully reflects the views of the U.S. side. However, the Korean negotiators believe that they should reserve the language which would guarantee the U.S. side's sympathetic consideration to any request for the transfer of custody which may be made by the Korean authorities in specific cases.

22. "With respect to Korean custody in security offenses, the Korean negotiators appreciate the acceptance by the U.S. side of the revised proposal made by the Korean side. However, we have noted that the acceptance by the U.S. side is conditioned upon the acceptance by the Korean negotiators of the two understandings:

(a) The first proposed understanding is not acceptable to the Korean negotiators, since we believe that in security offenses, the Korean authorities should be the only and final authorities to determine whether or not such custody is appropriate. This does not necessarily mean that we would

0108

not consult with U.S. authorities as to the necessity of such custody. But, as a matter of principle, we believe agreement with U.S. side is not necessary in a security case.

"(b) Regarding the second question, the Korean negotiators are prepared to accept the proposed understanding.

26. "With respect to custody in the hands of the Korean authorities, the Korean negotiators assure you that most cases in the hands of the Korean authorities would be transferr-d to the U.S. authorities except in specific cases where there is adequate reason to retain such custody. Even in such cases, if there arises any question as to the existence of adequate cause and necessity to retain the accused, the matter will be referred to the Joint Committee for review.

23. "f. Trial ~~Safe Guards~~ Safeguards

"The Korean negotiators appreciate the proposal made ~~by~~ by the U.S. negotiators ~~of~~ to effect the following changes in the Agreed Minute Re Paragraph 9 of the U.S. draft:

(a) Deletion of Subparagraph (a);

(b) In subparagraph (b), deletion of all language after the words 'shall have the right to appeal a conviction or sentence.'

24. "The Korean negotiators ~~request~~ hope that the U.S. negotiators would ~~display the same cooperative spirit and~~

0109

~~take into~~ consider~~ation~~ other outstanding issues regarding trial safe guards on which the Korean negotiators made their views clear at the 50th session and respond at an early meeting."

25. Mr. Habib stated that the U.S. negotiators would reserve until the next meeting a detailed reply to the remarks just made by the Korean Chief Negotiator. However, the U.S. negotiators would like to make some general observations regarding the positions stated by Mr. Chang.

26. Mr. Habib said the U.S. negotiators do not accept the principle that phraseology appearing in other status of forces agreements is definitive with regard to the Korean SOFA. The U.S. negotiators regarded precedents as useful, but not binding. In addition to the precedents found in the language of other agreements, the negotiators also had to take into account a body of experience. This experience included awareness of the way in which other status of forces agreements were actually working and accumulated knowledge of conditions in Korea. The task at hand was the negotiation of a status of forces agreement for Korea, not for Japan or any other country.

27. Mr. Habib noted that the statement made by the Korean negotiators was simply a repetition of views which they had stated previously and did not appear to take into

0110

account the expressed views of the U.S. negotiators on certain key issues. The U.S. negotiators would make detailed comments at the next meeting. Before doing so, they wished to ask a few questions and make some remarks in order to clarify certain points.

3. Regarding Paragraph 1(a), Mr. Habib noted that the Korean negotiators had expressed the wish to retain the phrase "all persons subject to the military law of the United States", despite the assurance given by the U.S. negotiators that no U.S. courts would be established in Korea and despite the desire of the U.S. negotiators to retain flexibility in case legislation should be passed in the future which would establish jurisdiction over U.S. civilians abroad. The objections of the Korean negotiators were apparently based on: (a) a feeling that the passage of such legislation was inconceivable, and (b) the possibility of a reversal of the 1960 Supreme Court decision. In stating these objections, the Korean negotiators were attempting to exercise the right of review of U.S. legislation, which was certainly not relevant to the question at hand. The Korean negotiators were seeking to differentiate between military personnel and civilians in the application of U.S. law. If U.S. law is to apply,

0111

it should apply equally to military personnel and civilians, who are in Korea for the accomplishment of the same mission under the provisions of the Mutual Security Treaty. The U.S. negotiators were concerned that the application of rights under the SOFA should not be discriminatory between the military personnel and the civilians who were in Korea under identical conditions and for the same purpose. Mr. Habib asked what the attitude of the Korean negotiators would be if the Supreme Court decision of 1960 had not been made.

29 30. Regarding Paragraph 1(b), Mr. Habib stated that the position of the U.S. negotiators that jurisdiction over the U.S. armed forces by the host government should be limited to the civil authorities of the government was a firm U.S. position in every country in which a SOFA is in force. The U.S. negotiators wanted to have it stated explicitly in the SOFA with the ROK. If the Korean negotiators were willing to give the assurances that they had given in this respect, why were they unwilling to spell the assurances out in the Agreement? The absence of the phrase "civil authorities" from other agreements is no reason why it should not be included in this Agreement. The experience of the past two years had clearly shown that the ROK Government does

0112

not hesitate to resort to military courts to try civil crimes. The Korean negotiators had argued that it would be difficult to explain this provision to the public and to the National Assembly. Why could the National Assembly not be told simply that the U.S. authorities were unwilling to pass jurisdiction from U.S. military courts to Korean military courts. The U.S. negotiators believed that such an explanation would be palatable and acceptable to the National Assembly. They believed the Korean objections to this provision to be shallow and urged the Korean negotiators to reconsider.

30. With regard to the question of the duty certificate, Mr. Habib reminded the Korean negotiators that the U.S. negotiators had not responded specifically to the proposed revision of the Agreed Minute Re Paragraph 3(a) (ii) of the Korean draft. Now that the U.S. negotiators had received further explanation of what the Korean negotiators had in mind, they would respond in detail to this proposed revision at the next meeting.

31. With regard to the waiver provision, Mr. Habib said the Korean negotiators appeared to be concerned over the question of automaticity. The concern of the U.S. negotiators was to obtain the maximum possible degree of

0113

waiver. The implication of the remarks made by the Korean Chief Negotiator was that the Korean authorities did not desire to try all cases that may arise and that only in special circumstances would they wish to try a case. The U.S. draft does not preclude this and provides the means whereby the Korean authorities could seek recall of their waiver ~~recall their waiver~~.

32. With regard to pre-trial custody, Mr. Habib noted that the Korean negotiators had made no concessions to meet what the U.S. negotiators consider to be a serious problem. With respect to this subject, also, the U.S. negotiators based their position on experience. The U.S. draft was clear. It provided that defendants in the custody of the U.S. authorities would be produced promptly at the request of the Korean authorities. The U.S. negotiators did not understand the Korean desire to retain custody, except in the case of security cases, with regard to which the U.S. negotiators had made a concession. The U.S. negotiators had also pointed out that the final sentence of Paragraph 5(c) of the U.S. draft was related to this question and would permit the Korean authorities to take custody when requested to do so. In view of the assurances on presentation of the accused already given by the U.S. negotiators, the Korean authorities could exercise jurisdiction just as effectively if the U.S. military authorities retain custody.

0114

33. Mr. Habib noted that the U.S. negotiators had considered the views of the Korean negotiators regarding trial safeguards and had given their reply. They believed there was no reason to withdraw elementary safeguards which are generally accepted as necessary under U.S. law and, in most cases, under ROK law. The trial safeguards listed in the U.S. draft were not onerous and did not detract from the exercise of jurisdiction by the Korean authorities. The objections of the Korean negotiators appeared to rest on narrow legalistic bases. A lack of safeguards for ROK citizens was no argument for the omission of those safeguards from an international agreement. More important criteria for judging these provisions included the question whether the provisions were onerous, unfair, or lacking precedents. The U.S. negotiators believed them to be not onerous, quite fair, and supported by sound precedents.

34. Mr. Habib asked whether the Korean negotiators wished to make any further comments to assist the U.S. negotiators in their consideration of the Korean position.

35. Mr. Chang replied that a wide gap separated the positions of the two sides. Perhaps the explanation given by the Korean negotiators had not been extensive enough or the U.S. negotiators had misunderstood the Korean position.

0115

The question of trial safeguards presented delicate problems. He proposed that this subject be taken up in informal discussions between the legal members of the negotiating teams.

36. Mr. Habib replied that the U.S. negotiators believed that more rapid progress could be made by discussing this question in the negotiating meetings. At the next meeting, the U.S. negotiators would be prepared to hold a point by point discussion of this subject.

37. Mr. Habib remarked that obviously a gap did exist between the two positions. The Korean negotiators were proposing that the U.S. negotiators go all the way toward meeting the Korean position. Such a course would not meet the U.S. requirements.

38. Mr. Chang replied that the Korean negotiators did not expect the U.S. negotiators to come all the way to meet the Korean position. Each side should consider the position of the other. The Korean negotiators believed that international precedents were important. They suggested that standard language be agreed to wherever possible.

39. Mr. Habib replied that standard language should not be used if standard conditions did not exist. The language had to be modified to suit specific situations existing in

0116

the country. He suggested that both sides think about these problems.

44. The next meeting was scheduled for August 7 at 3:00 p.m.

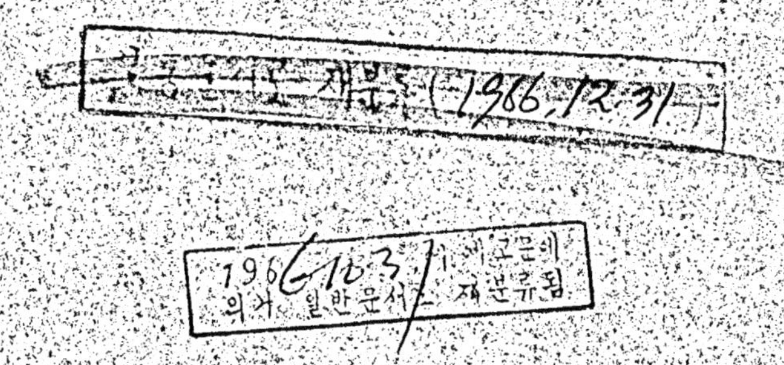

0117

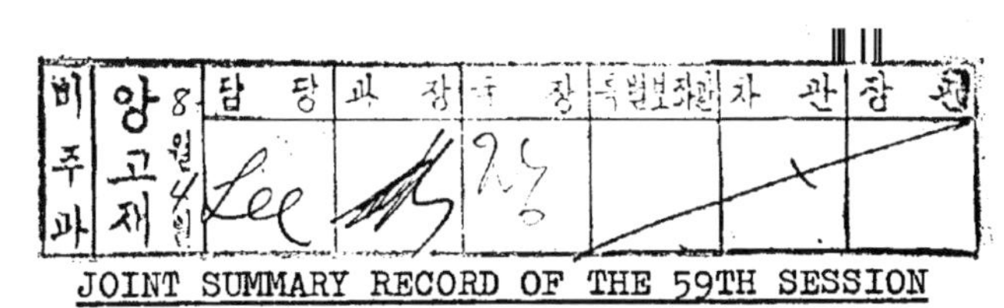

JOINT SUMMARY RECORD OF THE 59TH SESSION

1485

1/3

1. Time and Place: 3:00 - 4:45 P.M. July 28, 1964 at the Foreign Ministry's Conference Room (No.1)

2. Attendants:

ROK Side:

Mr. Chang, Sang Moon	Director European and American Affairs Bureau
Mr. Koo, Choong Whay	Chief, America Section Ministry of Foreign Affairs
Mr. Hur, Hyong Koo	Chief Prosecutors Section Ministry of Justice
Maj. Lee, Kye Hoon	Military Affairs Section Ministry of National Defense
Mr. Park, Sang Yong	3rd Secretary Ministry of Foreign Affairs
Mr. Ahn, Yun Gi	3rd Secretary Ministry of Foreign Affairs
Mr. Lee, Keun Pal (Rapporteur and Interpreter)	3rd Secretary Ministry of Foreign Affairs
Mr. Hwang, Young Jae	3rd Secretary Ministry of Foreign Affairs
Mr. Park, Won Chul	3rd Secretary Ministry of Foreign Affairs

U.S. Side:

Mr. Philip C. Habib	Counselor American Embassy
Brig. Gen. G.G. O'Connor	Deputy Chief of Staff 8th U.S. Army
Col. Howard Smigelow	Deputy Chief of Staff 8th U.S. Army
Capt. John Wayne	Assistant Chief of Staff USN/K
Col. Kenneth C. Crawford	Staff Judge Advocate 8th U.S. Army

0118

Mr. Frank R. La Macchia	First Secretary American Embassy
Mr. Benjamin A. Fleck! (Rapporteur and Press Officer)	First Secretary American Embassy
Mr. Robert A. Kinney	J-5 8th U.S. Army
Mr. Daniel A. O'Donohue	2nd Secretary American Embassy
Maj. Alton H. Harvey	Staff Judge Advocate's Office 8th U.S. Army
Mr. Kenneth Campen	Interpreter

1. Mr. Habib opened the meeting by introducing Major Harvey, who was replacing Lt. Colonel Wright as a member of the U.S. negotiating team. Mr. Chang welcomed Major Harvey to the negotiations.

Criminal Jurisdiction

2. Taking up the criminal jurisdiction article, Mr. Chang stated that at the previous session the Korean negotiators had expressed their initial disappointment at the response made by the U.S. negotiators to the proposals tabled by the Korean negotiators at the 50th and 52nd meetings. The Korean negotiators, after studying the U.S. position, would like to make a point by point comment on the U.S. response to their proposals.

3. Mr. Chang then made the following statement:

4. "a. All persons subject to the military law of the U.S., Para 1.(a)

"With respect to our proposal to substitute the phrase 'all persons subject to the military law of the United States' for the phrase 'the members of the U.S. armed forces and the civilian components,' the U.S. side gave an assurance that the U.S. Government has no intention

0119

to establish civil courts which could exercise jurisdiction in the Republic of Korea. At the same time, the U.S. negotiators indicated their preference for the language in their draft to the Korean proposal, on the grounds that legislation may be passed eventually in the U.S. which would provide that any accused U.S. civilian abroad could be taken to the U.S. for trial.

5. "We have no objection to the principle that the SOFA language should be flexible enough to accommodate all eventualities foreseen in the near future. However, it is inconceivable that such an uncertain eventuality as the legislation referred to by the U.S. negotiators should affect in any way our Status of Forces negotiations. Furthermore, decisions of the Supreme Court of the United States on the matter have been subject to reversal since 1956. Therefore, we can think not only of the possibility over which the U.S. negotiators are concerned but also of the possibility that the U.S. Supreme Court may eventually reverse its decision of 1960 so that civilian offenders may be tried by U.S. Court Martial overseas.

6. "Moreover, in our view, the proposed idea of taking the accused civilians back to the U.S. for trial is neither consonant with the established principle of judicial proceedings nor acceptable to any sovereign nation hosting foreign troops. We believe the contemporary principle and practice of trial in any given country demand that the trial should be held at the place where the offense is committed or at least at a place reasonably distant from the site of the crime. We also believe that if an accused who committed an offense in the territory of one sovereign

0120

country is brought to another sovereign country for trial there would arise a serious question as to possible infringement of sovereignty."

7. "b. <u>The civil Authorities of the Republic of Korea, Para. 1(b)</u>

"Regarding the provision of Paragraph 1(b), the United States negotiators stated that the language of paragraph 1(b) of the U.S. draft, 'the civil authorities of the Republic of Korea', sets forth the Korean Government's intention as expressed in assurances given by the Korean negotiators that the Korean Government will not exercise jurisdiction over U.S. military personnel by military tribunal under any circumstances.

8. "The assurance was intended to meet the requirement of the U.S. negotiators, who have expressed their concern over the possibility of subjecting their military personnel to Korean military tribunal.

9. "Inasmuch as such a significant assurance was given to your side, we have naturally expected that you would no longer insist on retaining the word 'civil'. Since this word 'civil' cannot be found in other SOFAs we wonder what were your understandings or arrangements with other countries in agreeing to the provision without the word 'civil'.

10. "If the Korean negotiators would accept such unprecedented wording as appeared in the U.S. draft, this would undoubtedly cause very delicate problems in the Korean Government as well as with the Korean people. Neither the sentiment of the Korean people nor the atmosphere of the National Assembly would tolerate acceptance of such a version.

0121

11. "c. <u>Official Duty Certificate, Agreed Minutes Re para. 3(a) (ii)</u>

"Regarding the official duty certificate, the U.S. side stated at the last session the following two points:

(1) The certificate will be conclusive unless modification is agreed upon;

(2) The accused should not be deprived of his entitlement to a prompt and speedy trial as a result of protracted reconsideration of the duty certificate.

12. "The Korean negotiators should like to concentrate on the first point alone at this meeting. The Korean negotiators have studied the U.S. statement, and we have found that the statement indicates an improvement over the U.S. Agreed Minute re Paragraph 3(a).

13. "The provision of the U.S. Agreed Minute re Paragraph 3(a) reads as follows: 'A certificate issued by or on behalf of his commanding officer etc... shall be conclusive for the purpose of determining primary jurisdiction.' However, the U.S. negotiators at the last session stated that unless modification is agreed upon either through request of the Korean authorities or otherwise, the certificate will be conclusive. The indication of possible modification at the request of the Korean authorities is an improvement from our point of view.

14. "In our view, any possible controversy over the duty certificate, though we do not expect to encounter many of them, should be solved by mutual consultation and to mutual satisfaction. Therefore, if a controversy arises

0122

over the certificate, the matter should be handed over to the Joint Committee for reconsideration. Whatever way we may take to solve this problem of duty certificate, we must find a mechanism under which mutual consultation and agreement are provided for resolution of controversy over the validity of the official duty certificate.

15. "d. The Concept of the Combat Zone and the Waiver of the Primary Jurisdiction

"At the previous session, the United States negotiators proposed that if the Korean negotiators would accept the Agreed Minute Re Paragraph 3 of the United States draft with respect to the waiver of primary jurisdiction, the U.S. side would delete the clause on the combat zone of Agreed Minute #1, Re Paragraph 1(b) and Agreed Minute #1, Re Paragraph 3(a). At the same time, the U.S. negotiators added that this proposal was a substantial concession by the U.S. side.

16. "The Korean negotiators appreciate the significant suggestion made by the U.S. side. We take the suggestion as an indication on the U.S. part to accommodate our concern over the proposed concept of the combat zone. Although the suggestion was conditioned upon the acceptance by the Korean side of the provision of the Agreed Minute Re Paragraph 3 of the U.S. draft, we welcome the qualified responsiveness of the U.S. side.

17. "However, to our regret, we cannot view the U.S. proposal as a significant concession, as the U.S. negotiators have claimed. Even if the U.S. negotiators withdraw the concept of the combat zone, the U.S. negotiators, by retaining the provisions of the Agreed Minute Re Paragraph 3 of the U.S. draft, would accomplish their ultimate purpose of

obtaining total waiver from the Korean authorities.
A quick review of the U.S. draft of the waiver clause would show clearly that the contents of the clause amount to what we call 'total waiver'.

18. "According to the provisions of U.S. draft:

(a) The Korean authorities have to waive automatically their primary jurisdiction upon the receipt of notice instead of the request for waiver from the U.S. side.

(b) The Korean authorities are also required to seek agreement of the Joint Committee in case they desire to recall the waiver for any particular case.

You have to note that the recall of waiver which has automatically been made by the Korean side is not granted by the U.S. side on the same automatic basis. In other words, while the Korean waiver is automatic, U.S. grant of recall is conditioned upon approval by the Joint Committee.

(c) Furthermore, the U.S. draft provides that the waiver thus granted by the Korean authorities shall be unconditional and final for all purposes and shall bar both the authorities and the nationals of the Republic of Korea from instituting criminal procedures. It is extremely unfair that the United States side, by the mere fact of waiver granted by the Korean authorities, intends not only to bar Korean nationals from initiating appropriate remedial actions, but also to prevent the authorities of the Korean Government from instituting criminal procedures even in a case where the U.S. has not tried the waivered case. In this regard, we are unable to find any international precedents similar to the U.S. draft in any other SOFA.

0124

19. "We are willing to assure you that we are prepared to waive the primary jurisdiction as generously as any NATO party does under the very simple provision in NATO SOFA. However, as a matter of principle, we believe that the Korean authorities, as the authorities of the receiving state, should have the right to determine whether or not to waive primary jurisdiction.

"This right can not be replaced by the automatic waiver clause which the U.S. side seeks. We should like to reiterate our position that whatever the final agreement we may reach on this subject, the agreement has to retain the language and mechanism that would provide for the principle of self-determination by the Korean authorities on waiver of primary jurisdiction.

20. "e. Pre-trial Custody, Paragraph 5(d) and 5(e)

"Regarding the subject of pre-trial custody, the U.S. chief negotiator stated that the revised draft of Paragraph 5(d) is an improvement over the original language but they still believed Paragraph 5(c) of the U.S. draft to be preferable. At the same time he stated that the U.S. side was prepared to agree to the revised Paragraph 5(e) of the Korean draft regarding custody in security offenses.

21. "With respect to pre-trial custody in the hands of the U.S., the revised Korean version of Paragraph 5(d) is almost identical with the language of the U.S. draft and fully reflects the views of the U.S. side. However, the Korean negotiators believe that they should reserve the language which would guarantee the U.S. side's sympathetic consideration to any request for the transfer of custody which may be made by the Korean authorities in specific cases.

22. "With respect to Korean custody in security offenses,

0125

the Korean negotiators appreciate the acceptance by the U.S. side of the revised proposal made by the Korean side. However, we have noted that the acceptance by the U.S. side is conditioned upon the acceptance by the Korean negotiators of the two understandings:

(a) The first proposed understanding is not acceptable to the Korean negotiators, since we believe that in security offenses, the Korean authorities should be the only and final authorities to determine whether or not such custody is appropriate. This does not necessarily mean that we would not consult with U.S. authorities as to the necessity of such custody. But, as a matter of principle, we believe agreement with U.S. side is not necessary in a security case.

(b) Regarding the second question, the Korean negotiators are prepared to accept the proposed understanding.

23. "f. Trial Safeguards

"The Korean negotiators appreciate the proposal made by the U.S. negotiators to effect the following changes in the Agreed Minute Re Paragraph 9 of the U.S. draft:

(a) Deletion of Subparagraph (a);

(b) In subparagraph (b), deletion of all language after the words 'shall have the right to appeal a conviction or sentence.'

24. "The Korean negotiators hope that the U.S. negotiators would consider other outstanding issues regarding trial safe guards on which the Korean negotiators made their views clear at the 50th session and respond at an early meeting."

0126

25. Mr. Habib stated that the U.S. negotiators would reserve until the next meeting a detailed reply to the remarks just made by the Korean Chief Negotiator. However, the U.S. negotiators would like to make some general observations regarding the positions stated by Mr. Chang.

26. Mr. Habib said the U.S. negotiators do not accept the principle that phraseology appearing in other status of forces agreements is definitive with regard to the Korean SOFA. The U.S. negotiators regarded precedents as useful, but not binding. In addition to the precedents found in the language of other agreements, the negotiators also had to take into account a body of experience. This experience included awareness of the way in which other status of forces agreements were actually working and accumulated knowledge of conditions in Korea. The task at hand was the negotiation of a status of forces agreement for Korea, not for Japan or any other country.

27. Mr. Habib noted that the statement made by the Korean negotiators was simply a repetition of views which they had stated previously and did not appear to take into account the expressed views of the U.S. negotiators on certain key issues. The U.S. negotiators would make detailed comments at the next meeting. Before doing so, they wished to ask a few questions and make some remarks in order to clarify certain points.

28. Regarding Paragraph 1(a), Mr. Habib noted that the Korean negotiators had expressed the wish to retain the phrase "all persons subject to the military law of the United States", despite the assurance given by the U.S. negotiators that no U.S. courts would be established in Korea and despite

0127

the desire of the U.S. negotiators to retain flexibility in case legislation should be passed in the future which would establish jurisdiction over U.S. civilians abroad. The objections of the Korean negotiators were apparently based on: (a) a feeling that the passage of such legislation was inconceivable, and (b) the possibility of a reversal of the 1960 Supreme Court decision. In stating these objections, the Korean negotiators were attempting to exercise the right of review of U.S. legislation, which was certainly not relevant to the question at hand. The Korean negotiators were seeking to differentiate between military personnel and civilians in the application of U.S. law. If U.S. law is to apply, it should apply equally to military personnel and civilians, who are in Korea for the accomplishment of the same mission under the provisions of the Mutual Security Treaty. The U.S. negotiators were concerned that the application of rights under the SOFA should not be discriminatory between the military personnel and the civilians who were in Korea under identical conditions and for the same purpose. Mr. Habib asked what the attitude of the Korean negotiators would be if the Supreme Court decision of 1960 had not been made.

29. Regarding Paragraph 1(b), Mr. Habib stated that the position of the U.S. negotiators that jurisdiction over the U.S. armed forces by the host government should be limited to the civil authorities of the government was a firm U.S. position in every country in which a SOFA is in force. The U.S. negotiators wanted to have it stated explicitly in the SOFA with the ROK. If the Korean

0128

negotiators were willing to give the assurances that they had given in this respect, why were they unwilling to spell the assurances out in the Agreement? The absence of the phrase "civil authorities" from other agreements is no reason why it should not be included in this Agreement. The experience of the past two years had clearly shown that the ROK Government does not hesitate to resort to military courts to try civil crimes. The Korean negotiators had argued that it would be difficult to explain this provision to the public and to the National Assembly. Why could the National Assembly not be told simply that the U.S. authorities were unwilling to pass jurisdiction from U.S. military courts to Korean military courts. The U.S. negotiators believed that such an explanation would be palatable and acceptable to the National Assembly. They believed the Korean objections to this provision to be shallow and urged the Korean negotiators to reconsider.

30. With regard to the question of the duty certificate, Mr. Habib reminded the Korean negotiators that the U.S. negotiators had not responded specifically to the proposed revision of the Agreed Minute Re Paragraph 3(a) (ii) of the Korean draft. Now that the U.S. negotiators had received further explanation of what the Korean negotiators had in mind, they would respond in detail to this proposed revision at the next meeting.

31. With regard to the waiver provision, Mr. Habib said the Korean negotiators appeared to be concerned over the question of automaticity. The concern of the U.S. negotiators was to obtain the maximum possible degree of waiver. The implication of the remarks made by the Korean

0129

Chief Negotiator was that the Korean authorities did not desire to try all cases that may arise and that only in special circumstances would they wish to try a case. The U.S. draft does not preclude this and provides the means whereby the Korean authorities could seek recall of their waiver.

32. With regard to pre-trial custody, Mr. Habib noted that the Korean negotiators had made no concessions to meet what the U.S. negotiators consider to be a serious problem. With respect to this subject, also, the U.S. negotiators based their position on experience. The U.S. draft was clear. It provided that defendants in the custody of the U.S. authorities would be produced promptly at the request of the Korean authorities. The U.S. negotiators did not understand the Korean desire to retain custody, except in the case of security cases, with regard to which the U.S. negotiators had made a concession. The U.S. negotiators had also pointed out that the final sentence of Paragraph 5(c) of the U.S. draft was related to this question and would permit the Korean authorities to take custody when requested to do so. In view of the assurances on presentation of the accused already given by the U.S. negotiators, the Korean authorities could exercise jurisdiction just as effectively if the U.S. military authorities retain custody.

33. Mr. Habib noted that the U.S. negotiators had considered the views of the Korean negotiators regarding trial safeguards and had given their reply. They believed there was no reason to withdraw elementary safeguards which are generally accepted as necessary under U.S. law and, in

0130

most cases, under ROK law. The trial safeguards listed in the U.S. draft were not onerous and did not detract from the exercise of jurisdiction by the Korean authorities. The objections of the Korean negotiators appeared to rest on narrow legalistic bases. A lack of safeguards for ROK citizens was no argument for the omission of those safeguards from an international agreement. More important criteria for judging these provisions included the question whether the provisions were onerous, unfair, or lacking precedents. The U.S. negotiators believed them to be not onerous, quite fair, and supported by sound precedents.

34. Mr. Habib asked whether the Korean negotiators wished to make any further comments to assist the U.S. negotiators in their consideration of the Korean position.

35. Mr. Chang replied that a wide gap separated the positions of the two sides. Perhaps the explanation given by the Korean negotiators had not been extensive enough or the U.S. negotiators had misunderstood the Korean position. The question of trial safeguards presented delicate problems. He proposed that this subject be taken up in informal discussions between the legal members of the negotiating teams.

36. Mr. Habib replied that the U.S. negotiators believed that more rapid progress could be made by discussing this question in the negotiating meetings. At the next meeting, the U.S. negotiators would be prepared to hold a point by point discussion of this subject.

37. Mr. Habib remarked that obviously a gap did exist between the two positions. The Korean negotiators were proposing that the U.S. negotiators go all the way toward meeting the Korean position. Such a course would not meet the U.S. requirements.

38. Mr.Chang replied that the Korean negotiators did not expect the U.S. negotiators to come all the way to meet the Korean position. Each side should consider the position of the other. The Korean negotiators believed that international precedents were important. They suggested that standard language be agreed to wherever possible.

39. Mr. Habib replied that standard language should not be used if standard conditions did not exist. The language had to be modified to suit specific situations existing in the country. He suggested that both sides think about these problems.

40. The next meeting was scheduled for August 7 at 3:00 p.m.

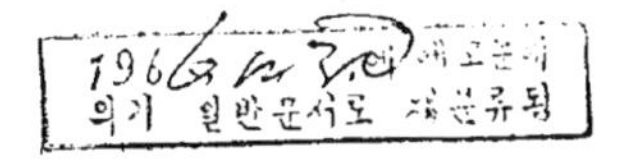

0132

기 안 용 지

자체 통제		기안처	미주과 이근팔	전화번호	근거서류접수일자
	과장	국장	차관	장관	
관계관 서명					
기안 년월일	1964. 8. 11.	시행 년월일		보존 년한	정서기장
분류 기호	외구미 722.2—	전통 제	8.14	종결	
경유 수신 참조	대통령 참조: 비서실장 국무총리 참조: 비서실장 사본: 법무부장관			발신	장관
제목	제 60 차 주둔군지위협정 체결 교섭 실무자회의 개최 보고				

1964. 8. 7. 하오 3 시 부터 동 5 시 30 분 까지 외무부 제 1 회의실에서 개최된 제 59 차 주둔군지위협정 체결 교섭실무자 회의에서 토의된 내용을 별첨과 같이 보고합니다.

유 첨: 제 60 차 주둔군지위협정 체결 교섭실무자회의 보고서. 1 부. 끝.

보통문서로 재분류 (1966. 12. 31)

1964. 8. 14 외무부

196 . 3 . 예고문에 의거 일반문서로 재분류됨

승인서식 1—1—3 (11 00900 03) (195mm×265mm16절지)

0133

제 60 차

한.미 간 주둔군지위협정 체결 교섭실무자회의

보 고 서

1. 일 시: 1964 년 8 월 7 일 하오 3 시 부터 동 5 시 30 분 까지.

2. 장 소: 외무부 제 1 회의실

3. 토의사항:

형사재판관할권

가. 관할권의 인적범위 및 미측의 행사기관

(1) 미측은 우리측이 제 59 차회의에서 일 주권국가 내에서 발생한 범죄에 관련된 피의자를 타 주권국가로 이송 재판한다는 것은 주권 침해의 문제를 야기하게 될 것임으로 미측의 주장은 수락할 수 없다고 한데 대하여 주권국가가 그 국민에 대하여 대인고권에 입각한 형사재판관할권을 보유한다는 것은 국제법상의 일반원칙이며 한국형법 제 3, 5, 6 조등에서 그러한 원칙을 인정하였음에도 불구하고 미측이 민간인 피의자를 본국으로 이송 재판하려는데 대하여 반대하는 이유를 알 수 없다고 주장하였다.

(2) 우리측은 형법이 내국인의국외범의처벌을규정하고 있지만 그 것은 타 주권국가의 승인 또는 피의자가 한국의 관할권 행사 범위 내에 들어 올 것을 전제로 한 것이며 결코 타 국가의 주권을 무시한 관할권의 일방적 행사를 규정한 것이 아니며 우리 나라가 승인하지 않는 것을 강요하려는 것은 주권 침해가 될 것임으로 미측이 입장을 재고할 것을 촉구하였다.

나. 한국의 관할권 행사기관

(1) 미측은 한국측이 어떠한 경우에도 미군관계 피의자를 군법재판에 회부하지 않을 것이라는 확약을 한 이상 한국측의 관할권 행사기관을 "한국민사당국"으로 하는 것에 반대할 이유가 없다고 주장 한데 대하여

(2) 우리측은 미측의 의도를 충족시키기 위하여 중대한 확약을 하였음에도 불구하고 미측이 계속 우리측이 수락할 수 없는 주장을 하고 있는바 쌍방은 다 같이 국민과 국회가 수락할 수 있는 협정의 용어를 모색토록 노력해야 할 것이며 만약 우리측 확약이

0134

64-3

제 60 차

한.미 간 주둔군지위협정 체결 교섭실무자회의

보 고 서

1. 일 시: 1964 년 8 월 7 일 하오 3 시 부터 동 5 시 30 분 까지.

2. 장 소: 외무부 제 1 회의실

3. 토의사항:

형사재판관할권

가. 관할권의 인적범위 및 미측의 행사기관

(1) 미측은 우리측이 제 59 차회의에서 일 주권국가 내에서 발생한 범죄에 관련된 피의자를 타 주권국가로 이송 재판한다는 것은 주권 침해의 문제를 야기하게 될 것임으로 미측의 주장은 수락할 수 없다고 한데 대하여 주권국가가 그 국민에 대하여 대인고권에 입각한 형사재판관할권을 보유한다는 것은 국제법상의 일반원칙이며 한국형법 제 3, 5, 6 조등에서 그러한 원칙을 인정하였음에도 불구하고 미측이 민간인 피의자를 본국으로 이송 재판하려는데 대하여 반대하는 이유를 알 수 없다고 주장하였다.

(2) 우리측은 형법이 내국인의 국외범의 처벌을 규정하고 있지만 그 것은 타 주권국가의 승인 또는 피의자가 한국의 관할권 행사 범위 내에 들어 올 것을 전 것이며 결코 타 국가의 주권을 무시한 관할권의 일방적 것이 아니며 우리 나라가 승인하지 않는 침해가 될 것임으로 미측의 입장을

나. 한국의 관할권 행사기관

(1) 미측은 한국측이 어 회부하지 않을 것 기관을 한국민 한데 대하여

(2) 우리측은 하였음 하고

0135

64-3-36(9)

회의록에 기록되는 대신 합의의사록에 삽입되면 미측은 미측의 주장을 철회할 용의가 있는가를 질문하여, 미측의 진의를 추궁하였다.

다. 공무 집행중 범죄

(1) 미측은 우리측이 제 59 차회의에서 미군이 발행하는 공무 집행중 범죄 증명서의 증명력을 부인하며고 시도하고 있다고 지적하고 벨줌, 덴마크, 불란서, 독일, 희랍, 이태리, 룩셈불크 등 미국이 협정을 맺고 있는 각국과의 실지 운영에 있어서 공무 집행중 범죄증명서에 대하여 이의가 제기된 바 없다고 주장하였다.

라. 제일차관할권의 포기

(1) 우리측은 제일차관할권의 포기문제가 관할권의 귀속을 결정하는데 있어서 중요한 역할을 할 것으로 보며 미측이 통고만 하면 자동적으로 관할권을 포기하게 될것이 않이라 미측이 포기를 요청하면 우리측이 스스로 관할권을 포기할 것인가를 결정할 수 있는 자유재량권을 보유하는 원칙 하에 이 문제가 해결되기를 바란다고 우리측 입장을 밝혔다.

마. 재판전 피의자의 신병 구금

(1) 미측은 한국측이 안전에 관한 재판전 피의자의 신병 구금 시 미측의 동의를 요한다는 미측 주장을 거부한데 대하여 한국당국은 실지운영상 그러한 자의 신병 구금을 위하여서는 미측과의 동의가 필요할 것이며 미군은 한국의 방위를 위하여 한국에 주둔하고 있는 만큼 미측의 동의를 요하는 것으로 하여도 미군이 한국의 안전을 해할 염려는 없을 것이라고 주장하였다.

(2) 우리측은 한.미 간의 특수한 관계로 보아 미측의 주장에 일리가 있다고 생각하지만 한국의 안전에 관한 한 우리측에 신병 구금의 결정권이 있어야 한다고 주장하였다.

바. 피의자의 권리

(1) 미측은 피의자의 권리중 즉시 신속한 재판을 받을 권리는 수습기간을 수료한 자격있는 법관으로 구성된 공정한 재판부에 의한 공개재판을 포함하여야 한다는 미측 초안 규정은 한국의 헌법과 법률이 이미 인정하고 있는 권리인 고로 협정상에 규정하기를 바란다고 주장하였으며

0136

64-3-6

회의록에 기록되는 대신 합의의사록에 삽입되면 미측은 미측의 주장을 철회할 용의가 있는가를 질문하여 미측의 진의를 추궁하였다.

다. 공무 집행중 범죄

(1) 미측은 우리측이 제 59 차회의에서 미군이 발행하는 공무 집행중 범죄 증명서의 증명력을 부인하려고 시도하고 있다고 지적하고 벨지움, 덴마크, 불란서, 독일, 희랍, 이태리, 룩셈불크 등 미국이 협정을 맺고 있는 각국과의 실지 운영에 있어서 공무 집행중 범죄증명서에 대하여 이의가 제기된 바 없다고 주장하였다.

라. 제일차관할권의 포기

(1) 우리측은 제일차관할권의 포기문제가 관할권의 귀속을 결정하는데 있어서 중요한 역활을 할 것으로 보며 미측이 통고만 하면 자동적으로 관할권을 포기하게 될것이 않이라 미측이 포기를 요청하면 우리측이 스스로 관할권을 포기할 것인가를 결정할 수 있는 자유재량권을 보유하는 원칙 하에 이 문제가 해결되기를 바란다고 우리측 입장을 밝혔다.

마. 재판전 피의자의 신병 구금

(1) 미측은 한국측이 안전에 관한 재판전 피의자의 신병 구금 시 미측의 동의를 요한다는 미측 주장을 거부한데 대하여 한국당국은 실지운영상 그러한 자의 신병 구금을 위하여서는 미측과의 동의가 필요할 것이며 미군은 한국의 방위를 위하여 한국에 주둔하고 있는 만큼 미측의 동의를 요하는 것으로 하여도 미군이 한국의 안전을 해할 염려는 없을 것이라고 주장하였다.

(2) 우리측은 한.미 간의 특수한 관계로 보아 미측의 주장에 일리가 있다고 생각하지만 한국의 안전에 관한 한 우리측에 신병 구금의 결정권이 있어야 한다고 주장하였다.

바. 피의자의 권리

(1) 미측은 피의자의 권리중 즉시 신속한 재판을 받을 권리는 수습기간을 수료한 자격있는 법관으로 구성된 공정한 재판부에 의한 공개재판을 포함하여야 한다는 미측 초안 규정은 한국의 헌법과 법률이 이미 권리인 고로 협정상에 규정하기를 바란다고 주장하였으며

0137 64-3-26. 미.모 110-1

(2) 미군관계 피의자는 한국의 군법재판에 복하지 않는다는 규정은 한국의 관할권 행사기관에 관한 문제와 관련하여 해결될 것 이라는데 쌍방이 의견을 같이 하였다.

(3) 미측은 또한 피의자에게 불리하게 이용될 증거는 재판 전 상당한 시일전에 피의자에게 통보되어야 한다는 권리는 한국 형사소송법 제 273 조에서 인정된 원칙임으로 협정 상에 명문화할 것을 계속 주장하였다.

4. 기타 사항: 차기 회의일자: 1964 년 8 월 14 일 하오 3 시 부터. 끝.

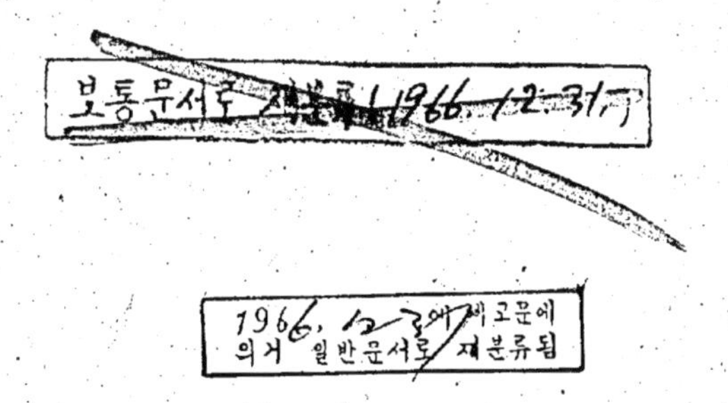

0138

64-3-70

(2) 미군관계 피의자는 한국의 군법재판에 복하지 않는다는 규정은 한국의 관할권 행사기관에 관한 문제와 관련하여 해결될 것 이라는데 쌍방이 의견을 같이 하였다.

(3) 미측은 또한 피의자에게 불리하게 이용될 증거는 재판 전 상당한 시일전에 피의자에게 통보되어야 한다는 권리는 한국 형사소송법 제 273 조에서 인정된 원칙임으로 협정 상에 명문화할 것을 계속 주장하였다.

4. 기타 사항: 차기 회의일자: 1964 년 8 월 14 일 하오 3 시 부터. 끝.

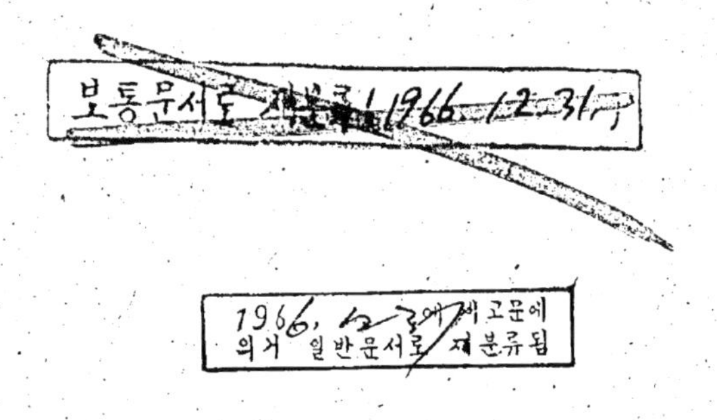

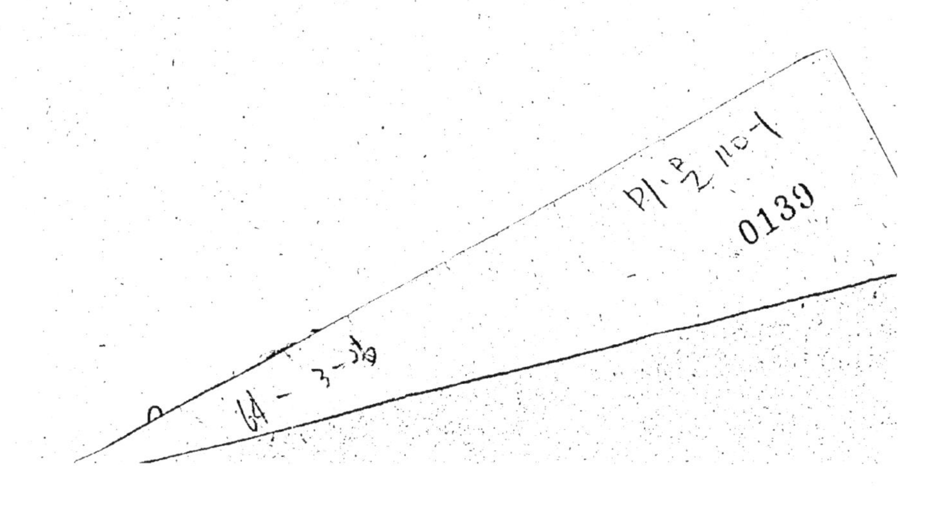

번 역

제 60 차 군대지위협정 실무자회의 합의 기록 (1964.8.7)

(형사 재판권 중 심문 방어 조항 번역문)

33. 심문 방어 제목에 관하여, "하비브"씨는 공개재판을 규정한 미국의 합의의사록 제 9 항(a)는 공공 또는 국가기밀이 관련된 경우으로 부터 일반 공중(一般公衆)을 제외하는 가능성을 배척하는 것은 아닌 것이라고 말하였다.

"하비브"씨는 한국측이 시보기간(試補期間)을 이수한 법관으로써 구성된 공평무사한 법정에 의한 공개재판을 요구한 이 합의의사록의 첫째 문장의 삭제를 제의한바 있다고 상기시켰다.

미국측은 한국 헌법 제 24 조 제 3항이 "모든 국민은 신속한 재판을 받을 권리를 가지며" "상당한 이유가 없는한 지체없이 ... 공개재판을 받을 권리를 가진다"라고 규정하고 있다는 사실을 알고 있었다.

그들은 또한 국민은 "헌법과 법률에 정한 법관에 의하여 법률에 의한" 재판을 받는 권리를 가진다고 규정한 제 24 조 제 1 항을 알고 있었다.

비록 위의 문제점이 한국 헌법에의하여 해결되고 있지만은, 미국측은 그 중요성에 비추워 상기 규정은 군대지위협정에도 도입되어야 할 것이라고 믿고 있다.

법관의 자격에 관하여는, 한국 헌법과 제안된 합의의사록 간의 불일치는 없다.

0140 66-7-7 141

번 역

제 60 차 군대지위 협정 실무자회의 약식 기록 (1964.8.7)

(형사 재판권 중 심판 방어 조항 발췌분)

33. 심판 방어 제목에 대하여, "하비브"씨는 공개재판을 규정한 미측안 합의의사록 제 9 항(a)는 공안 또는 국가기밀이 관련된 공판으로부터 일반 공중(一般公衆)을 제외하는 가능성을 배제하는 것은 아닌 것이라고 말하였다.

"하비브"씨는 한국측이 시보기간(試補期間)을 이수한 법관으로써 구성된 공평 무사한 법정에 의한 공개재판을 요구한 이 합의의사록의 첫째 문장의 삭제를 제의한바 있다고 상기시켰다.

미국측은 한국 헌법 제 24 조 제 3항이 "모든 국민은 신속한 재판을 받을 권리를 가지며" "상당한 이유가 없는한 지체없이 ... 공개재판을 받을 권리를 가진다"라고 규정하고 있다는 사실을 알고 있었다.

그들은 또한 국민은 "헌법과 법률에 정한 법관에 의하여 법률에 의한" 재판을 받는 권리를 가진다고 규정한 제 24 조 제 1 항을 알고 있었다.

비록 위의 문제점이 한국 헌법에의하여 해결되고 있지만은, 미국측은 그 중요성에 비추워 상기 규정은 군대지위협정에도 도입되어야 할 것이라고 믿고 있다.

법관의 자격에 관하여는, 한국 헌법과 제안된 합의의사록 간의 불일치는 없다.

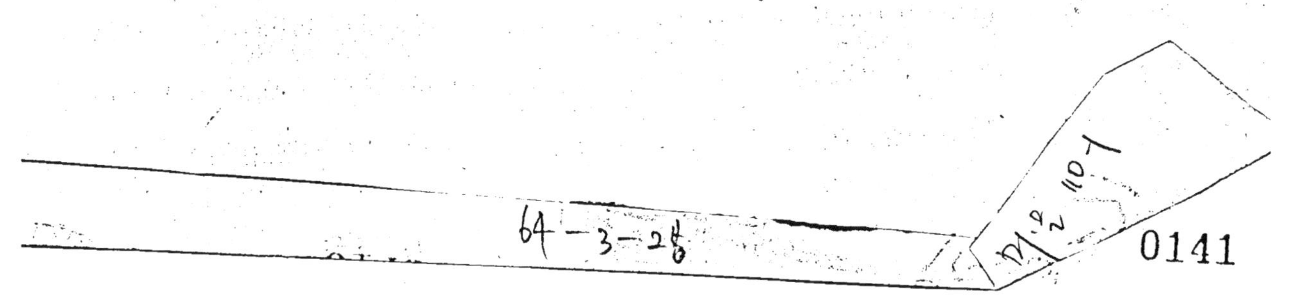

0141

미국측은 한국 헌법에서 사용하고 있는 용어와 같이 "유자격"법관이란 그들의 시보기간을 이수한 법관들이라고 생각한다.

제안한 합의의사록의 용어는 풍기 또는 국가기밀이 문제된다면, 일반 공중이 공개재판으로부터 제외될 수 있다는 경우의, 합중국에서의 관습과 모순되는 것은 아니다.

미국측이 보장받기를 원하는 것은 합중국 정부대표가 심판이 일반공중에게는 비공개로 하는 특별한 사정이 있거나 없거나를 불문하고, 모든 공판의 개정에 참여할 수 있는 권리에 있는 것이다.

34. "하비브"씨는 제안한 합의의사록 의 둘째 문장은 미국 인원(personnel)을 한국 군법회의에 의하여 심판하는 것을 금지하는 것이라고 견해를 말하였다.

본 규정은 이미 논의한바있는 "민간의"(civil)이란 용어를 제 1항(b)에 포함시킬 것인가의 문제와 직접 관련되어있다.

35. "장"씨는 한국측은 공개재판의 문제에 관하여 의견 차이가 있음을 시인하고 있었다.

한국측은 검토중에 있는 미국측의 논평을 받어 드리겠다.

한국측은 법원의 구성에 관한 미국측 성명서에 대하여 원칙적으로 반대가 없었다.

한국측은 제안한 합의의사록 Re 제 9항(a)는 제 1항 (b)에 "민간의"(이란 용어를 포함시키느냐 삭제하느냐의 문제에 관련되었다는 것에 동의하였다.

0142

0143

64-3-28 11-1

미국측은 한국 헌법에서 사용하고 있는 용어와 같이 "유자격"법관이란 그들의 시보기간을 이수한 법관들이라고 생각한다.

제안한 합의의사록의 용어는 풍기 또는 국가기밀이 문제된다면, 일반 공중이 공개재판으로부터 제외될 수 있다는 경우의, 합중국에서의 관습과 모순되는 것은 아니다.

미국측이 보장받기를 원하는 것은 합중국 정부대표가 심판이 일반공중에게는 비공개로 하는 특별한 사정이 있거나 없거나를 불문하고, 모든 공판의 개정에 참여할 수 있는 권리에 있는 것이다.

34. "하비브"씨는 제안한 합의의사록 의 둘째 문장은 미국 인원(personnel)을 한국 군법회의에 의하여 심판하는 것을 금지하는 것이라고 견해를 말하였다.

본 규정은 이미 논의한바있는 "민간의"(civil)이란 용어를 제 1항(b) 에 포함시킬 것인가의 문제와 직접 관련되어있다.

35. "장"씨는 한국측은 공개재판의 문제에 관하여 의견 차이가 있음을 시인하고 있었다.

한국측은 검토중에 있는 미국측의 논평을 받어 드리겠다.

한국측은 법원의 구성에 관한 미국측 성명서에 대하여 원칙적으로 반대가 없었다.

한국측은 제안한 합의의사록 Re 제 9항(a)는 제 1항 (b)에 "민간의"(이란 용어를 포함시키느냐 삭제하느냐의 문제에 관련되었다는 것에 동의하였다.

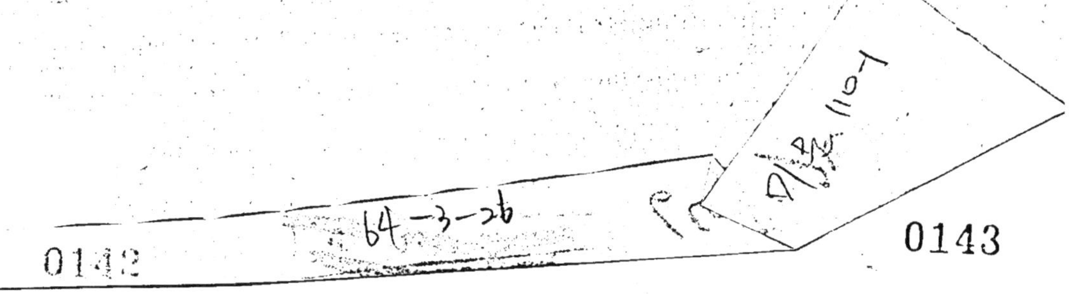

36. 제안된 미국측안 합의의사록 Re 제 9항(b)에 미치어, "하비브"씨는 한국측이 한국의 형사절차에는 대응규정(Counterpart)이 없고, 또한 본항이 현행 한국 법률의 정신에 배치된다는 이유로써 본항의 둘째 조항을 삭제하기를 제의한바 있었다.

"하비브"씨는 본 항은 증인의 진술서 등이 사건 서류 중에 포함되여 있는 경우 피고인의 변호인이 심판 전에 상기 진술서를 조사(examine)하고 사본할 권리를 보장하는 것이라고 지적하였다.

한국측은 본의하기를, 한국 형사소송법상 피고인은 그 에게 불리한 증거의 성질을 지실할 기회가 부여되여있고 또한 그것으로 충분하다는 것이다.

미국의 견지에서는, 제안된 합의의사록 의 본 둘째조항의 규정에 의하여 피고인에게 부여된 권리만 일반적인(common sense))권리인 것이다.

재판은 공판시까지 증거를 피고인 또는 그 변호인으로부터 격리시킴으로써 달성되는 것은 아니다.

37. "하비브"씨는 말하기를, 미국측은 문제된 조항은 한국법에 비교할 수 있는 것이라고 믿는다고 하였다.
그는 특이 형사소송법 제 273 조에 언급하였다. 동조는 다음과 같이 규정하고 있다.
"제 273 조 (공판기일전의 증거조사)
"(1) 법원은 신청에의하여, 검사, 피고인 또는 그 변호인으로 하여금 공판기일전에 피고인 또는 증인을 심문하도록 할 수 있고, 증거를 조사하도록 할 수 있다"

미국측이 요구하는 권리는 한국 형사소송법의 본 조문과 비교될 수 있고,

0144

(4) - 77

0145

또 정신상 합치않는 것이다.

그러므로 미국측은 한국측이 본 조항에 대한 반대를 재검토하기를 강조하였다.

38. "장"씨는 한국측은 이 문제를 앞으로 연구하기를 원한다고 답변하였다.

39. 이 문제에 관한 회답을 연기하기로 합의되였다.

차기 회합은 8월 14일, 오후 3시로 예정되였다.

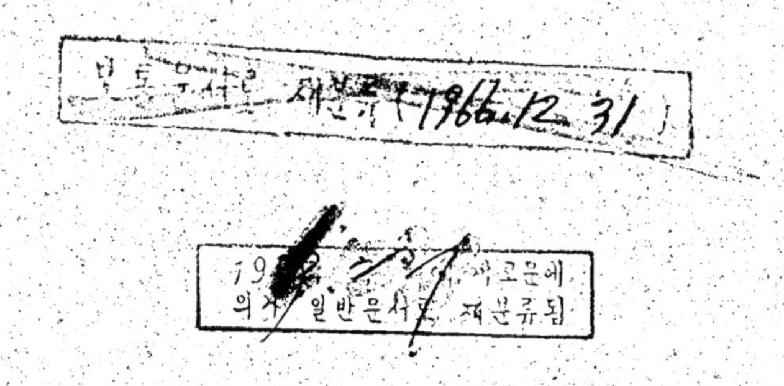

0146

64-2-26

64-3-26 (7)
0147

CONFIDENTIAL

STATUS OF FORCES NEGOTIATIONS: 60th Meeting

SUBJECT: Criminal Jurisdiction

PLACE: Ministry of Foreign Affairs

DATE: August 7, 1964

PARTICIPANTS:

Republic of Korea	United States
CHANG Sang-mun	Philip C. Habib
KU Chung-hoe	Captain John Wayne, USN
Major YI Kae-hun, ROKA	Colonel Kenneth C. Crawford, USA
HWANG Yong-chae	Benjamin A. Fleck
YI Kae-chol	Robert A. Kinney
YI Kun-pal (Interpreter)	Robert A. Lewis
~~HO Hyun-ku~~ Lee, Myung Hi	Major Alton H, Harvey, USA
Pak Won Chul	David Y.C. Lee (Interpreter)
Pak Sang Yong	
	Daniel A. O'Donohue, (Observer)

0148

Criminal Jurisdiction

1. Mr. Habib opened the meeting by stating that the U.S. negotiators wished to take up the Criminal Jurisdiction Article and go through it from the beginning, discussing the differences of view which had emerged during previous discussions.

2. With regard to Paragraph 1(a), Mr. Habib continued, the Korean negotiators had objected to the concept of jurisdiction contained in the U.S. draft, which would allow for the exercise of jurisdiction by the U.S. authorities at some future time outside the Republic of Korea. The Korean negotiators had stated at the 59th meeting that any future return of accused civilians to the United States for trial would be inconsistent with judicial principles and not acceptable to any sovereign nation hosting foreign troops. They also had stated that if a person accused of committing a crime in one sovereign country was taken to another sovereign country for trial "there would arise a serious question as to possible infringement of sovereignty".

3. Mr. Habib stated that the U.S. negotiators did not agree with this interpretation of the proposed provision. He pointed out that it is a recognized principle of international law that a sovereign state retains jurisdiction over its nationals whether they are within the territorial jurisdiction of the asserting state or within that of a foreign state. This jurisdiction is based upon the personal supremacy of a sovereign state over its own nationals rather than on any question of territorial sovereignty. The rights and duties of a national are solely determined by the law of his sovereign state and he is subjected to such penal jurisdiction for acts committed abroad as is provided for in that law.

4. Jurisdiction based upon the supremacy of a state over its nationals, Mr. Habib continued, is not in derogation of the sovereignty of the foreign state in which the offense is committed. Unless there are contrary treaty provisions, the state claiming jurisdiction based on nationality is under the obligation not to infringe upon the territorial supremacy of a foreign state by performing acts of sovereignty in the foreign state. This does not detract from the state's right under international law to punish its nationals when they are again within

its territorial jurisdiction for acts committed abroad.

5. Mr. Habib pointed out that the Republic of Korea has exercised this right through implementation of Korean law. The Korean negotiators had said that this would be contrary to international law and judicial principles. The U.S. negotiators, however, wished to point out that the laws of the Republic of Korea recognize this principle and make specific provisions for this very situation. Article 3, Criminal Code, Korean Law 293, reads as follows:

"Crimes Committed by Koreans Abroad

"This Code shall apply to all Korean nationals outside the territory of the Republic of Korea."

6. In fact, Mr. Habib continued, Korean law carries the principle of jurisdiction over crimes committed abroad much further than is applicable to the issue under discussion. Article 5 of the Korean Criminal Code provides that the Code shall apply to aliens who commit certain specified crimes outside the territory of the Republic of Korea. Article 6 reads as follows:

"Crimes Committed Abroad Against the Republic of Korea and Korean Nationals

"This Code shall apply to aliens who commit, outside the territory of Korea, against the Republic of Korea or her nationals, crimes other than those specified in the preceding article, except where they do not constitute crimes at the place of commission or where their prosecution or execution of the punishment imposed has been remitted."

7. Mr. Habib stated that the United States has no counterpart to Article 3 of the Korean Criminal Code. Whether or not this will be accomplished in future legislation is a matter wholly reserved to the United States Government in the exercise of its sovereign right of supremacy over its own nationals. If such legislation is passed, it would not derogate from the unquestioned sovereignty of the Republic of Korea. It is difficult to understand, he continued, why the ROK negotiators are concerned over a principle recognized by international law and specifically provided for in their own Criminal Code.

0150

10. Mr. Chang replied that the U.S. negotiators had quoted articles of the Korean Criminal Code to justify their position that an accused could be taken from one country to another for trial without causing any infringement upon the territorial jurisdiction of the former. ~~The U.S. negotiators had misinterpreted those articles.~~ The spirit underlying them was that the Government of the Republic of Korea would exercise jurisdiction over the accused when the accused come within reach of ROK sovereignty or under an extradition agreement. In other words, the Korean articles do not call for unilateral and involuntary waiver of territorial jurisdiction, while the U.S. draft in question and the explanation of the U.S. negotiators clearly demand unconditional waiver, voluntary or involuntary, of territorial jurisdiction on the part of the Republic of Korea. The Korean negotiators did not believe that the U.S. Government would automatically waiver jurisdiction over a Korean offender in the United States. In the absence of an extradition agreement between the two countries, which is the case at present, if the ROK Government tried to extradite a Korean civilian or soldier accused of an offense in the United States for trial in the Republic of Korea, the U.S. Government not only could, but would probably object. In case the U.S. Government feels, for one reason or another, that the territorial jurisdiction can not be waived, the accused Korean can not be brought to Korea for trial. In brief, waiver of territorial jurisdiction is traced to the consent of the territorial sovereign.

0151

8. Mr. Habib said the U.S. negotiators had clearly stated the purpose of the language in the U.S. draft, which was to provide for the possibility of future legislation in the United States. The Korean negotiators had objected on the grounds that there was no basis in judicial practice for such a provision and that it would derogate against the sovereignty of the Republic of Korea. The U.S. negotiators had clearly demonstrated that there was no lack of precedents in judicial practice and that the provision would not derogate against the sovereignty of the Republic of Korea.

9. Mr. Habib added that the U.S. negotiators believed the Korean negotiators might be basing their objection also on the fact that this provision does not appear in this form in other status of forces agreements. He reiterated the frequently expressed view of the U.S. negotiators that this agreement was being negotiated on the basis of accumulated experience and not on the basis of language in other agreements. There was nothing in this provision which was inconsistent with the spirit of other status of forces agreements, nor with the exercise of sovereignty by either government, nor with judicial precedents, including those contained in Korean law. Mr. Habib asked whether the Korean negotiators wished to comment.

10. Mr. Chang replied that the U.S. negotiators had quoted articles of the Korean Criminal Code to justify their position that an accused could be taken from one country to another for trial. The U.S. negotiators had misinterpreted those articles. They were valid only for certain offenses and the spirit underlying them was that the Government of the Republic of Korea would exercise jurisdiction over the accused only if the accused come within reach of ROK sovereignty. The Korean negotiators did not believe that the U.S. Government would automatically waive jurisdiction over a Korean offender in the United States. If the ROK Government tried to extradite a Korean soldier accused of an offense in the United States for trial in the Republic of Korea, the U.S. Government would probably object. The Korean negotiators desired that the Status of Forces Agreement with Korea contain standard language, insofar as possible.

0152

11. Mr. Habib replied that the negotiators were not arguing on the specifics of Korean law. Nor were they discussing the subject of extradition. They were discussing the principle of the right of each government to exercise its sovereignty, a principle which the Korean negotiators had questioned at the last meeting. The U.S. negotiators were not questioning the way in which the Korean authorities applied ROK law. With regard to the attitude of the U.S. Government, Mr. Habib reminded the Korean negotiators of the recent case of a member of the ROK Navy who had got into trouble in Guam. Although the charges against him had been of a very serious nature, including manslaughter, the U.S. Government, acting in response to the request of the ROK Government, had agreed to permit him to be returned to the Republic of Korea for trial.

12. Mr. Habib reiterated that the provision in question would result in no derogation of sovereignty and was based on judicial precedents. The Korean negotiators had raised the question of comparability with other status of forces agreements. In this case, the U.S. negotiators were not arguing in favor of their language on the basis of the existance of a different set of conditions in Korea than in other countries where U.S. armed forces are stationed. They wished to point out that at the time when the status of forces agreements with Japan and with the NATO governments were negotiated, the Supreme Court decision of 1960 had not yet been handed down. At the time when the agreement with Japan was negotiated, the U.S. negotiators had believed that U.S. military courts had jurisdiction over certain U.S. civilians. Therefore, in this respect the two agreements were not comparable.

13. Mr. Habib stated that similar reasoning lay behind the language of Paragraph 1(b) of the U.S. draft. The U.S. negotiators of the status of forces agreements with Japan and the NATO governments had not conceived of the possibility that military authorities (of the host country) could exercise jurisdiction. Inasmuch as that possibility does exist in the Republic of Korea, the U.S. negotiators, in drafting this more modern agreement, wish to make the language of the provision quite clear by having it read "the civil

0153

17. Mr. Chang stated that the Korean negotiators believed both sides were trying to negotiate an agreement that would be acceptable to their respective citizens and legislatures. They were trying to find acceptable wording regarding this question. The Korean negotiators believed that the effect would be the same, whether the assurance appeared in the text of the Agreement or in the Agreed Joint Summary. Inasmuch as the effect was same, the U.S. negotiators should and could be responsive to the concern of their counterparts. Utter disregard by the U.S. side of the Korean concern was not a constructive way of conducting negotiation. The Korean negotiators could not understand the U.S. insistance on the inclusion of the word "civil" in the text.

18. In an attempt to clarify the Korean position, Mr. Habib asked whether the Korean negotiators were proposing to include their assurance in the Agreed Joint Summary or as an Agreed Munite. Mr. Chang replied that they were neither making any suggestion nor proposal. They merely wished to clarify the U.S. position whether the U.S. negotiators would accept the assurance as an Agreed Minute and delete the word "civil" from the text. [~~Mr. Habib replied that this was a hypothetical question which he could not anser. If the Korean negotiators would propose an Agreed Minute, the U.S. negotiators would take it under consideration. Mr. Chang reiterated that he was in no position to do so.~~]

0154

authorities of the Republic of Korea". This is not an unreasonable provision and should be fairly easy to explain. It is fully consistent with the statements of the Korean negotiators for the negotiating record that the Korean authorities have no intention of subjecting U.S. personnel covered by this SOFA to military courts. The objection of the Korean negotiators to this provision appeared to be solely the fact that such language does not appear in the SOFA with Japan. The U.S. negotiators were of the opinion that this was not a valid objection.

14. Reverting to Paragraph 1(a), Mr. Chang stated that when an accused is taken from the host country to another country for trial, the host country voluntarily waives its jurisdiction. If such a case arose in the Republic of Korea and the ROK authorities were not prepared to waive ROK jurisdiction, the accused could not be taken to another country for trial. In effect, the language of the U.S. draft called for a voluntary waiver of jurisdiction over dependents by the ROK Government.

15. Mr. Chang asked whether the United States, following the 1960 Supreme Court decision, had received assurances from other governments with whom it has negotiated status of forces agreements that civilians may be taken to the United States for trial. Mr. Habib replied that, to his knowledge, the question had not arisen.

16. With regard to Paragraph 1(b), Mr. Chang stated that the Korean negotiators had given an unequivocal assurance for the negotiating record that under no circumstances would members of the U.S. armed forces be subject to trial by Korean military authorities, in the hope that the U.S. negotiators would agree to the deletion of the word "civil". Mr. Habib replied that the simplest way of handling this question was to leave the word "civil" in the text of the paragraph.

17. Mr. Chang stated that the Korean negotiators believed both sides were trying to negotiate an agreement that would be acceptable to their respective citizens and legislatures. They were trying to find acceptable wording regarding this question. The Korean negotiators believed that the effect would be the same, whether this language appeared in the text

of the Agreement or in the Agreed Joint Summary. However, the Korean negotiators could not agree to inclusion of the word "civil" in the text.

18. In an attempt to clarify the Korean position, Mr. Habib asked whether the Korean negotiators were proposing to include their assurance in the Agreed Joint Summary or as an Agreed Minute. Mr. Chang replied that they proposed the assurance for inclusion in the Agreed Joint Summary. However, they had the impression that this would not satisfy the U.S. negotiators. They were interested in knowing, therefore, whether the U.S. negotiators would accept the assurance as an Agreed Minute but they were not proposing it as an Agreed Minute. ~~Mr. Habib replied that this was a hypothetical question which he could not answer. If the Korean negotiators would propose an Agreed Minute, the U.S. negotiators would take it under consideration.~~

19. Mr. Habib stated that the U.S. negotiators wished to clarify further the U.S. position with regard to the duty certificate and to bring to the attention of the Korean negotiators certain precedents and other factors of which they might not be aware. The U.S. negotiators had stated their view that the duty certificate is conclusive. The Korean negotiators had taken the position that if the Korean authorities objected to a duty certificate, they should be able to refer the matter to the Joint Committee. If the Joint Committee could not reach agreement, the matter would then be referred to the Korean courts, under the terms of the third paragraph of the revised Agreed Minute Re Paragraph 3(a)(ii) of the Korean draft. The Korean negotiators had expressed the hope that the U.S. military authorities would be prepared to entertain requests for modification of duty certificates. The U.S. negotiators, Mr. Habib continued, did not wish to mislead the Korean negotiators regarding the firmness of the U.S. belief in the conclusive nature of the duty certificate. This belief was based on a lengthy body of experience. The U.S. negotiators wished to call the attention of the Korean negotiators to the following information.

20. In Belgium, Mr. Habib stated, duty ceritificates are prepared by the unit commanding officer and submitted to the Army Attache at the U.S. Embassy in

0156

Brussels. The Army Attache either submits the duty certificate to the local authorities or advises them informally regarding the duty status of the accused. The Belgian authorities have never questioned U.S. determinations regarding duty status of an accused.

21. In Denmark, Mr. Habib continued, no formal procedures have been established for the determination of official duty status and no official duty cases have arisen to date. If such a case should occur, the determination would be made by the U.S. Representative on the Joint Committee who would advise appropriate Danish authorities.

22. In France, the U.S. Staff Judge Advocate notifies the French prosecutor of official duty cases. The French Ministry of Justice issued a circular in 1956, which recognized the primary responsibility of the United States, as sending state, to determine the duty status of the accused. The French Court of Cassation in the case of James Martin (a partie civile prosecution brought by an injured claimant) decided that only the sending state may make the determination of the performance of official duty referred to in Article VII of the NATO Status of Forces Agreement and that the sending state's duty certificate is conclusive as a matter of law.

23. In Germany, Mr. Habib continued, criminal jurisdiction over U.S. personnel is exercised by the sending state only. However, the Agreement to Supplement the NATO Status of Forces Agreement in Germany provides as follows:

> "1. Whenever, in the course of criminal proceedings against a member of a force or of a civilian component, it becomes necessary to determine whether an offence has risen out of any act or omission done in the performance of official duty, such determination shall be made in accordance with the law of the sending State concerned. The highest appropriate authority of such sending State may submit to the German Court or authority dealing with the case a certificate thereon.
>
> "2. The German court or authority shall make its decision in conformity with the certificate. In exceptional cases, however, such certificate may, at the request of the German court or authority, be made the subject of review through discussions between the Federal Government and the

0157

XXXXXXXXXXXXXXXXXXXXXXX

diplomatic mission in the Federal Republic of the sending State."

24. Mr. Habib went on to point out that in Greece official duty certificates are issued by the Staff Judge Advocate and, if approved by the U.S. Representative on the Joint Committee, are submitted through diplomatic channels to the Ministry of Foreign Affairs. Greek authorities have never questioned official duty status determinations made by U.S. authorities.

25. In Italy, Mr. Habib continued, the determination of official duty status is made by a service Legal Officer or by the command Staff Judge Advocate on the basis of information provided by the unit commander. The determination is then submitted to the appropriate Italian official with a statement that the command will exercise its primary right of jurisdiction over the accused. It is well established in Italy that official duty certificates submitted by U.S. authorities are accepted without question by Italian authorities, including those issued with regard to acts or omissions which occur during travel incident to temporary duty or permanent change of station or while traveling between residence and place of duty in privately-owned vehicles.

26. In Luxembourg, official duty determinations are made by the U.S. Representative on the Joint Committee on the basis of information provided by the immediate commander of the individual concerned and are transmitted by him to the Chief Public Prosecutor of the appropriate arrondissement. Authorities of Luxembourg in all cases have accepted United States official duty determinations.

0158

27. Mr. Habib stated that he could go on, relating the precedents established in the Netherlands, Norway, Portugal, the United Kingdom, and the United States. Without taking the time to do that, he could state that again and again, in the countries cited, duty certificates are not questioned but are accepted as conclusive. In view of the many precedents he had cited and others which he had not cited, the U.S. negotiators did not believe that their requirement that the duty certificate be considered conclusive was an extraordinary requirement. He suggested that further discussion on this question be

29. Mr. Chang replied that the provisions regarding waiver were more important than those regarding the duty certificate because the waiver provisions would play a heavier role in determining which side would exercise jurisdiction than the other provisions would. This was a very sensitive subject. The Korean negotiators could not accept the automaticity of waiver provided for in the U.S. draft. They wished to reserve to the Korean authorities the right to determine whether or not to waive when requested to do so by the U.S. authorities. The Korean position was based not on a lack of precedents but on principle. The principle is that the waiver is granted by the ~~side~~ authorities who hold the jurisdiction and could not be exercised by the ~~side~~ authorities lacking the jurisdiction. The automatic waiver provisions proposed by the U.S. ~~side proposed~~ negotiators are diametrically opposite to this principle. Under the system of automatic waiver , the U.S. ~~side~~ authorities who lack the original jurisdiction ~~is~~ are to exercise waiver, while the Korean ~~side is~~ authorities are to ask for recall of waiver. The Korean negotiators had already stated, and wished to state again, that the Korean authorities would waive in as many cases as possible but they must retain the discretion whether or not to waive. The Korean negotiators therefore could not think of a SOFA with a waiver clause providing for an automatic waiver.

0159

deferred until the U.S. negotiators responded specifically to the revised Agreed Minute Re Paragraph 3(a)(ii) proposed by the Korean negotiators.

28. Turning to the waiver provisions, Mr. Habib recalled that the Korean negotiators had rejected the idea of an automatic waiver on the grounds that no precedent existed for such a provision. In the view of the U.S. negotiators, there was general agreement on the desirability of some sort of waiver provision. The U.S. negotiators had proposed a general waiver by the ROK Government, with the power to recall that waiver in special circumstances; the ROK negotiators had proposed that the U.S. authorities be given the power to request a waiver in special circumstances. Mr. Habib asked whether the Korean negotiators could elaborate on, or restate, their position in the light of the discussions which had taken place since these positions had first been stated.

29. Mr. Chang replied that the provisions regarding waiver were more important than those regarding the duty certificate because the waiver provisions would determine which side would exercise jurisdiction. This was a very sensitive subject. The Korean negotiators could not accept the automaticity of waiver provided for in the U.S. draft. They wished to reserve to the Korean authorities the right to determine whether or not to waive when requested to do so by the U.S. authorities. The Korean position was based not on a lack of precedents but on principle. The Korean negotiators had already stated, and wished to state again, that the Korean authorities would waive in as many cases as possible but they must retain the discretion whether or not to waive. The Korean negotiators therefore rejected any proposal which would provide for an automatic waiver.

30. Turning to the question of pre-trial custody, Mr. Habib recalled that the remaining difference of opinion pertains to the question of custody in security cases. The U.S. negotiators had indicated their willingness to agree to Paragraph 5(e) of the Korean draft, provided the Korean negotiators would agree to the inclusion in the

0160

31. Mr. Chang replied that in the light of the special and close relationship existing between the two countries, the Korean negotiators were not unprepared to reconsider this matter. They viewed it as a matter of principle, however. The Korean authorities were prepared to consult with U.S. military authorities concerning a security case and to recognize the U.S. right to participate in the determination of circumstances leading to custody by the Korean authorities but the final decision concerning custody must be made by the Korean authorities, not the U.S. authorities. Agreement between them was not necessary.

0161

Agreed Joint Summary of the following two understandings:

a. There must be mutual U.S.-ROK agreement as to the circumstances in which such custody is appropriate; and

b. Korean confinement facilities must be adequate by U.S. standards.

The Korean negotiators had accepted the second of these two understandings but had rejected the first on the grounds that the Korean authorities should be the only and final authorities to determine whether or not such custody is appropriate. Earlier, the Korean negotiators had stated that the Korean authorities required custody of individuals charged with security offenses in order to prevent further threats to the security of the Republic of Korea or to prevent destruction of evidence. It was inconceivable, Mr. Habib stated, that the United States Government would be a party to threats to the security of the Republic of Korea. The U.S. armed forces were not present in the Republic of Korea to pose a threat to its security. The U.S. authorities desired to participate in the determination of the circumstances under which Korean custody of the accused would be appropriate. This position did not reject the right of the Korean authorities to hold custody. As a matter of practical implementation, mutual discussion would be called for in a security case. Let both sides consider this question further.

31. Mr. Chang replied that in the light of the special and close relationship existing between the two countries, the Korean negotiators were not unprepared to reconsider this matter. They viewed it as a matter of principle, however. The Korean authorities were prepared to consult with U.S. military authorities concerning a security case but the final decision concerning custody must be made by the Korean authorities, not the U.S. authorities. Agreement between them was not necessary.

32. Mr. Habib replied that the U.S. negotiators believed that agreement was necessary - agreement as to the circumstances in which custody would be appropriate. In order to preclude the temptation to the Korean authorities to make a unilateral decision,

0162

there should be consultation. The U.S. negotiators were proposing these two understandings for inclusion in the Agreed Joint Summary in view of the importance of the Joint Summary as a document providing specific guidelines for those who will be charged with implementing the Agreement. Mr. Chang replied that the Korean negotiators fully shared the views of the U.S. negotiators concerning the impprtance of the Agreed Joint Summary and its function as a guide for implementation of the Agreement.

33. Turning to the subject of trial safeguards, Mr. Habib stated that the Agreed Minute Re Paragraph 9(a) in the U.S. draft, which would provide for a public trial, would not rule out the possibility of the public being excluded from a trial in which morals or state secrets are involved. Mr. Habib recalled that the Korean negotiators had proposed the deletion of the first sentence of this Agreed Minute, which calls for a public trial by an impartial tribunal composed of judges who have completed their probationary period. The U.S. negotiators were aware of the fact that Paragraph 3 of Article 24 of the ROK Constitution provides that "all citizens shall have the right to a speedy trial" and "shall have the right to a public trial... without delay in the absence of justifiable reasons". They were also aware of Paragraph 1 of Article 24, which provides that a citizen has the right to be tried"in conformity with the law by competent judges as qualified by the Constitution and law". Although these points are covered in the ROK Constitution, the U.S. negotiators believe that, in view of their importance, they should be included also in the Status of Forces Agreement. With regard to the competency of judges, there is no inconsistency between the ROK Constitution and the proposed Agreed Minute. The U.S. negotiators assume that "competent" judges, as the term is used in the Constitution, are judges who have completed their probationary period. Nor is the language of the proposed Agreed Minute inconsistent with practice in the United States, where the public may be excluded from a public trial if morals or state secrets are at isuue. What the U.S. negotiators were seeking to ensure was the right of a representative of

0163

the United States Government to be present at all sessions of a trial, whether or not under special circumstances it was closed to the general public.

34. Mr. Habib noted that the second sentence of the proposed Agreed Minute would prohibit the trial of U.S. personnel by a Korean military tribunal. This provision was directly related to the question of including the word "civil" in Paragraph 1(b), which the negotiators had already discussed.

35. Mr. Chang stated that the Korean negotiators recognized that there was a difference of opinion over the question of public trials. The Korean negotiators would take the comments of the U.S. negotiators under consideration. They had no objection in principle to the U.S. negotiators' statement regarding the composition of the court. They agreed that the second sentence of the proposed Agreed Minute Re Paragraph 9(a) was related to the question of including or deleting the word "civil" from Paragraph 1(b).

36. Turning to the proposed Agreed Minute Re Paragraph 9(b) of the U.S. draft, Mr. Habib noted that the Korean negotiators had proposed deletion of the second paragraph on the grounds that there is no counterpart in the Korean criminal procedures and that the paragraph is contrary to the spirit of existing ROK laws. Mr. Habib pointed out that this paragraph guarantees the counsel of an accused the right to examine and copy the statements of witnesses prior to trial when these statements are contained in the file of the case. The Korean negotiators had argued that under the Korean code of criminal procedure the accused is given the opportunity to know the nature of the evidence against him and that this is sufficient. In the view of the U.S. negotiators, the right provided to the accused by the provisions of the second paragraph of this proposed Agreed Minute is a common sense right. Justice is not achieved by keeping the evidence from the accused or his counsel until the time of trial.

37. Mr. Habib stated that the U.S. negotiators believed that the provision in question was comparable to the provisions of ROK law. He referred specifically to Article 273 of the ROK Code of Criminal Procedure, which states:

0164

"273. (Investigation of Evidence Before the Date of Public Trial)

"(1) The court may, upon application, permit the prosecutor or the accused or his counsel to examine the accused or other witnesses and to inspect evidence before the date fixed for trial..."

The right sought by the U.S. negotiators is comparable to, and consistent in spirit with, this provision of the Korean code. Therefore, the U.S. negotiators urged the Korean negotiators to reconsider their objections to this provision.

38. Mr. Chang replied that the Korean negotiators wished to study this matter further.

39. It was agreed to adjourn the meeting at this point. The next meeting was scheduled for August 14 at 3:00 p.m.

~~보통문서로 재분류(1966.12.31.)~~

1966.12.31 에 예고문에 의거 일반문서로 재분류됨

JOINT SUMMARY RECORD OF THE 60TH SESSION

1. Time and Place: 3:00 - 5:30 P.M. August 7, 1964 at the Foreign Ministry's Conference Room (No.1)

2. Attendants:

ROK Side:

Mr. Chang, Sang Moon	Director European and American Affairs Bureau
Mr. Koo, Choong Whay	Chief, America Section Ministry of Foreign Affairs
Mr. Lee, Myung Hi	Prosecutor Prosecutors Section Ministry of Justice
Maj. Lee, Kye Hoon	Military Affairs Section Ministry of National Defense
Mr. Park, Sang Yong	3rd Secretary Ministry of Foreign Affairs
Mr. Lee, Kae Chul	3rd Secretary Ministry of Foreign Affairs
Mr. Lee, Keun Pal (Rapporteur and Interpreter)	3rd Secretary Ministry of Foreign Affairs
Mr. Hwang, Young Jae	3rd Secretary Ministry of Foreign Affairs
Mr. Park, Won Chul	3rd Secretary Ministry of Foreign Affairs

U.S. Side:

Mr. Philip C. Habib	Counselor American Embassy
Capt. John Wayne	Assistant Chief of Staff USN/K
Col. Kenneth C. Crawford	Staff Judge Advocate 8th U.S. Army
Mr. Benjamin A. Fleck (Rapporteur and Press Officer)	First Secretary American Embassy
Mr. Robert A. Kinney	J-5 8th U.S. Army

0166

Mr. Robert A. Lewis	2nd Secretary American Embassy
Mr. Daniel A. O'Donohue	2nd Secretary American Embassy
Maj. Alton H. Harvey	Staff Judge Advocate's Office 8th U.S. Army
Mr. David Y.C. Lee (Interpreter)	2nd Secretary American Embassy

Criminal Jurisdiction

1. Mr. Habib opened the meeting by stating that the U.S. negotiators wished to take up the Criminal Jurisdiction Article and go through it from the beginning, discussing the differences of view which had emerged during previous discussions.

2. With regard to Paragraph 1(a), Mr. Habib continued, the Korean negotiators had objected to the concept of jurisdiction contained in the U.S. draft, which would allow for the exercise of jurisdiction by the U.S. authorities at some future time outside the Republic of Korea. The Korean negotiators had stated at the 59th meeting that any future return of accused civilians to the United States for trial would be inconsistent with judicial principles and not acceptable to any sovereign nation hosting foreign troops. They also had stated that if a person accused of committing a crime in one sovereign country was taken to another sovereign country for trial "there would arise a serious question as to possible infringement of sovereignty".

3. Mr. Habib stated that the U.S. negotiators did not agree with this interpretation of the proposed provision. He pointed out that it is a recongized principle of international law that a sovereign state retains jurisdiction over its nationals whether they are within the territorial jurisdiction of the asserting state or within that of a

foreign state. This jurisdiction is based upon the personal supremacy of a sovereign state over its own nationals rather than on any question of territorial sovereignty. The rights and duties of a national are solely determined by the law of his sovereign state and he is subjected to such penal jurisdiction for acts committed abroad as is provided for in that law.

4. Jurisdiction based upon the supremacy of a state over its nationals, Mr. Habib continued, is not in derogation of the sovereignty of the foreign state in which the offense is committed. Unless there are contrary treaty provisions, the state claiming jurisdiction based on nationality is under the obligation not to infringe upon the territorial supremacy of a foreign state by performing acts of sovereignty in the foreign state. This does not detract from the state's right under international law to punish its nationals when they are again within its territorial jurisdiction for acts committed abroad.

5. Mr. Habib pointed out that the Republic of Korea has exercised this right through implementation of Korean law. The Korean negotiators had said that this would be contrary to international law and judicial principles. The U.S. negotiators, however, wished to point out that the laws of the Republic of Korea recognize this principle and make specific provisions for this very situation. Article 3, Criminal Code, Korean Law 293, reads as follows:

"Crimes Committed by Koreans Abroad

"This Code shall apply to all Korean nationals outside the territory of the Republic of Korea."

0168

6. In fact, Mr. Habib continued, Korean law carries the principle of jurisdiction over crimes committed abroad much further than is applicable to the issue under discussion. Article 5 of the Korean Criminal Code provides that the Code shall apply to aliens who commit certain specified crimes outside the territory of the Republic of Korea. Article 6 reads as follows:

"Crimes Committed Abroad Against the Republic of Korea and Korean Nationals

"This Code shall apply to aliens who commit, outside the territory of Korea, against the Republic of Korea or her nationals, crimes other than those specified in the preceding article, except where they do not constitute crimes at the place of commission or where their prosecution or execution of the punishment imposed has been remitted."

7. Mr. Habib stated that the United States has no counterpart to Article 3 of the Korean Criminal Code. Whether or not this will be accomplished in future legislation is a matter wholly reserved to the United States Government in the exercise of its sovereign right of supremacy over its own nationals. If such legislation is passed, it would not derogate from the unquestioned sovereignty of the Republic of Korea. It is difficult to understand, he continued, why the ROK negotiators are concerned over a principle recognized by international law and specifically provided for in their own Criminal Code.

8. Mr. Habib said the U.S. negotiators had clearly stated the purpose of the language in the U.S. draft, which was to provide for the possibility of future legislation in the United States. The Korean negotiators had objected on the grounds that there was no basis in judicial practice for such a provision and that it would derogate against the sovereignty of the Republic of Korea. The U.S. negotiators

0169

had clearly demonstrated that there was no lack of precedents in judicial practice and that the provision would not derogate against the sovereignty of the Republic of Korea.

9. Mr. Habib added that the U.S. negotiators believed the Korean negotiators might be basing their objection also on the fact that this provision does not appear in this form in other status of forces agreements. He reiterated the frequently expressed view of the U.S. negotiators that this agreement was being negotiated on the basis of accumulated experience and not on the basis of language in other agreements. There was nothing in this provision which was inconsistent with the spirit of other status of forces agreements, nor with the exercise of sovereignty by either government, nor with judicial precedents, including those contained in Korean law. Mr. Habib asked whether the Korean negotiators wished to comment.

10. Mr. Chang replied that the U.S. negotiators had quoted articles of the Korean Criminal Code to justify their position that an accused could be taken from one country to another for trial without causing any infringement upon the territorial jurisdiction of the former. The spirit underlying them was that the Government of the Republic of Korea would exercise jurisdiction over the accused when the accused come within reach of ROK sovereignty or under an extradition agreement. In other words, the Korean articles do not call for unilateral and involuntary waiver of territorial jurisdiction, while the U.S. draft in question and the explanation of the U.S. negotiators clearly demand unconditional waiver, voluntary or involuntary, of territorial jurisdiction on the part of the Republic of Korea. The

0170

Korean negotiators did not believe that the U.S. Government would automatically waiver jurisdiction over a Korean offender in the United States. In the absence of an extradition agreement between the two countries, which is the case at present, if the ROK Government tried to extradite a Korean civilian or soldier accused of an offense in the United States for trial in the Republic of Korea, the U.S. Government not only could, but would probably object. In case the U.S. Government feels, for one reason or another, that the territorial jurisdiction can not be waived, the accused Korean can not be brought to Korea for trial. In brief, waiver of territorial jurisdiction is traced to the consent of the territorial sovereign.

11. Mr. Habib replied that the negotiators were not arguing on the specifics of Korean law. Nor were they discussing the subject of extradition. They were discussing the principle of the right of each government to exercise its sovereignty, a principle which the Korean negotiators had questioned at the last meeting. The U.S. negotiators were not questioning the way in which the Korean authorities applied ROK law. With regard to the attitude of the U.S. Government, Mr. Habib reminded the Korean negotiators of the recent case of a member of the ROK Navy who had got into trouble in Guam. Although the charges against him had been of a very serious nature, including manslaughter, the U.S. Government, acting in response to the request of the ROK Government, had agreed to permit him to be returned to the Republic of Korea for trial.

12. Mr. Habib reiterated that the provision in question would result in no derogation of sovereignty and was based on judicial precedents. The Korean negotiators had raised

the question of comparability with other status of forces agreements. In this case, the U.S. negotiators were not arguing in favor of their language on the basis of the existence of a different set of conditions in Korea than in other countries where U.S. armed forces are stationed. They wished to point out that at the time when the status of forces agreements with Japan and with the NATO governments were negotiated, the Supreme Court decision of 1960 had not yet been handed down. At the time when the agreement with Japan was negotiated, the U.S. negotiators had believed that U.S. military courts had jurisdiction over certain U.S. civilians. Therefore, in this respect the two agreements were not comparable.

13. Mr. Habib stated that similar reasoning lay behind the language of Paragraph 1(b) of the U.S. draft. The U.S. negotiators of the status of forces agreements with Japan and the NATO governments had not conceived of the possibility that military authorities of the host country could exercise jurisdiction. Inasmuch as that possibility does exist in the Republic of Korea, the U.S. negotiators, in drafting this more modern agreement, wish to make the language of the provision quite clear by having it read "the civil authorities of the Republic of Korea." This is not an unreasonable provision and should be fairly easy to explain. It is fully consistent with the statements of the Korean negotiators for the negotiating record that the Korean authorities have no intention of subjecting U.S. personnel covered by this SOFA to military courts. The objection of the Korean negotiators to this provision appeared to be solely the fact that such language does not

0172

appear in the SOFA with Japan. The U.S. negotiators were of the opinion that this was not a valid objection.

14. Reverting to Paragraph 1(a), Mr. Chang stated that when an accused is taken from the host country to another country for trial, the host country voluntarily waives its jurisdiction. If such a case arose in the Republic of Korea and the ROK authorities were not prepared to waive ROK jurisdiction, the accused could not be taken to another country for trial. In effect, the language of the U.S. draft called for a voluntary waiver of jurisdiction over dependents by the ROK Government.

15. Mr. Chang asked whether the United States, following the 1960 Supreme Court decision, had received assurances from other governments with whom it has negotiated status of forces agreements that civilians may be taken to the United States for trial. Mr. Habib replied that, to his knowledge, the question had not arisen.

16. With regard to Paragraph 1(b), Mr. Chang stated that the Korean negotiators had given an unequivocal assurance for the negotiating record that under no circumstances would members of the U.S. armed forces be subject to trial by Korean military authorities, in the hope that the U.S. negotiators would agree to the deletion of the word "civil". Mr. Habib replied that the simplest way of handling this question was to leave the word "civil" in the text of the paragraph.

17. Mr. Chang stated that the Korean negotiators believed both sides were trying to negotiate an agreement that would be acceptable to their respective citizens and legislatures. They were trying to find acceptable wording regarding this question. The Korean negotiators believed that the effect would be the same, whether the assurance appeared in the text

of the Agreement or in the Agreed Joint Summary. Inasmuch as the effect was same, the U.S. negotiators should and could be responsive to the concern of their counterparts. Utter disregard by the U.S. side of the Korean concern was not a constructive way of conducting negotiation. The Korean negotiators could not understand the U.S. insistance on the inclusion of the word "civil" in the text.

18. In an attempt to clarify the Korean position, Mr. Habib asked whether the Korean negotiators were proposing to include their assurance in the Agreed Joint Summary or as an Agreed Minute. Mr. Chang replied that they were neither making any suggestion nor proposal. They merely wished to clarify the U.S. position whether the U.S. negotiators would accept the assurance as an Agreed Minute and delete the word "civil" from the text.

19. Mr. Habib stated that the U.S. negotiators wished to clarify further the U.S. position with regard to the duty certificate and to bring to the attention of the Korean negotiators certain precedents and other factors of which they might not be aware. The U.S. negotiators had stated their view that the duty certificate is conclusive. The Korean negotiators had taken the position that if the Korean authorities objected to a duty certificate, they should be able to refer the matter to the Joint Committee. If the Joint Committee could not reach agreement, the matter would then be referred to the Korean courts, under the terms of the third paragraph of the revised Agreed Minute Re Paragraph 3(a)(ii) of the Korean draft. The Korean negotiators had expressed the hope that the U.S. military authorities would be prepared to entertain requests for modification of duty

0174

certificates. The U.S. negotiators, Mr. Habib continued, did not wish to mislead the Korean negotiators regarding the firmness of the U.S. belief in the conclusive nature of the duty certificate. This belief was based on a lengthy body of experience. The U.S. negotiators wished to call the attention of the Korean negotiators to the following information.

20. In Belgium, Mr. Habib stated, duty certificates are prepared by the unit commanding officer and submitted to the Army Attache at the U.S. Embassy in Brussels. The Army Attache either submits the duty certificate to the local authorities or advises them informally regarding the duty status of the accused. The Belgian authorities have never questioned U.S. determinations regarding duty status of an accused.

21. In Denmark, Mr. Habib continued, no formal procedures have been established for the determination of official duty status and no official duty cases have arisen to date. If such a case should occur, the determination would be made by the U.S. Representative on the Joint Committe, who would advise appropriate Danish authorities.

22. In France, the U.S. Staff Judge Advocate notifies the French prosecutor of official duty cases. The French Ministry of Justice issued a circular in 1956, which recognized the primary responsibility of the United States, as sending state, to determine the duty status of the accused. The French Court of Cassation in the case of James Martin (a _partie civile_ prosecution brought by an injured claimant) decided that only the sending state may make the determination of the performance of official duty referred to in Article VII of the NATO Status of Forces Agreement and that the sending state's duty certificate is conclusive as a matter of law.

0175

23. In Germany, Mr. Habib continued, criminal jurisdiction over U.S. personnel is exercised by the sending state only. However, the Agreement to Supplement the NATO Status of Forces Agreement in Germany provides as follows:

"1. Whenever, in the course of criminal proceedings against a member of a force or of a civilian component, it becomes necessary to determine whether an offence has risen out of any act or omission done in the performance of official duty, such determination shall be made in accordance with the law of the sending State concerned. The highest appropriate authority of such sending State may submit to the German Court or authority dealing with the case a certificate thereon.

"2. The German court or authority shall make its decision in conformity with the certificate. In exceptional cases, however, such certificate may, at the request of the German court or authority, be made the subject of review through discussions between the Federal Government and the diplomatic mission in the Federal Republic of the sending State."

24. Mr. Habib went on to point out that in Greece official duty certificates are issued by the Staff Judge Advocate and, if approved by the U.S. Representative on the Joint Committee, are submitted through diplomatic channels to the Ministry of Foreign Affairs. Greek authorities have never questioned official duty status determinations made by U.S. authorities.

25. In Italy, Mr. Habib continued, the determination of official duty status is made by a service Legal Officer or by the command Staff Judge Advocate on the basis of information provided by the unit commander. The determination is then submitted to the appropriate Italian official with a statement that the command will exercise its primary right of jurisdiction over the accused. It is well established in Italy that official duty certificates submitted by U.S. authorities are accepted without question by Italian authorities, including those issued with regard to acts or omissions which occur during travel incident to temporary duty in

0176

or permanent change of station or while traveling between residence and place of duty in privately-owned vehicles.

26. In Luxembourg, official duty determinations are made by the U.S. Representative on the Joint Committee on the basis of information provided by the immediate commander of the individual concerned and are transmitted by him to the Chief Public Prosecutor of the appropriate arrondissement. Authorities of Luxembourg in all cases have accepted United States official duty determinations.

27. Mr. Habib stated that he could go on, relating the precedents established in the Netherlands, Norway, Portugal, the United Kingdom, and the United States. Without taking the time to do that, he could state that again and again, in the countries cited, duty certificates are not questioned but are accepted as conclusive. In view of the many precedents he had cited and others which he had not cited, the U.S. negotiators did not believe that their requirement that the duty certificate be considered conclusive was an extraordinary requirement. He suggested that further discussion on this question be deferred until the U.S. negotiators responded specifically to the revised Agreed Minute Re Paragraph 3(a)(ii) proposed by the Korean negotiators.

28. Turning to the waiver provisions, Mr. Habib recalled that the Korean negotiators had rejected the idea of an automatic waiver on the grounds that no precedent existed for such a provision. In the view of the U.S. negotiators, there was general agreement on the desirability of some sort of waiver provision. The U.S. negotiators had proposed a general waiver by the ROK Government, with the

power to recall that waiver in special circumstances; the ROK negotiators had proposed that the U.S. authorities be given the power to request a waiver in special circumstances. Mr. Habib asked whether the Korean negotiators could elaborate on, or restate, their position in the light of the discussions which had taken place since these positions had first been stated.

29. Mr. Chang replied that the provisions regarding waiver were more important than those regarding the duty certificate because the waiver provisions would play a heavier role in determining which side would exercise jurisdiction than the other provisions would. This was a very sensitive subject. The Korean negotiators could not accept the automaticity of waiver provided for in the U.S. draft. They wished to reserve to the Korean authorities the right to determine whether or not to waive when requested to do so by the U.S. authorities. The Korean position was based not on a lack of precedents but on principle. The principle is that the waiver is granted by the authorities who hold the jurisdiction and could not be exercised by the authorities lacking the jurisdiction. The automatic waiver provisions proposed by the U.S. negotiators are diametrically opposite to this principle. Under the system of automatic waiver, the U.S. authorities, who lack the original jurisdiction, are to exercise waiver, while the Korean authorities are to ask for recall of waiver. The Korean negotiators had already stated, and wished to state again, that the Korean authorities would waive in as many cases as possible but they must retain the discretion whether or not to waive.

0178

The Korean negotiators therefore could not think of a SOFA with a waiver clause providing for an automatic waiver.

30. Turning to the question of pre-trial custody, Mr. Habib recalled that the remaining difference of opinion pertains to the question of custody in security cases. The U.S. negotiators had indicated their willingness to agree to Paragraph 5(e) of the Korean draft, provided the Korean negotiators would agree to the inclusion in the Agreed Joint Summary of the following two understandings:

> a. There must be mutual U.S.-ROK agreement as to the circumstances in which such custody is appropriate; and
>
> b. Korean confinement facilities must be adequate by U.S. standards.

The Korean negotiators had accepted the second of these two understandings but had rejected the first on the grounds that the Korean authorities should be the only and final authorities to determine whether or not such custody is appropriate. Earlier, the Korean negotiators had stated that the Korean authorities required custody of individuals charged with security offenses in order to prevent further threats to the security of the Republic of Korea or to prevent destruction of evidence. It was inconceivable, Mr. Habib stated, that the United States Government would be a party to threats to the security of the Republic of Korea. The U.S. armed forces were not present in the Republic of Korea to pose a threat to its security. The U.S. authorities desired to participate in the determination of the circumstances under which Korean custody of the accused would be appropriate. This position did not reject the right of the Korean authorities to hold custody. As a matter of practical implementation, mutual discussion would be called for in a security case. Let both sides consider this question further.

0179

31. Mr. Chang replied that in the light of the special and close relationship existing between the two countries, the Korean negotiators were not unprepared to reconsider this matter. They viewed it as a matter of principle, however. The Korean authorities were prepared to consult with U.S. military authorities concerning a security case and to recognize the U.S. right to participate in the determination of circumstances leading to custody by the Korean authorities but the final decision concerning custody must be made by the Korean authorities, not the U.S. authorities. Agreement between them was not necessary.

32. Mr. Habib replied that the U.S. negotiators believed that agreement was necessary - agreement as to the circumstances in which custody would be appropriate. In order to preclude the temptation to the Korean authorities to make a unilateral decision, there should be consultation. The U.S. negotiators were proposing these two understandings for inclusion in the Agreed Joint Summary in view of the importance of the Joint Summary as a document providing specific guidelines for those who will be charged with implementing the Agreement. Mr. Chang replied that the Korean negotiators fully shared the views of the U.S. negotiators concerning the importance of the Agreed Joint Summary and its function as a guide for implementation of the Agreement.

33. Turning to the subject of trial safeguards, Mr. Habib stated that the Agreed Minute Re Paragraph 9(a) in the U.S. draft, which would provide for a public trial, would not rule out the possibility of the public being excluded from a trial in which morals or state secrets are involved. Mr. Habib recalled that the Korean negotiators had proposed

0180

the deletion of the first sentence of this Agreed Minute, which calls for public trial by an impartial tribunal composed of judges who have completed their probationary period. The U.S. negotiators were aware of the fact that Paragraph 3 of Article 24 of the ROK Constitution provides that "all citizens shall have the right to a speedy trial" and "shall have the right to a public trial ... without delay in the absence of justifiable reasons". They were also aware of Paragraph 1 of Article 24, which provides that a citizen has the right to be tried" in conformity with the law by competent judges as qualified by the Constitution and law". Although these points are covered in the ROK Constitution, the U.S. negotiators believe that, in view of their importance, they should be included also in the Status of Forces Agreement. With regard to the competency of judges, there is no inconsistency between the ROK Constitution and the proposed Agreed Minute. The U.S. negotiators assume that "competent" judges, as the term is used in the Constitution, are judges who have completed their probationary period. Nor is the language of the proposed Agreed Minute inconsistent with practice in the United States, where the public may be excluded from a public trial if morals or state secrets are at issue. What the U.S. negotiators were seeking to ensure was the right of a representative of the United States Government to be present at all sessions of a trial, whether or not under special circumstances it was closed to the general public.

34. Mr. Habib noted that the second sentence of the proposed Agreed Minute would prohibit the trial of U.S. personnel by a Korean military tribunal. This provision was directly related to the question of including the word "civil" in Paragraph 1(b), which the negotiators had already discussed.

0181

35. Mr. Chang stated that the Korean negotiators recognized that there was a difference of opinion over the question of public trials. The Korean negotiators would take the comments of the U.S. negotiators under consideration. They had no objection in principle to the U.S. negotiators statement regarding the composition of the court. They agreed that the second sentence of the proposed Agreed Minute Re Paragraph 9(a) was related to the question of including or deleting the word "civil" from Paragraph 1(b).

36. Turning to the proposed Agreed Minute Re Paragraph 9(b) of the U.S. draft, Mr. Habib noted that the Korean negotiators had proposed deletion of the second paragraph on the grounds that there is no counterpart in the Korean criminal procedures and that the paragraph is contrary to the spirit of existing ROK laws. Mr. Habib pointed out that this paragraph guarantees the counsel of an accused the right to examine and copy the statements of witnesses prior to trial when these statements are contained in the file of the case. The Korean negotiators had argued that under the Korean code of criminal procedure the accused is given the opportunity to know the nature of the evidence against him and that this is sufficient. In the view of the U.S. negotiators, the right provided to the accused by the provisions of the second paragraph of this proposed Agreed Minute is a common sense right. Justice is not achieved by keeping the evidence from the accused or his counsel until the time of trial.

37. Mr. Habib stated that the U.S. negotiators believed that the provision in question was comparable to the provisions of ROK law. He referred specifically to Article 273 of the ROK Code of Criminal Procedure, which states:

0182

"273. (Investigation of Evidence Before the Date of Public Trial)

"(1) The court may, upon application, permit the prosecutor or the accused or his counsel to examine the accused or other witnesses and to inspect evidence before the date fixed for trial..."

The right sought by the U.S. negotiators is comparable to, and consistent in spirit with, this provision of the Korean code. Therefore, the U.S. negotiators urged the Korean negotiators to reconsider their objections to this provision.

38. Mr. Chang replied that the Korean negotiators wished to study this matter further.

39. It was agreed to adjourn the meeting at this point. The next meeting was scheduled for August 14 at 3:00 p.m.

5. 제6차 회의, 8.14

0184

기 안 용 지

관리번호 ~~1790~~

자체 통제		기안처	미주과 이근팔	전화번호	근거서류접수일자

	과장	국장	차관	장관		
	(서명)	(서명)	(서명)	(서명) 8/20		

관계관 서명	

기안 년월일	1964. 8. 19.	시행 년월일		보존 년한		정서	기장
분류 기호	외구미 722.2—	전체 통제	7821 종결				

경유 수신 참조	대통령 : 참조: 비서실장 국무총리 : 참조: 비서실장 사본: 법무부장관	발신	장관

제목	제 61 회 주둔군지위협정 체결 교섭 실무자회의 개최 보고

1964. 8. 14. 하오 3 시 부터 동 5 시 까지 외무부 제 1 회의실에서 개최된 제 61 차 주둔군지위협정 체결 교섭실무자회의에서 토의된 내용을 별첨과 같이 보고합니다.

유첨: 제 61 차 주둔군지위협정 체결 교섭실무자회의 보고서 1 부. 끝.

보통문서로 재분류 (1966.12.31.)

1966. 12. 31. 에 예고문에 의거 일반문서로 재분류됨

승인서식 1-1-3 (11-00900-03) (195mm×265mm16절지)

0185

제 61 차

한·미 간 주둔군지위협정 체결 교섭실무자회의

보 고 서

1. 일 시: 1964 년 8 월 14 일 하오 3 시 부터 동 5 시 까지.

2. 장 소: 외무부 제 1 회의실

3. 토의사항:

가. 민사청구권

(1) 우리측이 제51 차 회의에서 제시한 제안중 공무집행중 제 3 자에 대하여 끼친 손해의 배상 청구에 관하여 미측은 우리안에 의하면 손해배상액이 우리 법에 의하여 결정되면 미측에 통고되고 만약 미측에 불복이 있으면 국가배상심의위원회에서 재심할 것이며 그 결정은 최종적일 것으로 되어 있는데 미측으로서는 한국측의 손해배상액의 결정이 미측의 동의 없이 결정된다면 수락할 수 없으며 미측의 현 배상제도는 민사청구에 대하여 신속하고도 공정히 처리하고 있으므로 새로운 제도를 수립할 필요가 없다고 주장하고

(2) 우리측이 협정 발효 6 개월 후 부터 민사사건을 처리하려는데 대하여 미측은 우리 나라에 우리측이 제안한 바와 같은 효율적인 국가배상제도가 없고 6 개월내에 태세를 확립하려는 것은 불가능한 것임으로우리 주장은 수락할 수 없다고 말하고 우리 나라 현 제도에 관한 질문 및 참고자료의 제공을 의뢰하였다.

(3) 우리측은 우리측이 제안한 배상제도는 손해배상청구를 신속 공정하게 처리할 수 있는 제도이며 비록 현재는 효율적인 제도가 없다할지라도 협정 체결로 인하여 증가될 민사사건에 대비하여 기구 확장을 강구중임으로 협정 발효 6 개월 후이면 원활한 제도가 확립될 것이며 따라서 미측의 요구를 충족시킬 수 있을 것이라고 답변하였다.

나. 형사재판관할권

(1) 미측은 한국의 헌법과 법률이 보장하고 있는 피의자의 권리중 미측이 제안한 권리는 협정에 규정할 것을 요구하고 헌법이나

0186

64-3-)(

법률에서 보장되지 않은 권리도 교섭 결과에 따라 협정에

열거하고 필요하다면 특별법을 제정하여서라도 피의자의 권리를

보장하려는 것은 미측의 근본방침이며 이러한 원칙적인 문제에

대한 합의 없이는 피의자의 권리에 관하여 이 이상 토의할

필요가 없을 것이라고 주장하고 우리측 입장을 타진하였다.

(2) 우리측은 이에 대하여 이미 제 50 차 회의에서 밝힌 바와 같이

우리 나라 헌법과 법률이 보장한 권리는 불필요하게 협정에 열기할

필요가 없다는 입장에는 변함이 없으나 미측 견해를 참작하여

다음 회의에서 우리측 입장을 명백히 할 것이며 법률에서 보장

되지 않은 권리는 미측이 계속 검토할 것을 희망하면 검토 결과에

따라 해결책을 모색할 것을 제안하고 토의를 계속하기로 하였다.

(3) 미측은 피의자가 법무관리의 입회 없이 변호인과 면접할 수 있어야

하며 행형법의 수정을 통하여서라도 변호인이 피의자와 비밀히

상의할 수 있는 권리는 보장되어야 한다고 주장하였다.

(4) 미측은 또한 정부대표가 비공개재판을 포함한 모든 소송절차에

참석할 수 있는 권리가 보장되어야 하며 특히 법원이 안녕질서를

방해하거나 풍속을 해할 염려가 있을 때에 결정으로서 비공개

재판을 진행할 때에도 미군피의자의 보호를 위하여 공무를

집행하는 정부대표의 참석이 허용되어야 한다고 주장하고

(5) 기타 한국의 헌법과 법률이 보장하고 있는 각종 권리는 협정에

규정되어 있지 않아도 미군관계 피의자에게 보장되어야 한다고

주장하였다.

(6) 일심에서 언도된 형량보다 중한 형이 상급심에서 언도되어서는

않된다는 것은 검사가 불복 상소한 경우에도 적용되어야 하며

이 권리는 미국인이 향유하는 기본적 법의 원칙이며

(7) 또는 피의자는 정신적으로나 건강상 이유로 재판에 출석하기에

적당치 못한 경우에는 참석하지 않을 수 있는 권리가 보장되어야

하며

(8) 불법한 방법은 물론 부당한 방법에 의하여 채집된 것은

증거로서 사용되어서는 않된다고 미측은 계속 주장하였다. 0188

64-3-96

64-3-27
기.3 III-8
0189

(9) 미측은 또한 법률 적용의 착오는 상소의 이유가 되지만 사실의 오인으로 인한 상소는 부당하다고 말하고 그 것은 공소 위지의 책임이 있는 검사의 부주의로 증거 수집에 결함이 있게 되어 동일한 내용의 사건을 심급에 따라 수차 상소할 수 있는 것은 검사에게만 유리한 권한을 부여하는 반면 피의자는 불리한 입장에 노이게 될 것 입으로 미측은 사실의 오인으로 인한 상소를 인정할 수 없다고 주장하였다.

(10) 우리는 미측의 견해를 검토하여 다음 회의에서 우리측 입장을 밝히기로 하였다.

4. 기타 사항: 차기 회의 일자: 1964 년 8 월 28 일 하오 3 시. 끝

0190

64-3-77

비-3-27(3)　　　　미주 111-8 (3)

0191

제 61차 주둔군 지위협정 체결 교섭
실무자 회의록

11

형사재판관할권
미의자의 권리

하비부 미측수석대표는 형사재판관할권 조항에 관하여 전번회의에서 미측대표단은 미측이 협정상에 열거하기를 원하는 합의의사록의 피의자의 권리에 관하여 상세한 토의를 시작하였음을 상기시켰다. 그는 지난번 회의때 중단된 부분에서 부터 토의를 계속한것을 제의하였다. 하비부 미측수석대표는 한국측 대표단이 제 50차 회의 석상에서 합의의사록 제 9 (c) 및 (d) 항의 삭제를 제안한바 있으나 그후 회의에서는 한국대표단이 이제안을 재논한바 없다. 그러므로 미측대표단이 중요하다고 인정하는 동합의의사록에 대한 한국측 입장을 미측대표단은 정확히 이해할수가 없다. 동합의의사록은 피의자에게 영미법계의 가장 오래된 개념의 하나인 대질심문의 권리를 보장하려는 것으로서 한국형사소송법 제 161조부터 164조까지 제 291조, 제 293조 및 제 294조등 각조문에서 인정되고 있는 것이다.

장한국측 수석대표는 동합의의사록은 물론 기타 한국헌법과 관계법률이 보장하고 있는 피의자의 권리는 협정문으로 부터 삭제되어야 하며 그들을 협정에 규정하는 것은 불필요하게 반복하는 것이며 복잡한 것이라고 대답하였다.

"하비부" 미측수석대표는 그러한 피의자의 권리를 협정에 규정하는 것이 한국법에 관한한 중복될지 모르지만 본협정에 관한한 그렇지가 않은것이라고 대답하였다.

0192

한국법에서 보장되지 않은 피의자의 권리의 경우 법률이 개정될수 있다는 것이 생각되지 않는것이 아니다. 피의자의 권리는 중요하므로 협정에 규정하는 것은 미국정부가 협정의 체결에 합의하기 위한 중요한 요소인 것이다. "하비부"미측수석대표는 동문제는 근본적인 문제임을 지적하고 한국측대표단이 피의자의 권리를 협정에 규정하는 것을 문제화 하려는 것인지를 질문하였다. 과거 한국측대표단은 미측대표단의 요구를 수락한 것으로 알고, 미측대표단은 피의자의 권리를 규정할 것을 원칙적으로 동의하는 것으로 이해하였다. 한국대표단이 협정에 규정하는 것에 동의하지 않는한 미측이 이회의 석상에서 예정한바와 같이 축조적으로 상세하게 토의할 필요가 없을 것이다.

장한국측 수석대표는 한국측 초안은 미측초안 제9항에 열거된 모든 피의자의 권리가 한국헌법과 관계법률에 의하여 보장되고 있다는 것은 명백히 하고 있다고 답변하였다. ㅈ 50차 회의에서 한국측대표단은 본문 제9항에 규정된 피의자의 권리를 합의의사록에서 반복 규정하는 것과 한국헌법과 법률의 정신에 일치하는 피의자의 권리를 포함하는 것은 불필요한 것이라고 말한바 있다. 미측대표단은 한국의 헌법과 법률이 개정될 가능성에 대하여 염려하고 있음을 표명하였으나, 설사 개정된다 하여도 그러한 개정은 피의자를 위한 보호와 이익을 증진하는 결과가 될것이 틀림없다. 미측대표단은 모든 피의자의 권리를 열거하여야 할 합리적인 이유가 없다. 만약에 미측대표단이 한국측대표단의 입장에 동의하지 않는다면 만족스러운 해결이란 불가능한 것이다. 만약에 미측대표단이 제안한 피의자의 권리중 특히 중요하다고 생각하는 권리를 지적한다면 한국측대표단은 그러한

0193

합의의사록에 관하여 협의할 용의는 있다. "하비부"
미측 수석대표는 미측대표단이 한국법률의 변경이 인권
옹호를 더욱 위하는 것이 아니라는 것을 암시한 것은
아니라고 말하였다. 미측대표단은 한국측대표단의 진술은
그대로 받아드리는 바이지만 그것은 토의중인 문제와는
관계가 없는 것이라고 주장하였다. 그는 미측 합의의사록
제9항의 첫째문장은 특히 한국법에 관계되는 것인데
그것은 피의자에게 법에 의하여 한국국민에 부여된
모든 절차적 및 실제적 권리가 인정되어야 한다고 규정
하고 있다. 미측대표단은 주둔군지위협정이 피의자의
권리로서 어떤 기본적 권리를 규정하여야 한다고 믿는
바이다.

이러한 피의자의 권리는 한국법에 위배되지 않는
것이 아니다. 한국측대표단도 그러한 피의자의 권리가
한국법과 일치된다고 동의한바 있다. 한국측대표단은
미측대표단이 가장 중요하다고 믿는 피의자의 권리를
열거규정할이것을 당부한바 있다. 미측초안은 그러한 권리
의 열거를 규정한 것이다. 만약 한국측대표단이 미측
초안에 규정한 피의자의 권리중 어떤 특정의 권리에
반대한다면 미측대표단은 그러한 권리에 관하여 토의할
용의가 있다. 그러나 미측대표단이 협정에 피의자의
권리를 열거하려는 원칙을 결코 포기하지는 않을 것이다.
미측초안에 규정된 피의자의 권리중 한국정부의 주권을
침해하는 것은 아무것도 없다.

장한국측 수석대표는 한국의 헌법과 기타 관계
법률에 의하여 인정된 피의자의 권리에 관하여 견해의
차이가 있다고 답변하고 한국측 대표단은 다음 회의에서
한국측 입장을 제시하겠다고 말하였다. 만약 미측대표단이
한국의 헌법과 법률에 의하여 보장되지 않은 권리에

0194

관하여 토의하기를 원한다면 한국대표단도 그렇게 할 용의는 있다.

"하비부" 미측수석대표는 그러한 검토가 유익할 것이라고 말하였다. "하비부" 미측수석대표는 이미 지적한 바와 같이 합의의사록 9 (c) 및 (d) 항은 한국헌법에 위배되지는 않는다고 말하였다.

"하비부" 미측수석대표는 계속하여 한국대표단이 만약에 "비밀히" 라는 용어만 삭제된다면 미측합의 의사록 제9항 (c) 은 수락할수 있다고 말한바 있다고 지적하였다. 한국대표단은 현행 한국법체계는 면회시 피의자가 관계관의 감시하에 두어져야 한다고 주장한바 있다. 그러나 미측대표단은 만약에 변호사가 효율적이기 위하여서는 변호사는 담당피의자가 타인이 엿듣게 되는 두려움 없이 변호사에게 진실을 말할수 있도록 할수 있어야 만 한다고 믿는다. 행형법의 제한적 규정의 외면상 이유는 도주의 방지 및 증거인멸일 것이다. 그와 같은 목적은 피의자와 변호사를 경비원을 외부에 배치한 실내에 격리하면 이루워 질것이다. 이에 관련 하여 형사소송법의 규정은 비밀히 교통할수 있는 권리와 일치하겠지만 미군관계 인사에 관련된 사건을 위하여서는 입법이나 또는 행정적 관행을 통하여 행형법이 변경 되어야 한다.

그는 저명한 한국의 검사가 1963년 8월 28일자 법률신문의 기사에서 "변호사가 어떤 자의 입회 (행형 관리에 의한) 없이 수감자를 면접하고 직접 교통할수 있는 권리는 그러한 폐단을 제거하기 위하여 입법화 되어야 한다" 고 주장한바 있음을 지적하였다.

0195

끝으로 "하비부"미측 수석대표는 비밀히 고통할수 있는 원칙은 예를들면 "포로에 관한 제네바 협정에 있어서 국제법의 관행으로 인정되었다고 말하였다.

합의의사록 제9(f)항에 관하여 "하비부"미측수석대표는 동규정이 한국형사소송법과 일치하기 때문에 의견의 차이가 없다고 말하였다.

합의의사록 제9(g)항에 관하여 "하비부"미측 수석대표는 한국측대표단이 "정부대표의 참석없이 행하여진 진술은 피의자에 대한 유죄의 증거로서 채택될수 없다" 라는 부분에 대하여 이의를 표명한바 있다고 말하였다. 미측대표단은 미국정부대표는 공무에 종사하는 것이며 사전수사, 조사, 공판전변론 재판재체, 재판후 절차등에 항상 참석하게 되는 것이다. 한국측 대표단은 정부대표의 권리를 그러한 경우에 국한하려는것 같은데 미측입장은 정부대표는 비공개 재판을 포함한 모든 경우에 참석할수 있어야 한다는 것이다. 동규정을 협정에 삽입한 명백한 이유는 강제에 의한 자백이 진술되지 않도록 하기 위한 것이다.

"하비부"미측수석대표는 말하기를 미국측은 합의의사록제9항은 한국법률과 완전히 양립하는 것으로 믿는다. 그들은 다른 방법으로 적의한 심판기록을 유지하도록 약정한수 있으므로 (a)세항을 삭제하기도 이미 합의한바 있다.

(b)세항의 나머지 부분이 한국형사소송법과 양립할수 있다는 것에 관하여는 문제가 없었다.

(c) 및 (d)세항의 일반규정과 유사한 그것이 형사소송법 및 헌법에 포함되어 있다.

합의의사록 9항의(e)세항에 관하여, 한국측은 검사가 판결에 상소하는 문제전반을 토의하게 한 대안을 제의한바 있다.

0196

한국측 제안은 첫번째의 심민에서 미고가 행한 논의를 알게된 후에 미고인이 검사가 "무번째의 기회"를 가진다는 공정하지 못한 지위에 있게 될것이다.

검사가 상소하여 판결을 거듭하는 것은 모든 미군인 관계 인원에게는 흔히 있는 근본적인 법의원칙에 배치되는 것이며 이처럼 예측치 못하는 일로부터 보호함이 군대 지위협정에 포함시켜야 되는 본질적인 권리인 것이다.

"하비부"미측수석대표는 (f), (g) 및 (h) 세항에 관하여 한국법률 및 한국헌법과 양립되지 않는것은 없다고 말하였다.

"하비부"미측수석대표는 한국측이 (i) 세항을 미군관계 법인이 법원의 재판이외에 의한 처벌을 받지 않는다는 것을 의미하는 것으로 해석한다고 말한바를 상기시켰다.

이러한 해석은 옳은 것이 었다. 이규정은 심판에 의하지 아니하고 유죄를 선고하는 법안의 제정을 금지하는 것이다. 분명히 미국측은 [illegible] 모든 법인은 사법적 재판을 받아야 한다고 믿었다.

"하비부"미측수석대표는 (j) 세항과 한국헌법간에는 모순되는 점이 없다고 말하였다. (k) 세항에 관하여 "하비부"미측수석대표는 대안을 제의한바 있다. 양제안에는 용어상의 차이가 있었고 법적근거에 있어서는 차이가 없었다. 한국측이 제안한 용어는 한국측 제안의 엄격한 문자 그대로의 해석에 의하면 피고인의 출정 없이도 재판을 진행시킬수 있으므로 명확하지 아니 하였다.
(l) 세항에 관하여 "하비부 미측수석대표는 이규정의 법적 근거가 한국법률과 모순이 없다고 말하였다.
"하비부"미측수석대표는 한국측이 합의의사록 9항의 셋째 조항에서 "부당한"이라는 용어의 삭제를 제의한 바 있었다. 미국측은 반드시 위법은 아니지만 수많은

0197

부당한 행위가 있을수 있으므로, 협정안에 이용어를 그대로 남겨두는 것이 중요하다고 믿었다. 한국형사 소송법은 "진술이 특히 신빙할수 있을만한 사정하에서 행하여 졌을때에만" 자백은 증거로서 채증된다고 규정하고 있다. 이규정에 의하여 코합시키는 사정이란 부당한 행위를 모함한다.

"하비부" 미측수석대표는 한국측이 검사의 상소를 제한케 하는 합의의사록의 항의 넷째 조항의 삭제를 제의한바 있다. 미측은 형사소송법 제361조를 알고 있다. 그들은 법률적용의 착오를 이유로 검사가 상소하는 것에 대하여는 반대가 없다. 그러나 그들은 검사가 "사실의 오인" 또는 "형량의 부당"을 사유로 상소하는 것에 대하여 반대한다.

이러한 상소는 검사가 동일할 사건을 거듭 논의하는 허다한 기회를 부여할 것이다. 만일 이규정이 채택된다면 검사가 노력을 태만히 하는 경우에 피고인이 당연히 그에게 귀속할 유리한 보장을 받을 권리가 박탈당하는 반면 검사는 피고측의 죄상을 알게된 후에 다시 상소하는 기회를 가지게 된것이다.

"장" 한국측 수석대표는 한국측은 미측이 행한 충분한 설명에 사의를 표명하고 심판 방어에 관한 미측 입장을 검토하고 다음 회기에 그들의 의견을 표현하겠다고 말하였다.

0198

CONFIDENTIAL

STATUS OF FORCES NEGOTIATIONS: 61st Meeting

SUBJECTS: 1. Claims
2. Criminal Jurisidiction

PLACE: Ministry of Foreign Affairs

DATE: August 14, 1964

PARTICIPANTS:

Republic of Korea

CHANG Sang-mun
U Chung-hoe
Colonel KIM Won-kil, ROKA
CHU Mun-ki
O Chae-hi
HWANG Yong-chae
YI Kun=pal (Interpreter)
Huh Hyung Koo
Pak Won chul

9.

United States

Philip C. Habib
Brig. General Carroll H. Dunn, USA
Colonel Howard Smigelow, USA
Captain John Wayne, USN
Colonel Kenneth C. Crawford, USA
Frank R. LaMacchia
Benjamin A. Fleck
Robert A. Kinney
Robert A. Lewis
Major Alton Harvey, USA
Kenneth Campen (Interpreter)

11.

0199

1. Mr. Habib opened the 61st meeting by introducing Brigadier General Carroll H. Dunn, who was replacing Brigadier General G. G. O'Connor on the U.S. negotiating team. Mr. Chang warmly welcomed General Dunn on behalf of the Korean negotiators.

Claims

2. Taking up the Claims Article, Mr. Habib recalled that at the 51st meeting, the Korean negotiators had tabled proposed Agreed Minutes to this article. The first of these would provide that the decisions of the Korean claims authorities shall be final and conclusive. If the U.S. authorities disagree on the amount of a claim decided upon by the Korean claims authorities, the latter will reexamine the case but the results of their reexamination shall be final. According to the provisions of the second Agreed Minute proposed by the Korean negotiators, the ROK Government Claims Service would replace the U.S. Claims Service in the processing of claims six months from the date of entry into force of the Agreement, regardless of the state of readiness of the ROK Government Claims Service to assume such responsibilities.

3. Mr. Habib stated that the U.S. negotiators had carefully reviewed these proposals and had found them to be unacceptable. The primary objective in negotiating this article is to ensure an effective system of settling legitimate claims against the U.S. armed forces in Korea. The present system functions promptly and equitably. The Korean proposals would require changing from the present procedures, which have worked well for the past five years, to the recently established and as yet relatively untried ROK Government Claims Service procedures. The Korean negotiators had proposed that this change be made within six months of the effective date of the Agreement.

0200

4. The United States Government, Mr. Habib continued, has accumulated a great deal of experience over the past eleven years with the operation of claims machinery in other countries. It has found that the formula concept of

settling claims, as proposed by the Korean negotiators, is time-consuming and difficult to administer. This system compels the host nation to establish an expensive bureaucracy and often generates ill-will between the host nation and the United States. In Japan, the formula system is currently being administered in a manner much different from that described in the SOFA with Japan. Not one claim has yet been paid in Japan without prior concurrence of U.S. authorities.

5. The U.S. negotiators believe, Mr. Habib continued, that there is no question but that continuation of the present system, which is meeting the problem to the general satisfaction of all concerned, is infinitely preferable to switching over to the new, untried, and relatively complicated system proposed by the Korean negotiators. The U.S. negotiators believe that continued operation of the present U.S. Claims Service, with the U.S. Government underwriting the entire cost of the operation, will be in the best interests of both the ROK and U.S. Governments. Continuation of the present system will be much more likely to result in equitable and prompt settlement with legitimate Korean claimants than would the alternative system proposed by the Korean negotiators.

6. Mr. Chu replied that he would like to give a supplementary explanation of the Korean proposals. The U.S. negotiators had expressed the view that the reexamination system to be set up under the first Agreed Minute proposed by the Korean negotiators would delay final disposition of claims. They had also stated that the second proposed Agreed Minute would establish an untried system. It was true, he said, that the ROK Claims Service has no reexamination system as proposed in the Agreed Minute at present. However, the ROK authorities had ~~were~~ proposed the first Agreed Minute, considering that establishment of the reexamination system ~~planning to establish a system which~~ would ~~dispose of cases as quickly as possible. After~~ be necessary not only for final and prompt disposition of the cases but also ~~the SOFA came into force, the ROK authorities would be able to dispose of cases effectively~~ for opening a way to reconsider any disagreement by the U.S. authorities on the amount of a claim decided upon by the Korean authorities. The U.S. negotiators had expressed concern about the six-month provision in the Korean proposals. The Korean negotiators ~~authorities~~ considered six months to be sufficient time to enable the Korean authorities to establish an efficient system. Some of the U.S. negotiators had visited the Ministry of Justice in the autumn of 1963 and had witnessed the procedures then in effect. They had stated at that time that they believed no practical difference existed between

0201

the two systems. ~~In considering the Korean proposals,~~ Therefore, the Korean negotiators urged the U.S. negotiators to take into account the ~~feelings of the Korean people.~~ proposed mechanism envisaged by Korean proposals.

7. Mr. Habib replied that perhaps in theory no difference existed between the two claims systems. In practice, however, there was a great difference. It was a fact, he continued, that at the present time the Korean authorities had no effective claims service. The Korean negotiators had proposed the establishment of one within a given period of time but the U.S. negotiators believed this would be quite difficult to accomplish, in view of the possibility of the use of haphazard methods. In addition, there was the possibility that a case might be influenced unduly by public attention, which would result in a lack of adherence to standards.

8. Mr. Habib said that in order to assist them in considering the Korean position, the U.S. negotiators wished to have the answers to the following questions: concerning the operation of the State Compensation Committee, promulgated under law number 231, December 24, 1962, and established on April 27, 1963:

a. How many attorneys, investigators, interpreters, and translators are employed by the Committee?

b. Who pays the salaries of the personnel employed by the Committee?

c. How many claims have been processed by the Committee in 1963 and in 1964?

d. Does the amount of an award include attorneys' fees?

e. Has the ROK Government appropriated any money to settle claims awards in 1963 and 1964? If so, what was the appropriation act for each year and how much money was appropriated?

e. How many offices, including central and regional offices, have been established? How many employees are there in each office?

0202

f. Have rules and regulations been set forth by the Committee for the administration of the Act and the guidance of the employees administering the Act? If so, may the U.S. negotiators have a copy?

9. Mr. Habib stated that the U.S. negotiators believed the answers to the questions which he had just asked would demonstrate that the Korean authorities did not have an effective claims service. That is why the U.S. negotiators preferred to continue the present system. They were not suggesting that the U.S. authorities do not have an obligation to pay claims. Nor were they trying to seek means to avoid payment of claims.

10. Mr. Chu replied that the Korean negotiators would answer as many of the questions asked by the U.S. negotiators as possible. Last year, members of the U.S. negotiating team had visited the Ministry of Justice, had been given a briefing, and had closely examined the Korean procedures. They had been given the relevant Korean laws and other documents, as well as statistics regarding claims lodged, claims paid, and claims otherwise disposed of. The Korean authorities would be glad to provide these materials again, if necessary.

11. Mr. Habib replied that the U.S. negotiators wanted this material to be introduced officially so that it might be discussed officially.

12. Mr. Chu stated that the present Korean claims system was not inefficient for the number of cases currently being received. However, the Korean authorities were already taking the necessary steps for reorganizing and enlarging the system in order to improve it and enable it to handle an increase in cases. Present payments, he said, are based on accumulated experience and on decisions of the Korean courts. The questions asked by the U.S. negotiators would be answered at a later negotiating session.

13. Mr. Habib asked whether the Korean negotiators could give some indication of the amount of time currently required to process a claim under the existing ROK claims procedures. Mr. Chu replied that the average length of time was about three

0209

months.

Criminal Jurisdiction

14. Turning to the Criminal Jurisdiction Article, Mr. Habib recalled that at the previous meeting, the U.S. negotiators had begun a detailed discussion of the Agreed Minutes of the U.S. draft which enumerated the trial safeguards sought by the U.S. authorities. He proposed that that discussion be resumed at the point at which it had been halted at the last meeting.

15. Mr. Habib recalled that at the 50th meeting, the Korean negotiators had proposed deletion of the Agreed Minute Re Paragraph 9 (c) and (d). In subsequent discussion, they had not mentioned this proposal again. The U.S. negotiators, therefore, were uncertain of the Korean position regarding this Agreed Minute, which was an important paragraph in the view of the U.S. negotiators. It would guarantee to the accused the right of confrontation, one of the oldest concepts of the Anglo-Saxon legal system, which is recognized in Articles 161 through 164, 291, 293 and 294 of the ROK Code of Criminal Procedure.

16. Mr. Chang replied that this Agreed Minute, as well as others which provided safeguards guaranteed by the ROK Constitution and relevant laws, should be deleted from the Agreement. To include them would be unnecessarily repetitive and redundant.

17. Mr. Habib replied that inclusion of such safeguards in the Agreement might be redundant insofar as Korean law is concerned but not with regard to the Agreement. In the case of safeguards not guaranteed by Korean law, it is not inconceivable that the law could be amended. The trial safeguards were important and their inclusion in the Agreement was an important factor in enabling the U.S. Government to agree to the conclusion of the Agreement. Pointing out that this was a fundamental question, Mr. Habib asked whether the Korean negotiators were now questioning the listing of trial safeguards. Previously, the Korean negotiators had

0204

seemed to accept the problem of the U.S. negotiators and the U.S. negotiators had assumed that the Korean negotiators had agreed in principle to a listing of trial safeguards. Unless the Korean negotiators agreed to such a listing, there was little point in discussing the safeguards individually and in detail, as the U.S. negotiators had planned to do at this meeting.

18. Mr. Chang replied that the Korean draft clearly stated that all trial safeguards enumerated in Paragraph 9 of the U.S. draft were guaranteeed by the ROK Constitution and relevant laws. At the 50th meeting, the Korean negotiators had stated that it was not necessary to repeat in the Agreed Minutes the trial safeguards listed in Paragraph 9 or to include those safeguards which are consonant with the spirit of the ROK Constitution and relevant laws. The U.S. negotiators had expressed concern over the possibility that the laws and the Constitution might be changed. Even if they were changed, the Korean negotiators were sure that the changes would result in better protection and benefit for the accused. The U.S. negotiators had no reasonable grounds for listing all of these safeguards. If they did not agree with the position of the Korean negotiators, no satisfactory solution was possible. If the U.S. negotiators would indicate which of the proposed safeguards were of particular importance, the Korean negotiators were prepared to negotiate with regard to those Agreed Minutes.

19. Mr. Habib stated that the U.S. negotiators had not intimated that they believed changes in Korean laws would not be for the better. They accepted the statement of the Korean negotiators in this regard but it was not relevant to the question under discussion. He pointed out that the first sentence of the Agreed Minute Re Paragraph 9 of the U.S. draft specifically refers to ROK law, where it reads that the accused "shall be accorded every procedural and substantive right granted by law to the citizens of the Republic of Korea". The U.S. negotiators believed that the Status of Forces Agreement should provide certain fundamental rights as trial safeguards. These are not incompatible with ROK law. The Korean negotiators had agreed that they were compatible.

0205

The Korean negotiators had asked for a specific enumeration of those safeguards which the U.S. authorities believed to be most important. The U.S. draft provided this enumeration. If the Korean negotiators objected to certain of the safeguards listed in the U.S. draft, the U.S. negotiators were prepared to discuss them. However, there was no chance whatsoever that the U.S. negotiators would abandon the principle of enumerating trial safeguards in the Agreement. There is nothing in the safeguards listed, he added, which derogates from the sovereignty of the ROK Government.

20. Mr. Chang replied that a difference of opinion existed regarding those safeguards which were already guaranteed by the ROK Consitution and the relevant Korean laws and that the Korean negotiators would present their views at a later meeting. If the U.S. negotiators wished to discuss those safeguards which were not covered by the ROK Constitution or Korean law, the Korean negotiators were prepared to do so. Mr. Habib said that such discussion might be useful.

21. As already indicated, Mr. Habib said, the proposed Agreed Minute Re Paragraph 9 (c) and (d) was not incompatible with the ROK Constitution.

22. The Korean negotiators, Mr. Habib continued, had stated that the Agreed Minute Re Paragraph 9(e) would be acceptable if the word "confidentially" were deleted. They had argued that the present Korean legal system requires the accused to remain under surveillance of competent officers during an interview. However, the U.S. negotiators believed that if a counsel is to be effective, he must be able to have his client confide in him without fear of being overheard. The only apparent basis for the restrictive provisions of the Penal Administrative Law is to prevent escape and the stifling of evidence. The same objective could be accomplished by locking the accused and his counsel in a room with a guard outside. In this regard, although the Code of Criminal Procedure is compatible with the right of confidential communication, the Penal Administration Law should be changed for cases involving U.S. personnel, either by legislation or through administrative practice. Mr. Habib pointed out that a ranking Korean prosecutor, in an article in the Law Times of August 28, 1963, had stated:

"It may be argued that the rights of the defense

0206

counsel to meet the arrested without any participation (by the warden) and communicate directly should be legislated to prevent such troubles."

Finally, Mr. Habib continued, the principle of confidential communication is recognized as a "customary" rule of international law, for example in the Geneva Prisoner of War Convention.

23. Regarding the Agreed Minute Re Paragraph 9(f), Mr. Habib stated that there was no difference of opinion, since its provisions were consistent with the ROK Code of Criminal Procedure.

24. Regarding the Agreed Minute Re Paragraph 9(g), Mr. Habib stated that the Korean negotiators had expressed disagreement with that portion which reads: "no statement of the accused taken in the absence of such a representative shall be admissable as evidence in support of the guilt of the accused". The U.S. negotiators wished to point out that an official U.S. representative would be on duty and available at all times to be present at preliminary investigations, examinations, pre-trial hearings, the trial, and post-trial proceedings. The Korean negotiators appeared to wish to limit the right of this representative to be present at such sessions. The U.S. position was that an official representative should be able to attend all such sessions, including in camera sessions. The obvious reason for the inclusion of this provision in the Agreement is to ensure that no confession is obtained by coercion.

25. Mr. Habib stated that the U.S. negotiators believed the Agreed Minute Re Paragraph 9 to be fully compatible with ROK law. They had already agreed to delete subparagraph (a), since other ways could be arranged to maintain appropriate trial records. There was no question about the compatibility with the ROK Code of Criminal Procedure of the remaining portion of subparagraph (b). General provisions similar to those of subparagraphs(c) and (d) were contained in the Code of Criminal Procedure and the Constitution.

0207

26. With regard to subparagraph (e) of the Agreed Minute Re Paragraph

9, the Korean negotiators had proposed a counter-draft which brought into discussion the whole question of the prosecution appealing sentences. The Korean proposal would place the accused in the unfair position of the prosecutor having a "second chance", after becoming aware of the arguments used by the defense at the first trial. Increasing a sentence on appeal by the prosecution is contrary to the fundamental legal principles familiar to all American personnel and protection against such an eventuality is an essential right which should be included in the SOFA.

27. Mr. Habib noted that there was no incompatibility with the Korean laws and the ROK Constitution with regard to subparagraphs (f), (g), and (h).

28. Mr. Habib recalled that the Korean negotiators had stated that they interpreted subparagraph (i) as meaning that U.S. offenders should not be subject to punishment other than by decisions of a judicial court. This interpretation was correct. The provision is a prohibition against the enactment by a legislature of a bill which convicts a person of a crime without giving him a trial. Obviously, the U.S. negotiators believed that a judicial tribunal should be available to every offender.

29. Mr. Habib noted that there was no incompatibility between subparagraph (j) and the ROK Constitution.

30. With regard to subparagraph (k), Mr. Habib recalled that the Korean negotiators had proposed alternative language. There was a difference in language between the two versions but no difference in legal basis. The language proposed by the Korean negotiators was not specific enough, since under a strict reading of the Korean proposal, a trial could proceed without the accused being present.

31. With regard to subparagraph (l), Mr. Habib stated that there was no inconsistency in the legal basis of this provision with the Korean laws.

32. Mr. Habib recalled that the Korean negotiators had proposed the deletion of the word "improper" from the third unnumbered paragraph of the Agreed Minute Re Para-

0208

graph 9. The U.S. negotiators believed that it was important to retain this word in the draft, since there are a number of improper actions that are not necessarily illegal. The ROK Code of Criminal Procedure provides that a confession shall be received in evidence "only when the statement was made under such circumstances that it is undoubtedly believed to be true". The circumstances covered by this provision include improper acts.

33. Mr. Habib recalled that the Korean negotiators had proposed the deletion of the fourth unnumbered paragraph of the Agreed Minute Re Paragraph 9, which would limit appeals by the prosecution. The U.S. negotiators were aware of Article 361 of the Code of Criminal Procedure. They have no objection to appeals made by the prosecution for errors of law. They do object, however, to the prosecution making an appeal based on a "mistake of fact" or on the "unreasonableness of the sentence". Such appeals would allow the prosecution a number of chances to argue the same case. If such a provision were adopted, the accused would not be entitled to the advantage which is rightfully his if the prosecution is lax in its efforts; the prosecution would have a second chance after knowing the nature of the defense.

34. Mr. Chang stated that the Korean negotiators appreciated the extensive explanations given by the U.S. negotiators. They would consider the U.S. position on trial safeguards and express their views at a later meeting.

35. The next meeting was tentatively scheduled for August 21 at 3:00 p.m.

0209

JOINT SUMMARY RECORD OF THE 61ST SESSION

1. Time and Place: 3:00 - 5:00 P.M. August 14, 1964 at the Foreign Ministry's Conference Room (No.1)

2. Attendants:

ROK Side:

Mr. Chang, Sang Moon	Director European and American Affairs Bureau
Mr. Koo, Choong Whay	Chief, America Section Ministry of Foreign Affairs
Mr. Oh, Jae Hee	Chief, Treaty Section Ministry of Foreign Affairs
Col. Kim, Won Kil	Chief Military Affairs Section Ministry of National Defense
Mr. Choo, Moon Ki	Chief Legal Affairs Section Ministry of Justice
Mr. Hur, Hyong Koo	Chief Prosecutors Section Ministry of Justice
Mr. Lee, Keun Pal (Rapporteur and Interpreter)	3rd Secretary Ministry of Foreign Affairs
Mr. Hwang, Young Jae	3rd Secretary Ministry of Foreign Affairs
Mr. Park, Won Chul	3rd Secretary Ministry of Foreign Affairs

U.S. Side:

Mr. Philip C. Habib	Counselor American Embassy
Brig. Gen. Carroll H. Dunn	Deputy Chief of Staff 8th U.S. Army
Col. Howard Smigelow	Deputy Chief of Staff 8th U.S. Army
Capt. John Wayne	Assistant Chief of Staff USN/K

0210

Col. Kenneth C. Crawford	Staff Judge Advocate 8th U.S. Army
Mr. Franic R. La Macchia	First Secretary American Embassy
Mr. Benjamin A. Fleck (Rapporteur and Press Officer)	First Secretary American Embassy
Mr. Robert A. Kinney	J-5 8th U.S. Army
Mr. Robert A. Lewis	2nd Secretary American Embassy
Maj. Alton H. Harvey	Staff Judge Advocate's Office 8th U.S. Army
Mr. Kenneth Campen	Interpreter

1. Mr. Habib opened the 61st meeting by introducing Brigadier General Carroll H. Dunn, who was replacing Brigadier General G.G. O'Connor on the U.S. negotiating team. Mr. Chang warmly welcomed General Dunn on behalf of the Korean negotiators.

Claims

2. Taking up the Claims Article, Mr. Habib recalled that at the 51st meeting, the Korean negotiators had tabled proposed Agreed Minutes to this article. The first of these would provide that the decisions of the Korean claims authorities shall be final and conclusive. If the U.S. authorities disagree on the amount of a claim decided upon by the Korean claims authorities, the latter will reexamine the case but the results of their reexamination shall be final. According to the provisions of the second Agreed Minute proposed by the Korean negotiators, the ROK Government Claims Service would replace the U.S. Claims Service in the processing of claims six months from the date of entry into force of the Agreement, regardless of the state of readiness of the ROK Government Claims Service to assume such responsibilities.

0211

3. Mr. Habib stated that the U.S. negotiators had carefully reviewed these proposals and had found them to be unacceptable. The primary objective in negotiating this article is to ensure an effective system of settling legitimate claims against the U.S. armed forces in Korea. The present system functions promptly and equitably. The Korean proposals would require changing from the present procedures, which have worked well for the past five years, to the recently established and as yet relatively untried ROK Government Claims Service procedures. The Korean negotiators had proposed that this change be made within six months of the effective date of the Agreement.

4. The United States Government, Mr. Habib continued, has accumulated a great deal of experience over the past eleven years with the operation of claims machinery in other countries. It has found that the formula concept of settling claims, as proposed by the Korean negotiators, is time-consuming and difficult to administer. This system compels the host nation to establish an expensive bureaucracy and often generates ill-will between the host nation and the United States. In Japan, the formula system is currently being administered in a manner much different from that described in the SOFA with Japan. Not one claim has yet been paid in Japan without prior concurrence of U.S. authorities.

5. The U.S. negotiators believe, Mr. Habib continued, that there is no question but that continuation of the present system, which is meeting the problem to the general satisfaction of all concerned, is infinitely preferable to switching over to the new, untried, and relatively complicated system proposed by the Korean negotiators. The U.S. negotiators

0212

believe that continued operation of the present U.S. Claims Service, with the U.S. Government underwriting the entire cost of the operation, will be in the best interests of both the ROK and U.S. Governments. Continuation of the present system will be much more likely to result in equitable and prompt settlement with legitimate Korean claimants than would the alternative system proposed by the Korean negotiators.

6. Mr. Chu replied that he would like to give a supplementary explanation of the Korean proposals. The U.S. negotiators had expressed the view that the reexamination system to be set up under the first Agreed Minute proposed by the Korean negotiators would delay final disposition of claims. It was true, he said, that the ROK Claims Service has no reexamination system at present as proposed in the Agreed Minute. However, the ROK authorities had proposed the first Agreed Minute, considering that establishment of the reexamination system would be necessary not only for final and prompt disposition of the cases but also for opening a way to reconsider any disagreement by the U.S. authorities on the amount of a claim decided upon by the Korean authorities. They had also stated that the second proposed Agreed Minute would establish an untried system. The U.S. negotiators had expressed concern about the six-month provision in the Korean proposals. The Korean negotiators considered six months to be sufficient time to enable the Korean authorities to establish an efficient system. Some of the U.S. negotiators had visited the Ministry of Justice in the autumn of 1963 and had witnessed the procedures then in effect. They had stated at that time that they believed no practical difference existed between the two systems. Therefore, the Korean

negotiators urged the U.S. negotiators to take into account the proposed mechanism envisaged in the Korean proposals.

7. Mr. Habib replied that perhaps in theory no difference existed between the two claims sytems. In practice, however, there was a great difference. It was a fact, he continued, that at the present time the Korean authorities had no effective claims service. The Korean negotiators had proposed the establishment of one within a given period of time but the U.S. negotiators believed this would be quite difficult to accomplish, in view of the possibility of the use of haphazard methods. In addition, there was the possibility that a case might be influenced unduly by public attention, which would result in a lack of adherence to standards.

8. Mr. Habib said that in order to assist them in considering the Korean position, the U.S. negotiators wished to have the answers to the following questions: concerning the operation of the State Compensation Committee, promulgated under law number 231, December 24, 1962, and established on April 27, 1963:

a. How many attorneys, investigators, interpreters, and translators are employed by the Committee?

b. Who pays the salaries of the personnel employed by the Committee?

c. How many claims have been processed by the Committee in 1963 and in 1964?

d. Does the amount of an award include attorneys' fees?

e. Has the ROK Government appropriated any money to settle claims awards in 1963 and 1964? If so, what was the appropriation act for each year and how much money was appropriated?

0214

f. How many offices, including central and regional offices, have been established? How many employees are there in each office?

g. Have rules and regulations been set forth by the Committee for the administration of the Act and the guidance of the employees administering the Act? If so, may the U.S. negotiators have a copy?

9. Mr. Habib stated that the U.S. negotiators believed the answers to the questions which he had just asked would demonstrate that the Korean authorities did not have an effective claims service. That is why the U.S. negotiators preferred to continue the present system. They were not suggesting that the U.S. authorities do not have an obligation to pay claims. Nor were they trying to seek means to avoid payment of claims.

10. Mr. Chu replied that the Korean negotiators would answer as many of the questions asked by the U.S. negotiators as possible. Last year, members of the U.S. negotiating team had visited the Ministry of Justice, had been given a briefing, and had closely examined the Korean procedures. They had been given the relevant Korean laws and other documents, as well as statistics regarding claims lodged, claims paid, and claims otherwise disposed of. The Korean authorities would be glad to provide these materials again, if necessary.

11. Mr. Habib replied that the U.S. negotiators wanted this material to be introduced officially so that it might be discussed officially.

12. Mr. Chu stated that the present Korean claims system was not inefficient for the number of cases currently being received. However, the Korean authorities were already taking the necessary steps for reorganizing and enlarging

0215

the system in order to improve it and enable it to handle an increase in cases. Present payments, he said, are based on accumulated experience and on decisions of the Korean courts. The questions asked by the U.S. negotiators would be answered at a later negotiating session.

13. Mr. Habib asked whether the Korean negotiators could give some indication of the amount of time currently required to process a claim under the existing ROK claims procedures. Mr. Chu replied that the average length of time was about three months.

Criminal Jurisdiction

14. Turning to the Criminal Jurisdiction Article, Mr. Habib recalled that at the previous meeting, the U.S. negotiators had begun a detailed discussion of the Agreed Minutes of the U.S. draft which enumerated the trial safeguards sought by the U.S. authorities. He proposed that that discussion be resumed at the point at which it had been halted at the last meeting.

15. Mr. Habib recalled that at the 50th meeting, the Korean negotiators had proposed deletion of the Agreed Minute Re Paragraph 9(c) and (d). In subsequent discussion, they had not mentioned this proposal again. The U.S. negotiators, therefore, were uncertain of the Korean position regarding this Agreed Minute, which was an important paragraph in the view of the U.S. negotiators. It would guarantee to the accused the right of confrontation, one of the oldest concepts of the Anglo-Saxon legal system, which is recognized in Articles 161 through 164, 291, 293 and 294 of the ROK Code of Criminal Procedure.

0216

16. Mr. Chang replied that this Agreed Minute, as well as others which provided safeguards guaranteed by the ROK Constitution and relevant laws, should be deleted from the Agreement. To include them would be unnecessarily repetitive and redundant.

17. Mr. Habib replied that inclusion of such safeguards in the Agreement might be redundant insofar as Korean law is concerned but not with regard to the Agreement. In the case of safeguards not guaranteed by Korean law, it is not inconceivable that the law could be amended. The trial safeguards were important and their inclusion in the Agreement was an important factor in enabling the U.S. Government to agree to the conclusion of the Agreement. Pointing out that this was a fundamental question, Mr. Habib asked whether the Korean negotiators were now questioning the listing of trial safeguards. Proviously, the Korean negotiators had seemed to accept the problem of the U.S. negotiators and the U.S. negotiators had assumed that the Korean negotiators had agreed in principle to a listing of trial safeguards. Unless the Korean negotiators agreed to such a listing, there was little point in discussing the safeguards individually and in detail, as the U.S. negotiators had planned to do at this meeting.

18. Mr. Chang replied that the Korean draft clearly stated that all trial safeguards enumerated in Paragraph 9 of the U.S. draft were guaranteed by the ROK Constitution and relevant laws. At the 50th meeting, the Korean negotiators had stated that it was not necessary to repeat in the Agreed Minutes the trial safeguards listed in Paragraph 9 or to include those safeguards which are consonant with the

spirit of the ROK Constitution and relevant laws. The U.S. negotiators had expressed concern over the possibility that the laws and the Constitution might be changed. Even if they were changed, the Korean negotiators were sure that the changes would result in better protection and benefit for the accused. The U.S. negotiators had no reasonable grounds for listing all of these safeguards. If they did not agree with the position of the Korean negotiators, no satisfactory solution was possible. If the U.S. negotiators would indicate which of the proposed safeguards were of particular importance, the Korean negotiators were prepared to negotiate with regard to those Agreed Minutes.

19. Mr. Habib stated that the U.S. negotiators had not intimated that they believed changes in Korean laws would not be for the better. They accepted the statement of the Korean negotiators in this regard but it was not relevant to the question under discussion. He pointed out that the first sentence of the Agreed Minute Re Paragraph 9 of the U.S. draft specifically refers to ROK law, where it reads that the accused "shall be accorded every procedural and substantive right granted by law to the citizens of the Republic of Korea". The U.S. negotiators believed that the Status of Forces Agreement should provide certain fundamental rights as trial safeguards. These are not incompatible with ROK law. The Korean negotiators had agreed that they were compatible. The Korean negotiators had asked for a specific enumeration of those safeguards which the U.S. authorities believed to be most important. The U.S. draft provided this enumeration. If the Korean negotiators objected to

0218

certain of the safeguards listed in the U.S. draft, the U.S. negotiators were prepared to discuss them. However, there was no chance whatsoever that the U.S. negotiators would abandon the principle of enumerating trial safeguards in the Agreement. There is nothing in the safeguards listed, he added, which derogates from the sovereignty of the ROK Government.

20. Mr. Chang replied that a difference of opinion existed regarding those safeguards which were already guaranteed by the ROK constitution and the relevant Korean Laws and that the Korean negotiators would present their views at a later meeting. If the U.S. negotiators wished to discuss those safeguards which were not covered by the ROK Constitution or Korean law, the Korean negotiators were prepared to do so. Mr. Habib said that such discussion might be useful.

21. As already indicated, Mr. Habib said, the proposed Agreed Minute Re Paragraph 9(c) and (d) was not incompatible with the ROK Constitution.

22. The Korean negotiators, Mr. Habib continued, had stated that the Agreed Minute Re Paragraph 9(e) would be acceptable if the word "confidentially" were deleted. They had argued that the present Korean legal system requires the accused to remain under surveillance of competent officers during an interview. However, the U.S. negotiators believed that if a counsel is to be effective, he must be able to have his client confide in him without fear of being overheard. The only apparent basis for the restrictive provisions of the Penal Administrative Law is to prevent escape and the stifling of evidence. The same objective could be accomplished

0219

by locking the accused and his counsel in a room with a guard outside. In this regard, although the Code of Criminal Procedure is compatible with the right of confidential communication, the Penal Administration Law should be changed for cases involving U.S. personnel, either by legislation or through administrative practice. Mr. Habib pointed out that a ranking Korean prosecutor, in an article in the Law Times of August 28, 1963, had stated:

> "It may be argued that the rights of the defense counsel to meet the arrested without any participation (by the warden) and communicate directly should be legislated to prevent such troubles."

Finally, Mr. Habib continued, the principle of confidential communication is recognized as a "customary" rule of international law, for example in the Geneva Prisoner of War Convention.

23. Regarding the Agreed Minute Re Paragraph 9(f), Mr. Habib stated that there was no difference of opinion, since its provisions were consistent with the ROK Code of Criminal Procedure.

24. Regarding the Agreed Minute Re Paragraph 9(g), Mr. Habib stated that the Korean negotiators had expressed disagreement with that portion which reads: "no statement of the accused taken in the absence of such a representative shall be admissable as evidence in support of the guilt of the accused". The U.S. negotiators wished to point out that an official U.S. representative would be on duty and available at all times to be present at preliminary investigations, examinations, pre-trial hearings, the trial, and post-trial proceedings. The Korean negotiators appeared to wish to limit the right of this representative to be present at such sessions. The U.S. position was that an official

0220

representative should be able to attend all such sessions, including *in camera* sessions. The obvious reason for the inclusion of this provision in the Agreement is to ensure that no confession is obtained by coercion.

25. Mr. Habib stated that the U.S. negotiators believed the Agreed Minute Re Paragraph 9 to be fully compatible with ROK law. They had already agreed to delete subparagraph (a), since other ways could be arranged to maintain appropriate trial records. There was no question about the compatibility with the ROK Code of Criminal Procedure of the remaining portion of subparagraph (b). General provisions similar to those of subparagraphs (c) and (d) were contained in the Code of Criminal Procedure and the Constitution.

26. With regard to subparagraph (e) of the Agreed Minute Re Paragraph 9, the Korean negotiators had proposed a counter-draft which brought into discussion the whole question of the prosecution appealing sentences. The Korean proposal would place the accused in the unfair position of the prosecutor having a "second chance", after becoming aware of the arguments used by the defense at the first trial. Increasing a sentence on appeal by the prosecution is contrary to the fundamental legal principles familiar to all American personnel and protection against such an eventuality is an essential right which should be included in the SOFA.

27. Mr. Habib noted that there was no incompatibility with the Korean laws and the ROK Constitution with regard to subparagraphs (f), (g) and (h).

28. Mr. Habib recalled that the Korean negotiators had stated that they interpreted subparagraph (i) as meaning that U.S. offenders should not be subject to punishment

0221

other than by decisions of a judicial court. This interpretation was correct. The provision is a prohibition against the enactment by a legislature of a bill which convicts a person of a crime without giving him a trial. Obviously, the U.S. negotiators believed that a judicial tribunal should be available to every offender.

29. Mr. Habib noted that there was no incompatibility between subparagraph (j) and the ROK Constitution.

30. With regard to subparagraph (k), Mr. Habib recalled that the Korean negotiators had proposed alternative language. There was a difference in language between the two versions but no difference in legal basis. The language proposed by the Korean negotiators was not specific enough, since under a strict reading of the Korean proposal, a trial could proceed without the accused being present.

31. With regard to subparagraph (l), Mr. Habib stated that there was no inconsistency in the legal basis of this provision with the Korean laws.

32. Mr. Habib recalled that the Korean negotiators had proposed the deletion of the word "improper" from the third unnumbered paragraph of the Agreed Minute Re Paragraph 9. The U.S. negotiators believed that it was important to retain this word in the draft, since there are a number of improper actions that are not necessarily illegal. The ROK Code of Criminal Procedure provides that a confession shall be received in evidence" only when the statement was made under such circumstances that it is undoubtedly believed to be true". The circumstances covered by this provision include improper acts.

0222

33. Mr. Habib recalled that the Korean negotiators had proposed the deletion of the fourth unnumbered paragraph of the Agreed Minute Re Paragraph 9, which would limit appeals by the prosecution. The U.S. negotiators were aware of Article 361 of the Code of Criminal Procedure. They have no objection to appeals made by the prosecution for errors of law. They do object, however, to the prosecution making an appeal based on a "mistake of fact" or on the "unreasonableness of the sentence". Such appeals would allow the prosecution a number of chances to argue the same case. If such a provision were adopted, the accused would not be entitled to the advantage which is rightfully his if the prosecution is lax in its efforts and the prosecution would have a second chance after knowing the nature of the defense.

34. Mr. Chang stated that the Korean negotiators appreciated the extensive explanations given by the U.S. negotiators. They would consider the U.S. position on trial safeguards and express their views at a later meeting.

35. The next meeting was tentatively scheduled for August 28 at 3:00 p.m.

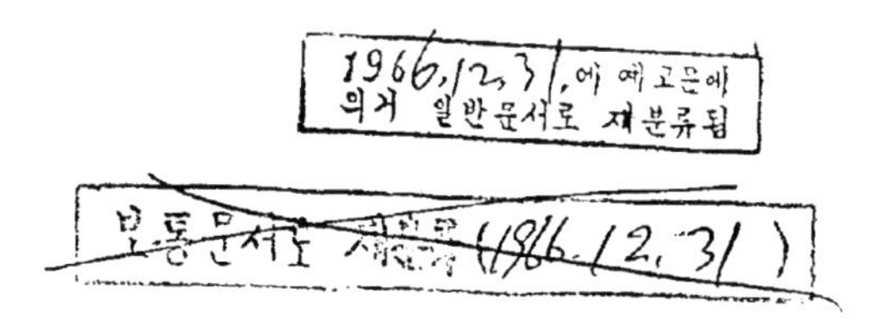

0223

6. 제62차 회의, 8.28

0224

SOFA NEGOTIATION

Agenda for the 62nd Session

16:00 August 28, 1964

1. Continuation of Discussions on:

   a. Claims Article

   b. Security Measures Article

2. Other Business

3. Agenda and Date of the Next Meeting

4. Press Release

0225

Aug. 28, 1964

US DRAFT

SAFETY AND SECURITY MEASURES FOR US FORCES

The United Ststes and the Republic of Korea will cooperate in taking such steps as may from time to time be necessary to ensure the security of the United States armed forces, the members thereof, the civilian component, the persons who are present in the Republic of Korea pursuant to Article________ (Invited Contractors), and their dependents and their property. The Government of the Republic of Korea agrees to seek such legislation and to take such other action as may be necessary to ensure the adequate security and protection within its territory of installations, equipment, property, records and official information of the United States, and, consistent with Article___ (Criminal Jurisdiction) to ensure the punishment of offenders under the applicable laws of the Republic of Korea.

0226

CONFIDENTIAL

ARTICLE

SECURITY MEASURES

"The United States and the Republic of Korea will cooperate in taking such steps as may from time to time be necessary to ensure the security of the United States armed forces, the members thereof, the civilian component, the persons who are present in the Republic of Korea pursuant to Article contractor, their dependents and their property. The Government of the Republic of Korea agrees to seek such legislation and to take such other action as may be necessary to ensure the adequate security and protection within its territory of installations, equipment, property, records, and official information of the United States, of the persons referred to in this paragraph, and their property and, consistent with Article criminal jurisdiction to ensure the punishment of offenders under the applicable laws of the Republic of Korea."

Contractor 40 명

all Contractor approx. 600 third nation 225

0227

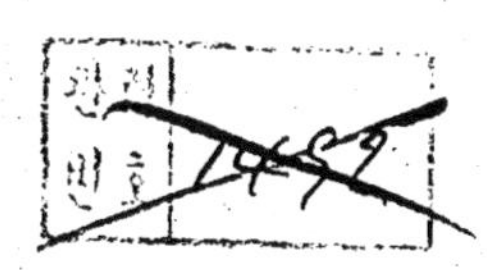

기 안 용 지

자체 통제		기안처	미주과 이근팔	전화번호	근거서류접수일자

	과장	국장	차관	장관		

관계관 서명	

기안 년월일	1964. 8. 31.	시행 년월일		보존 년한		정서	기장
분류 기호	외구미 722.2	전체 통제		종결			

경유 수신 참조	대 통 령 참조: 비서실장 국 무 총 리 참조: 비서실장 사본: 법 무 부 장 관	발신	장 관

제목	제 62 차 주둔군지위협정 체결 교섭 실무자회의 개최

1964. 8. 28. 하오 4 시부터 동 5 시 20 분 까지 외무부 제 1 회의실에서 개최된 제 62 차 주둔군지위협정 체결 교섭 실무자회의에서 토의된 내용을 별첨과 같이 보고합니다.

유 첨: 제 62 차 주둔군지위협정 체결 교섭실무자회의 보고서 1 부. 끝.

~~보통문서로 재분류 (1966. 12. 31)~~

1966, 12, 31 에 예고문에 의거 일반문서로 재분류됨

발송 1964. 9. 3. 외무부

승인서식 1—1—3 (11 00900 03) (195mm×265mm16절지)

0228

제 61 차

한.미 간 주둔군지위협정 체결 교섭실무자회의

보 고 서

1. 일 시: 1964.년 8 월 28 일 하오 4 시 부터 동 5 시 20 분 까지.

2. 장 소: 외무부 제 1 회의실

3. 토의사항:

가 민사청구권

(1) 우리측은 미측이 제 61 차 회의에서 현행 우리 나라 국가배상 제도에 관하여 질문을 제기한 사항에 대하여 우리측은 제 30차 회의에서 이미 상세히 설명한 바를 상기시키고 이어 다음과 같이 답변하였다.

(가) 국가배상위원회의 직원

국가배상위원회의 구성인원과 행정 심사 및 기타 요원에 관하여는 제 30 차 회의에서 충분히 설명하였으며 그 구성 원칙에는 그 당시와 다름이 없다. 현재 배상위원회의 직원은 조사원 9 명(법무관 2, 사무관 2, 주사 5) 지급 담당원 3 명 일반사무직원 2 명 계 14 명이다. 통역관이나 번역관은 현재 필요하지 않으므로 고용하지 않고 있다. 필요에 따라 고용할 수 있도록 조치가 진행중이다.

(나) 직원의 급료

직원은 전원이국가공무원이므로 국가공무원보수규정에 의하여 국가가 지급한다.

(다) 1963 년도 및 1964 년도의 사건 접수 및 처리 상황

1963 년 5 월 1 일 부터 12 월 31 일 까지 283 건을 접수 처리하였으며 1964 년도에는 6 월 31 일 현재 207 건 을 접수하여 그중 139 건을 처리하고 68 건은 진행중에 있다. 즉 과거 1 년 2 개월간에 총 490 건을 접수하여 422 건을 완결하고 나머지 68 건이 진행중에 있다.

(라) 변호사의 비용

국가배상위원회에서 결정하는 배상금 중에는 변호사의 비용은 포함되지 않는다.

0229

64-3-78

64-3-25 (3)

미국: 월 111-7

0230

(마) 1963 년도 및 1964 년도 지급예산

1963 년도의 지급예산은 30,390,000 원이 었으며 1964 년도의 지급예산 은 25,910,200 원이다. 1964 년도 예산은 1963 년도 보다 약간 적으나 실지로 하등의 영향이 없을 것이며 만일 부족 시에는 추가 조치할 것이다.

(바) 사무소의 수

현재는 중앙사무소 하나로 운영되고 있으나 중앙사무소의 개선과 국가배상제도의 확장을 위한 조치가 진행되고 있다.

(사) 운영관계 법령

1951.9.8. 일자 법률 제 231 호 국가배상법을 뒷바침하기 위하여 국가배상금 청구에 관한 절차법, 국가배상금 청구에 관한 절차법 시행령, 국가배상금 청구에 관한 절차법 시행규칙등을 위시하여 민법과 법원의 많은 판례 및 자료와 풍부한 경험이 있어 합리적으로 처리하고 있다.

(2) 또한 미측이 우리 나라에 효과적인 청구제도가 없다고 하는데 대하여 우리측은 우리 나라 현제도가 많은 청구사건을 신속히 효율적으로 처리하고 있음을 강조하고 작년도에 미측대표단이 법무부를 방문하여 한국배상제도의 효율성을 인정한 바 있음을 상기시켰다.

(3) 한국당국은 본 협정이 발효된 후 증가될 청구사건에 대비하여 과중한 부담없이 현제도를 다소 개선 확장하므로서 충분히 그 임무를 수행할 수 있을 것임을 강조하고 한.미간의 수차의 비공식회의를 통하여 미측이 제시한 요구사항을 검토한 후 51 차 회의에서 우리측 주장을 제시한 것임을 설명하고 미측의 재고를 촉구하였다.

(4) 기타 우리측은 미측의 배상제도에 관한 참고자료의 제공을 요청 하였다.

나. 보호조치

(1) 미측은 주한미군관계 신체 및 재산의 보호조치에 관하여 지금까지의 미측 주장을 종합하여 미군을 위한 한국당국의 현 보호조치가 부족 하다는 것이 아니며 따라서 미측은 주한미군의 보호를 위한 입법

0231

64-3-7f

64-3-29 미무 III-7

0232

조치를 요구함에 있어서도 한국정부가 어떠한 특별한 대우를 하여 줄 것을 주장하는 것은 아니라고 천명하였다.

(2) 미측은 또한 한미간의 공동방어의 임무 수행을 위하여 필요하다면 상호간의 합의에 의하여 한국이 입법조치를 취할 것을 기록에 남기자는 것이며 그러한 입법조치로 말미아마 혜택을 받게 되는 것은 미군 뿐만 아니라 한국국민도 다 같이 포함될 것이라고 말하고 그러한 양해하에 한국측 주장을 수락할 용의가 있음을 시사하였다.

(3) 우리측은 미측의 태도가 건설적임을 지적하고 충분히 검토한 후 다음 기회에 우리측 입장을 제시한기로 하였다.

4. 기타 사항:

차기 회의 일자: 1964 년 9 월 11 일 하오 3 시 부터. 끝.

보통문서로 재분류(1966.12.31.)

1966.12.31에 예고문에 의거 일반문서로 재분류됨

0233

64-3-80

64-3-28(3) 미주 문 111-9 13).

0234

STATUS OF FORCES NEGOTIATIONS: 62nd Meeting

SUBJECTS: 1. Claims
2. Security Measures

PLACE: Ministry of Foreign Affairs

DATE: August 28, 1964

PARTICIPANTS:

Republic of Korea	United States
CHANG Sang-mun	Philip C. Habib
KU Chung-hoe	Brig. General Carroll H. Dunn, USA
Colonel KIM Won-kil, ROKA	Colonel Howard Smigelow, USA
CHU Mun-ki	Colonel Kenneth C. Crawford, USA
O Chae-hi	Frank R. LaMacchia
HWANG Yong-chae	Robert A. Kinney
Major LEE Ke-hoon, ROKA	Major Alton Harvey, USA
YI Kun-pal (Interpreter)	Kenneth Campen (Interpreter)
PAK Won-chol	Lt Col Martin S. Drucker, USA, (Observer)
	Lt Col Charles Thompson, USA, (Observer)

1. Mr. Habib opened the 62nd meeting by introducing Lt Col Martin S. Drucker and Lt Col Charles Thompson, of the US Armed Forces Claims Service in Korea. Mr. Chang welcomed them on behalf of the Korean negotiators.

CLAIMS

2. Taking up the Claims Article, Mr. Chang stated that Mr. Chu ~~introduced Mr. Chu Mun-ki, of the Ministry of Justice, who~~ would make a statement on the Claims Article. Mr. Chu stated that: The Korean negotiators had already given a through explanation of the Korean claims compensation system and of its practical implementation at the 30th session. They felt that the US negotiators had grasped the whole picture of the Korean claims system, which functions efficiently at present. However, in order to respond to the questions raised at the 61st session by the Chief US negotiator regarding the Korean claims system, the Korean negotiators were ready to present the following additional explanations on those matters which had not been covered at the 30th session:

0235

a. Employees of the Compensation Committee,

No significant change has been made in the organization of the State Compensation Committee or in personnel employed either for administrative or for investigational purposes of the claims service, since the detailed explanation which had been given to the US negotiators at the 30th session. At present, there are 9 investigators (2 legal officers, 2 class three officials, and 5 other officers), and 5 clerks (3 for payment administration and 2 for general administration). Interpreters and translators are currently not employed since there has been no necessity for such personnel for settlement of the civil claims currently received.

b. Salaries of Employees,

All of the employees of the Korean claims authorities are employees of the Korean Government. Therefore, their salaries are paid by the Government in accordance with the relevant laws and regulations.

c. Claims Processed in the Years 1963 and 1964.

In 1963, 283 cases had been received and processed during the period from May 1 to December 31, 1963.

As of 30 June 1964, 207 cases had been received and 139 cases had been processed thus far in 1964. In addition, 68 cases were under consideration on 30 June 1964.

In other words, during the past 14 months, 490 claims cases have been received and processing of 422 has been completed. Detailed tabulation of the claims which have been received and considered by the Committee are as shown on the table.

0236

Number of Claims Processed in 1963 and 1964

YEAR	NO. OF CLAIMS RECEIVED	DISPOSITION				PENDING
		AWARDED	REJECTED	WITHDREW	TOTAL	
1963 (1 May-31 Dec)	283	189	81	13	283	-
1964 (1 Jan-30 Jun)	207	91	27	21	139	68
TOTAL	490	280	108	34	422	68

d. Fees for Attorney.

In the claims awards made by the Committee, attorney's fees are not included.

e. Appropriations for awards in 1963 and 1964.

In the 1963 and 1964 budgets, 30,390,000 Won and 25,910,200 Won, respectively, were appropriated for awards. Although the amount of the budget for fiscal year 1964 is little less than that for 1963, this will not affect the payment of claims awards. If additional appropriations should be necessary, the Korean authorities would take appropriate measures.

f. Number of Claims Offices.

As had been explained at the 30th session, there is one central office in the Ministry of Justice. However, as the Korean negotiators pointed out at the 61st session, actions designed to improve the central office as well as enlarge the system are now being taken by the Korean authorities.

g. Rules and Regulations.

In order to implement the State Compensation Law, No. 231, promulgated on September 8, 1951, there are following laws and regulations:

0237

(1) Law relating to Procedures for Claims on Damages by the State, No. 1223, promulgated on Dec 24, 1962.

(2) Regulations relating to the Application of the Law No. 1223, Cabinet Ordinance No. 1187, promulgated on February 5, 1963, and amended by Presidential Decree No. 1773, April 21, 1964.

(3) Regulations relating to the Application of the Law No. 1223, Ministry of Justice Regulation No. 63, April 27, 1964, amended by Ministry of Justice Regulation No. 79, May [illegible], 1964.

Mr. Chu further stated that,

3. As the Korean negotiators explained in detail at the 30th session, in addition to these laws and regulations, the Korean Civil Code, decisions of the courts, and other data serve as guidance for reasonable settlement of claims. At the 61st session, the Chief US negotiator had stated that the US negotiators believed the answers to the questions which they had raised would demonstrate that the Korean authorities did not have an effective claims service. However, the Korean negotiators believe that the foregoing answers, and their explanation of the State Compensation Committee at the 30th session, surely demonstrates the effectiveness of the present Korean claims system. The Korean claims authorities have been settling, promptly, equitably, and efficiently, the claims for various damages arising our of acts or omissions of 600,000 members of the Korean Armed Forces and more than 200,000 officials of the Government done in the performance of their official duties, as well as for other damages arising out of acts, omissions, or occurrences for which the Korean Government is legally responsible. The Korean negotiators wish to remind the US negotiators of the fact that some of the US negotiators visited the Ministry of Justice last Fall, and were given two briefings on the Korean State Compensation Committee system and its operation, they also observed an actual State Compensation Committee meeting dealing with civil claims, and

recognized the efficiency of the system.

4. The Korean negotiators believe, Mr. Chu continued, that after the Status of Forces Agreement comes into force, the possible increase in number of claims which would be filed with the Korean authorities could be efficiently processed by the Korean authorities, ~~The Korean negotiators have indicated this could be done,~~ without imposing any excessive administrative burden on the Korean authorities, with some improvement and enlargement of the present Korean system.

5. The Korean negotiators also wish to point out, Mr. Chu stated, that the Korean claims agencies are staffed with judges, prosecutors, attorneys, with profound experience and abundance of knowledge of judicial precedents accumulated over the past ten years. Therefore, the Korean negotiators are confident that the Korean authorities, with the help of the experienced personnel available in the field of civil claims, could promptly and equitably dispose of claims arising out of the stationing of the comparably not too large number of the US milit ary personnel in Korea.

6. Mr. Chu said that the Korean legal experts had met informally several times with members of the US negotiating team and exchanged their views regarding their respective positions. As the result of these meetings, the Korean negotiators had made their position clear at the 51st session by proposing two [three] agreed minutes, after carefully studying the views expressed by the US negotiators in these informal discussions. The Korean negotiators wish to ask the US negotiators to study further the proposals made by the Korean negotiators and respond favorably at a later meeting.

7. Mr Chu ~~also indicated he wished to~~ ask the US negotiators ~~some~~ questions. The US negotiators stated at the 61st meeting that the formula system in the Japan SOFA worked much differently in practice than as indicated

in the text of the US-Japan Claims Article. The ROK negotiators would like to have detailed information on procedures for settlement of claims in Japan. Mr. Chu also asked about procedures for reexamination of claims by the US Claims Service in Korea, including the point of whether the same personnel who participated in the original decision also handles reexaminations upon appeal. He also asked about the number of personnel in the US Claims Service in Korea, including the number who hold qualification as attorneys, prosecutors, and judges. Mr. Chu also asked about the number of claims processed, amounts involved, and average time taken to process a claim from time of receipt until it is settled. Mr. Chu also presented the US negotiators with Korean language copies of ROK GOvernment laws and regulations on claims.

8. Mr. Habib thanked Mr. Chu for his explanation and for the copies of the ROK Government claims materials. The US negotiators will reply in detail at the next meeting.

9. Mr. Habib asked if the documents in the Korean language just provided by Mr. Chu contained information on ROK standards used in determination of the amounts of claims awards. Mr. Chu answered that the materials do not contain such standards, or guidelines, but as explained in detail at the 30th session, the ROK claims offical used the Hofmann formula in deciding the amount of awards.

10. Mr. Habib stated that the US Armed Forces Claims Service has a published set of awards for various claims, and that such a standard set of regulations and guidelines tends to prevent discrimination, or wide variation in claims awards. Mr. Chu explained that the ROK State Compensation Committee determined the amount of awards, not by their own arbitrary decisions, but by the Hofmann formula, using the precedents established by the ROK civil courts. He emphasized that there was no room for discrimination in the operation of the Korean claims system. Mr. Habib asked if this could be demonstrated through

6

0240

example? It was agreed this subject would be discussed more fully at a later meeting.

11. Mr. Habib indicated that, while the ROK negotiators had supplied general statistics on total claims, detailed statistics on individual claims cases of various types would also be useful. The ROK negotiators indicated such information would be supplied at a later meeting.

SECURITY MEASURES

12. Mr. Habib indicated he wanted to clarify the present US position on the Security Measures Article, since the two sides had discussed three different drafts of this Article, formally and informally, as well as related articles in other SOFA's and a proposed understanding for the Agreed Joint Summary.

13. Mr. Habib said that the only US draft now under consideration is the one tabled at the 25th negotiating session on 26 June 1963.

14. The ROK negotiators, at the 46th session on 13 March 1964, stated that they would agree to the inclusion of the phrase "the persons who are present in the Republic of Korea pursuant to Article_______ (Invited Contractors)", and the phrase "consistent with Article______"(Criminal Jurisdiction Article)", as desired by the US, if the US negotiators would agree to delete the phrase "of the persons referred to in this paragraph, and their property", as desired by the ROK side. The US negotiators are willing to agree to the deletion from the US draft of the phrase "of the persons referred to in this paragraph and their property", as proposed by the ROK negotiators, if the ROK negotiators agree to the inclusion in the Agreed Joint Summary of the mutual understand first tabled at the 55th negotiating session on 19 June 1964.

15. Mr. Habib stated that both ROK and US authorities are fully aware that the defense of Korea is a joint effort involving Americans as well as Koreans, and it is believed both ROK and US officials want to insure that the US and ROK forces have the capability to discharge effectively their mutual obligations under the US-ROK Mutual Security Pact. The first sentence of the Security Measures Article to which we have both agreed, demonstrated this fact by stating that:

"The United States and the Republic of Korea will cooperate in taking such steps as may from time to time be necessary to ensure the security of the United States armed forces, the members thereof, the civilian component, the persons who are present in the Republic of Korea pursuant to Article________(Invited Contractors), their dependents and their property."

16. Mr. Habib stated that the US negotiators feel that it is entirely proper and correct for the confidential negotiating record to show clear agreement between ROK and US Governments on the following understanding:

"In cooperating with each other under this Article, the two Governments agree that each will take such measures as may be necessary to ensure the security and protection of the US armed forces, the members thereof, the civilian component, the persons who are present in the Republic of Korean pursuant to Article_____(Invited Contractors), their dependents and their property."

17. Mr. Habib stated that the foregoing language means just what it says and no more. The US negotiators wish to assure the Korean negotiators that such an understanding does not envisage the passage of legislation which would be applicable only to offenses against US personnel. Any legislation would of course be equally applicable to Koreans as well as Americans. We seek no special privileges in this regard. At the same time, the US cannot believe that the ROK Government would knowingly fail to take any measures that would be necessary to assist in accomplishment of our mutual defense objectives. This, of course, would include the passage of legislation if such were necessary. This does not mean that the US is ~~of the opinion~~ implying that current ROK legislation in this area is deficient. But times and conditions do change. The US simply wishes ROK assurance for the record that in the event of changed conditions

9

0243

the ROK will, in cooperation with the US, take such measures as the then existing circumstances dictate to be necessary. This is the sort of understanding which underlies the basic fabric of ROK-US defense agreements and cooperative efforts, and which surely reflects the views of both of our Governments.

18. Mr. Habib concluded his statement by emphasizing that the two sides now appeared to be in agreement on the text of the article, and at least on the spirit behind the understnading for the agreed record. Therefore, it is hoped that with this elaboration of the US views, the Koreans and US negotiators ~~could~~ can acheive early agreement on this Article and go on to discussion of other articles where real differences in US-ROK views still exist~~ed~~.

19. Mr. Chang thanked the US side for their review of the status of this Article and for the US statement, which he ~~stated~~ felt took a very constructive approach toward resolving this problem. He indicated that the Korean negotiators would take this question under advisement and reply at the next meeting. ~~Mr. Chang raised a question about the last phrase in the US draft, which reads: "to ensure the punishment of offenders under the applicable laws of the Republic of Korea."~~ Mr. Habib explained that, of course, offenders could only be punished "under the applicable laws of the Republic of Korea", and that there was no intent in the proposed language to prejudge the case of such offenders.

20. It was agreed that the secretaries for the ROK and US sides, respectively, would meet ~~to~~ later to decide the date for the next meeting.

0244

7. With regard to the statement made by the Chief US negotiator at the 61st session in connection with the US Claims Service in Korea, Mr. Chu asked the US negotiators the following questions:

a. The US negotiators stated that the formula system in the Japan SOFA worked much differently in practice than as indicated in the text of the US-Japan Claims Article. Could the US negotiators present detailed information on the working procedures for settlement of claims in Japan?

b. The US negotiators had stated that the present US Claims Service meets the problem to the general satisfaction of all concerned. Does this mean that there are no claimants who have been dissatisfied so far? How does the US Claims Service dispose of claims which are not settled to the satisfaction of the claimant at present? Does the US Claims Service have a reexamination system? If so, who participates in the reexamination? Are they the same personnel who participate in the original decision? How many cases have been reexamined? Could the US negotiators give a detailed contents of the cases reexamined?

c. How many persons are there in the US Claims Service in Korea who hold qualifications as attorneys, prosecutors and judges?

d. How many claims were processed by the US Claims Service in Korea since its activation? Are there detailed statistics on individual claims cases of various types, including amounts involved?

e. The Korean negotiators would also like to have information regarding the cases for which the highest and

0245

the lowest amount were paid, including the copies of the claim files thereof.

f. How long does it take, on the average, to process a claim by the US Claims Service in Korea?

0246

10.

Mr. Chu asked if the U.S. side could furnish the Korean Negotiators with the copies of such a published set of standards used by the U.S. Armed Forces Claims Service.

~~비 밀 CONFIDENTIAL~~

Security Measures

19. However, Mr. Chang pointed out that the last phrase of the article was not still agreed upon, as the Korean draft reads "for the punishment of offenders under the applicable laws of the ROK" while the U.S. draft reads "to ensure the punishment ...." The Korean negotiators, Mr. Chang continued, prefer their draft on the ground that it is the responsibility borne soly by the Korean Government to ensure the punishment of certain offenses under the applicable law and the responsibility could not properly be placed as a negotiable subject.

0247

SOFA NEGOTIATION

Agenda for the 62nd Session

16:00 August 28, 1964

1. Continuation of Discussions on:
   a. Claims Article
   b. Security Measures Article
2. Other Business
3. Agenda and Date of the Next Meeting
4. Press Release

0248

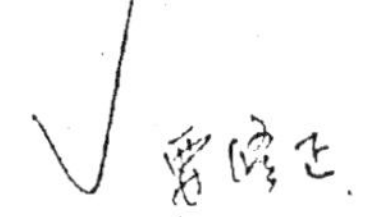

JOINT SUMMARY RECORD OF THE 62ND SESSION

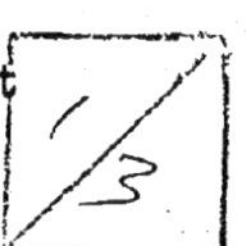

1. Time and Place: 4:00 - 5:20 P.M. August 28, 1964 at the Foreign Ministry's Conference Room (No.1)

2. Attendants:

ROK Side:

Mr. Chang, Sang Moon	Director European and American Affairs Bureau
Mr. Koo, Choong Whay	Chief, America Section Ministry of Foreign Affairs
Mr. Oh, Jae Hee	Chief Treaty Section Ministry of Foreign Affairs
Col. Kim, Won Kil	Chief Military Affairs Section Ministry of National Defense
Mr. Choo, Moon Ki	Chief Legal Affairs Section Ministry of Justice
Maj. Lee, Kye Hoon	Military Affairs Section Ministry of National Defense
Mr. Lee, Keun Pal (Rapporteur and Interpreter)	3rd Secretary Ministry of Foreign Affairs
Mr. Hwang, Young Jae	3rd Secretary Ministry of Foreign Affairs
Mr. Park, Won Chul	3rd Secretary Ministry of Foreign Affairs

U.S. Side:

Mr. Philip C. Habib	Counselor American Embassy
Brig. Gen. Carroll H. Dunn	Deputy Chief of Staff 8th U.S. Army
Col. Howard Smigelow	Deputy Chief of Staff 8th U.S. Army
Col. Kenneth C. Crawford	Staff Judge Advocate 8th U.S. Army

0249

Mr. Franic R. La Macchia	First Secretary American Embassy
Mr. Robert A. Kinney (Rapporteur and Press Officer)	J-5 8th U.S. Army
Maj. Alton H. Harvey	Staff Judge Advocate's Office 8th U.S. Army
Mr. Kenneth Campen	Interpreter
Lt. Col. Martin S. Drucker	Observer
Lt. Col. Charles Thompson	Observer

1. Mr. Habib opened the 62nd meeting by introducing Lt. Col. Martin S. Drucker and Lt. Col. Charles Thompson, of the US Armed Forces Claims Service in Korea. Mr. Chang welcomed them on behalf of the Korean negotiators.

<u>Claims</u>

2. Taking up the Claims Article, Mr. Chang stated that Mr. Chu would make a statement on the Claims Article. Mr. Chu stated that the Korean negotiators had already given a thorough explanation of the Korean claims compensation system and of its practical implementation at the 30th session. They felt that the US negotiators had grasped the whole picture of the Korean claims system, which functions efficiently at present. However, in order to respond to the questions raised at the 61st session by the Chief US negotiator regarding the Korean claims system, the Korean negotiators were ready to present the following additional explanations on those matters which had not been covered at the 30th session:

a. <u>Employees of the Compensation Committee</u>.

No significant change has been made in the organization of the State Compensation Committee or in personnel employed either for administrative or for investigational purposes of the claims service, since the detailed explanation which

0250

had been given to the US negotiators at the 30th session. At present, there are 9 investigators (2 legal officers, 2 class three officials, and 5 other officers), and 5 clerks (3 for payment administration and 2 for general administration). Interpreters and translators are currently not employed since there has been no necessity for such personnel for settlement of the civil claims currently received.

b. Salaries of Employees.

All of the employees of the Korean claims authorities are employees of the Korean Government. Therefore, their salaries are paid by the Government in accordance with the relevant laws and regulations.

c. Claims Processed in the Years 1963 and 1964.

In 1963, 283 cases had been received and processed during the period from May 1 to December 31, 1963.

As of 30 June 1964, 207 cases had been received and 139 cases had been processed thus far in 1964, 68 cases were under consideration on 30 June 1964.

In other words, during the past 14 months, 490 claims cases have been received and processing of 422 has been completed. Detailed tabulation of the claims which have been received and considered by the Committee are as shown on the table.

Number of Claims Processed in 1963 and 1964

YEAR	NO. OF CLAIMS RECEIVED	DISPOSITION				PENDING
		AWARDED	REJECTED	WITHDREW	TOTAL	
1963 (1 May-31 Dec.)	283	189	81	13	283	-
1964 (1 Jan.-30 Jun.)	207	91	27	21	139	68
TOTAL	490	280	108	34	422	68

0251

d. Fees for Attorney.

In the claims awards made by the Committee, attorney's fees are not included.

e. Appropriations for awards in 1963 and 1964.

In the 1963 and 1964 budgets, 30,390,000 Won and 25,910,200 Won, respectively, were appropriated for awards. Although the amount of the budget for fiscal year 1964 is a little less than that for 1963, this will not affect the payment of claims awards. If additional appropriations should be necessary, the Korean authorities would take appropriate measures.

f. Number of Claims Offices.

As had been explained at the 30th session, there is one central office in the Ministry of Justice. However, as the Korean negotiators pointed out at the 61st session, actions designed to improve the central office as well as enlarge the system are now being taken by the Korean authorities.

g. Rules and Regulations.

In order to implement the State Compensation Law, No. 231, promulgated on September 8, 1951, there are following laws and regulations:

(1) Law relating to Procedures for Claims on Damages by the State, No. 1223, promulgated on Dec. 24, 1962.

(2) Regulations relating to the Application of the Law No. 1223, Cabinet Ordinance No. 1187, promulgated on February 5, 1963, and amended by Presidential Decree No. 1773, April 21, 1964.

(3) Regulations relating to the Application of the Law No. 1223, Ministry of Justice Regulation No. 63, April 27, 1964, amended by Ministry of Justice Regulation No. 79, May ___, 1964.

0252

Mr. Chu also presented the US negotiators with Korean language copies of ROK Government laws and regulations on claims.

3. Mr. Chu further stated that, as the Korean negotiators explained in detail at the 30th session, in addition to these laws and regulations, the Korean Civil Code, decisions of the courts, and other data serve as guidance for reasonable settlement of claims. At the 61st session, the Chief US negotiator had stated that the US negotiators believed the answers to the questions which they had raised would demonstrate that the Korean authorities did not have an effective claims service. However, the Korean negotiators believe that the foregoing answers, and their explanation of the State Compensation Committee at the 30th session, surely demonstrate the effectiveness of the present Korean claims system. The Korean claims authorities have been settling, promptly, equitably, and efficiently, the claims for various damages arising out of acts or omissions of 600,000 members of the Korean Armed Forces and more than 200,000 officials of the Government done in the performance of their official duties, as well as for other damages arising out of acts, omissions, or occurrences for which the Korean Government is legally responsible. The Korean negotiators wish to remind the US negotiators of the fact that some of the US negotiators visited the Ministry of Justice last Fall, and were given two briefings on the Korean State Compensation Committee system and its operation, they also observed an actual State Compensation Committee meeting dealing with civil claims, and recognized the efficiency of the system.

0253

4. The Korean negotiators believe, Mr. Chu continued, that after the Status of Forces Agreement comes into force, the possible increase in number of claims which would be filed with the Korean authorities could be efficiently processed by the Korean authorities, without imposing any excessive administrative burden on the Korean authorities, with some improvement and enlargement of the present Korean system.

5. The Korean negotiators also wish to point out, Mr. Chu stated, that the Korean claims agencies are staffed with judges, prosecutors, and attorneys, with profound experience and abundance of knowledge of judicial precedents accumulated over the past ten years. Therefore, the Korean negotiators are confident that the Korean authorities, with the help of the experienced personnel available in the field of civil claims, could promptly and equitably dispose of claims arising out of the stationing of the comparably not too large number of the US military personnel in Korea.

6. Mr. Chu said that the Korean legal experts had met informally several times with members of the US negotiating team and exchanged their views regarding their respective positions. As the result of these meetings, the Korean negotiators had made their position clear at the 51st session by proposing three agreed minutes, after carefully studying the views expressed by the US negotiators in these informal discussions. The Korean negotiators wish to ask the US negotiators to study further the proposals made by the Korean negotiators and respond favorably at a later meeting.

7. With regard to the statement made by the Chief US negotiator at the 61st session in connection with the US Claims Service in Korea, Mr. Chu asked the US negotiators the following questions:

0254

a. The US negotiators stated that the formula system in the Japan SOFA worked much differently in practice than as indicated in the text of the US-Japan Claims Article. Could the US negotiators present detailed information on the working procedures for settlement of claims in Japan?

b. The US negotiators had stated that the present US Claims Service meets the problem to the general satisfaction of all concerned. Does this mean that there are no claimants who have been dissatisfied so far? How does the US Claims Service dispose of claims which are not settled to the satisfaction of the claimant at present? Does the US Claims Service have a reexamination system? If so, who participates in the reexamination? Are they the same personnel who participate in the original decision? How many cases have been reexamined? Could the US negotiators give a detailed contents of the cases reexamined?

c. How many persons are there in the US Claims Service in Korea who hold qualifications as attorneys, prosecutors and judges?

d. How many claims were processed by the US Claims Service in Korea since its activation? Are there detailed statistics on individual claims cases of various types, including amounts involved?

e. The Korean negotiators would also like to have information regarding the cases for which the highest and the lowest amount were paid, including the copies of the claim files thereof.

f. How long does it take, on the average, to process a claim by the US Claims Service in Korea?

0255

8. Mr. Habib thanked Mr. Chu for his explanation and for the copies of the ROK Government claims materials. The US negotiators will reply in detail at the next meeting.

9. Mr. Habib asked if the documents in the Korean language just provided by Mr. Chu contained information on ROK standards used in determination of the amounts of claims awards. Mr. Chu answered that the materials do not contain such standards, or guidelines, but as explained in detail at the 30th session, the ROK claims official used the Hofmann formula in deciding the amount of awards.

10. Mr. Habib stated that the US Armed Forces Claims Service has a published set of awards for various claims, and that such a standard set of regulations and guidelines tends to prevent discrimination, or wide variation in claims awards. Mr. Chu asked if the U.S. side could furnish the Korean negotiators with the copies of such a published set of standards used by the U.S. Armed Forces Claims Service. He explained that the ROK State Compensation Committee determined the amount of awards, not by their own arbitrary decisions, but by the Hofmann formula, using the precedents established by the ROK civil courts. He emphasized that there was no room for discrimination in the operation of the Korean claims system. Mr. Habib asked if this could be demonstrated through example? It was agreed this subject would be discussed more fully at a later meeting.

11. Mr. Habib indicated that, while the ROK negotiators had supplied general statistics on total claims, detailed statistics on individual claims cases of various types would also be useful. The ROK negotiators indicated such information would be supplied at a later meeting.

0256

Security Measures

12. Mr. Habib indicated he wanted to clarify the present US position on the Security Measures Article, since the two sides had discussed three different drafts of this Article, formally and informally, as well as related articles in other SOFA's and a proposed understanding for the Agreed Joint Summary.

13. Mr. Habib said that the only US draft now under consideration is the one tabled at the 25th negotiating session on 26 June 1963.

14. The ROK negotiators, at the 46th session on 13 March 1964, stated that they would agree to the inclusion of the phrase "the persons who are present in the Republic of Korea pursuant to Article ____ (Invited Contractors)", and the phrase "consistent with Article ___ (Criminal Jurisdiction Article)", as desired by the US, if the US negotiators would agree to delete the phrase "of the persons referred to in this paragraph, and their property", as desired by the ROK side. The US negotiators are willing to agree to the deletion from the US draft of the phrase "of the persons referred to in this paragraph and their property", as proposed by the ROK negotiators, if the ROK negotiators agree to the inclusion in the Agreed Joint Summary of the mutual understanding first tabled at the 55th negotiating session on 19 June 1964.

15. Mr. Habib stated that both ROK and US authorities are fully aware that the defense of Korea is a joint effort involving Americans as well as Koreans, and it is believed both ROK and US officials want to insure that the US and ROK forces have the capability to discharge effectively their mutual obligations under the US-ROK Mutual Security Pact. The first sentence of the Security Measures Article to which we have both agreed, demonstrated this fact by stating that:

0257

"The United States and the Republic of Korea will cooperate in taking such steps as may from time to time be necessary to ensure the security of the United States armed forces, the members thereof, the civilian component, the persons who are present in the Republic of Korea pursuant to Article ____ (Invited Contractors), their dependents and their property."

16. Mr. Habib stated that the US negotiators feel that it is entirely proper and correct for the confidential negotiating record to show clear agreement between ROK and US Governments on the following understanding:

"In cooperating with each other under this Article, the two Governments agree that each will take such measures as may be necessary to ensure the security and protection of the US armed forces, the members thereof, the civilian component, the persons who are present in the Republic of Korean pursuant to Article ____ (Invited Contractors), their dependents and their property."

17. Mr. Habib stated that the foregoing language means just what it says and no more. The US negotiators wish to assure the Korean negotiators that such an understanding does not envisage the passage of legislation which would be applicable only to offenses against US personnel. Any legislation would of course be equally applicable to Koreans as well as Ameridans. We seek no special privileges in this regard. At the same time, the US cannot believe that the ROK Government would knowingly fail to take any measures that would be necessary to assist in accomplishment of our mutual defense objectives. This, of course, would include the passage of legislation if such were necessary. This does not mean that the US is implying that current ROK legislation

0258

in this area is deficient. But times and conditions do change. The US simply wishes ROK assurance for the record that in the event of changed conditions the ROK will, in cooperation with the US, take such measures as the then existing circumstances dictate to be necessary. This is the sort of understanding which underlies the basic fabric of ROK-US defense agreements and cooperative efforts, and which surely reflects the views of both of our Governments.

18. Mr. Habib concluded his statement by emphasizing that the two sides now appeared to be in agreement on the text of the article, and at least on the spirit behind the understanding for the agreed record. Therefore, it is hoped that with this elaboration of the US views, the Koreans and US negotiators can achieve early agreement on this Article and go on to discussion of other articles where real differences in US-ROK views still exist.

19. Mr. Chang thanked the US side for their review of the status of this Article and for the US statement, which he felt took a very constructive approach toward resolving this problem. He indicated that the Korean negotiators would take this question under advisement and reply at the next meeting. However, Mr. Chang pointed out that the last phrase of the Article was not still agreed upon, as the Korean draft reads "for the punishment of offenders under the applicable laws of the ROK" while the US draft reads "to ensure the punishment ..." the Korean negotiators, Mr. Chang continued, prefer their draft on the ground that it is the responsibility borne soly by the Korean Government to ensure the punishment of certain offenses under the applicable law and the responsibility could not properly be placed as a negotiable subject. Mr. Habib

0259

explained that, of course, offenders could only be punished "under the applicable laws of the Republic of Korea", and that there was no intent in the proposed language to prejudge the case of such offenders.

20. It was agreed that the secretaries for the ROK and US sides, respectively, would meet later to decide the date for the next meeting.

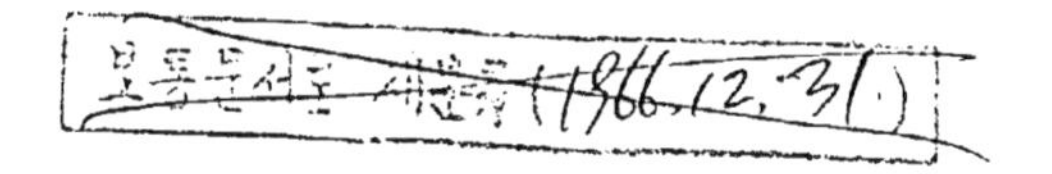

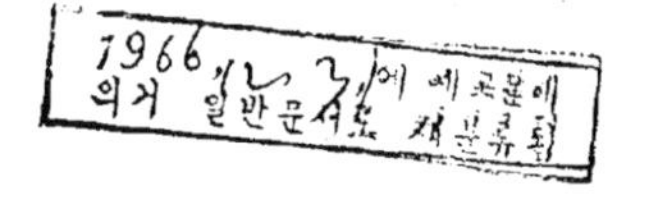

0260

청 구 권

한국측은 제50차 회의에서 한국국가배상위원회에 관한 제도 및 그운영실태등을 세밀히 설명하였으므로 미국측으로서는 별의문이 없을줄로 믿고 있으나 미국측이 제61차 회의에서 재차 동위원회에 관하여 질문하였으므로 미국측 질문에 응하여 제50차 회의시의 한국국가배상위원회에 관한 설명에 추가하여 답변하겠다.

a. 국가배상위원회의 직원

국가배상위원회의 구성인원과 행정, 심사 및 기타 요원에 관하여는 제50차 회의시에 충분히 설명하였으며 그 구성원칙에는 그당시와 다른점이 없다.

현재 배상위원회의 직원은 조사원9명(법무관 2, 사무관2, 주사5) 지급담당원3명, 일반 사무직원2명으로서 계 14명이다.

통역관이나 번역관은 현재 필요하지 않으므로 고용하지 않고있다.

b. 직원의 급료

직원은 전원의 국가공무원이므로 국가공무원 보수규정에 의하여 국가가 지급하고 있다.

c. 1963년 및 1964년도의 사건접수 및 처리

1963년도에는 283건을 접수 처리하였다. 이는 1963년5월1일부터 12월31일까지의 통계이다.

1964년도에는 6월30일 현재 207건을 접수하였으며 그중 139건을 처리하고 68건은 미결로 남아 있었다.

이는 1년2개월간에 총490건을 접수하여 422건은 완전처리하고 그남어지는 진행중에 있음을 알수있다. 자세한 내용은 통계표와 같다.

0261

구분 / 년도	접수	처리				진행중
		인정	기각	취하	계	
1963 년도 (5.1-12.31)	283	189	81	13	283	없음
1964 년도 (1.1-6.30)	207	91	27	21	139	68
합계	490	280	108	34	422	

d. 변호사의 비용

국가배상위원회에서 결정하는 배상금 중에는 변호사의 비용은 포함되지 않는다.

e. 1963 년도 및 1964 년도 지급예산

1963 년도의 지급예산은 30,390,000 원이었으며 1964 년도의 지급예산은 25,910,200 원이다. (1964 년도 예산은 작년도보다 적으나 현재 지급하여야 할 예산에는 하등의 영향이 없다 부족시는 추가조치한다)

f. 사무소의 수 (중앙 및 지방)

제 30 차 회의시에 설명한바와 같이 현재는 중앙사무소 하나로 운영한다. 그러나 중앙사무소의 개선과 지방사무소의 신설을 위한 조치는 제 61 차 회의시의 말한바와 같이 현재 이미 취하고 있는 중이다.

g. 운영 규정

1951.9.8 일 법률 제 231 호 국가배상법을 뒤받침하기 위하여,

(1) 1962.12.24 일 법률제 1223 호 국가배상금 청구에 관한 절차법.

(2) 1963.2.5 일 각령제 1187 호, 1964.4.21 일 대통령 제 1773 호 개정, 국가배상금 청구에 관한 절차법 시행령.

0262

(3) 1963.4.27 법무부령 제63호, 1964.5, 법무부령 제79호개정, 국가배상금 청구에 관한 절차법 시행규칙등의 법규가 있으며, 그운영은 제30차 회의시에 상세히 설명한 바와 같이 한국민법(제5장 불법행위)과 경험 및 기타 자료등을 참고로 하여 합리적으로 하고 있다. 이제 관계자료를 전달하오니 참고하시기 바랍니다.

미측은 제61차 회의에서 그들의 질문에 대한 한국측의 답변은 한국당국이 효과적인 청구제도를 갖고있지 않음을 입증하게 될것이라고 말하였다.

이와같은 미측질문에 대한 답변과 제30차 회의시의 한국제도에 대한 설명을 종합하여 볼때, 현재 한국 국가배상위원회는 60만 한국국군과 28여만의 중앙 및 지방정부 공무원이 공무집행중에 불법적인 민간 재산에 대한 손해행위로 일어나는 청구사건과 기타 정부가 책임지게 되는 많은 청구사건을 신속히 효율적으로 처리해 나가고 있음을 입증하고 있는 것이다.

또한 미측의 비공식회담 교섭대표들이 실제로 법무부를 방문하고 2차에걸친 "부리핑"과 국가배상위원회의 회의진행상황을 직접 목격하고 한국배상제도의 효율성을 인정한바 있다. 따라서 앞으로 한국측 청구권 조항 초안에 의하여 비교적 소수의 미군과 그들의 구성원 및 피고용자의 의한 손해에 대한 청구사건을 처리하게 된다 하여도 한국당국은 과중한 부담없이 현행제도를 다소 개선하므로서 충분히 그임무를 수행할수 있을 것이며, 한국에는 수10년간의 민사청구 사건 처리에 경험이 있는 검사, 판사, 변호사등이 많으며 충분한 민사판례가 있어 신속하고 공정하게 사건처리를

0263

효율적으로 할수 있을 것이다. 한국측은 여러차례에 걸친 미국고섭대표 및 청구관계 실무자들과의 비공식적인 접촉에서 미국측이 제시한 세가지 요구사항을 검토한후 51차회의에서 세가지 합의의사록을 제시함으로서 이에 대한 한국측의 입장을 명백히 표시한 것이다.

(1) 미측 합의의사록 (비공식 회의에서 제시한 합의의사록 1설명)

(2) " (비공식 회의에서 제시한 합의의사록 2설명)

(3) " (비공식 회의에서 제시한 합의의사록 3설명)

따라서 미측은 한국의 청구제도를 좀더 연구하고 한국안에 대한 해답을 하여 주기 바란다.

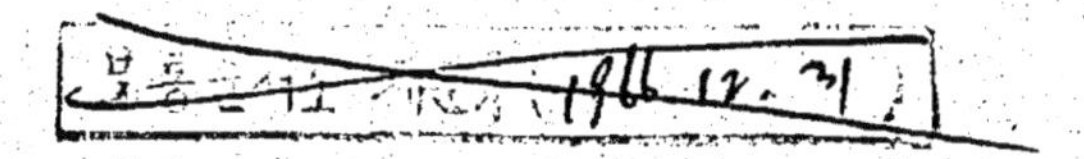

1966,12,31에 예고문에 의거 일반문서로 재분류됨

0264

Claims Article

Regarding the Claims Article at the 30th session, the Korean negotiators had already given a thorough explanation of the Korean claims compensation system and of its practical implementation. Therefore, they believed that the U.S. negotiators had grasped the whole picture of the Korean claims system which functions efficiently at the present.

However, in order to respond to the questions raised by the Chief U.S. negotiator at the 61st session regarding the Korean claims system, the Korean negotiators are ready to give an additional explanation on those matters which had not been covered at the 30th session:

a. Employees of the Compensation Committee

Regarding the organization of the State Compensation Committee and personnel employed either for administrative or for investigational purposes of the claims service, a detailed explanation had been given to the U.S. negotiators by the Korean negotiators at the 30th session, and since then, no significant change has been made.

At present, there are 9 investigators (2 legal officers, 2 class three officials, and 5 other officers), and 5 clerks (3 for payment administration and 2 for general administration).

Interpreters and translators are currently not employed since there has no such necessity been arisen for settlement of the civil claims currently received.

b. Salaries of Employees

All of employees of the Korean claims authorities are employees of the Korean Government. Therefore, their salaries are paid by the Government in accordance with the relevant laws and regulations.

0265

c. Claims Processed in the Years 1963 and 1964

In 1963, 283 cases had been received and disposed during the period beginning May 1 to December 31, 1963.

In 1964, as of June 30, 207 cases had been received and 139 cases had been disposed. The remaining 63 cases have been under process.

In other words, during the past 14 months, 422 cases of claims have been received and disposed completely. Detailed tabulation of the claims which have been processed by the Committee are as shown on the table.

d. Fees for Attorney

In the claims award decided by the Committee, attorney's fees are not included.

e. Appropriations for award in 1963 and 1964

In the budget of 1963 and 1964, 30,390,000 Won and 25,910,200 Won were appropriated for award, respectively. (The amount of budget for the fiscal year of 1964 is a little less than that of 1963, but this will not affect the payment of claims award. If additional appropriation would be necessary, the Korean authorities would take appropriate measures.

f. Number of Claims Office

As had been explained at the 30th session, there is one central office in the Ministry of Justice. However, as the Korean negotiators had pointed out at the 61st session, actions for improvement of the central office as well as for enlargement of the system is now being taken by the Korean authorities.

g. Rules and Regulations

In order to implement the State Compensation Law, No.231, promulgated on September 8, 1951, there are following laws and regulations:

0266

(1) Law relating to Procedures for Claims on Damages by the State, No. 1223, promulgated on December 24, 1962.

(2) Regulations relating to the Application of the Law No. 1223, Cabinet Ordinance No. 1187, promulgated on February 5, 1963, and amended by Presidential Decree No. 1773, April 21, 1964.

(3) Regulations relating to the Application of the Law No. 1223, Ministry of Justice Regulation No. 63, April 27, 1964, amended by Ministry of Justice Regulation No. 79, May 1964.

In addition to these laws and regulations as the Korean negotiators had explained in detail at the 30th session, there are the Korean Civil Code, Decisions of the court, [redacted] and other data as guidance for reasonable settlement of claims.

At the 61st session, the Chief U.S. negotiator had stated that the U.S. negotiators believed the answers to the questions which they had raised would demonstrate that the Korean authorities did not have an effective claims service.

However, the Korean negotiators believe that the answers given by them just now and their explanation of the State Compensation Committee at the 30th session would surely be sufficient enough to demonstrate the effectiveness of the present Korean claims system. The Korean claims authorities have been settling promptly, equitably, and efficiently the claims for the various damages arising out of acts or omissions of 600,000 members of the Korean Armed Forces and more than 200,000 officials of the [redacted] Government, done in the performance of their official duties, as well as for other many damages arising out of act, omission, or occurrence for which the Korean Government are legally responsible.

The Korean negotiators wishes to remind the U.S. negotiators of the fact that the U.S. negotiators had visited at the fall of last year the Ministry of Justice, had been given briefings twice on the Korean State Compensation Committee system and its aperation and had actually observed the State Compensation Committee meeting dealing with civil claims, and had recognized the efficiency of the system.

The Korean negotiators believe that after coming into force of the Status of Forces Agreement, a possible increase in number of claims which would be filed with the Korean authorities could be efficiently dealt with by the Korean authorities under the provisions proposed by the Korean negotiators without imposing any excessive administrative burden on the Korean authorities if some improvement and enlargement of the present Korean system could be achieved.

The Korean negotiators also wishes to point out that the Korean authorities are staffed by judges, prosecutors, attorneys with their profound experiences and abundant knowledges of judicial precedents accumulated for over ten years. Therefore, the Korean negotiators are confident that the Korean authorities, with the help of those experienced personnel available in the field of civil claims, could promptly and equitably dispose of claims arising out of the stationing of the comparably not too large number of the U.S. military personnel in Korea.

In the past, the Korean legal experts had informally met several times with the members of the U.S. negotiators and exchanged their views regarding their respective positions.

0268

As the result of these meetings, the Korean negotiators had made their position clear at the 51st session by proposing the three agreed minutes after carefully studying the ~~informally proposed by~~ concern expressed by the U.S. negotiators through informal discussions.

(1) The costs under paragraph 5 to be borne by the United States shall not exceed 75% of the amounts mutually agreed upon by claims authorities of both governments as being properly payable under that paragraph.

(2) The provisions of paragraph 5 of this article will become effective upon mutual agreement in the Joint Committee that the claims service of the Government of the Republic of Korea is prepared to undertake the procedures provided for in that paragraph. Until such time the United States agrees to pay just and reasonable compensation in settlement of civil claims (other than contractual claims) arising out of acts or omissions of members of the United States Forces done in the performance of official duty or out of any other act, omission or occurrence for which the United States Forces are legally responsible. In making such payments United States authorities would exercise the broad authority provided under United States laws relating to Foreign Claims and regulations issued thereunder. In settling claims which are described as arising "... out of any act, omission or occurrence for which the United States Forces are legally responsible,"

0269

United States authorities will take into consideration local law and practice.

(3) For the purposes of paragraph 5 of this Article, members of the Korean Augmentation to the United States Army (KATUSA) shall be considered as members of the United States armed forces, and members of the Korean Service Corps (KSC) shall be considered as employees of the armed forces of the Republic of Korea.

Therefore, the Korean negotiators wishes to ask the U.S. negotiators to study further the proposals made by the Korean negotiators and respond favorably at a later meeting.

0270

Claims Article

Regarding the Claims Article, the Korean negotiators had already given at the 30th session a thorough explanation of the Korean claims compensation system and of its practical implementation. Therefore, they believed that the U.S. negotiators had grasped the whole picture of the Korean claims system which functions efficiently at the present.

However, in order to respond to the questions raised at the 61st session by the Chief U.S. negotiator regarding the Korean claims system, the Korean negotiators are ready to give an additional explanation on those matters which had not been covered at the 30th session:

a. Employees of the Compensation Committee

Regarding the organization of the State Compensation Committee and personnel employed either for administrative or for investigational purposes of the claims service, a detailed explanation had been given to the U.S. negotiators by the Korean negotiators at the 30th session, and since then, no significant change has been made.

At present, there are 9 investigators (2 legal officers, 2 class three officials, and 5 other officers), and 5 clerks (3 for payment administration and 2 for general administration).

Interpreters and translators are currently not employed since there has no such necessity been arisen for settlement of the civil claims currently received.

b. Salaries of Employees

All of employees of the Korean claims authorities are employees of the Korean Government. Therefore, their salaries are paid by the Government in accordance with the relevant laws and regulations.

0271

c. Claims Processed in the Years 1963 and 1964

In 1963, 283 cases had been received and disposed during the period beginning May 1 to December 31, 1963.

In 1964, as of June 30, 207 cases had been received and 139 cases had been disposed. The remaining 63 cases have been under process.

In other words, during the past 14 months, 422 cases of claims have been received and disposed completely. Detailed tabulation of the claims which have been processed by the Committee are as shown on the table.

d. Fees for Attorney

In the claims award decided by the Committee, attorney's fees are not included.

e. Appropriations for award in 1963 and 1964

In the budget of 1963 and 1964, 30,390,000 Won and 25,910,200 Won were appropriated for award, respectively. (The amount of budget for the fiscal year of 1964 is a little less than that of 1963, but this will not affect the payment of claims award. If additional appropriation would be necessary, the Korean authorities would take appropriate measures.

f. Number of Claims Office

As had been explained at the 30th session, there is one central office in the Ministry of Justice. However, as the Korean negotiators had pointed out at the 61st session, actions for improvement of the central office as well as for enlargement of the system is now being taken by the Korean authorities.

g. Rules and Regulations

In order to implement the State Compensation Law, No. 231, promulgated on September 8, 1951, there are following laws and regulations:

0272

(1) Law relating to Procedures for Claims on Damages by the State, No. 1223, promulgated on December 24, 1962.

(2) Regulations relating to the Application of the Law No. 1223, Cabinet Ordinance No. 1187, promulgated on February 5, 1963, and amended by Presidential Decree No. 1773, April 21, 1964.

(3) Regulations relating to the Application of the Law No. 1223, Ministry of Justice Regulation No. 63, April 27, 1964, amended by Ministry of Justice Regulation No. 79, May 1964.

In addition to these laws and regulations as the Korean negotiators had explained in detail at the 30th session, there are the Korean Civil Code, Decisions of the court, and other data as guidance for reasonable settlement of claims.

At the 61st session, the Chief U.S. negotiator had stated that the U.S. negotiators believed the answers to the questions which they had raised would demonstrate that the Korean authorities did not have an effective claims service.

However, the Korean negotiators believe that the answers given by them just now and their explanation of the State Compensation Committee at the 30th session would surely be sufficient enough to demonstrate the effectiveness of the present Korean claims system. The Korean claims authorities have been settling promptly, equitably, and efficiently the claims for the various damages arising out of acts or omissions of 600,000 members of the Korean Armed Forces and more than 200,000 officials of the Government done in the

0273

performance of their official duties, as well as for other many damages arising out of act, omission, or occurrence for which the Korean Government are legally responsible.

The Korean negotiators wishes to remind the U.S. negotiators of the fact that the U.S. negotiators had visited at the fall of last year the Ministry of Justice, had been given briefings twice on the Korean State Compensation Committee system and its operation and had actually observed the State Compensation Committee meeting dealing with civil claims, and had recognized the efficiency of the system.

The Korean negotiators believe that after coming into force of the Status of Forces Agreement, a possible increase in number of claims which would be filed with the Korean authorities could be efficiently dealt with by the Korean authorities under the provisions proposed by the Korean negotiators without imposing any excessive administrative burden on the Korean authorities if some improvement and enlargement of the present Korean system could be achieved.

The Korean negotiators also wishes to point out that the Korean authorities are staffed by judges, prosecutors, attorneys with their profound experiences and abundant knowledges of judicial precedents accumulated for over ten years. Therefore, the Korean negotiators are confident that the Korean authorities, with the help of those experienced personnel available in the field of civil claims, could promptly and equitably dispose of claims arising out of the stationing of the comparably not too large number of the U.S. military personnel in Korea.

In the past, the Korean legal experts had informally met several times with the members of the U.S. negotiators.

0274

정/리/보/존/문/서/목/록

기록물종류	문서-일반공문서철	등록번호	923 9596	등록일자	2006-07-27
분류번호	741.12	국가코드	US	주제	
문서철명	한.미국 간의 상호방위조약 제4조에 의한 시설과 구역 및 한국에서의 미국군대의 지위에 관한 협정 (SOFA) 전59권. 1966.7.9 서울에서 서명 : 1967.2.9 발효 (조약 232호) *원본				
생산과	미주과/조약과	생산년도	1952 - 1967	보존기간	영구
담당과(그룹)	조약	조약	서가번호	--	
참조분류					
권차명	V.25 실무교섭회의, 제63-68차, 1964.9-12월				
내용목차	1. 제63차 회의, 9.11 (p.2~33) 2. 제64차 회의, 10.16 (p.34~88) 3. 제65차 회의, 10.23 (p.89~124) 4. 제66차 회의, 11.24 (p.125~169) 5. 제67차 회의, 12.16 (p.170~219) 6. 제68차 회의, 12.23 (p.220~253) * 일지 : 1953.8.7 이승만 대통령-Dulles 미국 국무장관 공동성명 - 상호방위조약 발효 후 군대지위협정 교섭 약속 1954.12.2 정부, 주한 UN군의 관세업무협정 체결 제의 1955.1월, 5월 미국, 제의 거절 1955.4.28 정부, 군대지위협정 제의 (한국측 초안 제시) 1957.9.10 Hurter 미국 국무차관 방한 시 각서 수교 (한국측 제의 수락 요구) 1957.11.13, 26 정부, 개별 협정의 단계적 체결 제의 1958.9.18 Dawling 주한미국대사, 형사재판관할권 협정 제외 조건으로 행정협정 체결 의사 전달 1960.3.10 정부, 토지, 시설협정의 우선적 체결 강력 요구 1961.4.10 장면 국무총리-McConaughy 주한미국대사 공동성명으로 교섭 개시 합의 1961.4.15, 4.25 제1, 2차 한.미국 교섭회의 (서울) 1962.3.12 정부, 교섭 재개 촉구 공한 송부 1962.5.14 Burger 주한미국대사, 최규하 장관 면담 시 형사재판관할권 문제 제기 않는 조건으로 교섭 재개 통고 1962.9.6 한.미국 간 공동성명 발표 (9월 중 교섭 재개 합의) 1962.9.20~ 1965.6.7 제1-81차 실무 교섭회의 (서울) 1966.7.8 제82차 실무 교섭회의 (서울) 1966.7.9 서명 1967.2.9 발효 (조약 232호)					

마/이/크/로/필/름/사/항

촬영연도	*롤 번호	화일 번호	후레임 번호	보관함 번호
2006-11-22	I-06-0069	02	1-253	

0001

1. 제63차 회의, 9.11

0002

관리번호 1339

기 안 지

기 안 자	미주과 황영재	전화번호		공 보	필 요	불필요
		과 장	국 장	차 관	장 관	
		9/15	9/15	9월1		
협 조 자 서 명					보존년한	
기 안 년 월 일	1964. 9. 15.	시 행 년월일		통제관	정 서	기 장
분류기호 문서번호	외구미 722.2					
경 유 수 신 참 조	대 통 령 (참조: 비서실장) 국무총리 (참조: 비서실장) 사본: 법 무 부 장 관			발 신	장 관	
제 목	제 63 차 주둔군지위협정 체결 교섭 실무자회의 개최 보고					

1964. 9. 11. 하오 3시부터 동 4시 30분 가지 외무부 제1회의실에서 개최된 제 63 차 주둔군지위협정 체결 교섭 실무자회의에서 토의된 내용을 별첨과 같이 보고 합니다.

유첨: 제63차 주둔군지위협정 체결교섭 실무자회의 보고서 1부, 끝

일반문서로 재분류(1966. 12. 31.)

1966, 12, 31, 에 예고문에 의거 일반문서로 재분류됨

발송 No. 497 1964. 9 16 외무부

공통서식 1—2 (갑) (16절지)

0003

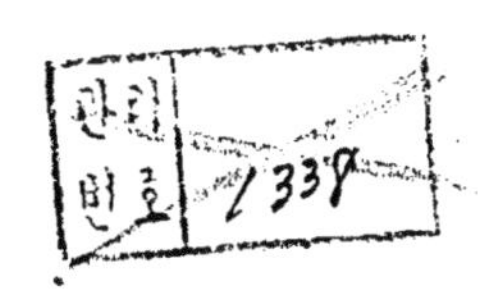

기 안 지

기 안 자	미주과 황영재	전화번호		공 보	필 요	불필요
	과장	국장	차관	장관		
		전결				
협 조 자 서 명					보존년한	
기 안 년 월 일	64. 9. 16.	시행 년월일		통제관	정서	기장
분류기호 문서번호	외구미 722.2					
경유 수신 참조	법무부장관			발신	장 관	
제 목	제63차 주둔군지위협정 체결 실무자 교섭회의 결과보고 사본 송부					

별첨은 1964년 9월 11일 개최된 제63차 미주둔군 지위협정 체결을 위한 실무자 교섭회의의 결과보고 사본을 송부하오니 귀부에서 적의 참고하시기 바랍니다.

유첨 - 제63차 주둔군지위협정 실무자교섭회의 결과보고 사본 1부. 끝

공통서식 1—2 (갑) (16절지)

0004

제 63 차

한·미간 주둔군지위협정 체결 교섭 실무자
회의 보고서

1. 일시 1964. 9. 11. 하오 3시부터 4시 30분까지
2. 장소 외무부 제1회의실
3. 토의사항

가. 민사청구권

(1) 미측은 현행미군 소청제도는 한국인의 민사 청구사건을 공정하게 또 효율적으로 처리하고 있으므로 이를 계속시키는 것이 타당함을 재차 주장하는 동시에 62차 회의에서 우리측이 질문한 주한미군의 소청사무에 관하여 요지 다음과 같이 답변하였다.

(가) 미일 협정의 실제운영상태
일본에 있어서는 미·일 양국에서 청구사건을 각각 별도로 조사하고 그조사결과에 따라 양국의 관계당국이 국가의 책임한계와 보상금액에 합의하고 있는 것으로 알고 있다.

(나) 주한미군 소청처리에 대한 불만건수, 재심제도 및 관계서류
미군소청사무소의 결정에 불복을 제기한 건수는 전체사건의 5퍼센트이며, 이런사건에 대해서는 대개 그사건을 처리한 심사위원이 재심 처리하게 된다. 이런사건에 대한 서류는 사건해결후 60일 혹은 사건기각 및 재심요구 접수후 120일이 경과한 후에 미국으로 보내기 때문에 그렇게 빨리 제시할수는 없다.

(다) 주한미군 소청소내의 검사, 변호사 혹은 만사자격 소유자의 수
현재 4명이 변호사 자격을 갖고 있으며

0005

그중 3명이 심사위원으로 있다.

(라) 1963년 및 1964년의 사건 처리 현황

1963년에는 839건을 심사하여 680건에 대하여 청구를 인정 그중 649건에 대하여 보상금을 지불하였으며 159건의 청구는 인정치 않았다. 보상금 총지불액수는 1963년에 19,264,162 원이다.

1964년에는 9월 1일 현재 911건을 심사하여 589건을 인정 576건에 대하여 보상금을 지불하고 기각건수는 322건이다. 금년의 보상금 지불 류계는 25,865,548. 원이다.

(마) 지금까지 지불한 최고 및 최저 보상금액 및 그관계 서류

최고 보상금 지불사건은 627,376원이며, 최저는 200원이었으며 그관계서류는 한국측이 요청하면 제시할수 있으나 이들 완결된 사건에 대한 기록을 미국에서 가져오려면 대개 30일이 소요된다.

(바) 사건 처리 평균소요기간

사건 종류에 따라 상이하나, 보통사건접수 60일후에 심사결과를 청구자에게 통보한다.

(사) 보상금 사정에 관한 기준

한국근로기준법에 규정된 보상기준을 참고로 하여 보상금을 사정한다.

(2) 한국측은 한국제도는 보상금 사정기준에 있어 공포된 규정은 없으나 실제로는 관례에 의하여 효율적으로 운영되는 기준이 있으며, 한국측의 국가배상위원회의 위원들은 법조계의 경험이 풍부하며, 한국의 국가배상위원회의 보상금 결정에 불만이 있을 때에는 청구자는 3심제인 한국 민사재판을 통하여 공정한 재판을 받을수 있음을 지적하고 한국안에 대하여 재고할것을 촉구함.

64-3-8

0007

0008

(3) 미측은 한국제도는 보상금 사정에 관한 기준이 법적 뒷받침을 받고 있지 못하고 있음을 지적하는 동시, 현행 주한미군이 사용하는 제도에 결점이 없는한 구태여 한국제도로 교체할 근본적인 이유가 없음을 주장하였으며,

(4) 한국측은 이에 대하여 양제도가 유사하며 모두 잘운영되는 것은 사실이나 피해자인 한국국민은 어디까지나 한국법에 의하여 구제되도록 함이 타당한 것이며, 언어상 의장벽 및 잘알려지지 않은 외국제도에 의하여 청구사건을 해결하는 것보다는 피해자들이 더욱잘 이해하고 있는 한국법에 의하여 해결토록 하는것이 더욱 용이할 것이다. 또한 미측은 한국제도에 대하여 오직 보상금 지불기준이 법제화되지 않음을 지적하고 있으나 이는 용이하게 해결될수 있는 문제로 보고 있으며, 미측도 이런법규의 유무를 아직 구체적으로 표시하지 않았음을 지적하였다.

(5) 미측은 청구권 문제에 대한 토의는 더계속하여도 현재로서는 진전을 볼수가 없음을 지적하고 양측이 이문제의 해결을 위한 가일층의 검토를 할수 있도록 차후회의로 연기할것을 제의, 한국측은 이에 동의하였음.

나. 보호조치

(1) 한국측은 62차회의에서 설명한 미국측입장에 대하여 다음과 같이 제안함.

(가) 협정본문 마지막 부분의 미국정부재산에 대한 범법자의 처벌문제와 관련하여 미측이 제안하는 "... to ensure the punishment of..." 를 한국안과 같이

0009

64-3-29 미국·운 III-6

0010

" ... for the punishment of" 로 할것을 제안 하고,

(나) 미측이 55차회의에서 제안한 양해사항에 대하여는 미측자신이 군대구성원, 군속, 가족 및 초청계약자들을 "이원" 에 대한 특별대우를 원하지 않고 있으며 또한 한국측이 필요한 조치를 취할 것이라는 사실을 인정하고 있는 이상 동양해사항이 불필요할 뿐만 아니라, 상기 양해사항은 미국당국이 일방적인 조치를 취할수 있는 것으로 오해하게 될 가능성이 있으며 이와 관련한 어떤문제가 야기될 때에는 합동위원회에서 해결할수 있음을 지적하고 미측의 양해사항을 철회할것을 제안하였음.

(2) 미측은 그들의 "인원"에 대하여 특별법을 요구하는 것은 아니며, 한국측 제안을 검토하겠음을 시사하였음. 끝

보통문서로 재분류(1966.12.31.)

1966.12.31.에 예고문에 의거 일반문서로 재분류됨

0011

64-3-110

STATUS OF FORCES NEGOTIATIONS: 63rd Meeting

SUBJECTS:
1. Correction of Record
2. Claims
3. Security Measures

PLACE: Ministry of Foreign Affairs

DATE: September 11, 1964

PARTICIPANTS:

Republic of Korea	United States
CHANG Sang-mun	Philip C. Habib
KU Chung-hoe	Brig. General Carroll H. Dunn, USA
Colonel KIM Won-kil, ROKA	Colonel Howard Smigelow, USA
CHU Mun-ki	Captain John Wayne, USN
KIM Se-~~...~~ Kwon	Benjamin A. Fleck
O Chae-hi	Robert A. Kinney
Major YI Kae-hun, ROKA	Robert A. Lewis
HWANG Yong-chae	Major Alton Harvey, USA
KIM Yun-taik (Interpreter)	Kenneth Campen (interpreter)
	Lt. Colonel Charles Thompson, USA

0013

1. Mr. Chang opened the meeting by introducing Mr. Kim Se-Kwon, a Prosecutor from the Ministry of Justice, and Mr. Kim Yun-taik, who would serve as interpreter for the Korean negotiators in the place of Mr. Yi Kun-pal. Mr. Habib welcomed these gentlemen to the negotiations and, in turn, introduced Lt. Colonel Charles Thompson, of the U.S. Claims Service, who would participate in the discussion of the Claims Article. Mr. Chang welcomed Lt. Colonel Thompson.

Correction of Summary Record

2. Mr. Habib stated that before proceeeding with the agenda agreed upon, the U.S. negotiators would like to correct an error which they had discovered in the Agreed Joint Summary of the 60th meeting. The first sentence of paragraph 23 of that Summary reported a statement that in Germany criminal jurisdiction over U.S. personnel is exercised by the sending state only. This, of course, was untrue, as both the U.S. and Korean negotiators were well aware. The topic under discussion at the time had been duty certificates and the discussion which followed the statement in question had made it plain that the United States does not have exclusive criminal jurisdiction in the Federal Republic of Germany. Accordingly, the U.S. negotiators proposed that the two secretaries amend the Agreed Joint Summary of the 60th meeting by deleting from paragraph 23 the words: "criminal jurisdiction over U.S. personnel is exercised by the sending state only. However". Mr. Chang replied that the Korean negotiators agreed to the proposed correction.

Claims

3. Taking up the Claims Article, Mr. Habib stated that he would like to make a few remarks related to the previous discussion of this article. The U.S. negotiators had sought to make clear that the U.S. Government is determined to continue to meet its recognized responsibilities to provide prompt and equitable settlement of any justified claims against the U.S. armed forces in Korea. The U.S. Armed Forces Claims Service, Korea, is currently fulfilling these responsibilities in an efficient

0014

and effective manner. The U.S. armed forces wish to continue this operation [in order] to fulfill the legal obligations of the U.S. Government in the settlement of claims. The U.S. Claims Service has operated in such a manner as to insure the continuance of the current friendly relations between the Korean people and the U.S. armed forces. The U.S. negotiators are convinced that this friendly relationship is, in part, a result of the fact that the Korean people know that legitimate claims against the U.S. armed forces will be speedily and fairly settled. At the previous meeting, the U.S. negotiators had promised to try to answer specific questions. Lt. Colonel Thompson would now answer the questions posed by the Korean negotiators.

4. Lt. Colonel Thompson stated that with reference to the first question asked by the Korean negotiators, concerning the operation of the claims system in Japan, it is the understanding of the U.S. negotiators that the U.S. armed forces and the Japanese authorities each conducts a separate claims investigation. When these investigations have been concluded, the Japanese claims agency and the U.S. claims agency reach agreement as to the liability and the amount of any award.

5. With reference to the Korean inquiry regarding the settlement of claims in Korea, Lt. Colonel Thompson stated that there are some dissatisfied claimants. However, objections are received only in 5 percent of the cases. Obviously, not all claims are justified nor can they all be settled by payment of the amount claimed. Claims are thoroughly re-examined upon the receipt of a complaint [made] by a claimant. This re-examination is made by the commissioner who originally acted on the claim. If the same commissioner is not available, the review will be made by another commissioner. He is authorized to change a prior determination upon the receipt of new and material evidence, or to correct manifest errors in calculation, or [because of] fraud or collusion. It is estimated that ten cases are re-examined each month. This includes cases re-examined [for] the first time and those being re-examined for the second and subsequent times. Detailed contents of all cases are not immediately available, as the files are

0015

sent to the United States within 60 days after settlement or 120 days after disapproval or receipt of the last letter from the claimant requesting review. It may be noted that the principal complaints of claimants are based on findings of negligence on the part of the claimants to a degree which prevents payment of the claim.

6. In response to the third question posed by the Korean negotiators, Lt. Colonel Thompson stated that four members of the U.S. Claims Service are qualified attorneys and three of these serve as Claims Commissioners. There are no Claims Commissioners who are not attorneys. Furthermore, these four attorneys at present have a combined total of fifty-nine years of legal experience. In addition, the services of seven U.S. attorneys and one Korean attorney assigned to the office of the Staff Judge Advocate, Eighth United States Army, are available for general legal advice.

7. Regarding the number of claims made against the U.S. armed forces, Lt. Colonel Thompson tabled the following data showing the number of claims processed during 1963 and up to September 1, 1964:

	Claims Adjudicated	Claims Allowed	Claims Disallowed	Claims Paid	Amount Paid	
					Won	Dollars
1963	839	680	159	649	19,264,162	148,185.86
1964 (as of Sept. 1)	911	589	322	576	25,865,548	101,433.52

Lt. Colonel Thompson stated that statistical reports for the period from June 1, 1959, through 1962 have been sent to the United States and are not immediately available. The largest amount paid on a claim was Won 627,376 ($4,844.60), paid to Mr. Na In-duk, who had been assaulted and shot in the leg by two U.S. soldiers who were absent without leave from their units. Mr. Na's leg had to be amputated. The lowest payment had been Won 200 ($1.54), paid to Mr. Yi Chong-hwa for damage to his barley field by a U.S. tank. The files on both of these cases have been sent to the United States and details, therefore, are not available at this time. Lt. Colonel Thompson said that individual

0016

files can be made available for review by the Korean authorities, upon request. However, if the cases have been completed, it will take approximately 30 days to obtain the records from the United States.

8. Regarding the time it takes to process a claim, Lt. Colonel Thompson stated that this varies, based on the complexity of the investigation and the factual situation. He pointed out that there may be delays caused by difficulties in investigation or by the claimant's failure to provide promptly required documents. These variables make it impossible to fix an absolute time of processing. It may be fairly estimated, however, that a claim is normally settled and the claimant notified within sixty days after the claim has been received by the Claims Service.

9. Regarding the question of the standards adhered to by the Claims Service, Lt. Colonel Thompson stated that the allowable compensation normally represents the cost of repairing the property or the cost of restoring it to the condition it was in immediately prior to the damage. The claimant establishes these costs by presenting receipts for amounts expended to repair or estimates of the cost of repair submitted by reputable contractors or other qualified repairmen. Compensation, for lost or completely destroyed property is computed at the actual value of the property at the time of the loss or destruction. The value of growing crops and trees is similarly computed. The compensation payable for personal injury and death, Lt. Colonel Thompson continued, is not as amenable to mathematical calculation as are the costs of property damage. To obtain as much consistency as possible, standard elements are utilized to form a sound basis on which to compute awards. In this regard, the Claims Service follows the disability grades and compensation tables set forth in the Korean Labor Standards Act and implementing Presidential Decree No. 889, used by the Republic of Korea Workman's Compensation Board. Such tables can be obtained readily from the appropriate ROK Government offices. The Claims Commissions are charged with the responsibility of evaluating each case in the light of standard elements to arrive

0017

at a fair settlement.

10. Mr. Chu replied that the Korean negotiators would study the statements made by Lt. Colonel Thompson and perhaps would ask further questions at a later meeting. Mr. Chu said that he wished to make a few remarks in addition to those which he had made at the previous meeting.

11. Mr. Chu recalled that the U.S. negotiators had asked what criteria the Korean Claims Service used for computation of claims payments. In reply, he had explained the Korean practices. It was true that there were no Korean legal provisions for settling claims. However, when the payment of claims against the U.S. armed forces was turned over to the Korean Claims Service, such claims would be handled effectively and without prejudice. He said that the highest amount paid by the Korean Claims Service in settlement of a claim was Won 450,000, in a traffic accident case resulting in death. More detailed data on cases handled by the Korean Claims Service would be provided as soon as compiled.

12. Mr. Chu said he would like to acquaint the U.S. negotiators with the personal backgrounds of members of the Korean Claims Settlement Commission. The Chairman was Mr. Kwon, the present Vice Minister of Justice, formerly a law professor for 7 years, a lawyer for 3 years, and a public prosecutor for 15 years. Mr. Lee, The Director of the Bureau of Legal Affairs, had been a law professor for 6 years and a prosecutor for 13 years. Member Yun had been a prosecutor for 19 years, as had member Lee, the present Director of the Bureau of Correction. Member Lim, head of the Appellate Court, had served for 15 years as a judge. Member Kim, currently Vice Chief of the Staff Judge Advocate's Section, ROK Army Headquarters, had served previously for 11 years as a Judge Advocate. Member Kim, a lawyer and formerly a Justice of the Supreme Court, had served as a lawyer for 20 years and a judge for 10 years. In view of the backgrounds of these people, who could doubt that claims would be handled by them in an equitable and just manner? Handling of claims against the U.S. armed forces by the Korean Claims Service would not compromise U.S. interests.

0018

13. Mr. Chu stated that in case a claimant was dissatisfied, he could file an objection with a Korean court for decision of the matter through legal procedures. As the U.S. negotiators knew, there were three levels of courts in the ROK judicial system. Thus, a claimant could file his objection three separate times.

14. On the basis of the information which the Korean negotiators had provided concerning the Korean claims system, Mr. Chu asked the U.S. negotiators to reconsider their position. Mr. Habib asked if the Korean negotiators could provide any examples of cases which had been appealed to the courts. What had been the findings of the court? Mr. Chu replied that only one such case had occurred to date, and that adjudication in that case had not yet been completed.

15. Mr. Habib recalled that Mr. Chu had stated that at present, there were no fixed legal provisions for the payment of claims but that the Korean authorities intended to settle claims equitably. Mr. Habib pointed out that the lack of legal standards leaves open the possibility of settlement of individual claims on bases not related to any standards. He asked whether the Korean negotiators could furnish any data which would indicate the range of payments actually made for claims of the same type. Mr. Chu replied that these data would appear in the statistics which the Korean authorities were in the process of compiling.

16. Mr. Habib said he wished to ask a more fundamental question. To date, the Korean negotiators had not indicated why they wished to make a change from the claims system which is in operation. The U.S. negotiators had explained how the U.S. Claims Service operates. They had indicated that the U.S. armed forces are prepared to continue to operate this system, which imposes no financial burden whatsoever on the Korean authorities. Did the Korean negotiators find anything wrong in the operation of U.S. Claims Service? The only argument against its continuation which they had made to date was that this problem was handled differently in other countries. The U.S. negotiators did not believe that was a good argument. They believe

it to be significant that in only 5 percent of the cases have claimants ojected to the manner in which their claim has been handled by the U.S. Claims Service. The U.S. negotiators would be interested in knowing what the similar figure was with regard to claims handled by the Korean Claims Service. As the U.S. negotiators had previously pointed out, the U.S. armed forces were not trying to evade their responsibility with regard to the payment of claims. They and the U.S. negotiators preferred not to exchange a system which was working effectively and equitably and obviously to the satisfaction of the claimants for one which was only in its beginning stages.

17. Mr. Chu replied that the Korean negotiators were well aware that the two claims systems under discussion were similar. Mr. Habib pointed out that the U.S. negotiators had not expressed any such judgment and did not believe the two systems to be similar. Mr. Chu said this was the belief of the Korean negotiators. He added that the absence of objections, as indicated by the 5 percent figure cited by the U.S. negotiators, does not necessarily mean that all of the remaining 95 percent of the claimants were satisfied. They had to contend, after all, with such things as the language barrier and lack of knowledge of how the system worked.

18. Mr. Habib demurred. In the absence of objections, he said, one can only assume satisfaction. He pointed out that the U.S. Claims Service provides interpreters, explains fully the procedures to be followed, and gives whatever other assistance may be necessary to claimants.

19. Mr. Chu then stated that, as a matter of principle, what happens in a given country should be settled by the authorities of that country. Mr. Habib again demurred. He pointed out that the matters under discussion involved two countries and that how matters involving the two countries were settled was a question to be settled by agreement between the two governments. He reminded the Korean negotiators that the U.S. armed forces were in Korea under the terms of an international agreement.

0020

20. Mr. Chu said the Korean negotiators understood the position stated by the U.S. negotiators and that the two sides were in the process of negotiating an agreement which would make an exception to the principle which he had just stated. The Korean negotiators believed there were no differences between the two systems but the Korean system contained more remedies for handling objections by dissatisfied claimants. The Korean Claims Service personnel understand their own people better than U.S. personnel and can more easily persuade claimants to accept the payments awarded.

21. Mr. Chang added that the Korean negotiators believed that by now the U.S. negotiators realized that the Korean Claims Service was an efficient, working system. However, the U.S. negotiators appeared still to have misgivings regarding the lack of legal standards. Claims were paid by the Korean Claims Service on the basis of practices developed over many years. Lack of legal standard on the part of the Korean Claims System does not necessarily mean that the awards were given without any standard. The U.S. negotiators had not indicated that the U.S. claims service had any legal standards either.

22. Mr. Habib pointed out that Lt. Colonel Thompson had covered this subject as the last point in the statement which he had made earlier in the meeting. Mr. Chang replied that the Korean authorities had standards but they were not standards which had been promulgated as law by the National Assembly. He asked what legally promulgated standards were followed by the U.S. Claims Service. He pointed out that the matters under discussion involved Korean nationals and that the Korean negotiators believed it to be ridiculous that Korean nationals should be dealt with under procedures that were not Korean. However, the Korean negotiators agreed that the interest of the foreign government involved must be recognized. How that interest could be expressed was open to negotiation.

23. Mr. Habib remarked that the negotiators appeared to have exhausted the possibilities for discussion of this article at this time and suggested that further discussion be deferred until a later meeting, after each side had the opportunity for further study. Mr. Chang agreed.

0021

Security Measures

24. Turning to the Security Measures Article, Mr. Chang stated that the Korean negotiators had studied the position expounded by the U.S. negotiators at the 62nd meeting. As a result, the Korean negotiators had reached the conclusion that the last phrase of the Article must read as in the Korean draft, "...for the punishment of...", as the Korean negotiators had indicated at the 62nd meeting. With regard to the understanding proposed by the U.S. negotiators for the Agreed Joint Summary at the 55th meeting, the Korean negotiators believed the understanding is not necessary in the light of the content of the text and the representation made by the U.S. negotiators at the last meeting, as the U.S. negotiators had stated that they seek no special privileges with regard to the security measures for U.S. personnel and that they fully recognize that the Korean authorities would not fail to cooperate with the U.S. armed forces in taking necessary measures for security of the U.S. military personnel.

25. Mr. Chang stated that the Korean negotiators still found objectionable points in the proposed understanding. First, the phrase "...each will take such measures as may be necessary..." seems to involve some possible factor of misunderstanding that the United States authorities might institute unilateral measures without prior agreement with the Korean authorities. The Korean negotiators did not think that the United States negotiators intended the proposed understanding to bring about such an effect. If the interpretation of the Korean negotiators was correct and the U.S. negotiators were seeking prior agreement with the Korean authorities to effect mutual cooperation, the Korean negotiators believed that the provisions of the Article istself would be sufficient and [thus] no such ambiguous understanding should be included as a confidential agreement in the Agreed Joint Summary.

26. Secondly, Mr. Chang continued, while the proposed understanding provides that each side may institute measures for "persons" as well as for the U.S. armed forces, it was noted that the second sentence of the text already

0022

provides that the ROK Government will take legislative measures regarding the U.S. armed forces, if necessary. With regard to "persons", the Korean position still stood, as the Korean negotiators had repeatedly explained it in the past. The ROK Government is prepared to take legislative measures for them only when it considers such measures necessary. Accordingly, (inclusion of) the phrase "such measures" in the understanding is not acceptable to the Korean side, if the term includes legislative measures for persons. Moreover, should any problem arise in the course of implementing the Article, the Korean negotiators believe that the Joint Committee could deal with it effectively. The Korean authorities will take such measures as they deem necessary and other, joint measures may be taken if such are necessary. As the Korean negotiators are convinced that the Korean authorities will ask the United States for its cooperation whenever such is deemed necessary and that the United States will respond favorably, the Korean negotiators believed that such mutual cooperation is sufficiently provided for in the text of the Article. Therefore, the Korean negotiators suggested that the U.S. negotiators, taking the Korean position into consideration, withdraw their proposal for a separate understanding.

27. Mr. Habib replied that the U.S. negotiators had attempted to make clear that what they were proposing was not discriminatory legislation for U.S. "persons" only, but legislation which would include Korean and U.S. persons alike. Mr. Chang stated that the Korean negotiators understood this. Mr. Habib then stated that the U.S. negotiators would study the Korean position, as just explained by Mr. Chang.

28. It was agreed that the two secretaries would meet and fix the date of the next meeting.

JOINT SUMMARY RECORD OF THE 63RD SESSION

1. Time and Place: 3:00 - 4:30 P.M. September 11, 1964 at the Foreign Ministry's Conference Room (No.1)

2. Attendants:

ROK Side:

Mr. Chang, Sang Moon	Director European and American Affairs Bureau
Mr. Koo, Choong Whay	Chief, America Section Ministry of Foreign Affairs
Mr. Oh, Jae Hee	Chief Treaty Section Ministry of Foreign Affairs
Col. Kim, Won Kil	Chief Military Affairs Section Ministry of National Defense
Mr. Choo, Moon Ki	Chief Legal Affairs Section Ministry of Justice
Mr. Kim, Se Kwon	Prosecutor Claims Section Ministry of Justice
Maj. Lee, Kye Hoon	Military Affairs Section Ministry of National Defense
Mr. Hwang, Young Jae	3rd Secretary Ministry of Foreign Affairs
Mr. Park, Won Chul	3rd Secretary Ministry of Foreign Affairs
Mr. Kim, Yoon Taik (Interpreter)	3rd Secretary Ministry of Foreign Affairs

U.S. Side:

Mr. Philip C. Habib	Counselor American Embassy
Brig. Gen. Carroll H. Dunn	Deputy Chief of Staff 8th U.S. Army
Col. Howard Smigelow	Deputy Chief of Staff 8th U.S. Army

0024

Capt. John Wayne	Assistant Chief of Staff USN/K
Mr. Benjamin A. Fleck (Rapporteur and Press Officer)	First Secretary American Embassy
Mr. Robert A. Kinney	J-5 8th U.S.Army
Mr. Robert A. Lewis	Second Secretary American Embassy
Maj. Alton H. Harvey	Staff Judge Advocate's Office 8th U.S. Army
Mr. Kenneth Campen	Interpreter
Lt. Col. Charles Thompson	Claims Service 8th U.S. Army

1. Mr. Chang opened the meeting by introducing Mr. Kim Se-kwon, a Prosecutor from the Ministry of Justice, and Mr. Kim Yun-taik, who would serve as interpreter for the Korean negotiators in the place of Mr. Yi Kun-pal. Mr. Habib welcomed these gentlemen to the negotiations and, in turn, introduced Lt. Colonel Charles Thompson, of the U.S. Claims Service, who would participate in the discussion of the Claims Article. Mr. Chang welcomed Lt. Colonel Thompson.

Correction of Summary Record

2. Mr. Habib stated that before proceeding with the agenda agreed upon, the U.S. negotiators would like to correct an error which they had discovered in the Agreed Joint Summary of the 60th meeting. The first sentence of paragraph 23 of that Summary reported a statement that in Germany criminal jurisdiction over U.S. personnel is exercised by the sending state only. This, of course, was untrue, as both the U.S. and Korean negotiators were well aware. The topic under discussion at the time had been duty certificates and the discussion which followed the statement in question

had made it plain that the United States does not have exclusive criminal jurisdiction in the Federal Republic of Germany. Accordingly, the U.S. negotiators proposed that the two secretaries amend the Agreed Joint Summary of the 60th meeting by deleting from paragraph 23 the words: "criminal jurisdiction over U.S. personnel is exercised by the sending state only. However", Mr. Chang replied that the Korean negotiators agreed to the proposed correction.

Claims

3. Taking up the Claims Article, Mr. Habib stated that he would like to make a few remarks related to the previous discussion of this article. The U.S. negotiators had shought to make clear that the U.S. Government is determined to continue to meet its recognized responsibilities to provide prompt and equitable settlement of any justified claims against the U.S. armed forces in Korea. The U.S. Armed Forces Claims Service, Korea, is currently fulfilling these responsibilities in an efficient and effective manner. The U.S. armed forces wish to continue this operation in order to fulfill the legal obligations of the U.S. Government in the settlement of claims. The U.S. Claims Service has operated in such a manner as to insure the continuance of the current friendly relations between the Korean people and the U.S. armed forces. The U.S. negotiators are convinced that this friendly relationship is, in part, a result of the fact that the Korean people know that legitimate claims against the U.S. armed forces will be speedily and fairly settled. At the previous meeting, the U.S. negotiators had promised to try to answer specific questions. Lt. Colonel

0026

Thompson would now answer the questions posed by the Korean negotiators.

4. Lt. Colonel Thompson stated that with reference to the first question asked by the Korean negotiators, concerning the operation of the claims system in Japan, it is the understanding of the U.S. negotiators that the U.S. armed forces and the Japanese authorities each conducts a separate claims investigation. When these investigations have been concluded, the Japanese claims agency and the U.S. claims agency reach agreement as to the liability and the amount of any award.

5. With reference to the Korean inquiry regarding the settlement of claims in Korea, Lt. Colonel Thompson stated that there are some dissatisfied claimants. However, objections are received only in 5 percent of the cases. Obviously, not all claims are justified nor can they all be settled by payment of the amount claimed. Claims are thoroughly re-examined upon the receipt of a complaint made by a claimant. This re-examination is made by the commissioner who originally acted on the claim. If the same commissioner is not available, the review will be made by another commissioner. He is authorized to change a prior determination upon the receipt of new and material evidence, or to correct manifest errors in calculation, or because of fraud or collusion. It is estimated that ten cases are re-examined each month. This includes cases re-examined for the first time and those being re-examined for the second and subsequent times. Detailed contents of all cases are not immediately available, as the files are sent to the United States within 60 days after settlement or 120 days after disapproval or receipt of the last letter from the claimant requesting review. It may be noted that the principal complaints of claimants are based

on findings of negligence on the part of the claimants to a degree which prevents payment of the claim.

6. In response to the third question posed by the Korean negotiators, Lt. Colonel Thompson stated that four members of the U.S. Claims Service are qualified attorneys and three of these serve as Claims Commissioners. There are no Claims Commissioners who are not attorneys. Furthermore, these four attorneys at present have a combined total of fifty-nine years of legal experience. In addition, the services of seven U.S. attorneys and one Korean attorney assigned to the office of the Staff Judge Advocate, Eighth United States Army, are available for general legal advice.

7. Regarding the number of claims made against the U.S. armed forces, Lt. Colonel Thompson tabled the following data showing the number of claims processed during 1963 and up to September 1, 1964:

	Claims Adjudicated	Claims Allowed	Claims Disallowed	Claims Paid	Amount Paid Won	Dollars
1963	839	680	159	649	19,264,162	148,185.8(
1964 (as of Sept.1)	911	589	322	576	25,865,548	101,433.5:

Lt. Colonel Thompson stated that statistical reports for the period from June 1, 1959, through 1962 have been sent to the United States and are not immediately available. The largest amount paid on a claim was Won 627,376 ($4,844.60), paid to Mr. Na In-duk, who had been assaulted and shot in the leg by two U.S. soldiers who were absent without leave from their units. Mr. Na's leg had to be amputated. The lowest payment had been Won 200 ($1.54), paid to Mr. Yi Chong-hwa for damage to his barley field by a U.S. tank. The files on both of these cases have been sent to the United States and details, therefore, are not available at this time. Lt. Colonel Thompson

0028

said that individual files can be made available for review by the Korean authorities, upon request. However, if the cases have been completed, it will take approximately 30 days to obtain the records from the United States.

8. Regarding the time it takes to process a claim, Lt. Colonel Thompson stated that this varies, based on the complexity of the investigation and the factual situation. He pointed out that there may be delays caused by difficulties in investigation or by the claimant's failure to provide promptly required documents. These variables make it impossible to fix an absolute time of processing. It may be fairly estimated, however, that normally a claim is settled and the claimant notified within sixty days after the claim has been received by the Claims Service.

9. Regarding the question of the standards adhered to by the Claims Service, Lt. Colonel Thompson stated that the allowable compensation normally represents the cost of repairing the property or the cost of restoring it to the condition it was in immediately prior to the damage. The claimant establishes these costs by presenting receipts for amounts expended to repair or estimates of the cost of repair submitted by reputable contractors or other qualified repairmen. Compensation for lost or completely destroyed property is computed at the actual value of the property at the time of the loss or destruction. The value of growing crops and trees is similarly computed. The compensation payable for personal injury and death, Lt. Colonel Thompson continued, is not as amenable to mathematical calculation as are the costs of property damage. To obtain as much consistency as possible, standard elements are utilized to form a sound basis on which to compute awards. In this regard, the Claims

0029

Service follows the disability grades and compensation tables set forth in the Korean Labor Standards Act and implementing Presidential Decree No. 889, used by the Republic of Korea Workman's Compensation Board. Such tables can be obtained readily from the appropriate ROK Government offices. The Claims Commissions are charged with the responsibility of evaluating each case in the light of standard elements to arrive at a fair settlement.

10. Mr. Chu replied that the Korean negotiators would study the statements made by Lt. Colonel Thompson and perhaps would ask further questions at a later meeting. Mr. Chu said that he wished to make a few remarks in addition to those which he had made at the previous meeting.

11. Mr. Chu recalled that the U.S. negotiators had asked what criteria the Korean Claims Service used for computation of claims payments. In reply, he had explained the Korean practices. It was true that there were no Korean legal provisions for settling claims. However, when the payment of claims against the U.S. armed forces was turned over to the Korean Claims Service, such claims would be handled effectively and without prejudice. He said that the highest amount paid by the Korean Claims Service in settlement of a claim was Won 450,000, in a traffic accident case resulting in death. More detailed data on cases handled by the Korean Claims Service would be provided as soon as compiled.

12. Mr. Chu said he would like to acquaint the U.S. negotiators with the personal backgrounds of members of the Korean Claims Settlement Commission. The Chairman was Mr. Kwon, the present Vice Minister of Justice, formerly a

0030

law professor for 7 years, a lawyer for 3 years, and a public prosecutor for 15 years. Mr. Lee, the Director of the Bureau of Legal Affairs, had been a law professor for 6 years and a prosecutor for 13 years. Member Yun had been a prosecutor for 19 years, as had member Lee, the present Director of the Bureau of Correction. Member Lim, head of the Appellate Court, had served for 15 years as a judge. Member Kim, currently Vice Chief of the Staff Judge Advocate's Section, ROK Army Headquarters, had served previously for 11 years as a Judge Advocate. Member Kim, a lawyer and formerly a Justice of the Supreme Court, had served as a lawyer for 20 years and a judge for 10 years. In view of the backgrounds of these people, who could doubt that claims would be handled by them in an equitable and just manner? Handling of claims against the U.S. armed forces by the Korean Claims Service would not compromise U.S. interests.

13. Mr. Chu stated that in case a claimant was dissatisfied, he could file an objection with a Korean court for decision of the matter through legal procedures. As the U.S. negotiators knew, there were three levels of courts in the ROK judicial system. Thus, a claimant could file his objection three separate times.

14. On the basis of the information which the Korean negotiators had provided concerning the Korean claims system, Mr. Chu asked the U.S. negotiators to reconsider their position. Mr. Habib asked if the Korean negotiators could provide any examples of cases which had been appealed to the courts. What had been the findings of the court? Mr. Chu replied that only one such case had occurred to date, and that adjudication in that case had not yet been completed.

0031

15. Mr. Habib recalled that Mr. Chu had stated that at present there were no fixed legal provisions for the payment of claims but that the Korean authorities intended to settle claims equitably. Mr. Habib pointed out that the lack of legal standards leaves open the possibility of settlement of individual claims on bases not related to any standards. He asked whether the Korean negotiators could furnish any data which would indicate the range of payments actually made for claims of the same type. Mr. Chu replied that these data would appear in the statistics which the Korean authorities were in the process of compiling.

16. Mr. Habib said he wished to ask a more fundamental question. To date, the Korean negotiators had not indicated why they wished to make a change from the claims system which is in operation. The U.S. negotiators had explained how the U.S. Claims Service operates. They had indicated that the U.S. armed forces are prepared to continue to operate this system, which imposes no financial burden whatsoever on the Korean authorities. Did the Korean negotiators find anything wrong in the operation of U.S. Claims Service? The only argument against its continuation which they had made to date was that this problem was handled differently in other countries. The U.S. negotiators did not believe that was a good argument. They believe it to be significant that in only 5 percent of the cases have claimants objected to the manner in which their claim has been handled by the U.S. Claims Service. The U.S. negotiators would be interested in knowing what the similar figure was with regard to claims handled by the Korean Claims Service. As the U.S. negotiators had previously pointed out, the U.S. armed forces were not trying to evade their responsibility with regard to the payment of claims. They and the U.S. negotiators preferred not to exchange a system which was working effectively and

0032

equitably and obviously to the satisfaction of the claimants for one which was only in its beginning stages.

17. Mr. Chu replied that the Korean negotiators were well aware that the two claims systems under discussion were similar. Mr. Habib pointed out that the U.S. negotiators had not expressed any such judgment and did not believe the two systems to be similar. Mr. Chu said this was the belief of the Korean negotiators. He added that the absence of objections, as indicated by the 5 percent figure cited by the U.S. negotiators, does not necessarily mean that all of the remaining 95 percent of the claimants were satisfied. They had to contend, after all, with such things as the language barrier and lack of knowledge of how the system worked.

18. Mr. Habib demurred. In the absence of objections, he said, one can only assume satisfaction. He pointed out that the U.S. Claims Service provides interpreters, explains fully the procedures to be followed, and gives whatever other assistance may be necessary to claimants.

19. Mr. Chu then stated that, as a matter of principle, what happens in a given country should be settled by the authorities of that country. Mr. Habib again demurred. He pointed out that the matters under discussion involved two countries and that how matters involving the two countries were settled was a question to be settled by agreement between the two governments. He reminded the Korean negotiators that the U.S. armed forces were in Korea under the terms of an international agreement.

20. Mr. Chu said the Korean negotiators understood the position stated by the U.S. negotiators and that the two sides were in the process of negotiating an agreement which

0033

would make an exception to the principle which he had just stated. The Korean negotiators believed there were no differences between the two systems but the Korean system contained more remedies for handling objections by dissatisfied claimants. The Korean Claims Service personnel understand their own people better than U.S. personnel and can more easily persuade claimants to accept the payments awarded.

21. Mr. Chang added that the Korean negotiators believed that by now the U.S. negotiators realized that the Korean Claims Service was an efficient, working system. However, the U.S. negotiators appeared still to have misgivings regarding the lack of legal standards. Claims were paid by the Korean Claims Service on the basis of practices developed over many years. Lack of legal standard on the part of the Korean Claims system does not necessarily mean that the awards were given without any standard. The U.S. negotiators had not indicated that the U.S. Claims Service had any legal standards either.

22. Mr. Habib pointed out that Lt. Colonel Thompson had covered this subject as the last point in the statement which he had made earlier in the meeting. Mr. Chang replied that the Korean authorities had standards but they were not standards which had been promulgated as law by the National Assembly. He asked what legally promulgated standards were followed by the U.S. Claims Service. He pointed out that the matters under discussion involved Korean nationals and that the Korean negotiators believed it to be ridiculous that Korean nationals should be dealt with under procedures that were not Korean. However, the Korean negotiators agreed that the interest of the foreign government involved must be recognized. How that interest could be expressed was open to negotiation.

0034

23. Mr. Habib remarked that the negotiators appeared to have exhausted the possibilities for discussion of this article at this time and suggested that further discussion be deferred until a later meeting, after each side had the opportunity for further study. Mr. Chang agreed.

Security Measures

24. Turning to the Security Measures Article, Mr. Chang stated that the Korean negotiators had studied the position expounded by the U.S. negotiators at the 62nd meeting. As a result, the Korean negotiators had reached the conclusion that the last phrase of the Article must read as in the Korean draft, "... for the punishment of ...", as the Korean negotiators had indicated at the 62nd meeting. With regard to the understanding proposed by the U.S. negotiators for the Agreed Joint Summary at the 55th meeting, the Korean negotiators believed the understanding is not necessary in the light of the content of the text and the representation made by the U.S. negotiators at the last meeting, as the U.S. negotiators had stated that they seek no special privileges with regard to the security measures for U.S. personnel and that they fully recognize that the Korean authorities would not fail to cooperate with the U.S. armed forces in taking necessary measures for security of the U.S. military personnel.

25. Mr. Chang stated that the Korean negotiators still found objectionable points in the proposed understanding. First, the phrase "... each will take such measures as may be necessary..." seems to involve some possible factor of misunderstanding that the United States authorities might institute unilateral measures without prior agreement with

0035

the Korean authorities. The Korean negotiators did not think that the United States negotiators intended the proposed understanding to bring about such an effect. If the interpretation of the Korean negotiators was correct and the U.S. negotiators were seeking prior agreement with the Korean authorities to effect mutual cooperation, the Korean negotiators believed that the provisions of the Article itself would be sufficient and that no such ambiguous understanding should be included as a confidential agreement in the Agreed Joint Summary.

26. Secondly, Mr. Chang continued, while the proposed understanding provides that each side may institute measures for "persons" as well as for the U.S. armed forces, it was noted that the second sentence of the text already provides that the ROK Government will take legislative measures regarding the U.S. armed forces, if necessary. With regard to "persons", the Korean position still stood, as the Korean negotiators had repeatedly explained it in the past. The ROK Government is prepared to take legislative measures for them only when it considers such measures necessary. Accordingly, inclusion of the phrase "such measures" in the understanding is not acceptable to the Korean side, if the term includes legislative measures for persons. Moreover, should any problem arise in the course of implementing the Article, the Korean negotiators believe that the Joint Committee could deal with it effectively. The Korean authorities will take such measures as they deem necessary and other, joint measures may be taken if such are necessary. As the Korean negotiators are convinced that the Korean authorities will ask the United States for its cooperation whenever such is deemed

0036

necessary and that the United States will respond favorably, the Korean negotiators believed that such mutual cooperation is sufficiently provided for in the text of the Article. Therefore, the Korean negotiators suggested that the U.S. negotiators, taking the Korean position into consideratioh, withdraw their proposal for a separate understanding.

27. Mr. Habib replied that the U.S. negotiators had attempted to make clear that what they were proposing was not discriminatory legislation for U.S. "persons" only, but legislation which would include Korean and U.S. persons alike. Mr. Chang stated that the Korean negotiators understood this. Mr. Habib then stated that the U.S. negotiators would study the Korean position, as just explained by Mr. Chang.

28. It was agreed that the two secretaries would meet and fix the date of the next meeting.

2. 제64차 회의, 10.16

0038

협 조 전 | 응신기일

분류기호 외구미 제목 행정협정에 관한 문의

수신 조약과장 발신일자 64.6.22. (협조제의)

미주둔군지위협정 노무조항에 관한 미국측 초안 Agreed Minutes 제2항에 관하여 아래 사항을 검토 회시하여 주시기 바람.

미주과장 (발신명의) 구 충 회

(제1의견)

1. 미측은 그간 양측의 비공식 회담을 통하여, 본조항을 제시한 이유는 외국에 있는 미국 국민들이 노무조항에 관하여 접수국의 법률과 관습 및 관례에 따르리는 하나 미국의 주권이 침해되는 것은 아니라는 것을 명백히 하기 위함이며, 혹 미국국회의원들의 질의가 있는 시 설명할수 있는 길을 마련하기 위한 것이라 함.

(제2의견)

2. 본조항은 타국이 체결한 행정협정에서 선례를 볼수없는 조항으로서 다음 사항에 대한 검토가 요청됨.

가. 한국노동법과 관습 및 관례준수와 국제법상의 Immunities 와의 관련성.

나. 본조항 삽입여부에 대한 귀의견. 끝

공통서식 1—23 (16절지)

277

0039

ARTICLE

1. The United States armed forces, the organizations provided for in Article ____ and the persons referred to in the first paragraph of Article ___ may employ civilian personnel under this Agreement. Such civilian personnel shall be nationals of the Republic of Korea.

does not preclude 64/5/18

2. The employers provided for in the paragraph 1 shall recruit employees to the maximum extent practicable with the assistance of the authorities of the Republic of Korea. In case employers exercise direct recruitment and employment of employees, employers shall provide such relevant information as may be required for labour administration to the Office of Labour Affairs of the Republic of Korea.

64/5/18

3rd Inf. la.

3. The obligations for the withholding and payment of income tax and social security contributions, and, unless otherwise agreed upon in this article, the conditions of employment and work, such as those relating to wages and supplementary payments, the conditions for the welfare and protection of workers, and the rights of workers concerning labour relations shall be those laid down by the legislation of the Republic of Korea.

ARTICLE

1. In this Article the expressio

(a) "employer" refers to the United States armed forces (including non-appropriated fund activities) and the persons referred to in the first paragraph of Article ____.

(b) "employee" refers to any civilian (other than a member of the civilian component) employed by an employer, except (1) a member of the Korean Service Corps, ~~who is an employ of the Government of Korea,~~ and (2) a domestic employed by an individual mem of the United States armed forces, civilian component or dependent thereof.

2. Employers will recruit employees to the maximum extent practicable with the assistance of the authorities of the Republic of Korea. In case employers exercise direct recruitment of employees, employers will provide such relevant information to the Office of Labor Affairs of the Republic of Korea.

3. The condition of employment, the compensation, and the labor-management practices shall be established by the United States armed forces for their employees in general conform with the labor laws, customs and practices of the Republic of Korea; ~~provided however, that an employer may terminate employment whenever the continuation of such employment would materially impair the accomplishment of~~

0040

~~the mission of the United States armed forces.~~

4\. (a) An employee shall have the same right to strike as an employee in a comparable position in the employment of the armed forces of the Republic of Korea. Such an employee may voluntarily organize and join a union or other employee group whose objectives are not inimical to the interests of the United States. Membership or nonmembership in such groups shall not be a cause for discharge or non-employment or suspension from work.

(b) Employers will maintain procedures designed to assure the just and timely resolution of employee grievances.

4\. Should the United States armed forces dismiss a worker and a decision of a court or a Labour Commission of the Republic of Korea to the effect that the contract of employment has not terminated become final, the following procedures shall apply:

(a) The United States armed forces shall be informed by the Government of the Republic of Korea of the decision of the court or Commission;

(b) Should the United States armed forces not desire to return the worker to duty, they shall so notify the Government of the Republic of Korea within ten days after being informed by the latter of the decision of the court or Commission, and may temporarily withhold the worker from duty;

(c) Upon such notification, the Government of the Republic of Korea and the United States armed forces shall consult together without delay with a view to finding a practical solution of the case;

(d) Should such a solution not be reached within a period of thirty days from the date of commencement of the consultations under (c) above, the worker will not be entitled to return to duty. In such case, the Government of the United States shall pay to the Government of the Republic of Korea an amount equal to the cost of employment of the worker for a period of time to be agreed between the two Governments through the Joint Committee.

5. (a) Should the Republic of Korea adopt measures allocating labor, the United States armed forces shall be accorded employment privileges no less favorable than those enjoyed by the armed forces of the Republic of Korea.

Agreement

(전시근로동원 배제)

(b) In the event of a national emergency, employees who have acquired vital skills essential to the mission of the indispensable United States armed forces shall be determined on an individual basis to be exempt from Republic of Korea military reserve training, (mobilization recall) service or other compulsory service. The United States armed forces shall furnish to the Republic of Korea lists of those employees deemed vital ~~essential~~.

All Italian civilian personnel ... are required to fulfill their military service obligation as determined by Italian law. However the appropriate Italian authority, when requested on an individual basis by the Allied Hqs, may exempt individual employees from reserve training, mobilization recall, from compulsory labor direction and civil defense duties.

5. The United States Government shall ensure that the contractors referred to in Article ____ employ the Korean personnel to the maximum extent practicable in connection with their activities under this Agreement. The provisions of paragraph 2 of this Article shall be applied to the employment by the contractors of the said Korean personnel.

6. Members of the civilian component shall not be subject to Korean laws or regulations with respect to their terms and conditions of employment.

Agreed Minutes

1. It is understood that the Government of the Republic of Korea shall be reimbursed for costs incurred under relevant contracts between appropriate authorities of the Korean Government and the United States armed forces or the

Agreed Minutes

1. The Republic of Korea will make available, at designated induction points, qualified personnel for Korean Service Corps units in numbers sufficient to meet the requirements of United States armed forces. The employment of a

X

27-4

0043

and the persons, respectively

organizations provided for in Articles ___ and in connection with the employment of workers to be provided for the United States armed forces or such organizations and persons.

2. It is understood that the term "the legislation of the Republic of Korea" mentioned in Paragraph 2, Article ___ includes decisions of the courts and the Labor Commissions of the Republic of Korea, subject to the provisions of Paragraph 3, Article ___.

~~3. It is understood that the provisions of Article ___, paragraph 3 shall only apply to discharges for security~~

3. It is understood that the Gov't of the ROK shall be reimbursed for direct costs incurred in providing assistance requested pursuant to paragraph 2.

3. With regard to any dispute between the employers except the contractors providef for in Paragraph 1 and employees or any recognized employee organization under the provisions of this Agreement, settlement shall be accomplished in the following manner:

a. The dispute shall be referred to the Office of Labour Affairs, Ministry of Health and Social Affairs, or the Labour Committee of the Republic of Korea.

b. In the event the dispute is not settled by the procedures described in (a) above, the dispute shall referred to the Joint Committee, or such sub-committee as may be established thereunder, for resolution.

As understanding in the Summary Record:
"With regard to the provisions in paragraph ___ of the Agreed Minute, 'any recognized employee organization' shall refer to any employee organization recognized by the authorities of the Republic of Korea."

domestic by an individual member of the United States armed forces, civilian component or dependent thereof shall be governed by applicable Korean laws and in addition by wage scales and control measures promulgated by the United States armed forces.

2. The undertaking of the United States Government to conform to Korean labor laws, customs, and practices, does not imply any waiver by the United States Government of its immunities under international law. moreover

With regard to any major dispute between employers and any recognized employee organization which cannot be settled through the use of existing procedures of the United States armed forces, settlement shall be accomplished in the following manner:

a. The dispute shall be referred to the Office of Labor Affairs, Ministry of Health and Social Affairs, Republic of Korea, for conciliation.

b. In the event that the dispute is not settled by the procedure described in (a) above, the matter may be referred to a Special Committee appointed by the Office of Labor Affairs, Ministry of Health and Social Affairs, Republic of Korea for mediation. This committee shall be tri-partite in composition and shall consist of equal representation from the recognized employee organization, the Office of Labor, and United States Forces Korea.

c. In the event that the dispute is not settled by the procedures described in (a) and (b) above the dispute shall be referred to the Joint Committee, or such sub-committee as may be established thereunder for resolution of the dispute. In resolving the dispute, the Joint Committee, or such sub-committee as may be established thereunder, shall give due consideration to the laws and regulations of the Republic of Korea.

d. During the period in which a dispute is being handled by procedures mentioned in paras (a), (b) and (c) above recognized employee organizations and employees shall not indulge in any practices disruptive of normal work requirements.

0044

e. Failure of any recognized employee organization or employee to abide by the decision of the Joint Committee or any sub-committee established thereunder on any dispute, or action in violation of para (d) above shall be considered just cause for the withdrawal of recognition of that organization and the discharge of the employee.

and the persons, respective

organizations provided for in Articles ____ and ____ in connection with the employment of workers to be provided for the United States armed forces or such organizations and persons.

2. It is understood that the term "the legislation of the Republic of Korea" mentioned in Paragraph 2, Article ____ includes decisions of the courts and the Labor Commissions of the Republic of Korea, subject to the provisions of Paragraph 3, Article ____.

~~3. It is understood that the provisions of Article ____, paragraph 3 shall only apply to discharges for security~~

3. It is understood that the Gov't of the ROK shall be reimbursed for direct costs incurred in providing assistance requested pursuant to paragraph 2.

the U.S. Gov't may terminate employment whenever the continuation of such employment would materially impair the accomplishment of the mission of the U.S. Armed Forces. ×46

×45

3. It is understood that the Gov't of the ROK shall be reimbursed for direct costs incurred in providing assistance requested pursuant to paragraph 2.

3. With regard to any dispute between the employers except the contractors providef for in Paragraph 1 and employees or any recognized employee organization under the provisions of this Agreement, settlement shall be accomplished in the following manner:

a. The dispute shall be referred to the Office of Labour Affairs, Ministry of Health and Social Affairs, or the Labour Committee of the Republic of Korea.

b. In the event the dispute is not settled by the procedures described in (a) above, the dispute shall referred to the Joint Committee, or such sub-committee as may be established thereunder, for resolution.

0045

As understanding in the Summary Record:

"With regard to the provisions in paragraph ___ of the Agreed Minute, 'any recognized ~~employee~~ organization' shall refer to any ~~employee~~ organization recognized by the authorities of the Republic of Korea."

64/5/18 3.0.0.

41-42

may 18 '64

ARTICLE

1. The United States armed forces, the organizations provided for in Article ___ and the persons referred to in the first paragraph of Article ___ may employ civilian personnel under this Agreement. Such civilian personnel shall be nationals of the Republic of Korea.

ARTICLE

1. In this Article the expressio

(a) "employer" refers to the United States armed forces (including non-appropriated fund activities) and the persons referred to in the first paragraph of Article ___.

(b) "employee" refers to any Korean national civilian (~~other than a member of the civilian component~~) employed by an employer, except (1) a member of the Korean Service Corps, ~~who is an employ of the Government of Korea,~~ and (2) a domestic employed by an individual mem

US 측 이 삭제

2. Local labour requirements of the United States armed forces and of the said organizations shall be ~~satisfied to the~~ maximum extent practicable, with the assistance of the Korean authorities. In case the United States military authorities exercise direct recruitment and employment of labors, they shall provide the Republic of Korea with the relevant information required for labor administration.

美側 提案 保留中

Presented by the ROK side at the 3rd informal meeting on may 18 '64

2. The employers provided for in the paragraph 1 ~~will~~ shall recruit employees to the maximum extent practicable with the assistance of the authorities of the Republic of Korea. In case employers exercise direct recruitment and employment of employees, employers ~~will~~ shall provide such relevant information as may be required for labour administration to the Office of Labour Affairs of the Republic of Korea.

0046

ARTICLE

1. In this Article the expressio

(a) "employer" refers to the

nited States armed forces (including

2. Local labour requirements of the United States armed forces and of the said organizations shall be satisfied with the assistance of the Korean authorities.

The obligations for the withholding and payment of income tax and social security contributions, and, unless otherwise agreed upon in this article, the conditions of employment and work, such as those relating to wages and supplementary payments, the conditions for the protection of workers, and the rights of workers concerning labour relations shall be those laid down by the legislation of the Republic of Korea.

recruitment, employment and management of employees directly.

3. The condition of employment, the compensation, and the labor-management practices shall be established by the United States armed forces for their employees in general conform with the labor laws, customs and practices of the Republic of Korea; provided however, that an employer may terminate employment whenever the continuation of such employment would materially impair the accomplishment of

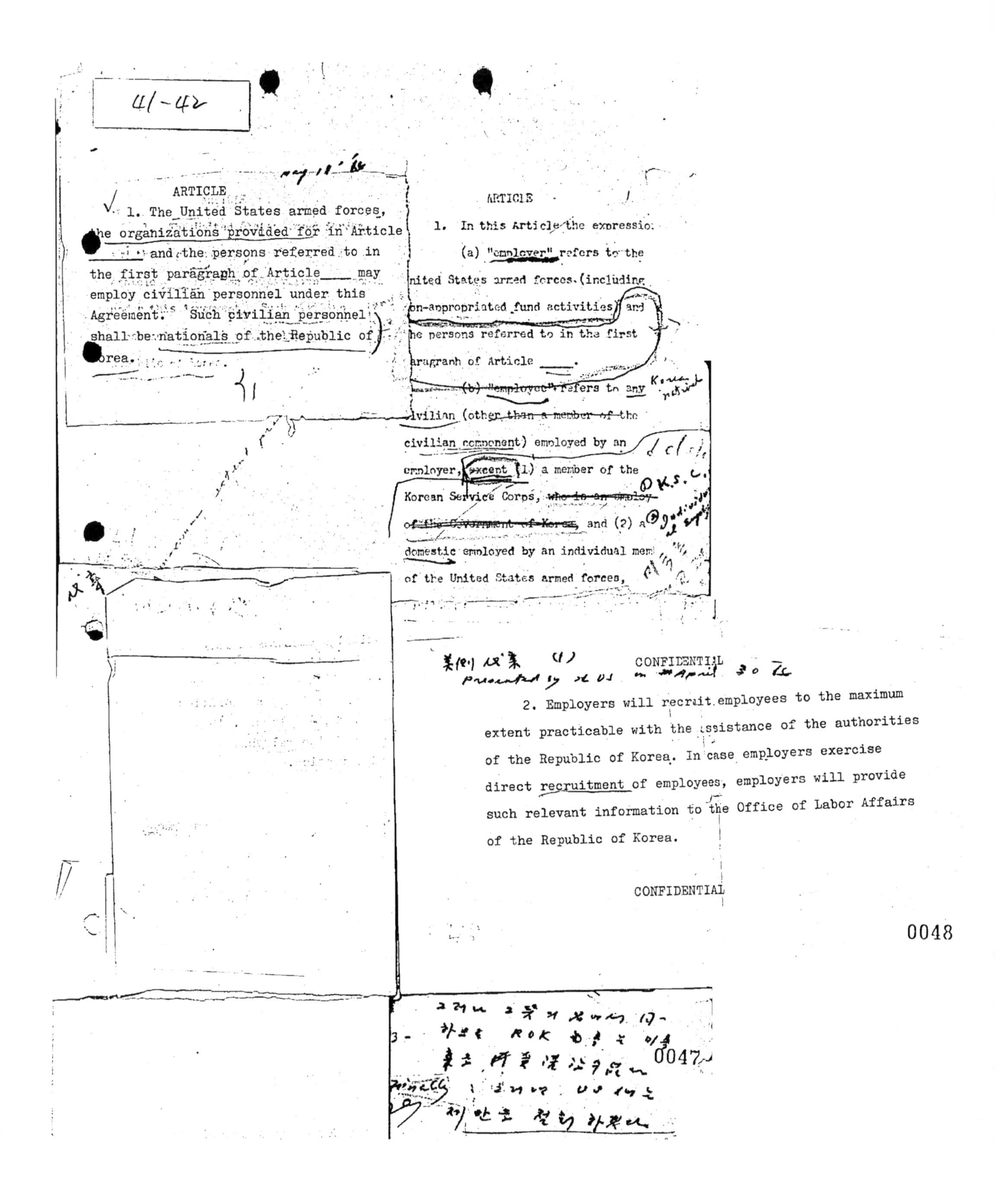

41-42

ARTICLE

1. The United States armed forces, the organizations provided for in Article ___ and the persons referred to in the first paragraph of Article ___ may employ civilian personnel under this Agreement. Such civilian personnel shall be nationals of the Republic of Korea.

ARTICLE

1. In this Article the expression

(a) "employer" refers to the United States armed forces (including non-appropriated fund activities) and the persons referred to in the first paragraph of Article ___.

(b) "employee" refers to any civilian (other than a member of the civilian component) employed by an employer, except (1) a member of the Korean Service Corps, who is an employ of the Government of Korea, and (2) a domestic employed by an individual member of the United States armed forces,

CONFIDENTIAL

2. Employers will recruit employees to the maximum extent practicable with the assistance of the authorities of the Republic of Korea. In case employers exercise direct recruitment of employees, employers will provide such relevant information to the Office of Labor Affairs of the Republic of Korea.

CONFIDENTIAL

0048

0047

the mission of the United States armed forces.

4. (a) An employee shall have the same right to strike as an employee in a comparable position in the employment of the armed forces of the Republic of Korea. Such an employee may voluntarily organize and join a union or other employ group whose objectives are not inimical to the interests of the United States. Membership or nonmembership in such groups shall not be a cause for discharge or non-employment.

(b) Employers will maintain procedures designed to assure the just and timely resolution of employee grievances.

5. Should the United States armed forces dismiss a worker and a decision of a court or a Labour Commission of the Republic of Korea to the effect that the contract of employment has not terminated become final, the following procedures shall apply:

(a) The United States armed forces shall be informed by the Government of the Republic of Korea of the decision of the court or Commission;

(b) Should the United States armed forces not desire to return the worker to duty, they shall so notify the Government of the Republic of Korea within ten days after being informed by the latter of the decision of the court or Commission, and may temporarily withhold the worker from duty;

(c) Upon such notification, the Government of the Republic of Korea and the United States armed forces shall consult together without delay with a view to finding a practical solution of the case;

(d) Should such a solution not be reached within a period of thirty days from the date of commencement of the consultations under (c) above, the worker will not be entitled to return to duty. In such case, the Government of the United States shall pay to the Government of the Republic of Korea an amount equal to the cost of employment of the worker for a period of time to be agreed between the two Governments through the Joint Committee.

OK

5. (a) Should the Republic of Korea adopt measures allocating labor, the United States armed forces shall be accorded employment privileges no less favorable than those enjoyed by the armed forces of the Republic of Korea.

(b) In the event of a national emergency, employees who have acquired skills essential to the mission of the United States armed forces shall be exempt from Republic of Korea military service or other compulsory service. The United States armed forces shall furnish to the Republic of Korea lists of those employees deemed essential.

5. The United States Government shall ensure that the contractors referred to in Article ____ employ the Korean personnel to the maximum extent practicable in connection with their activities under this Agreement. The provisions of paragraph 2 of this Article shall be applied to the employment by the contractors of the said Korean personnel.

6. Members of the civilian component shall not be subject to Korean laws or regulations with respect to their terms and conditions of employment.

Agreed Minutes

1. It is understood that the Government of the Republic of Korea shall be reimbursed for costs incurred under relevant contracts between appropriate authorities of the Korean Government and the United States armed forces or the

Agreed Minutes

1. The Republic of Korea will make available, at designated induction points, qualified personnel for Korean Service Corps units in numbers sufficient to meet the requirements of United States armed forces. The employment of a

0051

0052

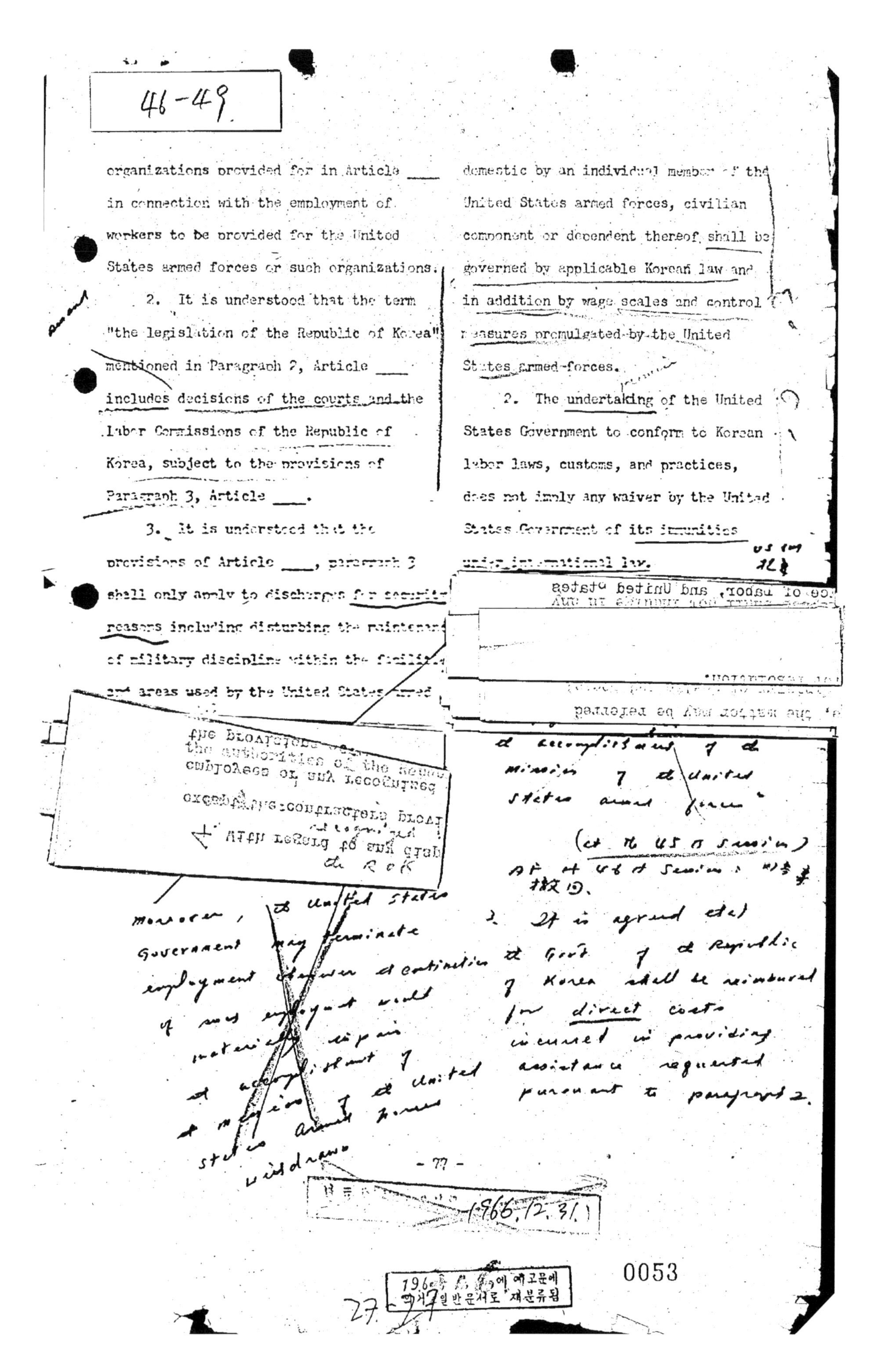

46-49

organizations provided for in Article ____ in connection with the employment of workers to be provided for the United States armed forces or such organizations.

2. It is understood that the term "the legislation of the Republic of Korea" mentioned in Paragraph 2, Article ____ includes decisions of the courts and the Labor Commissions of the Republic of Korea, subject to the provisions of Paragraph 3, Article ____.

3. It is understood that the provisions of Article ____, paragraph 3 shall only apply to discharges for security reasons including disturbing the maintenance of military discipline within the facilities and areas used by the United States armed

domestic by an individual member of the United States armed forces, civilian component or dependent thereof shall be governed by applicable Korean law and in addition by wage scales and control measures promulgated by the United States armed forces.

2. The undertaking of the United States Government to conform to Korean labor laws, customs, and practices, does not imply any waiver by the United States Government of its immunities under international law.

- 77 -

1966.12.31

0053

1966.12.31에 예고문에 의거 일반문서로 재분류됨

organizations provided for in Article ____ in connection with the employment of workers to be provided for the United States armed forces or such organizations.

2. It is understood that the term "the legislation of the Republic of Korea" mentioned in Paragraph 2, Article ____ includes decisions of the courts and the Labor Commissions of the Republic of Korea, subject to the provisions of Paragraph 3, Article ____.

3. It is understood that the provisions of Article ____, paragraph 3 shall only apply to discharges for security reasons including disturbing the maintenance of military discipline within the facilities and areas used by the United States armed forces.

domestic by an individual member of the United States armed forces, civilian component or dependent thereof shall be governed by applicable Korean law and in addition by wage scales and control measures promulgated by the United States armed forces.

2. The undertaking of the United States Government to conform to Korean labor laws, customs, and practices, does not imply any waiver by the United States Government of its immunities under international law.

US 側 ~~~

The U.S. revised proposal on May 20, '64

the ROK counter proposal at the 3rd informal meeting on May 18 '64

AGREED MINUTE

4. With regard to any dispute between the employers except the contractors provided for in Paragraph 1 and employees or any recognized employee organization under the provisions of this Agreement, settlement shall be accomplished in the following manner:

a. The dispute shall be referred to the Office of Labour Affairs, Ministry of Health and Social Affairs, or the Labour Committee of the Republic of Korea.

b. In the event the dispute is not settled by the procedures described in (a) above, the dispute shall be referred to the Joint Committee, ~~or such sub-committee~~ as may be established thereunder, for resolution.

As understanding in the Summary Record:

"With regard to the provisions in paragraph ____ of the Agreed Minute, 'any recognized employee organization' shall refer to any employee organization recognized by the authorities of the Republic of Korea."

US 案 : recognized by the US authorities and approved by the ROK

0054

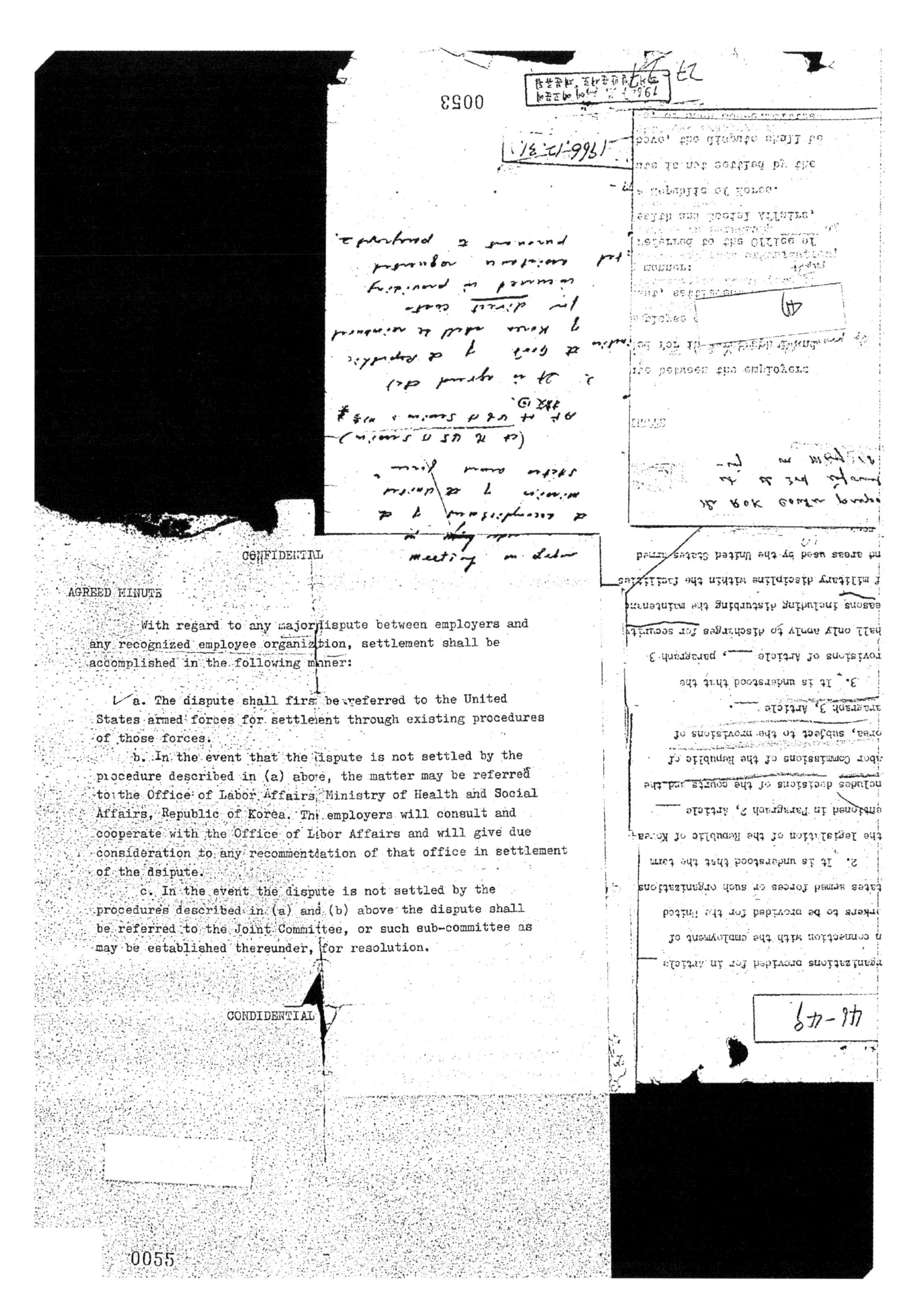

0053

CONFIDENTIAL

AGREED MINUTE

With regard to any major dispute between employers and any recognized employee organization, settlement shall be accomplished in the following manner:

a. The dispute shall first be referred to the United States armed forces for settlement through existing procedures of those forces.

b. In the event that the dispute is not settled by the procedure described in (a) above, the matter may be referred to the Office of Labor Affairs, Ministry of Health and Social Affairs, Republic of Korea. The employers will consult and cooperate with the Office of Labor Affairs and will give due consideration to any recommendation of that office in settlement of the dsipute.

c. In the event the dispute is not settled by the procedures described in (a) and (b) above the dispute shall be referred to the Joint Committee, or such sub-committee as may be established thereunder, for resolution.

CONDIDENTIAL

0055

46-49

organizations provided for in Article ___ in connection with the employment of workers to be provided for the United States armed forces or such organizations.

2. It is understood that the term "the legislation of the Republic of Korea" mentioned in Paragraph 2, Article ___ includes decisions of the courts and the Labor Commissions of the Republic of Korea, subject to the provisions of Paragraph 3, Article ___.

3. It is understood that the provisions of Article ___, paragraph 3 shall only apply to discharges for security reasons including disturbing the maintenance of military discipline within the facilities and areas used by the United States armed forces.

domestic by an individual member of the United States armed forces, civilian component or dependent thereof shall be governed by applicable Korean law and in addition by wage scales and control measures promulgated by the United States armed forces.

2. The undertaking of the United States Government to conform to Korean labor laws, customs, and practices, does not imply any waiver by the United States Government of its immunities under international law.

The U.S. revised proposal on May 20, '64

CONFIDENTIAL

Agreed Minute

With regard to any major dispute between employers and any recognized employee organization which cannot be settled through the use of existing procedures of the United States armed forces, settlement shall be accomplished in the following manner:

a. The dispute shall be referred to the Office of Labor Affairs, Ministry of Health and Social Affairs, Republic of Korea, for conciliation.

b. In the event that the dispute is not settled by the prodedure described in (a) above, the matter may be referred to a Special Committee appointed by the Office of Labor Affairs, Ministry of Health and Social Affairs, Republic of Korea for mediation. This committee shall be tri-partite in composition and shall consist of equal representation from the recognized employee organization, the Office of Labor, and United States Forces Korea.

c. In the event that the dispute is not settled by the procedures described in (a) and (b) above the dispute shall be referred to the Joint Committee, or such sub-committee as may be established thereunder for resolution of the dispute. In resolving the dispute, the Joint Committee, or such sub-committee as may be established thereunder, shall give due consideration to the laws and regulations of the Republic of Korea.

d. During the period in which a dispute is being handled by by procedures mentioned in paras (a), (b) and (c) above recognized employee organizations and employees shall not indulge in any practices disruptive of normal work requirements.

e. Failure of any recognized employee organization or employee to abide by the decision of the Joint Committee or any sub-committee established thereunder on any dispute, or action in violation of para(d) above shall be considered just cause for the withdrawal of of recognition of that organization and the discharge of the employee.

0056

ARTICLE ____

1. The United States armed forces, the organizations provided for in Article ____ and the persons referred to in the first paragraph of Article ____ may employ civilian personnel under this Agreement. Such civilian personnel shall be nationals of the Republic of Korea, ~~but does not preclude employment of citizens of the United States~~.

2. The employers provided for in the paragraph 1 shall recruit to the maximum extent practicable with the assistance of the authorities of the Republic of Korea. In case employers exercise direct recruitment and employment of workers, employers shall provide such relevant information as may be necessary for labour administration to the Office of Labour Affairs of the Republic of Korea.

3. Unless otherwise agreed upon in this article, The condition of employment and work, such as those relating to wages and supplementary payments, compensations, and the conditions for the protection and welfare of workers and the Rights of workers concerning labor Relations shall conform with those laid down by the legislation of the Republic of Korea.

~~Workers shall have the right to strike and to organize and join workers organizations including unions recognized by the authorities of the Republic of Korea and whose objects are not inimical to the mission of the United States armed forces. Membership in such unions or organizations shall in no way affect the worker.~~

~~4. (a) In case the service of a worker is no longer required, the employer shall provide the worker with a written notice of termination of employment, with the reasons specified. Such notice shall be provided to a worker with service up to two years thirty days prior to the actual date of termination and to a worker with service over two years sixty days prior to~~

2773

0057

to the actual date of termination. The employer shall pay such a worker one month's wages for each year of services.

(b) The worker is required to give the employer the notice of intent to resign seven days in advance of the intended date of resignation.

(c) The worker involuntarily terminated of employment have the right to appeal to the Joint Committee when he deems his termination unjustified. The Joint Committee shall determine within two weeks from the date of the appeal submitted in writing whether the termination was justified, and when found contarary, the worker shall be reinstated immediately.

tax and other deductions from the wages of the workers.

U.S. (b) In the event of a national emergency, workers who have acquired special skills essential to the mission of the United States armed forces shall be deferred on an individual basis from the Republic of Korea military reserve training, ~~mobilization recall~~ or other compulsory service. The United States armed forces shall furnish the Republic of Korea with lists of those workers deemed essential.

OK U.S. 5. Should the Republic of Korea adopt measures allocating labor, the United States armed forces shall be accorded employment privileges no less favorable than those enjoyed by the armed forces of the Republic of Korea.

OK U.S. 6. Members of the civilian component shall not be subject to Korean laws with respect to their terms and conditions of employment.

Agreed Minutes

OK U.S. 1. It is understood that the Government of the Republic of Korea shall be reimbursed for direct costs incurred in providing assistance pursuant to paragraph 2, Article _____.

2. Provisions of Article — shall not apply to citizens of the United States provided for in this Article —.

27-14

0058

~~2. It is understood that the service of a worker is no longer required is when he is not desirable in employment for security reasons including disturbing the maintenance of military discipline within the facilities and areas used by the United States armed forces.~~

2. With regard to any dispute between the employers except the contractors provided for in Paragraph 1, Article —, and workers or any recognized workers organization including labor unions under the provisions of this Agreement, which cannot be settled through the use of existing procedures of the U.S. armed forces, settlement shall be accomplished in the following manner:

(a) The dispute shall be referred to the Office of Labour Affairs, Ministry of Health and Social Affairs, Republic of KOREA, for conciliation.

(b) In the event that the dispute is not settled by the procedure described in (a) above, the matter may be referred to a Special Labor Committee appointed by the Office of Labor Affairs, Ministry of Health and Social Affairs, Republic of Korea, for mediation. This committee shall be tri-partite in composition and shall consist of equal representation from the recognized ~~employee~~ workers organizations including Labor Unions, the Office of Labor Affairs, and the United States ~~Forces Korea~~ armed forces.

(c) In the event that the dispute is not settled by the procedures described in (a) and (b) above the dispute shall be referred to the Joint Committee, or such sub-committee as may be established thereunder for arbitration to resolve the dispute. The decisions of the Joint Committee or sub-committee thereunder are binding.

0059

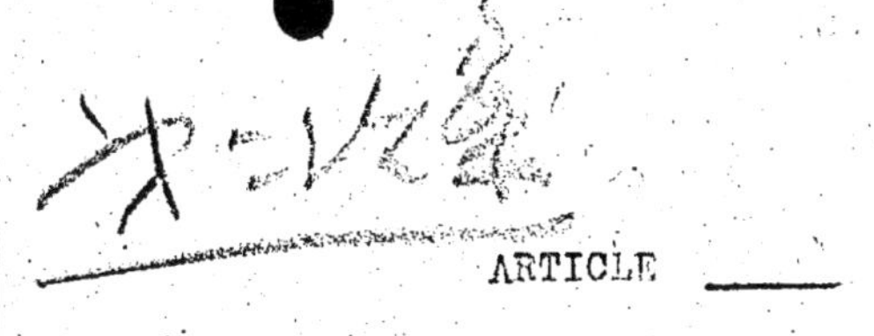

관리 번호 3091

ARTICLE ____

1. The United States armed forces, the organizations provided for in Article ____ and the persons referred to in the first paragraph of Article ____ may employ civilian personnel under this Agreement. Such civilian personnel shall be nationals of the Republic of Korea, ~~but does not preclude employment of citizens of the United States.~~

2. The employers provided for in the paragraph 1 shall recruit to the maximum extent practicable with the assistance of the authorities of the Republic of Korea. In case employers exercise direct recruitment and employment of workers, employers shall provide such relevant information as may be necessary for labour administration to the Office of Labour Affairs of the Republic of Korea.

3. Unless otherwise agreed upon in this Article, the conditions of employment and work, such as those relating to wages and supplementary payments, ~~and~~ the conditions for the protection and welfare of workers, compensations, and the rights of workers concerning labor relations shall conform with those laid down by the legislation of the Republic of Korea.

4. (a) The United States authorities shall withhold and pay over to the authorities of the Republic of Korea all income tax and other deductions from the wages of the workers.

(b) In the event of a national emergency, workers who have acquired special skills essential to the mission of the United States armed forces shall be deferred on an individual basis from the Republic of Korea military reserve training, mobilization recall or other compulsory service.

7/31 미측에게 수교

27-1

0060

The United States armed forces shall furnish the Republic of Korea with lists of those workers deemed essential.

5. Should the Republic of Korea adopt measures allocating labor, the United States armed forces shall be accorded employment privileges no less favorable than those enjoyed by the armed forces of the Republic of Korea.

6. Members of the civilian component shall not be subject to Korean laws with respect to their terms and conditions of employment.

Agreed Minutes

1. It is understood that the Government of the Republic of Korea shall be reimbursed for direct costs incurred in providing assistance pursuant to paragraph 2, Article ____.

2. Provisions of Article ____ shall not apply to citizens of the United States provided for in ~~this~~ Para. 1, Article ____.

3. With regard to any dispute between the employers except the ~~contractors provided for~~ persons referred to in Paragraph 1, Article ____, and workers or ~~any recognized workers organization including~~ labor unions under the provisions of this Agreement, which cannot be settled through the use of existing procedures of the U.S. armed forces, settlement shall be accomplished in the following manner:

(a) The dispute shall be referred to the Office of Labour Affairs, Ministry of Health and Social Affairs, Republic of Korea, for conciliation.

(b) In the event that the dispute is not settled by the procedure described in (a) above, the matter may be referred to a Special Labor Committee appointed by the Office of Labor Affairs, Ministry of Health and Social

7/31 미측에 수교

272

0061

Affairs, Republic of Korea, for mediation. This committee shall be tri-partite in composition and shall consist of equal representation from the recognized workers organization including labor unions, the Office of Labor Affairs, and the United States armed forces.

(c) In the event that the dispute is not settled by the procedures described in (a) and (b) above the dispute shall be referred to the Joint Committee, or such sub-committee as may be established thereunder for arbitration to resolve the dispute. The decisions of the Joint Committee or sub-committee threunder ~~are~~ shall be binding.

277

0062

ARTICLE ____

1. The United States armed forces, the organizations provided for in Article ____ and the persons referred to in the first paragraph of Article ____ may employ civilian personnel under this Agreement. Such civilian personnel shall be nationals of the Republic of Korea, (~~but does not preclude employment of citizens of the United States.~~)

2. The employers provided for in the paragraph 1 shall recruit to the maximum extent practicable with the assistance of the authorities of the Republic of Korea. In case employers exercise direct recruitment and employment of workers, employers shall provide such relevant information as may be necessary for labour administration to the Office of Labour Affairs of the Republic of Korea.

3. Unless otherwise agreed upon in this Article, the conditions of employment and work, such as those relating to wages and supplementary payments, ~~and~~ the conditions for the protection and welfare of workers, compensations, and the rights of workers concerning labor relations shall conform with those laid down by the legislation of the Republic of Korea.

4. (a) The United States authorities shall withhold and pay over to the authorities of the Republic of Korea all income tax and other deductions from the wages of the workers.

(b) In the event of a national emergency, workers who have acquired special skills essential to the mission of the United States armed forces shall be deferred on an individual basis from the Republic of Korea military reserve training, mobilization recall or other compulsory service.

27-4

0063

The United States armed forces shall furnish the Republic of Korea with lists of those workers deemed essential.

5. Should the Republic of Korea adopt measures allocating labor, the United States armed forces shall be accorded employment privileges no less favorable than those enjoyed by the armed forces of the Republic of Korea.

6. Members of the civilian component shall not be subject to Korean laws with respect to their terms and conditions of employment.

Agreed Minutes

1. It is understood that the Government of the Republic of Korea shall be reimbursed for direct costs incurred in providing assistance pursuant to paragraph 2, Article ____.

2. Provisions of Article ____ shall not apply to citizens of the United States provided for in Para. 1 ~~this~~ Article ____.

3. With regard to any dispute between the employers except the persons referred to in ~~contractors provided for~~ ~~the first Para~~ in Paragraph 1, Article ____, and workers or any recognized workers organization including labor unions under the provisions of this Agreement, which cannot be settled through the use of existing procedures of the U.S. armed forces, settlement shall be accomplished in the following manner:

(a) The dispute shall be referred to the Office of Labour Affairs, Ministry of Health and Social Affairs, Republic of Korea, for conciliation.

(b) In the event that the dispute is not settled by the procedure described in (a) above, the matter may be referred to a Special Labor Committee appointed by the Office of Labor Affairs, Ministry of Health and Social

미31 미측64수고

노동쟁의 조정법 10조

27-5

0064

Affairs, Republic of Korea, for mediation. This committee shall be tri-partite in composition and shall consist of equal representation from the recognized workers organization including labor Unions, the Office of Labor Affairs, and the United States armed forces.

(c) In the event that the dispute is not settled by the procedures described in (a) and (b) above the dispute shall be referred to the Joint Committee, or such sub-committee as may be established thereunder for arbitration to resolve the dispute. The decisions of the Joint Committee or sub-committee threunder ~~are~~ shall be binding.

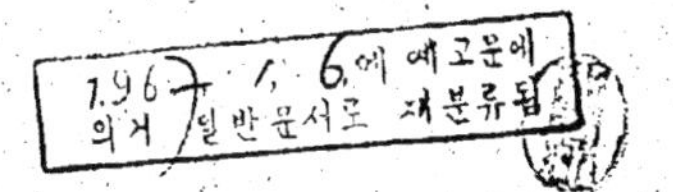

27-6

0065

1. The United States armed forces, the organizations provided for in Article ___ and the persons referred to in the first paragraph of Article ___ may employ civilian personnel under this Agreement. Such civilian personnel shall be nationals of the Republic of Korea, but does not preclude employment of citizens of the United States.

2716

0066

2. The employers provided for in the paragraph 1 shall recruit to the maximum extent practicable with the assistance of the authorities of the Republic of Korea. In case employers exercise direct recruitment and employment of workers employers shall provide such relevant information as may be necessary for labour administration to the Office of Labour Affairs of the Republic of Korea.

0067

2717

3. Unless otherwise agreed upon in this Article, the conditions of employment and work, such as those relating to wages and supplementary payments, the conditions for the protection and welfare of workers, compensations, and the rights of workers concerning labor relations shall conform with those laid down by the legislation of the Republic of Korea.

2718

0068

4. (a) The United States authorities shall withhold and pay over to the authorities of the Republic of Korea all income tax and other deductions from the wages of the workers.

(b) In the event of a national emergency, workers who have acquired special skills essential to the mission of the United States armed forces shall be deferred on an individual basis from the Republic of Korea ~~military reserve training,~~ mobilization recall or other compulsory service. The United States armed forces shall furnish the Republic of Korea with lists of those workers deemed essential.

2719

0069

5. Should the Republic of Korea adopt measures allocating labor, the United States armed forces shall be accorded employment privileges no less favorable than those enjoyed by the armed forces of the Republic of Korea.

0070

27-20

6. Members of the civilian component shall not be subject to Korean laws with respect to their terms and conditions of employment.

0071

Agreed Minutes

1. It is understood that the Government of the Republic of Korea shall be reimbursed for direct costs incurred in providing assistance pursuant to paragraph 2, Article ________.

27-22

0072

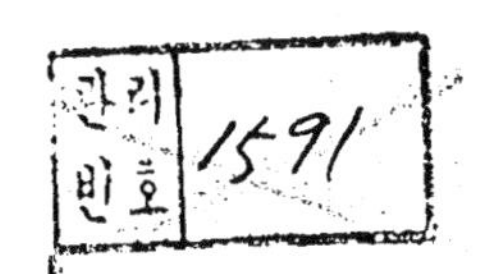

관리 번호 1591

기 안 용 지

자체 통제		기안처	미주과 이근팔	전화번호	근거서류접수일자

	과장	국장	차관	장관		
	1021	전결				

관계관 서명	
기안 년월일	1964. 10. 21.
시행 년월일	검열
보존 년한	
정서 기장	
분류 기호	외구미 722.2—
전체 통제	1964.10.22 종결
경유 수신 참조	대통령: 비서실장 국무총리: 비서실장 사본: 보건사회부장관(참조: 노동청장)
발신	장관
제목	제 64 차 주둔군지위협정 체결 교섭 실무자회의 결과보고

1964. 10. 16. 하오 4 시 부터 동 5 시 까지 외무부 제 1 회의실에서 개최된 제 64 차 주둔군지위협정 체결 교섭 실무자회의에서 토의된 내용을 별첨과 같이 보고합니다.

유 첨: 제 64 차 주둔군지위협정 체결 교섭 실무자회의 보고서

~~첨부물에서 분리하면 일반문서로 재분류~~ 603

1964.12.31에 예고문에 의거 일반문서로 재분류됨

승인서식 1—1—3 (11 00900—03) (195mm×265mm16절지)

0073

기 안 용 지

자체 통제		기안처	미주과 이근팔	전화번호	근거서류접수일자
	과장	국장	차관	장관	
	1021	전결			
관계관 서명					
기안 년월일	1964. 10. 21.	시행 년월일		보존 년한	정서 기장
분류 기호	외구미 722.2—	전체 통제		종결	
경유 수신 참조	보건사회부장관 노동청장	발신	장관		
제목	제 64 차 주둔군지위협정 체결 교섭 실무자회의 결과보고				

1964 년 10 월 16 일 개최된 제 64 차 주둔군지위협정 체결 교섭 실무자회의 결과 보고서 사본을 송부하오니 참고하시기 바랍니다.

유첨: 제 64 차 주둔군지위협정 체결 교섭 실무자회의 결과 보고서 사본 1 부. 끝.

1964.10.22
외무부

첨부물에서 분리되면 보통문서로 재분류

승인서식 1—1—3 (11 00900 03) (195mm×265mm16절지)

0074

외 무 부

외구미 722.2 1964.10.21.

수신 보건사회부장관

참조 노동청장

제목 제64차 주둔군지위협정 체결 교섭 실무자회의 결과보고

1964년 10월 16일 개최된 제64차 주둔군지위협정 체결 교섭 실무자회의 결과보고서 사본을 송부하오니 참고하시기 바랍니다.

유첨 - 제64차 주둔군지위협정 체결 교섭 실무자회의 결과보고서 1통. 끝

외 무 부 장 관 이 동 원

0075

외 무 부

외구미 722.2 1964. 10. 21.

수신 대통령, 국무총리
참조 비서실장
사본 보건사회부장관
제목 제64차 주둔군지위협정 체결 교섭 실무자회의 결과 보고

1964. 10. 16 하오 4시부터 동 5시까지 외무부 제1 회의실에서 개최된 제64차 주둔군지위협정 체결 교섭 실무자회의에서 토의된 내용을 별첨과 같이 보고합니다.

유첨 – 제64차 주둔군지위협정 체결 교섭 실무자회의 보고서 1통. 끝.

첨부물에서 분리되면 보통문서로 재분류

외무부장관 이 동 원

0076

제 64 차

한·미 간 주둔군지위협정 체결 교섭실무자회의

보 고 서

1. 일 시: 1964 년 10 월 16 일 하오 4 시 부터 동 5 시 까지.

2. 장 소: 외무부 제 1 회의실.

3. 토의사항:

노무 조달

(1) 미측은 우리측이 주장하여 온 입장을 검토한 바에 따라 다음과 같이 수정 사항을 제안하였다.

(가) 미군은 노무자의 모집 고용과 관리를 직접 할 수 있으며 필요하면 한국정부의 조력을 얻어 할 수 있다. 직접 고용의 경우는 필요한 관계 정보를 한국노동청에 제출할 것이다.

(나) 미군은 협정의 규정과 미군의 기본적 노무관리의 필요에 위배되지 않는 한도내에서 고용조건 보상 및 노무관리에 관하여 한국의 법률 및 관행에 따를 것이다.

(다) 미군당국은 한국의 소득세에 관한 법이 요구하는 세금을 노무자의 급료로 부터 공제하여 한국정부에 지불할 것 이다.

(라) 미군은 한국 법에 규정된 근로기준을 준수할 것 이지만 미국정부는 ~~주권국가인 고로~~ 외국의 법정의 (또는 노동위원회) 관할권에 복종 할 수는 없다.

(2) 우리측은 미국측이 수정안을 제시한데 대하여 사의를 표하고 동 제안에 대하여 우리측 입장을 다음과 같이 설명하였다.

(가) 미측이 제안한 노무자의 모집 고용 및 관리와 세금의 공제에 관한 수정안은 양측 실무자 간에 개최되된 비공식회의에서 토의된 사항을 토대로 한 것으로서 별다른 새로운 양보라고 할 수 없다.

(나) 우리측은 미군의 방위목적을 위한 필요에 대하여 가능한한 협조코저 하나 미군 노무자도 일반 노무자와 같이 한국의 노동법이 보장하는 모든 권리를 향유해야 하며 노사간의

0077

64-3-114

64-3-32 (2)

미국문 111-5 (2)

-1531

0078

분쟁이 원만히 해결되지 않을 경우 파업을 할 수 있어야 한다는 것이 우리측의 근본적인 태도이다.

(다) 우리는 미군을 한국법정의 재판권에 복하게 하려는 의도는 없다. 미국이 한국의 노동관계 법규에 규정된 근로기준을 준수할 용의가 있다면 간단 명료하게 미군은 노무관리에 관하여 한국법을 준수할 것이며 분쟁이 발생할 경우에는 노동청, 특별노동위원회, 합동위원회의 절차를 순차적으로 밟아 해결한다" 라고 하면 될 것 이다.

(3) 양측은 한.미간의 견해 차의를 검토하여 다음 회의에서 계속 토의 하기로 하였다.

4. 기타 사항:

차기 회의 일자: 1964 년 10 월 23 일 하오 4 시. 끝

보통문서로 재분류 (1966.12.31.)

1966,12.31에 예고문에 의거 일반문서로 재분류됨

0079

64-3-04

64-3-32

미국문 111-5(2)

0080

제 64 차

한 · 미간 주둔군지위협정 체결 교섭 실무자회의

보고서

1. 일시 1964 년 10 월 16 일 하오 4 시부터 동 5 시까지
2. 장소 외무부 제 1 회의실
3. 토의사항

노무조달

(1) 미측은 우리측이 주장하여 온 입장을 검토한 바에 따라 다음과 같이 수정사항을 제안하였다.

(가) 미군은 노무자의 모집 고용과 관리를 직접할수 있으며 필요하면 한국정부의 조력을 얻어 할수 있다. 직접 고용의 경우는 필요한 관계 정보를 한국노동청에 제출할 것이다.

(나) 미군은 협정의 규정과 미군의 기본적 노무관리의 필요에 위배되지 않는 한도내에서 고용조건 보상 및 노무관리에 관하여 한국의 법률 및 관항에 따를 것이다.

(다) 미군당국은 한국의 소득세에 관한 법이 요구하는 세금을 노무자의 급료로 부터 공제하여 한국정부에 지불할 것이다.

(라) 미군은 한국법에 규정된 근로기준을 준수할 것이지만 미국정부는 외국의 법정 또는 노동위원회의 관할권에 복종할수는 없다.

(2) 우리측은 미국측이 수정안을 제시한데 대하여 사의를 표하고 동제안에 대하여 우리측 입장을 다음과 같이 설명하였다.

(가) 미측이 제안한 노무자의 모집 고용 및 관리와 세금의 공제에 관한 수정안은 양측 실무자간에 개최된 비공식 회의에서 토의된 사항을 토대로 한 것으로서 별다른 새로운 양보라고 할수 없다.

0081

(나) 우리측은 미군의 방위목적을 위한 필요에 대하여 가능한한 협조조치 하나 미군노무자도 일반 노무자와 같이 한국의 노동법이 보장하는 모든 권리를 향유해야 하며 노사간의 분쟁이 원만히 해결되지 않을 경우 파업을 할수 있어야 한다는 것이 우리측의 근본적인 태도이다.

(다) 우리는 미군을 한국법정의 재판권에 복하게 하려는 의도는 없다. 미국이 한국의 노동관계 법규에 규정된 근로기준을 준수할 의의가 있다면 간단 명료하게 "미군은 노무관리에 관하여 한국법을 준수할 것이며 분쟁이 발생할 경우에는 노동청, 특별노동위원회, 합동위원회의 절차를 순차적으로 밟아 해결한다" 라고 하면 될것이다.

(3) 양측은 한•미간의 견해차이를 검토하여 다음 회의에서 계속 토의하기로 하였다.

4. 기타 사항

차기회의일자 1964년 10월 23일 하오 4시. 끝

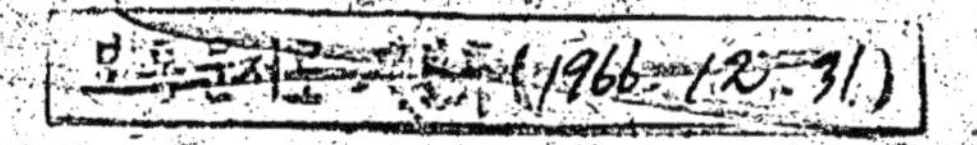

1966.12.31에 예고문에 의거 일반문서로 재분류됨

0082

CONFIDENTIAL

STATUS OF FORCES NEGOTIATIONS: 64th Meeting

SUBJECT: Labor

PLACE: Ministry of Foreign Affairs

DATE: October 16, 1964

PARTICIPANTS:

Republic of Korea

CHANG Sang-mun
KU Chung-hoe
Colonel KIM Won-kil, ROKA
HWANG YONG-chae
YI Kun-pal (Interpreter)
HU Sung John
KIM Dai Chung

United States

Philip C. Habib
Brig. General Carroll H. Dunn, USA
Colonel Howard Smigelow, USA
Captain John Wayne, USN
Benjamin A. Fleck ← Frank R. LaMacchia
Robert A. Kinney
Robert A. Lewis
Major Alton Harvey, USA
David Y.S. Lee (Interpreter)

Julio Hernandez, Observer

0083

1. Mr. Habib opened the discussion by recalling that the Labor Article had been discussed previously in formal negotiating sessions and in subsequent informal discussions, during which the respective positions of the two sides had been clarified. The U.S. negotiators had studied the views expressed by the Korean negotiators in the light of the situation in Korea and the requirements of the U.S. armed forces in the joint defense of the Republic of Korea. He said the U.S. negotiators would now table several proposed changes in the U.S. draft of this article which were designed to meet the needs of the Korean negotiators and to be consistent with the joint U.S.-ROK defense requirements.

2. Mr. Habib recalled that the U.S. negotiators had tabled a revised Paragraph 2 at the 45th meeting. This revised paragraph would provide for assistance by the ROK authorities in recruitment of USFK Korean employees. At that meeting a new Agreed Minute had also been tabled, which would provide that the ROK Government be reimbursed for direct costs incurred in providing the assistance requested pursuant to Paragraph 2. At the 46th meeting, the ROK negotiators had indicated their desire that the U.S. military authorities, when accomplishing direct recruitment and employment of personnel, should provide the ROK Government with relevant information required for labor administration. During subsequent discussion of this point in informal sessions, the ROK negotiators had indicated that the relevant information would be information required mainly for administrative and planning purposes, covering such details as the number of employees hired, the places of employment, and the job classifications. The U.S. negotiators wish to cooperate, Mr. Habib continued, with the ROK Government in meeting its requirements for ROK labor administration. Therefore, they wished to table at this time the following proposed revision of Paragraph 2, which includes an entirely new second sentence:

> "2. Employers may accomplish the recruitment, employment and management of employees directly, and upon request of the employer, with the assistance of the authorities of the Republic of Korea. In case employers accomplish

0084

direct recruitment of employees, employers will provide available relevant information as may be required for labor administration to the Office of Labor Affairs of the Republic of Korea."

3. With regard to Paragraph 3 of the Labor Article, Mr. Habib said the U.S. negotiators believe that USFK personnel standards parallel or exceed those of the ROK Labor Standards Act, a fact which they believe the ROK Office of Labor Affairs would be happy to confirm. The U.S armed forces will continue to conform to Korean labor standards and practices and to Korean labor laws as they are generally observed by Korean employers, subject to the basic management needs of the U.S. armed forces. In order to make this commitment more explicit, Mr. Habib continued, the U.S. negotiators were tabling at this time the following entirely new proposed Paragraph 3:

"3. To the extent not inconsistent with the provisions of this article or the basic management needs of the United States Armed Forces, the conditions of employment, compensation, and labor-management practices established by the United States Armed Forces for their employees will conform with the labor laws, customs, and practices of the Republic of Korea."

4. Mr. Habib recalled that the ROK negotiators had requested the U.S. negotiators to agree to the withholding of income taxes of Korean employees of the U.S. armed forces, in accordance with ROK law. The United States Government recognizes the general soundness of the principle of the employer withholding employee contributions for income taxes. Assuming the responsibility for withholding such contributions of the 33,000 Korean employees of the U.S. armed forces will be a major administrative burden. However, the U.S. armed forces desire to cooperate with the ROK Government in every possible way. Therefore, the U.S. negotiators wished to table the following new Agreed Minute:

"Employers will withhold from the pay of their employees, and pay over to the Government of the Republic of Korea, withholdings required by the legislation of the Repub-

0085

lic of Korea."

5. Mr. Chang replied that the Korean negotiators appreciated the action of the U.S. negotiators in tabling these proposed revisions. He recalled that both sides had met informally and exchanged views on these matters. The proposed new Paragraph 2 and the Agreed Minute tabled by the U.S. negotiators were apparently based on these exchanges of views but the Korean negotiators noted that there were some changes in wording. They would study the tabled revisions and comment at a later meeting.

6. With regard to Paragraph 3, Mr. Chang said the Korean negotiators felt no hesitation in accommodating U.S. needs for defense purposes to the extent practicable. The basic position of the Korean negotiators was that laborers employed by the U.S. armed forces should enjoy all the rights guaranteed by the relevant Korean labor laws for other Korean employees, ~~Korean employees working for other employers,~~ including the right to strike if disputes cannot be resolved satisfactorily. There appeared to be a continuing difference between the positions of the two sides. ~~The Korean negotiators would study the revision of Paragraph 3 tabled by the U.S. negotiators and comment at a later meeting.~~

7. Mr. Habib replied that the U.S. negotiators had made clear that the U.S. armed forces will conform to the ROK Labor Standards Act. They had pointed out that present USFK practice parallels or exceeds the basic standards set forth in that Act. At the same time, the U.S. negotiators have emphasized that the United States Government cannot submit to the jurisdiction of a foreign court ~~government~~ or labor tribunal. In previous discussions, the negotiators had explored possible procedures for settling labor disputes. Obviously, the U.S. armed forces would like to see disputes settled as amicably as possible. In formulating their position, the Korean negotiators should take into account two factors. First, the U.S. negotiators have made quite clear that the U.S. armed forces will conform to the basic standards of

0086

Korean law. Secondly, the U.S. Government cannot submit to jurisdiction of foreign courts or labor tribunals. The U.S. negotiators believed that their position on these two points is not inconsistent. They also believe that in practice, any problems will be taken care of, since both sides intend to work together in good faith.

8. Mr. Chang replied that the Korean negotiators fully understood the two basic points of the U.S. position, as described by Mr. Habib. They did not doubt that the U.S. armed forces would conform to the basic standards set forth in Korean law and they agreed that some aspects of the personnel procedures of the U.S. armed forces exceed those basic standards. Also, Mr. Chang continued, the ROK authorities have no intention of subjecting U.S. authorities to the jurisdiction of Korean courts in connection with labor disputes. Reaching agreement on this point would be much simpler if the U.S. negotiators would agree to a provision that the U.S. armed forces would conform to ROK laws with the understanding that disputes would be solved by the Joint Committee instead of being taken to court. In the informal discussions, the Korean negotiators had suggested that in case a dispute arises, it be referred to the Office of Labor Affairs, ROK Ministry of Health and Social Affairs. If not settled by the Office of Labor Affairs, it would then be referred to a Special Labor Committee. If the Labor Committee could not settle it, the dispute would then be referred to the Joint Committee, whose decision would be final and binding.

9. Mr. Habib replied that obviously, the U.S. armed forces stand ready to be advised and helped by the relevant ROK Ministries in the event of a dispute. Nothing in the U.S. draft of the Labor Article would prevent this. Nor does it prevent discussion of disputes by the Joint Committee. The U.S. draft does provide for conformance. If the ROK authorities were not satisfied that the U.S. armed forces are conforming, the presumption ~~is that they would~~ raise the matter in the Joint Committee or in a subcommittee.

0087

There was nothing in the U.S. draft which would prevent such discussion. The U.S. negotiators had indicated that the U.S. armed forces could not conform to those provisions of ROK law which would subject the U.S. Government to ROK courts or labor tribunals. The Korean negotiators had indicated their understanding that such subjection would not be in keeping with the normal relationship between sovereign governments. It appeared to the U.S. negotiators, therefore, that agreement had been reached on the provisions of the text of this paragraph and that what the negotiators were now discussing was how best to implement those provisions. All agreed that the Joint Committee was the implementing body. Therefore, it should be left to the Joint Committee to decide how to implement those provisions.

10. Mr. Chang replied that the U.S. negotiators had misunderstood the comments of the Korean negotiators if they believed that the latter had agreed to the language of the proposed revision of Paragraph 3. He said there still existed a wide gap between the positions of the two sides with regard to the solution of labor disputes which was directly related to the agreement on Paragraph 3. The Korean negotiators ~~still favored the detailed procedures which they had suggested for the settlement of disputes~~ felt that the words "the basic management needs" were ambiguous. However, they would study the drafts and comment at allater meeting.

11. The next meeting was scheduled for October 23 at 3:00 p.m.

0088

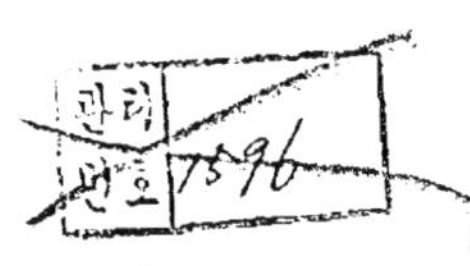

1/3

JOINT SUMMARY RECORD OF THE 64TH SESSION

1. Time and Place: 4:00 - 5:00 P.M. October 16, 1964 at the Foreign Ministry's Conference Room (No.1)

2. Attendants:

ROK Side:

Mr. Chang, Sang Moon	Director European and American Affairs Bureau
Mr. Hu, Sung John	Director Labor Administration Bureau Office of Labor Affairs
Mr. Koo, Choong Whay	Chief, America Section Ministry of Foreign Affairs
Mr. Kim, Dai Chung	Chief Labor Administration Section Office of Labor Affairs
Col. Kim, Won Kil	Chief Military Affairs Section Ministry of National Defense
Mr. Lee, Keun Pal (Rapporteur and Interpreter)	3rd Secretary Ministry of Foreign Affairs
Mr. Hwang, Young Jae	3rd Secretary Ministry of Foreign Affairs

U.S. Side:

Mr. Philip C. Habib	Counselor American Embassy
Brig. Gen. Carroll H. Dunn	Deputy Chief of Staff 8th U.S. Army
Col. Howard Smigelow	Deputy Chief of Staff 8th U.S. Army
Capt. John Wayne	Assistant Chief of Staff USN/K
Col. Kenneth C. Crawford	Staff Judge Advocate 8th U.S. Army
Mr. Frank R. LaMacchia	First Secretary American Embassy

0089

Mr. Benjamin A. Fleck (Rapporteur and Press Officer)	First Secretary American Embassy
Mr. Robert A. Kinney	J-5 8th U.S. Army
Mr. Robert A. Lewis	Second Secretary American Embassy
Maj. Alton H. Harvey	Staff Judge Advocate's Office 8th U.S. Army
Mr. David Y.S. Lee (Interpreter)	Second Secretary American Embassy
Mr. Julio Hernandez (Observer)	Labor Adviser 8th U.S. Army

1. Mr. Habib opened the discussion by recalling that the Labor Article had been discussed previously in formal negotiating sessions and in subsequent informal discussions, during which the respective positions of the two sides had been clarified. The U.S. negotiators had studied the views expressed by the Korean negotiators in the light of the situation in Korea and the requirements of the U.S. armed forces in the joint defense of the Republic of Korea. He said the U.S. negotiators would now table several proposed changes in the U.S. draft of this article which were designed to meet the needs of the Korean negotiators and to be consistent with the joint U.S.-ROK defense requirements.

2. Mr. Habib recalled that the U.S. negotiators had tabled a revised Paragraph 2 at the 45th meeting. This revised paragraph would provide for assistance by the ROK authorities in recruitment of USFK Korean employees. At that meeting a new Agreed Minute had also been tabled, which would provide that the ROK Government be reimbursed for

0090

direct costs incurred in providing the assistance requested pursuant to Paragraph 2. At the 46th meeting, the ROK negotiators had indicated their desire that the U.S. military authorities, when accomplishing direct recruitment and employment of personnel, should provide the ROK Government with relevant information required for labor administration. During subsequent discussion of this point in informal sessions, the ROK negotiators had indicated that the relevant information would be information required mainly for administrative and planning purposes, covering such details as the number of employees hired, the places of employment, and the job classifications. The U.S. negotiators wish to cooperate, Mr. Habib continued, with the ROK Government in meeting its requirements for ROK labor administration. Therefore, they wished to table at this time the following proposed revision of Paragraph 2, which includes an entirely new second sentence:

> "2. Employers may accomplish the receuitment, employment and management of employees directly, and upon request of the employer, with the assistance of the authorities of the Republic of Korea. In case employers accomplish direct recruitment of employees, employers will provide available relevant information as may be required for labor administration to the Office of Labor Affairs of the Republic of Korea."

3. With regard to Paragraph 3 of the Labor Article, Mr. Habib said the U.S. negotiators believe that USFK personnel standards parallel or exceed those of the ROK Labor Standards Act, a fact which they believe the ROK Office of Labor Affairs would be happy to confirm. The U.S. armed forces will continue to conform to Korean labor standards and practices and to Korean labor laws as they are generally observed by Korean employers, subject to the basic management needs of the U.S. armed forces. In

0091

order to make this commitment more explicit, Mr. Habib continued, the U.S. negotiators were tabling at this time the following entirely new proposed Paragraph 3:

> "3. To the extent not inconsistent with the provisions of this article or the basic management needs of the United States Armed Forces, the conditions of employment, compensation, and labor-management practices established by the United States Armed Forces for their employees will conform with the labor laws, customs, and practices of the Republic of Korea."

4. Mr. Habib recalled that the ROK negotiators had requested the U.S. negotiators to agree to the withholding of income taxes of Korean employees of the U.S. armed forces, in accordance with ROK law. The United States Government recognizes the general soundness of the principle of the employer withholding employee contributions for income taxes. Assuming the responsibility for withholding such contributions of the 33,000 Korean employees of the U.S. armed forces will be a major administrative burden. However, the U.S. armed forces desire to cooperate with the ROK Government in every possible way. Therefore, the U.S. negotiators wished to table the following new Agreed Minute:

> "Employers will withhold from the pay of their employees, and pay over to the Government of the Republic of Korea, withholdings required by the income tax legislation of the Republic of Korea."

5. Mr. Chang replied that the Korean negotiators appreciated the action of the U.S. negotiators in tabling these proposed revisions. He recalled that both sides had met informally and exchanged views on these matters. The proposed new Paragraph 2 and the Agreed Minute tabled by the U.S. negotiators were apparently based on these exchanges of views but the Korean negotiators noted that there were some changes in wording. They would study the tabled revisions and comment at a later meeting.

0092

6. With regard to Paragraph 3, Mr. Chang said the Korean negotiators felt no hesitation in accommodating U.S. needs for defense purposes to the extent practicable. The basic position of the Korean negotiators was that laborers employed by the U.S. armed forces should enjoy all the rights guaranteed by the relevant Korean labor laws for other Korean employees, including the right to strike if disputes cannot be resolved satisfactorily. There appeared to be a continuing difference between the positions of the two sides.

7. Mr. Habib replied that the U.S. negotiators had made clear that the U.S. armed forces will conform to the ROK Labor Standards Act. They had pointed out that present USFK practice parallels or exceeds the basic standards set forth in that Act. At the same time, the U.S. negotiators have emphasized that the United States Government cannot submit to the jurisdiction of a foreign court or labor tribunal. In previous discussions, the negotiators had explored possible procedures for settling labor disputes. Obviously, the U.S. armed forces would like to see disputes settled as amicably as possible. In formulating their position, the Korean negotiators should take into account two factors. First, the U.S. negotiators have made quite clear that the U.S. armed forces will conform to the basic standards of Korean law. Secondly, the U.S. Government cannot submit to jurisdiction of foreign courts or labor tribunals. The U.S. negotiators believed that their position on these two points is not inconsistent. They also believe that in practice, any problems will be taken care of, since both sides intend to work together in good faith.

0093

8. Mr. Chang replied that the Korean negotiators fully understood the two basic points of the U.S. position, as described by Mr. Habib. They did not doubt that the U.S. armed forces would conform to the basic standards set forth in Korean law and they agreed that some aspects of the personnel procedures of the U.S. armed forces exceed those basic standards. Aslo, Mr. Chang continued, the ROK authorities have no intention of subjecting U.S. authorities to the jurisdiction of Korean courts in connection with labor disputes. Reaching agreement on this point would be much simpler if the U.S. negotiators would agree to a provision that the U.S. armed forces would conform to ROK laws with the understanding that disputes would be solved by the Joint Committee instead of being taken to court. In the informal discussions, the Korean negotiators had suggested that in case a dispute arises, it be referred to the Office of Labor Affairs, ROK Ministry of Health and Social Affairs. If not settled by the Office of Labor Affairs, it would then be referred to a Special Labor Committee. If the Labor Committee could not settle it, the dispute would then be referred to the Joint Committee, whose decision would be final and binding.

9. Mr. Habib replied that obviously, the U.S. armed forces stand ready to be advised and helped by the relevant ROK Ministries in the event of a dispute. Nothing in the U.S. draft of the Labor Article would prevent this. Nor does it prevent discussion of disputes by the Joint Committee. The U.S. draft does provide for conformance. If the ROK authorities were not satisfied that the U.S.

0094

armed forces are conforming, the presumption is that they would raise the matter in the Joint Committee or in a subcommittee. There was nothing in the U.S. draft which would prevent such discussion. The U.S. negotiators had indicated that the U.S. armed forces could not conform to those provisions of ROK law which would subject the U.S. Government to ROK courts or labor tribunals. The Korean negotiators had indicated their understanding that such subjection would not be in keeping with the normal relationship between sovereign governments. It appeared to the U.S. negotiators, therefore, that agreement had been reached on the provisions of the text of this paragraph and that what the negotiators were now discussing was how best to implement those provisions. All agreed that the Joint Committee was the implementing body. Therefore, it should be left to the Joint Committee to decide how to implement those provisions.

10. Mr. Chang replied that the U.S. negotiators had misunderstood the comments of the Korean negotiators if they believed that the latter had agreed to the language of the proposed revision of Paragraph 3. He said there still existed a wide gap between the positions of the two sides with regard to the solution of labor disputes which was directly related to agreement on Paragraph 3. The Korean negotiators felt that the words "the basic management needs" were ambiguous. However, they would study the drafts and comment at a later meeting.

11. The next meeting was scheduled for October 23 at 3:00 p.m.

협 조 전	응 신 기 일

문서번호 외구미 722.2-821 제 목 주둔군지위협정 체결 교섭

수 신: 기획관리실장 발 신: 구미국장 년 월 일 1964. 9. 4. 제 1 의견

한.미 간 주둔군지위협정 체결 교섭에 임할 우리측 입장을 수립하기 위하여 참고코저 하오니 다음 사항에 관하여 법무부 및 총무처에 질의코저 하오니 이에 대한 귀견을 회보하여 주시기 바랍니다.

다 음

국방부 및 그 예하 각군에 근무하는 고용원(노무자)으로서 국가공무원법상 일반직공무원이 아닌 고용원이 신분에 관한 현행 관계법령 하에서 노동문제에 관련하여 쟁의행위를 포함한 집단적행위를 할 수 있는지 그 여부와 그 법적 근거. 끝.

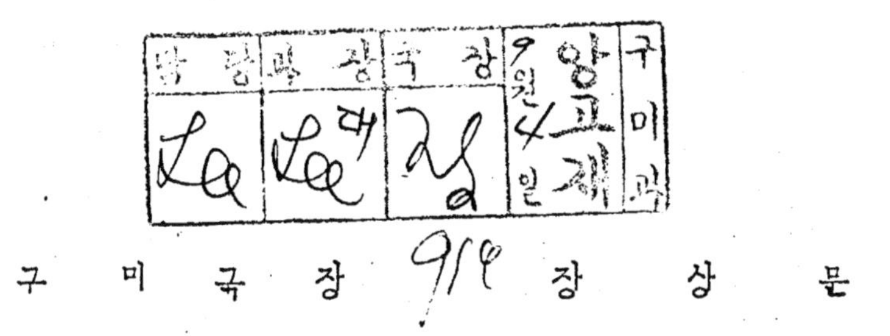

구 미 국 장 장 상 문

승인서식 1-34 (11-13330-01) (195mm×265mm16절지)

0096

협 조 전

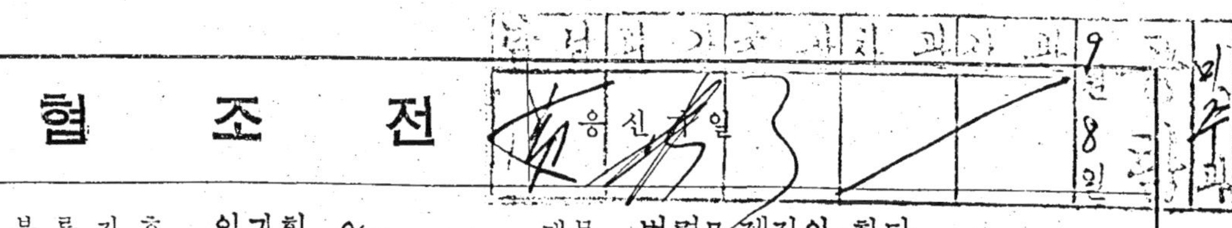

분류기호 외기획 84 제목 법령문제질의 회답

수신 구미국장 발신일자 1964. 9. 7 (협조제의)

대: 외구미 722.2 —821

대호 협조전으로 문의하신 건에 관하여 아래와 같이 회답해 드립니다.

(발신명의)

1. 별정직공무원의 범주에 속하는 단순한 노무에 종사하는 공무원(국가공무원법 제2조 제8호)은 국가공무원법 제3조의 규정에 의하여 동법 제7장, 복무에 관한 규정, 의 적용을 받으므로 동법 제66조와 공무원복무규정 제27조에 의거하여 동규정 별표에 지정한 노무공무원(교통부, 체신부, 전매청, 및 국립의료원 소속) 이외의 노무공무원은 노동쟁의에 참여할수 없음.
따라서 국방부 및 예하 각군에 근무하는 노무공무원은 노동쟁의에 참여할수 없다고 봄.

(제1의견)

2. 그러나 특별권력관계하에 있는 노무공무원은 물론 상기규정의 적용을 받는다 할지라도 사계약에 의하여 채용한 노무자에 대하여는 그 적용 여부가 의심되나 이들에 대하여는 상기 규정의 적용에서 제외된다고 보는것이 타당할것임.

(제2의견)

기획관리실장 문 철 순

공통서식 1—23 (16절지)

0097

3. 제65차 회의, 10.23

0098

Labor Procurement Article (15th Session, 64, 10.23)

1. The Korean negotiators, after carefully studying the revised proposals tabled by the U.S. negotiators at the 64th session regarding Labor Procurement Article, wish to comment on them:

2. Regarding the revised provisions of paragraph 2 of the U.S. draft, the Korean negotiators now wish to table their counter proposals. The Korean negotiators found no substantial difference between the paragraph of the U.S. draft and that of Korean draft. However, the Korean negotiators consider their draft prefeable because the Korean draft can fully meet the U.S. requirement to hire directly and also meet the concern of the Korean negotiators who wish to place the expression first of the employment with the assistance of the Korean authorities to the maximum extent "practicable". Therefore, the Korean negotiators request the U.S. negotiators to reconsider and accept it.

3. With respect to agreed minute tabled by the U.S. negotiators at the previous session regarding payment of the withholding of the income tax to the Korean government, although the wording differs from that of the Korean draft, the Korean negotiators are ready to accept the U.S. draft, subject to the rearrangement of the number of agreed minute.

12-5

which the Korean Negotiators consider to be the most important paragraph

4. With respect to the provisions of paragraph 3 of the U.S. draft, the U.S. negotiators have stated that the U.S. armed forces will conform with the Korean laws, customs, and practices to the extent not inconsistent with the provisions of this Article or the basic management needs of the United States armed forces. The Korean Negotiators felt that meaning of the phraseology "the basic management needs of the U.S. armed forces is ambiguous. ~~and could be the source of dispute over interpretation of this paragraph.~~ If the Korean negotiators would accept this wording, there would be the possibility that the U.S. armed forces could deprive employees of any rights, including right to strike. Therefore, the Korean negotiators are unable to accept the praceology.

The U.S. negotiators have reiterated their positions that first, the U.S. armed forces will conform to the basic standards of Korean law, and secondly, the U.S. government cannot submit to jurisdiction of foreign courts or labor tribunals. The Korean negotiators, have already made it very clear that the Korean negotiators also have no intention what-so-ever of subjecting the U.S. Government to the jurisdiction of Korean courts or labor tribunals. The Korean negotiators, therefore, made a counter provision to the U.S. Para. 3 in order to accommodate the concern of U.S. negotiators and now wish to table it, and the Korean negotiators also propose an agreed minute which provides that any labor dispute should be referred to the Joint Committee as the final authorities and its decision shall be binding. The Korean negotiators are convinced that the detailed procedures to solve the disputes as shown in the proposed agreed minute could fully meet the U.S. concern over the possibility of subjecting the U.S. government to the Korean Courts or labor tribunals.

0100

The Korean negotiators ask the U.S. side to study carefully and accept the proposal.

12-7

0101

Oct 23, 1964

Labor Article.

Paragraph 2

The employers provided for in the paragraph 1 shall recruit and employ to the maximum extent practicable with the assistance of the authorities of the Republic of Korea. In case employers exercise direct recruitment and employment of employees, employers shall provide such relevant information as may be necessary for labour administration to the Office of Labour Affairs of the Republic of Korea.

Paragraph 3

The conditions of employment and work, such as those relating to wages and supplementary payments, the conditions for the protection and welfare of employees, compensations, and the rights of employees, concerning labor relations shall, unless otherwise agreed upon in this Article, conform with those laid down by the legislation of the Republic of Korea.

0102

Oct 23, '96

I

Agreed Minute

With regard to any dispute between the employers except the persons referred to in Paragraph 1, Article _____, and employees or labor unions which cannot be settled through the use of existing procedures of the U.S. armed forces, settlement shall be accomplished in the following manner.

(a). The dispute shall be referred to the Office of Labor Affairs, Ministry of Health and Social Affairs, Republic of Korea, for conciliation.

(b) In the event that the dispute is not settled by the procedure described in (a) above, the matter may be referred to a Special Labor Committee appointed by the Office of Labor Affairs, Ministry of Health and Social Affairs, Republic of Korea, for mediation. This committee shall be tri-partite in composition and shall be consisted of equal representation from Labor Unions, the Office of Labor Affairs, and the United States armed forces.

(c) In the event that the dispute is not settled by the procedures described in (a) and (b) above, the dispute shall be referred to the Joint Committee, or such sub-committee as may be established thereunder for arbitration to resolve the dispute. The decisions of the Joint Committee or sub-committee thereunder shall be binding.

0103

ARTICLE____

Labor Procurement

1. In this Article the expression:

(a) "employer" refers to the United States armed forces (including nonappropriated fund activities) and the persons referred to in the first paragraph of Article________.

(b) "employee" refers to any civilian (other than a member of the civilian component) employed by an employer, except (1) a member of the Korean Service Corps, who is an employee of the Government of Korea, and (2) a domestic employed by an individual member of the United States armed forces, civilian component or dependent thereof.

2. Employers may accomplish the recruitment, employment and management of employees directly.

3. The condition of employment, the compensation, and the labor-management practices shall be established by the United States armed forces for their employees in general conformity with the labor laws, customs and practices of the Republic of Korea; provided however, that an employer may terminate employment whenever the continuation of such employment would materially impair the accomplishment of the mission of the United States armed forces.

4. (a) An employee shall have the same right to strike as an employee in a comparable position in the employment of the armed forces of the Republic of Korea. Such an employee may voluntarily organize and join a union or other employee group whose objectives are not inimical to the interests of the United States. Membership or nonmembership in such groups shall not be a cause for discharge or non-employment.

0104

(b) Employers will maintain procedures designed to assure the just and timely resolution of employee grievances.

5. (a) Should the Republic of Korea adopt measures allocating labor, the United States armed forces shall be accorded employment privileges no less favorable than those enjoyed by the armed forces of the Republic of Korea.

(b) In the event of a national emergency, employees who have acquired skills essential to the mission of the United States armed forces shall be exempt from Republic of Korea military service or other compulsory service. The United States armed forces shall furnish to the Republic of Korea lists of those employees deemed essential.

6. Members of the civilian component shall not be subject to Korean laws or regulations with respect to their terms and conditions of employment.

AGREED MINUTES

1. The Republic of Korea will make available, at designated induction points, qualified personnel for Korean Service Corps units in numbers sufficient to meet the requirements of United States armed forces. The employment of a domestic by an individual member of the United States armed forces, civilian component or dependent thereof shall be governed by applicable Korean law and in addition by wage scales and control measures promulgated by the United States armed forces.

2. The undertaking of the United States Government to conform to Korean labor laws, customs, and practices, does not imply any waiver by the United States Government of its immunities under international law.

0105

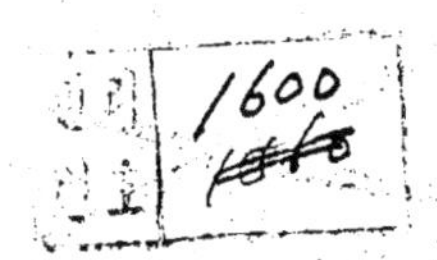

기 안 용 지

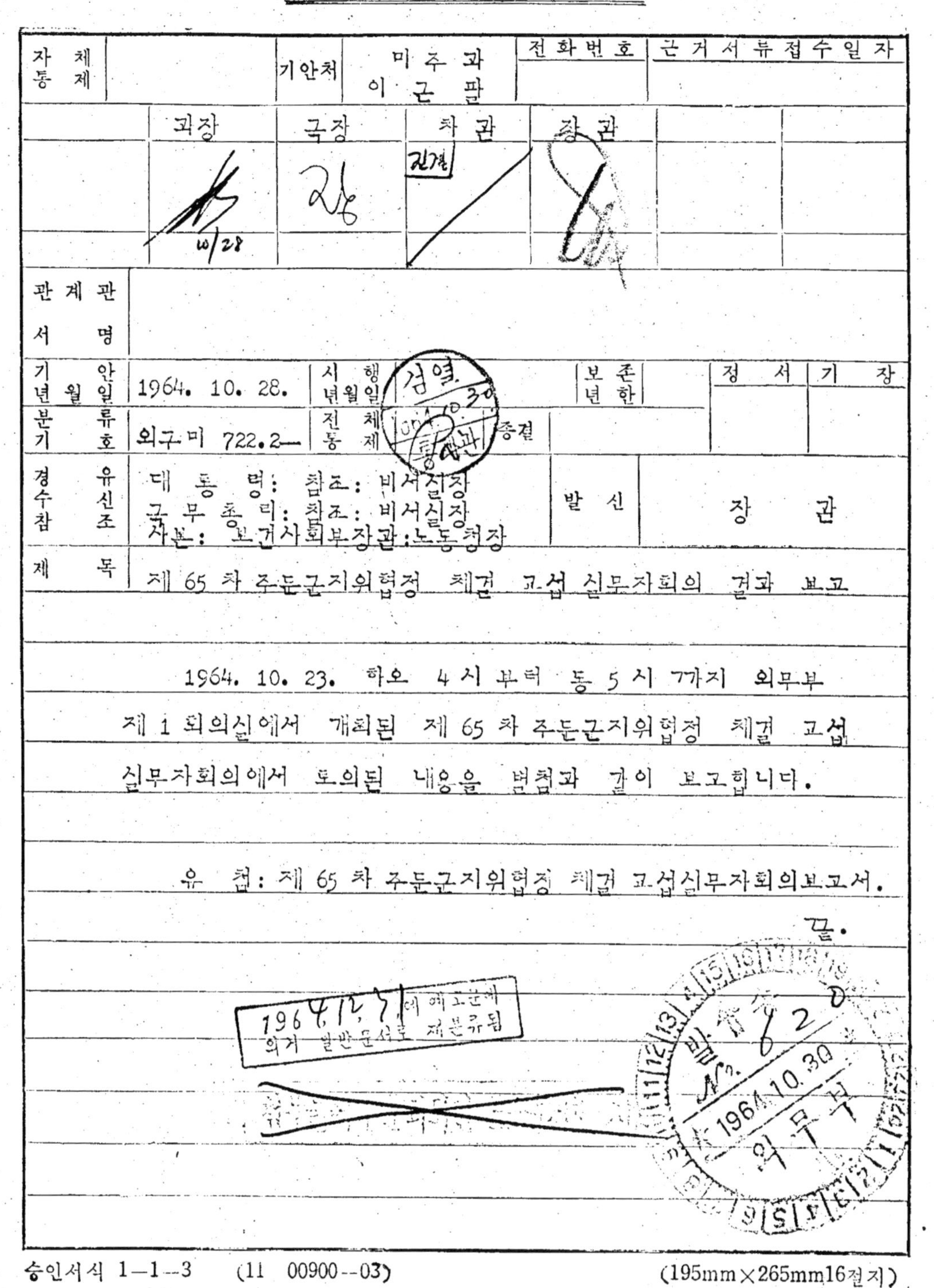

자체 통제		기안처	미주과 이근팔	전화번호	근거서류접수일자
	과장	국장	차관	장관	
관계관 서명					
기안 년월일	1964. 10. 28.	시행 년월일		보존 년한	정서 기장
분류 기호	외구미 722.2—	전체 통제		종결	
경수 유신 참조	대 통 령: 참조: 비서실장 국 무 총 리: 참조: 비서실장 사본: 보건사회부장관: 노동청장	발신	장 관		
제목	제 65 차 주둔군지위협정 체결 교섭 실무자회의 결과 보고				

1964. 10. 23. 하오 4 시 부터 동 5 시 까지 외무부 제 1 회의실에서 개최된 제 65 차 주둔군지위협정 체결 교섭 실무자회의에서 토의된 내용을 별첨과 같이 보고합니다.

유 첨: 제 65 차 주둔군지위협정 체결 교섭실무자회의보고서.

끝.

1964.12.31. 에 예고문에 의거 일반문서로 재분류됨

발송 No. 62 1964.10.30 외무부

승인서식 1-1-3 (11 00900-03) (195mm×265mm16절지)

0106

외 무 부

외구미 722.2　　　　　　　　　　　　　　　　　　　1964. 10. 30.

수신 대통령, 국무총리

참조 비서실장

사본 보건사회부장관

제목 제 65 차 주둔군지위협정 체결 교섭 실무자회의 결과 보고

1964. 10. 29, 하오 4시부터 동 5시까지 외무부 제 1 회의실에서 개최된 제 65 차 주둔군지위협정 체결 교섭 실무자회의에서 토의된 내용을 별첨과 같이 보고합니다.

유첨 - 제 65 차 주둔군지위협정 체결교섭 실무자회의 보고서. 끝

첨부물에서 분리되면 보통문서로 재분류

외 무 부 장 관　　이 동 원

0107

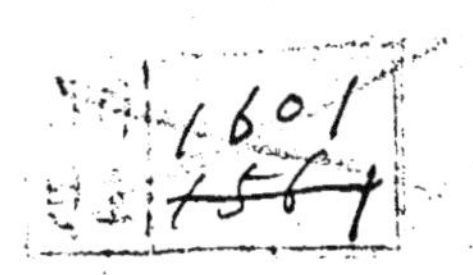

기 안 용 지

자체 통제		기안처	미주과 이근팔	전화번호	근거서류접수일자
	과장	국장	차관	장관	
관계관 서명					
기안 년월일	1964. 10. 28.	시행 년월일	검열 1964.10.30.	보존 년한	정서 기장
분류 기호	외구미 722.2—	전체 통제		종결	
경유 수신 참조	보건사회부장관 노동청장			발신	장관
제목	제 65 차 주둔군지위협정 체결 교섭실무자회의 결과 보고				

1964. 10. 23. 개최된 제 65 차 주둔군지위협정 체결 교섭 실무자회의 결과 보고서 사본을 송부하오니 참고하시기 바랍니다.

유 첨: 제 65 차 주둔군지위협정 체결 교섭 실무자회의 결과 보고서 사본 1부. 끝.

1964.12.31.에 예고문에 의거 일반문서로 재분류됨

발송 1964.10.30 외무부

승인서식 1-1-3 (11 00900-03) (195mm×265mm16절지)

0108

외 무 부

외구미 722.2 1964. 10. 30.

수신 보건사회부장관

참조 노동청장

제목 제65차 주둔군지위협정 체결 교섭 실무자회의 결과 보고

1964. 10. 23, 개최된 제65차 주둔군지위협정 체결 교섭 실무자회의 결과 보고서 사본을 송부하오니 참고하시기 바랍니다.

유첨 - 제65차 주둔군지위협정 체결 교섭 실무자회의 결과보고서 사본 1부. 끝

첨부물에서 분리되면 보통문서로 재분류

외 무 부 장 관 이 동 원

0109

제 65 차

한.미 간 주둔군지위협정 체결 고섭실무자회의

보 고 서

1. 일 시: 1964 년 10 월 23 일 하오 4 시 부터 동 5 시 까지.
2. 장 소: 외무부 제 1 회의실
3. 토의사항:

노무 조달

(1) 우리측은 미국측이 제 64 차 회의에서 수정 제안한 대안을 검토한 후 우리측 입장을 다음과 같이 제시하였다.

(가) 미군당국은 "가능한 최대한도로" 한국정부의 조력 하에 노무자를 모집 고용하여야 하며 미군이 노무자를 직접 고용할 경우에는 노동행정에 필요한 정보를 노동청에 제공하여야 한다.

(나) 한국의 세법이 요구하는 소득세액을 노무자의 임금에서 공제하여 한국관계당국에 지불할 것을 규정한 미측 제안은 이를 수락한다.

(다) 미군노무자의 임금 및 제수당에 관한 고용과 노동의 조건, 노무자의 보호와 후생조건, 보상, 및 노동관계에 있어서의 노무자의 권리등 근로조건은 특히 본 협정에서 별도로 합의되지 않는 한 한국법이 정하는 바에 따라야 한다.

(라) 우리측은 미국이 주권국가임으로 외국의 법정 또는 노동위원회의 관할권에 복할 수 없다는 미측 입장을 참작하여 미군관계 노사간의 분쟁을 다음과 같은 절차에 따라 해결할 것을 제의하였다.

(ㄱ) 분쟁은 제일차적으로 알선을 위하여 노동청에 회부된다.

(ㄴ) 알선절차에서 해결되지 않는 경우에는 노동청 미군당국 및 노무자측의 3 자대표로 구성된 특별노동위원회에 조정을 위하여 회부된다.

(ㄷ) 상기 절차에서도 분쟁이 해결되지 않을 경우에는 중재를 위하여 합동위원회에 회부되며 합동위원회의 결정은 구속력을 갖는다.

0110

64-3-10

64-3-33

미국·문 111-4(2)

0111

(2) 미측은 우리측 제안에 대하여 다음과 같이 논평하고 다음 기회에 미측 태도를 밝힐 것이라고 답변하였다.

(가) 미측은 필요할 경우 한국정부의 조력을 얻어 노무자를 고용할 것이지만 한국정부의 조력은 고도의 기술자의 모집 및 복직자의 우선 고용등 문제를 제외한 단순한 노무자의 고용의 경우에만 한정될 것 이다.

(나) 미군은 한국의 노동법에서 규정된 근로기준을 준수할 용의가 있으나 미군사명의 특수성에 비추어 미군의 기본적 노무관리의 필요성에 위배되지 않는 한도 내에서만 한국의 노동법을 준수할 수 있다.

(다) 한국측이 제안한 분쟁 해결 절차중 특별노동위원회의 조정은 미군을 노동위원회의 관할권에 복하게 하는 결과가 될 것임으로 노동청의 알선절차에서 해결되지 않을 경우에는 직접 합동위원회의 중재에 회부되기를 희망한다.

(3) 한.미 쌍방은 상기 문제점을 중심으로 입장을 재검토하여 다음 기회에 토의하기로 하였다.

4. 기타 사항: 차기 회의 일자: 1964 년 11 월 13 일 하오 3 시. 끝.

예고문서로 재분류(1966.12.31.)

1966.12.31. 에 예고문에 의거 일반문서로 재분류됨

0112

64-3-91

H-3-37(2)

미국:문 11-4(2)

0113

제 65 차

한·미간 주둔군지위협정 체결 교섭 실무자회의

보 고 서

1. 일시 1964년 10월 23일 하오 4시부터 동 5시까지

2. 장소 외무부 제1회의실

3. 토의사항

노무조항

(1) 우리측은 미국측이 제64차 회의에서 수정제안한 대안을 검토한후 우리측 입장을 다음과 같이 제시하였다.

(가) 미군당국은 "가능한 한 최대한도로 한국정부의 조력하에 노무자를 모집 고용하여야 하며 미군이 노무자를 직접 고용한 경우에는 노동행정에 필요한 정보를 노동청에 제공하여야 한다.

(나) 한국의 세법이 요구하는 소득세액을 노무자의 임금에서 공제하여 한국관계당국에 지불할것을 규정한 미측 제안은 이를 수락한다.

(다) 미군노무자의 임금 및 제수당에 관한 고용과 노동의 조건, 노무자의 보호와 수상조건, 보상, 및 노동관계에 있어서의 노무자의 권리등 근로조건은 특히 본협정에서 별도로 합의되지 않는 한 한국법이 정하는 바에 따라야 한다.

(라) 우리측은 미국이 주권국가임으로 외국의 법정 또는 노동위원회의 관할권에 복할수 없다는 미측 입장을 참작하여 미군관계 노사간의 분쟁을 다음과 같은 절차에 따라 해결할 것을 제의하였다.

(1) 분쟁은 제일차적으로 알선을 위하여 노동청에 회부된다.

(나) 알선절차에서 해결되지 않는 경우에는 노동청 미군당국 및 노무자측의 3자대표로 구성된 특별노동위원회에 조정을 위하여 회부된다.

(다) 상기 절차에서도 분쟁이 해결되지 않을 경우에는 중재를 위하여 합동위원회에 회부되며 합동위원회의 결정은 구속력을 갖는다.

(2) 미측은 우리측 제안에 대하여 다음과 같이 논평하고 다음 기회에 미측 태도를 밝힐 것이라고 답변하였다.

(가) 미측은 필요할 경우 한국정부의 조력을 얻어 노무자를 고용할 것이지만 한국정부의 조력은 고도의 기술자의 모집 및 복직자의 우선고용등 문제를 제외한 단순한 노무자의 고용의 경우에만 한정될 것이다.

(나) 미군은 한국의 노동법에서 규정된 근로기준은 준수할 용의가 있으나 미군사면의 특수성에 비추어 미군의 기본적 노무관리의 필요성에 위배되지 않는 한도내에서만 한국의 노동법을 준수할 수 있다.

(다) 한국측이 제안한 분쟁해결 절차중 특별노동위원회의 조정은 미군을 노동위원회의 관할권에 복하게 하는 결과가 될것임으로 노동청의 알선절차에서 해결되지 않을 경우에는 직접 합동위원회의 중재에 회부되기를 희망한다.

(3) 한·미 쌍방은 상기 문제점을 중심으로 입장을 재검토하여 다음 기회에 토의하기로 하였다.

4. 기타사항

차기회의일자 1964 년 11 월 19 일,하오 3 시 . 끝

0115

CONFIDENTIAL

STATUS OF FORCES NEGOTIATIONS: 65th Meeting

SUBJECT: Labor

PLACE: Ministry of Foreign Affairs

DATE: October 23, 1964

PARTICIPANTS:

Republic of Korea	United States
CHANG Sang-mun	Philip C. Habib
KU Chung-hoe	Brig. General Carroll H. Dunn, USA
~~Colonel KIM Won-kil, ROKA~~	Colonel Howard Smigelow, USA
Hu Sung-john	Captain John Wayne, USN
KIM Dai-chung	Colonel Kenneth C. Crawford, USA
O Chae-hi	Frank R. LaMacchia
HWANG Yong-chae	Benjamin A. Fleck
YI Kun-pal (Interpreter)	Robert A. Kinney
PARK Won-chul	Major Alton Harvey, USA
Major Lee Kae-hoon	David Y.S. Lee (Interpreter)
	O. C. Reed, Observer

0116

1. Mr. Chang opened the meeting by stating that the Korean negotiators had studied the revisions of the U.S. draft of the Labor Article which the U.S. negotiators had proposed at the previous meeting.

2. Regarding Paragraph 2, although the Korean negotiators believed there was no great substantive difference, they did wish to include language providing for recruitment with the assistance of ROK authorities "to the maximum extent practicable". Therefore, they wished to table at this time the following proposed Paragraph 2:

> "2. The employers provided for in paragraph 1 shall recruit and employ to the maximum extent practicable with the assistance of the authorities of the Republic of Korea. In case employers exercise direct recruitment and employment of employees, employers shall provide such relevant information as may be necessary for labor administration to the Office of Labor Affairs of the Republic of Korea."

Mr. Chang stated that the Korean draft could fully meet the U.S. requirement to hire employees directly.

3. Mr. Chang stated that the question of adding an Agreed Minute regarding the withholding of income tax payments had been discussed previously. Although its language the Agreed Minute tabled by the U.S. negotiators at the 64th meeting differed from the language originally proposed by the Korean negotiators, they found no substantial difference. Therefore, they accepted ~~agreed to the U.S. proposal~~.

4. Mr. Chang remarked that the most important paragraph to be discussed at this meeting was Paragraph 3. The revised draft tabled by the U.S. negotiators states that the United States armed forces will conform with the labor laws, customs, and practices of the Republic of Korea "to the extent not inconsistent with the provisions of this article or the basic management needs of the United States Armed Forces". The Korean negotiators found the term "basic management needs of the United States Armed Forces" to be ambiguous. They feared that the use of this phraseology could be the source of disputes over interpretation of this paragraph. Mr. Chang remarked that when the U.S. negotiators had tabled this revised draft, they had said that the U.S. armed forces will conform with the

basic standards of Korean law and that the United States Government cannot submit to the jurisdiction of foreign courts or labor tribunals. The Korean negotiators, Mr. Chang continued, had made it clear that the ROK authorities had no intention of trying to force agencies of the U.S. Government to submit to Korean courts or labor tribunals. In order to provide for other means of settling labor disputes, the Korean negotiators wished to table the following proposed revision of Paragraph 3 and a related Agreed Minute:

> "3. The conditions of employment and work, such as those relating to wages and supplementary payments, the conditions for the protection and welfare of employees, compensations, and the rights of employees, concerning labor relations shall, unless otherwise agreed upon in this Article, conform with those laid down by the legislation of the Republic of Korea."
>
> "Agreed Minute
>
> "With regard to any dispute between the employers except the persons referred to in Paragraph 1, Article ___, and employees or labor unions which cannot be settled through the use of existing procedures of the U.S. armed forces, settlement shall be accomplished in the following manner.
>
> "(a). The dispute shall be referred to the Office of Labor Affairs, Ministry of Health and Social Affairs, Republic of Korea, for conciliation.
>
> "(b). In the event that the dispute is not settled by the procedure described in (a) above, the matter may be referred to a Special Labor Committee appointed by the Office of Labor Affairs, Ministry of Health and Social Affairs, Republic of Korea, for mediation. This committee shall be tri-partite in composition and shall be consisted of equal representation from Labor Unions, the Office of Labor Affairs, and the United States armed forces.
>
> "(c). In the event that the dispute is not settled by the procedures described in (a) and (b) above, the dispute shall be referred to the Joint Committee, or such sub-committee as may be established thereunder for arbitration to resolve the dispute. The decisions of the Joint Committee or sub-committee thereunder shall be binding.

The Korean negotiators, Mr. Chang continued, were convinced that the detailed procedures which were designed to resolve disputes outside of the jurisdiction of Korean courts or labor tribunal, could fully meet the U.S. concern over the possibility of subjecting the U.S. Government to Korean courts or labor tribunals.

0118

6. Mr. Habib stated that the U.S. negotiators would give the Korean proposals careful study. At this time, he wished to make some preliminary remarks concerning them. With regard to Paragraph 2, the U.S. negotiators had tabled a draft which was intended to indicate that in recruiting personnel, the U.S. armed forces are prepared to use the ROK Labor Offices whenever practicable. This use would be dependent on the ability of the Labor Offices to provide labor of the type needed by the U.S. armed forces. The Korean negotiators had previously indicated that the ROK Labor Offices are now prepared to recruit only unskilled and semi-skilled labor. At present, the requirement of the U.S. armed forces is for skilled labor and specially-trained technical personnel. Use of the Labor Offices would also be limited by the fact that there is a low attrition rate among employees of the U.S. armed forces and the fact that there is a large group of former employees who have reemployment rights and whose reemployment would be effected outside of the procedure of using the Labor Offices. The U.S. draft provides that when the armed forces need the assistance of the ROK authorities in hiring personnel, they will ask for such assistance and it will be provided. The U.S. draft quite clearly provides for direct hire while the language proposed by the Korean negotiators, "to the maximum extent practicable", authorizes direct hire only by implication. A clear statement of the procedures to be followed would be greatly preferable to a statement granting authority to the U.S. armed forces only by implication.

7. In addition, Mr. Habib continued, the language proposed by the Korean negotiators omits any statement of the right of the employer to manage his employees. The U.S. proposal contains such a statement. The U.S. negotiators considered this an important point because a literal reading of the Korean draft could lead to the interpretation that the U.S. armed forces would manage their employees with the assistance of ROK authorities.

8. Mr. Habib said that he hoped that the Korean negotiators were not

under any misapprehension that the U.S. armed forces in Korea were just an ordinary employer.

9. Turning to Paragraph 3, Mr. Habib said that the revised draft proposed by the U.S. negotiators made it clear that the U.S. armed forces in Korea were prepared to conform not only with Korean labor laws but also with customs and practices. The Korean negotiators had objected to the phrase "basic management needs of the U.S. armed forces". The U.S. negotiators wished to point out that the needs of the U.S. armed forces in connection with the accomplishment of their mission could involve management decisions which are unforeseeable. The U.S. negotiators had thought that the primary need of the Korean negotiators was the inclusion in this article of an explicit statement of the willingness of the U.S. armed forces to conform with Korean labor laws and practices. They had not thought that the Korean negotiators wished to place a straightjacket on the U.S. armed forces, which have a unique function and unique needs. The U.S. negotiators saw no ambiguity in the phrase "basic management needs", which was directly related to the question of conformity. If the U.S. armed forces were committed to conformity with Korean laws and practices, as proposed in the U.S. draft, any question regarding the fulfillment of that commitment would be the subject of discussion and amicable settlement in the Joint Committee. The U.S. negotiators believed the language proposed by the Korean negotiators would establish a requirement which was too rigid for a subject which is much more complicated in practice than the Korean draft would indicate. The U.S. draft is explicit enough to meet the needs of the Korean authorities and would leave implementation to the Joint Committee.

10. Taking up the Agreed Minute tabled by the Korean negotiators, Mr. Habib said that although the U.S. negotiators believed that spelling out (in the SOFA) procedures for the settlement of labor disputes was unnecessary, they did not

0120

disagree in principle. In order to assist them in their study of the Korean proposal, Mr. Habib continued, he wished to ask a few preliminary questions.

11. With regard to labor disputes, Mr. Habib pointed out that the U.S. armed forces now informally receive advice and assistance from the ROK Office of Labor Affairs. Subparagraph (a) of the Korean draft, therefore, appeared to be consistent with current practice. However, the U.S. negotiators felt misgivings about subparagraph (b) because, by introducing mediation procedures, it appeared to border on a requirement that the U.S. armed forces be brought before a Korean tribunal. As the Korean negotiators were aware, the U.S. negotiators could not agree to any such requirement. The proposal contained in subparagraph (b) would place the employer at a disadvantage. The U.S. negotiators would give their considered views regarding this Agreed Minute at a later meeting. Their preliminary reaction was that if inclusion of detailed procedures for settlement of disputes were ultimately agreed to, it would be preferable to omit any reference to mediation procedures by providing that an unsettled dispute be taken directly from unsuccessful conciliation efforts by the Office of Labor Affairs to consideration by the Joint Committee. The negotiators might profitably seek to draft a simpler statement of procedures which would lead to the submission of an unsettled dispute to the Joint Committee.

12. Mr. Chang replied that the Agreed Minute tabled by the Korean negotiators had been based on the procedures followed in the Republic of Korea, in keeping with the provisions of Korea law, which, in principle, provided for the three steps of conciliation, mediation, and arbitration. However, under Korean law there were no grounds for enforcement of settlements arrived at through conciliation or mediation. Only in the case of arbitration awards was there any legal ground for enforcement. The Korean negotiators would take into account the views just expressed by the U.S. negotiators.

0121

13. Mr. Chang said the U.S. negotiators had suggested that the Korean draft of Paragraph 2 might prohibit the direct hire of civilian employees by the U.S. armed forces. The Korean negotiators could not conceive that the Korean draft in any way would prohibit direct hire. They believed this to be a technical question of wording rather than one of substance. They would study the comments of the U.S. negotiators.

14. Mr. Habib replied that he had said that the Korean draft provided for direct hire only by implication, whereas the U.S. negotiators desired an explicit authorization.

15. Referring to Mr. Habib's comment that the Korean draft of Paragraph 2 omitted any statement of the right of the employer to manage his employees, Mr. Chang stated that this omission had been intentional because the Korean negotiators needed clarification by the U.S. negotiators of what the latter meant when they referred to "management". The Korean negotiators believed that the extent of management in terms of labor relations is a highly technical subject, especially when disputes are involved. They were fearful, however, that if the concept of management were included in this paragraph, it might be interpreted to include disciplinary measures, including the right to fire employees in certain circumstances. Therefore, the Korean negotiators had purposely omitted any reference to management from their draft in order to hold further discussion on the subject.

16. Mr. Habib pointed out that, as in many other instances throughout the SOFA, one paragraph (Paragraph 2) is designed to grant certain authority to the U.S. armed forces and the following paragraph (Paragraph 3) explains how the authority is to be exercised. Unless granted the authority to manage their employees, the U.S. armed forces would find it difficult to carry out the managerial functions referred to in Paragraph 3. Mr. Reed then explained that the U.S. armed forces defined [illegible] as including hire, placement, promotion,

0122

and separation of employees.

17. Mr. Chang mentioned that Mr. Habib had pointed out that the U.S. armed forces were not an ordinary employer. The Korean negotiators were well aware of this. If the U.S. armed forces were an ordinary employer, this discussion would be unnecessary. The Korean negotiators had expressly stated that the U.S. armed forces would not be subjected to Korean courts or labor tribunals. They had also said that, in view of the uniqueness of the U.S. armed forces as an employer, they would consider omitting mediation procedures from the provisions for settlement of disputes. If it could be said that the Korean draft does not seem to take into account the uniqueness of the U.S. armed forces as an employer, it could also be said that the U.S. draft does not take into consideration the general labor practices provided for by Korean laws. Each side, therefore, should study the matter carefully.

18. Mr. Habib remarked that the Korean draft of Paragraph 3 covered the same ground as the U.S. draft but used more words in doing so. Mr. Chang replied that it was necessary to be specific because the Korean negotiators would have great difficulty in explaining to the National Assembly the meaning of the words "basic management needs of the United States armed forces". Mr. Habib reiterated that while the U.S. armed forces were prepared to commit themselves to conform to Korean laws and practices, it was necessary to include a qualification which provided for unforeseeable contingencies. Mr. Chang replied that the qualification suggested by the U.S. negotiators was much too general, for it could be applied to any situation. Mr. Habib replied that implementation of the Agreement must be left to the Joint Committee. If the ROK authorities believed that the U.S. armed forces were not carrying out their commitment, they retained the right to raise the question in the Joint Committee.

19. The meeting was adjourned after the U.S. negotiators indicated that

0123

they would give careful study to the Korean proposals.

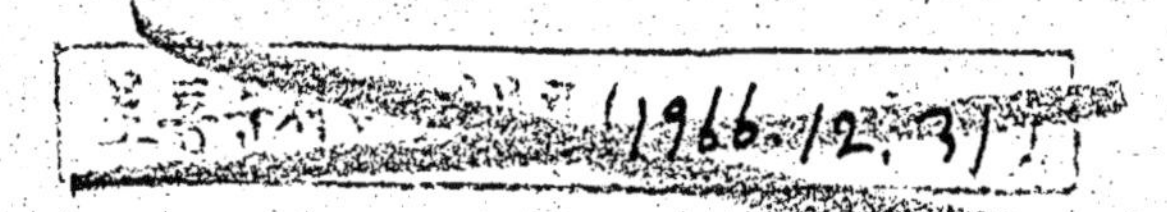

1966, 12, 31,에 예고문에 의거 일반문서로 재분류됨

0124

관리번호 1603

1/3

JOINT SUMMARY RECORD OF THE 65TH SESSION

1. Time and Place: 4:00 - 5:00 P.M. October 23, 1964 at the Foreign Ministry's Conference Room (No.1)

2. Attendants:

ROK Side:

Mr. Chang, Sang Moon	Director European and American Affairs Bureau
Mr. Hu, Sung John	Director Labor Administration Bureau Office of Labor Affairs
Mr. Koo, Choong Whay	Chief, America Section Ministry of Foreign Affairs
Mr. Kim, Dai Chung	Chief Labor Administration Section Office of Labor Affairs
Mr. Oh, Jae Hee	Chief Treaty Section Ministry of Foreign Affairs
Maj. Lee, Kye Hoon	Military Affairs Section Ministry of National Defense
Mr. Lee, Keun Pal (Rapporteur and Interpreter)	3rd Secretary Ministry of Foreign Affairs
Mr. Hwang, Young Jae	3rd Secretary Ministry of Foreign Affairs
Mr. Park, Won Chul	3rd Secretary Ministry of Foreign Affairs

U.S. Side:

Mr. Philip C. Habib	Counselor American Embassy
Brig. Gen. Carroll H. Dunn	Deputy Chief of Staff 8th U.S. Army
Col. Howard Smigelow	Deputy Chief of Staff 8th U.S. Army
Capt. John Wayne	Assistant Chief of Staff USN/K

0125

Col. Kenneth C. Crawford	Staff Judge Advocate 8th U.S. Army
Mr. Frank R. LaMacchia	First Secretary American Embassy
Mr. Benjamin A. Fleck (Rapporteur and Press Officer)	First Secretary American Embassy
Mr. Robert A. Kinney	J-5 8th U.S. Army
Maj. Alton H. Harvey	Staff Judge Advocate's Office 8th U.S. Army
Mr. David Y.S. Lee (Interpreter)	Second Secretary American Embassy
Mr. Ogden C. Reed	Civilian Personnel Director 8th U.S. Army

1. Mr. Chang opened the meeting by stating that the Korean negotiators had studied the revisions of the U.S. draft of the Labor Article which the U.S. negotiators had proposed at the previous meeting.

2. Regarding Paragraph 2, although the Korean negotiators believed there was no great substantive difference, they did wish to include language providing for recruitment with the assistance of ROK authorities "to the maximum extent practicable". Therefore, they wished to table at this time the following proposed Paragraph 2:

> "2. The employers provided for in paragraph 1 shall recruit and employ to the maximum extent practicable with the assistance of the authorities of the Republic of Korea. In case employers exercise direct recruitment and employment of employees, employers shall provide such relevant information as may be necessary for labor administration to the Office of Labor Affairs of the Republic of Korea."

0126

Mr. Chang stated that the Korean draft could fully meet the U.S. requirement to hire employees directly.

3. Mr. Chang stated that the question of adding an Agreed Minute regarding the withholding of income tax payments had been discussed previously. Although its language differed from the language originally proposed by the Korean negotiators, they found no substantial difference. Therefore, they accepted the Agreed Minute tabled by the U.S. negotiators at the 64th meeting.

4. Mr. Chang remarked that the most important paragraph to be discussed at this meeting was Paragraph 3. The revised draft tabled by the U.S. negotiators states that the United States armed forces will conform with the labor laws, customs, and practices of the Republic of Korea "to the extent not inconsistent with the provisions of this article or the basic management needs of the United States Armed Forces." The Korean negotiators found the term "basic management needs of the United States Armed Forces" to be ambiguous. They feared that the use of this phraseology could be the source of disputes over interpretation of this paragraph. Mr. Chang remarked that when the U.S. negotiators had tabled this revised draft, they had said that the U.S. armed forces will conform with the basic standards of Korean law and that the United States Government cannot submit to the jurisdiction of foreign courts or labor tribunals.

5. The Korean negotiators, Mr. Chang. continued, had made it clear that the ROK authorities had no intention of trying to force agencies of the U.S. Government to submit to Korean courts or labor tribunals. In order to provide for other means of settling labor disputes, the Korean negotiators wished to table the following proposed

revision of Paragraph 3 and a related Agreed Minute:

"3. The conditions of employment and work, such as those relating to wages and supplementary payments, the conditions for the protection and welfare of employees, compensations, and the rights of employees, concerning labor relations shall, unless otherwise agreed upon in this Article, conform with those laid down by the legislation of the Republic of Korea."

"Agreed Minute

"With regard to any dispute between the employers except the persons referred to in Paragraph 1, Article _____, and employees or labor unions which cannot be settled through the use of existing procedures of the U.S. armed forces, settlement shall be accomplished in the following manner.

"(a). The dispute shall be referred to the Office of Labor Affairs, Ministry of Health and Social Affairs, Republic of Korea, for conciliation.

"(b). In the event that the dispute is not settled by the procedure described in (a) above, the matter may be referred to a Special Labor Committee appointed by the Office of Labor Affairs, Ministry of Health and Social Affairs, Republic of Korea, for mediation. This committee shall be tri-partite in composition and shall be consisted of equal representation from Labor Unions, the Office of Labor Affairs, and the United States armed forces.

"(c). In the event that the dispute is not settled by the procedures described in (a) and (b) above, the dispute shall be referred to the Joint Committee, or such sub-committee as may be established thereunder for arbitration to resolve the dispute. The decisions of the Joint Committee or sub-committee thereunder shall be binding."

The Korean negotiators, Mr. Chang continued, were convinced that the detailed procedures which were designed to resolve disputes outside of the jurisdiction of Korean courts or labor tribunal could fully meet the U.S. concern over the possibility of subjecting the U.S. Government to Korean courts or labor tribunals.

0128

6. Mr. Habib stated that the U.S. negotiators would give the Korean proposals careful study. At this time, he wished to make some preliminary remarks concerning them. With regard to Paragraph 2, the U.S. negotiators had tabled a draft which was intended to indicate that in recruiting personnel, the U.S. armed forces are prepared to use the ROK Labor Offices whenever practicable. This use would be dependent on the ability of the Labor Offices to provide labor of the type needed by the U.S. armed forces. The Korean negotiators had previously indicated that the ROK Labor Offices are now prepared to recruit only unskilled and semi-skilled labor. At present, the requirement of the U.S. armed forces is for skilled labor and specially-trained technical personnel. Use of the Labor Offices would also be limited by the fact that there is a low attrition rate among employees of the U.S. armed forces and the fact that there is a large group of former employees who have reemployment rights and whose reemployment would be effected outside of the procedure of using the Labor Offices. The U.S. draft provides that when the armed forces need the assistance of the ROK authorities in hiring personnel, they will ask for such assistance and it will be provided. The U.S. draft quite clearly provides for direct hire while the language proposed by the Korean negotiators, "to the maximum extent practicable", authorizes direct hire only by implication. A clear statement of the procedures to be followed would be greatly preferable to a statement granting authority to the U.S. armed forces only by implication.

7. In addition, Mr. Habib continued, the language proposed by the Korean negotiators omits any statement of the right of the employer to manage his employees. The U.S. proposal contains such a statement. The U.S. negotiators considered this an important point because a literal reading of the Korean draft could lead to the interpretation that the U.S. armed forces would manage their employees with the assistance of ROK authorities.

8. Mr. Habib said that he hoped that the Korean negotiators were not under any misapprehension that the U.S. armed forces in Korea were just an ordinary employer.

9. Turning to Paragraph 3, Mr. Habib said that the revised draft proposed by the U.S. negotiators made it clear that the U.S. armed forces in Korea were prepared to conform not only with Korean labor laws but also with customs and practices. The Korean negotiators had objected to the phrase "basic management needs of the U.S. armed forces." The U.S. negotiators wished to point out that the needs of the U.S. armed forces in connection with the accomplishment of their mission could involve management decisions which are unforeseeable. The U.S. negotiators had thought that the primary need of the Korean negotiators was the inclusion in this article of an explicit statement of the willingness of the U.S. armed forces to conform with Korean labor laws and practices. They had not thought that the Korean negotiators wished to place a straightjacket on the U.S. armed forces, which have a unique function and unique needs. The U.S. negotiators saw no ambiguity in the phrase "basic management needs", which was directly related to the question of conformity. If the U.S. armed forces were committed to conformity with Korean laws and practices, as proposed in the U.S. draft, any question regarding the fulfillment of that commitment would be the subject of discussion and

0130

amicable settlement in the Joint Committee. The U.S. negotiators believed the language proposed by the Korean negotiators would establish a requirement which was too rigid for a subject which is much more complicated in practice than the Korean draft would indicate. The U.S. draft is explicit enough to meet the needs of the Korean authorities and would leave implementation to the Joint Committee.

10. Taking up the Agreed Minute tabled by the Korean negotiators, Mr. Habib said that although the U.S. negotiators believed that spelling out in the SOFA procedures for the settlement of labor disputes was unnecessary, they did not disagree in principle. In order to assist them in their study of the Korean proposal, Mr. Habib continued, he wished to ask a few preliminary questions.

11. With regard to labor disputes, Mr. Habib pointed out that the U.S. armed forces now informally receive advice and assistance from the ROK Office of Labor Affairs. Subparagraph (a) of the Korean draft, therefore, appeared to be consistent with current practice. However, the U.S. negotiators felt misgivings about subparagraph (b) because, by introducing mediation procedures, it appeared to border on a requirement that the U.S. armed forces be brought before a Korean tribunal. As the Korean negotiators were aware, the U.S. negotiators could not agree to any such requirement. The proposal contained in subparagraph (b) would place the employer at a disadvantage. The U.S. negotiators would give their considered views regarding this Agreed Minute at a later meeting. Their preliminary reaction was that if inclusion of detailed procedures for settlement

0131

of disputes were ultimately agreed to, it would be preferable to omit any reference to mediation procedures by providing that an unsettled dispute be taken directly from unsuccessful conciliation efforts by the Office of Labor Affairs to consideration by the Joint Committee. The negotiators might profitably seek to draft a simpler statement of procedures which would lead to the submission of an unsettled dispute to the Joint Committee.

12. Mr. Chang replied that the Agreed Minute tabled by the Korean negotiators had been based on the procedures followed in the Republic of Korea, in keeping with the provisions of Korea law, which, in principle, provided for the three steps of conciliation, mediation, and arbitration. However, under Korean law there were no grounds for enforcement of settlements arrived at through conciliation or mediation. Only in the case of arbitration awards was there any legal ground for enforcement. The Korean negotiators would take into account the views just expressed by the U.S. negotiators.

13. Mr. Chang said the U.S. negotiators had suggested that the Korean draft of Paragraph 2 might prohibit the direct hire of civilian employees by the U.S. armed forces. The Korean negotiators could not conceive that the Korean draft in any way would prohibit direct hire. They believed this to be a technical question of wording rather than one of substance. They would study the comments of the U.S. negotiators.

14. Mr. Habib replied that he had said that the Korean draft provided for direct hire only by implication, whereas

0132

the U.S. negotiators desired an explicit authorization.

15. Referring to Mr. Habib's comment that the Korean draft of Paragraph 2 omitted any statement of the right of the employer to manage his employees, Mr. Chang stated that this omission had been intentional because the Korean negotiators needed clarification by the U.S. negotiators of what the latter meant when they referred to "management". The Korean negotiators believed that the extent of management in terms of labor relations is a highly technical subject, especially when disputes are involved. They were fearful, however, that if the concept of management were included in this paragraph, it might be interpreted to include disciplinary measures, including the right to fire employees in certain circumstances. Therefore, the Korean negotiators had purposely omitted any reference to management from their draft in order to hold further discussion on the subject.

16. Mr. Habib pointed out that, as in many other instances throughout the SOFA, one paragraph (Paragraph 2) is designed to grant certain authority to the U.S. armed forces and the following paragraph (Paragraph 3) explains how the authority is to be exercised. Unless granted the authority to manage their employees, the U.S. armed forces would find it difficult to carry out the managerial functions referred to in Paragraph 3. Mr. Reed then explained that the U.S. armed forces defined management as including hire, placement, promotion, and separation of employees.

0133

17. Mr. Chang mentioned that Mr. Habib had pointed out that the U.S. armed forces were not an ordinary employer. The Korean negotiators were well aware of this. If the U.S. armed forces were an ordinary employer, this discussion would be unnecessary. The Korean negotiators had expressly stated that the U.S. armed forces would not be subjected to Korean courts or labor tribunals. They had also said that, in view of the uniqueness of the U.S. armed forces as an employer, they would consider omitting mediation procedures from the provisions for settlement of disputes. If it could be said that the Korean draft does not seem to take into account the uniqueness of the U.S. armed forces as an employer, it could also be said that the U.S. draft does not take into consideration the general labor practices provided for by Korean laws. Each side, therefore, should study the matter carefully.

18. Mr. Habib remarked that the Korean draft of Paragraph 3 covered the same ground as the U.S. draft but used more words in doing so. Mr. Chang replied that it was necessary to be specific because the Korean negotiators would have great difficulty in explaining to the National Assembly the meaning of the words "basic management needs of the United States armed forces." Mr. Habib reiterated that while the U.S. armed forces were prepared to commit themselves to conform to Korean laws and practices, it was necessary to include a qualification which provided for unforeseeable contingencies. Mr. Chang replied that the qualification suggested by the U.S. negotiators was much too general, for it could be applied to any situation.

0134

Mr. Habib replied that implementation of the Agreement must be left to the Joint Committee. If the ROK authorities believed that the U.S. armed forces were not carrying out their commitment, they retained the right to raise the question in the Joint Committee.

19. The meeting was adjourned after the U.S. negotiators indicated that they would give careful study to the Korean proposals.

4. 제66차 회의, 11.24

0136

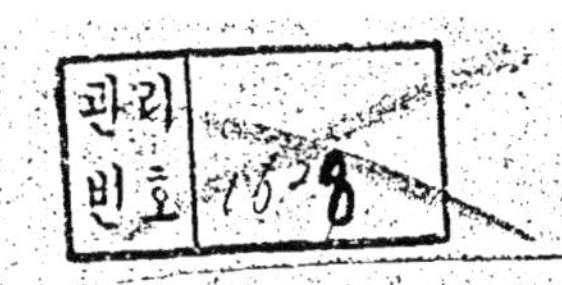

기 안 용 지

자체 통제		기안처	미주과 이근팔	전화번호	근거서류접수일자
	과장	국장	차관	장관	
	26/11				
관계관 서명					
기안 년월일	1964. 11. 26.	시행 년월일		보존 년한	정서 기장
분류 기호	외구미 722.2—	전체 통제	1964.11.28 종결		
경유 수신 참조	대 통 령: 참조: 비서실장 국 무 총 리: 참조: 비서실장 사본: 법무부장관			발신	장 관
제목	제 66 차 주둔군지위협정 체결 교섭 실무자회의 결과 보고				

1964. 11. 24. 하오 3 시 부터 동 4 시 15 분 까지 외무부 제 1 회의실에서 개최된 제 66 차 주둔군지위협정 체결 교섭 실무자회의에서 토의된 형사재판관할권 및 민사청구권에 관한 내용을 별첨과 같이 보고합니다.

1964.11.28

유 첨 : 제 66 차 주둔군지위협정 체결교섭실무자회의 보고서.

끝.

1966.12.31 에 예고문에 의거 일반문서로 재분류됨

승인서식 1—1—3 (11 00900—03) (195mm×265mm16절지)

0137

기 안 용 지

자 체 통 제		기안처	미주과 이근팔	전화번호	근거서류접수일자
	과장	국장	차관	장관	
관계관 서 명					
기 안 년 월 일	1964. 11. 26.	시 행 년월일	1964.11.28	보 존 년 한	정 서 기 장
분 류 기 호	외구미 722.2—	전 체 통 제	종결		
경 유 수 신 참 조	법무부장관			발 신	장 관
제 목	제 66 차 주둔군지위협정 체결 교섭 실무자회의 결과 보고				

1964. 11. 24. 개최된 제 66 차 주둔군지위협정 체결 교섭 실무자회의 결과 보고서 사본을 송부하오니 참고하시기 바랍니다.

유 첨: 제 66 차 주둔군지위협정 체결 교섭 실무자회의 결과 보고서 사본. 1 부. 끝.

승인서식 1—1—3 (11 00900—03) (195mm×265mm16절지)

0138

외 무 부

외구미 722.2 1964. 11.28.

수신 대통령, 국무총리

참조 비서실장

사본 법무부장관

제목 제66차 주둔군지위협정 체결 교섭 실무자 회의 결과보고

1964.11.24, 하오 3시부터 동 4시 15분까지 외무부 제1회의실에서 개최된 제66차 주둔군지위협정 체결 교섭 실무자회의에서 토의된 형사재판관할권 및 민사청구권에 관한 내용을 별첨과 같이 보고합니다.

유첨 - 제66차 주둔군지위협정 체결 교섭 실무자회의 보고서 1부. 끝

외 무 부 장 관 이 동 원

0139

외 무 부

외구미 722.2 1964. 11. 28.

수신 법무부장관
제목 제66차 주둔군지위협정 체결 고섭 실무자회의 결과 보고

1964. 11. 24, 개최된 제66차 주둔군지위협정 체결 고섭 실무자회의 결과보고서 사본을 송부하오니 참고하시기 바랍니다.

유첨 - 제66차 주둔군지위협정 체결 고섭 실무자회의 결과 보고서 사본 1부. 끝

(1966.12.31 일반문서로 재분류)

외 무 부 장 관 이 동 원

0140

제 66 차

한 · 미간 주둔군지위협정 체결 고섭 실무자회의

보 고 서

1. 일시 1964 년 11 월 24 일 하오 3 시부터 동 4 시 15 분까지

2. 장소 외무부 제 1 회의실

3. 토의사항

가. 형사재판관할권

우리측은 상금 합의를 보지 못하고 있는 형사 재판관할권 중 특히 한국의 관할권 행사기관, 공무집행중 범죄, 및 관할권의 포기등 중요 조항에 관한 우리측 입장을 다음과 같이 재강조하고 우리측 입장을 조속한 시일내에 수락하여 고섭을 타결할 것을 미측에 촉구하였다.

1) 한국의 관할권 행사기관

(1) 과거 미측이 세계각국과 군대지위협정을 체결함에 있어서 미군범법자에 대한 접수국의 관할권 행사기관을 "민사당국"에 만 극한시키며 한 것이 미국의 입장이 었으며 한국에 있어서도 미군범법자에 대하여 군사재판권이 행사될 가능성이 존재하는 한 한국의 관할권 행사기관을 "한국의 민사당국"이라고 협정상 명시하기를 희망한다고 미측이 주장한데 대하여 우리측은 "여하한 경우에도 미군범법자를 한국군법재판에 회부하지는 않을 것"을 회의록이나 기타 협정이외의 형태로 보장할 용의가 있음을 재강조하고 그대신 미측으로 하여금 우리나라 관할권 행사기관을 우리주장대로 "한국당국"으로 규정함에 동의할 것을 요구하였다.

0141

64-3-10

64-3-34 (4)　　미3기타 III-3 (4)

0142

2) 공무집행중 범죄

(1) 우리측은 제 52차 회의에서 공무집행중 범죄에 대한 관할권을 결정함에 있어서 (ㄱ) 공무집행중 범죄 증명서의 발행권을 국제선례에 따라 미군당국에 인정하고 (ㄴ) 증명서의 효력은 반증이 없는한 충분한 증거가 되며 (ㄷ) 한국당국이 반증을 제시하는 경우 합동위원회에서 결정한다는 것을 내용으로 하는 대안을 제시한바 있다.

(2) 미측은 제 58차 회의에서 우리의 대안을 심의하는전제로서 (ㄱ) 증명서는 수정되지 않는한 계속 확정적이며 (ㄴ) 신속한 재판을 받을 피의자의 권리가 재심 지연으로 인하여 박탈되어서는 않된다는 조건을 제시하였으며 제 60차 회의에서도 협정체결 각국의 공무집행중 범죄 처리에 관한 선례를 인용하여 미측 주장을 고집한 바를 상기시키고,

(3) 우리는 세계각국의 선례에 따라 대다수의 경우 미측이 발행한 증명서의 효력을 인정할 용의가 있지만 반증이 제시된 경우에도 미군당국이 일방적으로 결정할수 있는 제도에 반대하며 오로지 양측의 원만한 합의에 의하여서만 해결되어야 한다는 우리측 원칙에 변함이 없음을 지적하고 미측의 재고를 요청하였다.

3) 관할권의 포기

(1) 우리측은 관할권의 포기에 관한 미측 제안에는 한국당국이 특히 중대하다고 인정하여 재판해야 할 특수한 경우에 관할권을 행사할수 있는 보장이 없음을 지적하고

(2) 미측이 과거 수차에 걸쳐 최대한도의 관할권

0143

64-3-93

4-3-34 미.모 111-3

0144

의 모기를 한국당국으로 부터 획득하려는 것이 미측의 관심사라고 주장한데 대하여 우리측은 국제선례에 따라 관할권을 관대하게 미측에 모기할 용의가 있으나 한국측은 다만 접수국으로서 관할권의 모기여부를 결정할수 있는 재량권이 인정되어야 한다고 강조하였다.

4) 상기와 같은 우리측 입장에 대하여 미측은 한국측 입장을 이해하는 바이며 가까운 시일내에 교섭에 관한 훈령이 있을것으로 믿는다고 답변하였다.

나. 민사청구권

민사청구권 조항에 있어서는 미측은 지금까지 주한미군의 현행 소청제도를 그대로 계속 적용할 것을 주장하여 왔는바;

(1) 한국측이 제안하는 제도는 (ㄱ) 시간이 많이 들며, (ㄴ) 운영하는데 경비가 많이 들게된다는 미측 주장에 대하여 현행한국제도는 효율적이며 공정하게 잘운영되고 있어 이러한 문제점은 충분히 극복할수 있다는 사실을 이미 설명하였음을 상기시키고,

(2) 한국의 제도가 경험이 적은 동시에 배상금 지급기준이 법령으로 제정되어 있지 않아 현행 미군제도 보다 단점이 많다는 미측 주장에 대하여서는 우리측은 이러한 미국측 주장이 극히 타당하지 않으며 양국간의 우호관계의 증진을 위하여도 주한미군당국은 공정하고도 합리적인 민사청구제도를 마련하는 것이 필요할 것임을 강조하였다.

(3) 한국측이 제안한 제도는 한국법에 따라 피해자가 공정한 절차에 의거 구제될수 있도록 되어 있으나

0145

0146

미국측 제도는 그들의 군대규칙에 의거한 절차
에 따라 청구문제를 미군당국이 일방적으로
해결하게 되어 있는 모순이 있음을 지적하고
한국제도의 우월성을 강조하고 한국안에 의거하여
토의를 진행할 것을 제안하였다. 끝

0147

64-2-18

6A-3-34(4)

미3·무 111-3(4)

0148

제 66 차

한·미간 주둔군지위협정 체결 교섭 실무자회의

보고서

1. 일시 1964년 11월 24일 하오 3시부터 4시 15분까지
2. 장소 외무부 제1회의실
3. 토의사항

가. 형사재판관할권

우리측은 상금 합의를 보지 못하고 있는 형사재판관할권중 특히 한국의 관할권 행사기관, 공무집행중 범죄, 및 관할권의 포기등 중요조항에 관한 우리측 입장을 다음과 같이 재강조하고 우리측 입장을 조속한 시일내에 수락하여 교섭을 타결할 것을 미측에 촉구하였다.

1) 한국의 관할권 행사기관

(1) 과거 미측이 세계각국과 군대지위협정을 체결함에 있어서 미군범법자에 대한 접수국의 관할권 행사기관을 "민사당국"에 만 국한시키려 한것이 미국의 입장이 었으며 한국에 있어서도 미군범법자에 대하여 군사재판권이 행사될 가능성이 존재하는 한 한국의 관할권 행사기관은 "한국의 민사당국" 이라고 협정상 명시하기를 희망한다고 미측이 주장한데 대하여 우리측은 "여하한 경우에도 미군범법자를 한국군법재판에 회부하지는 않은것"을 회의록이나 기타 협정이외의 협대로 보장할 용의가 있음을 재강조하고 그대신 미측으로 하여금 우리나라 관할권 행사기관은 우리주장대로 "한국당국"으로 규정함에 동의할것을 요구하였다.

0149

2) 공무집행중 범죄

(1) 우리측은 제 52차 회의에서 공무집행중 범죄에 대한 관할권을 결정함에 있어서 (ㄱ) 공무집행중 범죄 증명서의 발행권은 국제선례에 따라 미군당국에 인정하고 (ㄴ) 증명서의 효력은 반증이 없는한 충분한 증거가 되며 (ㄷ) 한국당국이 반증을 제시하는 경우 합동위원회에서 결정한다는 것을 내용으로 하는 대안을 제시한바 있다.

(2) 미측은 제 55차 회의에서 우리의 대안을 심의하는 전제로서 (ㄱ) 증명서는 수정되지 않는한 계속 확정적이며 (ㄴ) 신속한 재판을 받을 피의자의 권리가 재심 지연으로 인하여 박탈되어서는 안된다는 조건을 제시하였으며 제 60차 회의에서도 협정체결 각국의 공무집행중 범죄 처리에 관한 선례를 인용하여 미측 주장을 고집한 바를 상기시키고,

(3) 우리는 세계각국의 선례에 따라 대다수의 경우 미측이 발행한 증명서의 효력을 인정할 용의가 있지만 반증이 제시된 경우에도 미군당국이 일방적으로 결정할수 있는 제도에 반대하며 오로지 양측의 원만한 합의에 의하여서만 해결되어야 한다는 우리측 원칙에 변함이 없음을 지적하고 미측의 재고를 요청하였다.

3) 관할권의 포기

(1) 우리측은 관할권의 포기에 관한 미측 지안에는 한국당국이 특히 중대하다고 인정하여 재판해야할 특수한 경우에 관할권을 행사할수 있는 보장이 없음을 지적하고

0150

(2) 미측이 과거 수차에 걸쳐 최대한도의 관할권의 포기를 한국당국으로 부터 획득 하려는 것이 미측의 관심사라고 주장한데 대하여 우리측은 국지선례에 따라 관할권은 관대하게 미측에 포기할 용의가 있으나 한국측은 다만 접수국으로서 관할권의 포기 여부를 결정할수 있는 재량권이 인정되어야 한다고 강조하였다.

4) 상기와 같은 우리측 입장에 대하여 미측은 한국측 입장을 이해하는 바이며 가까운 시일내에 교섭에 관한 훈령이 있을 것으로 믿는다고 답변하였다.

나. 민사청구권

민사청구권 조항에 있어서는 미측은 지금까지 주한미군의 현행 소청제도를 그대로 계속 적용할 것을 주장하여 왔는바;

(1) 한국측이 제안하는 제도는 (ㄱ) 시간이 많이 들며, (ㄴ) 운영하는데 경비가 많이 들게된다는 미측 주장에 대하여 현행한국제도는 효율적이며 공정하게 잘 운영되고 있어 이러한 문제점은 충분히 극복할수 있다는 사실을 이미 설명 하였음을 상기시키고,

(2) 한국의 제도가 경험이 적은 동시에 배상금 지급 기준이 법령으로 제정되어 있지 않아 현행미군 제도 보다 단점이 많다는 미측 주장에 대하여서는 우리측은 이러한 미국측 주장이 극히 타당하지 않으며 양국간의 우호관계의 증진을 위하여도 주한미군당국은 공정하고도 합리적인 민사청구 제도를 마련하는 것이 필요한 것임을 강조 하였다.

0151

(5) 한국측이 제안한 제도는 한국법에 따라 피해자가 공정한 절차에 의거 구제될수 있도록 되어 있으나 미국측 제도는 그들의 군대규칙에 의거한 절차에 따라 청구문제를 미군당국이 일방적으로 해결하게 되어 있는 모순이 있음을 지적하고 한국제도의 우월성을 강조하고 한국안에 의거하여 토의를 진행할것을 제안하였다. 끝

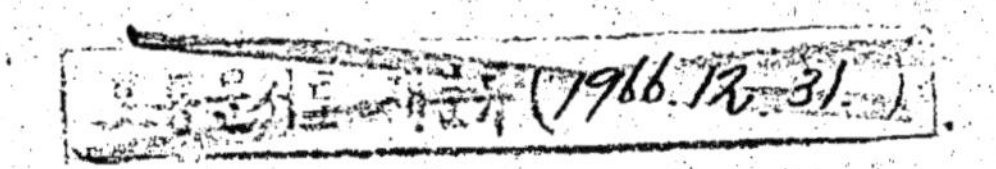

1966.12.31.에 예고문에 의거 일반문서로 재분류됨

0152

CONFIDENTIAL

STATUS OF FORCES NEGOTIATIONS: 66th Meeting

SUBJECTS: 1. Criminal Jurisdiction
2. Claims

PLACE: Ministry of Foreign Affairs

DATE: November 24, 1964

PARTICIPANTS:

Republic of Korea	United States
CHANG Sang-mun	Philip C. Habib
Colonel KIM Won-kil, ROKA	Brig. General Carroll H. Dunn, USA
KU Chung-hoe	Colonel Howard Smigelow, USA
Yi Nam-ki	Captain John Wayne, USN
YUN Un-yong	Colonel Kenneth C. Crawford, USA
CHU Mun-ki	Frank R. LaMacchia
O Chae-hi	Benjamin A. Fleck
YI Myong-hi	Robert A. Kinney
HWANG Yong-chae	Goodwin Shapiro
YI Kun-pal (Interpreter)	Major Alton Harvey, USA
	David Y.S. Lee (Interpreter)

0153

1. Mr. Chang opened the meeting by introducing Mr. Yun Un-yong, who has replaced Mr. Yun Tu-sik as Director of the Prosecutors' Bureau, Ministry of Justice. Mr. Chang stated that Mr. Yun Un-yong would play the major role for the Ministry of Justice in the negotiations. Mr. Chang then announced the impending departure of Mr. KU Chung-hoe for an overseas assignment. Remarking that Mr. Ku had participated in the negotiations for a longer period than anyone else on the Korean negotiating team, Mr. Chang stated that his Korean colleagues would sorely miss Mr. Ku's contributions to the negotiations. He then introduced as Mr. Ku's successor on the negotiating team and as Chief of the Foreign Ministry's America Section, Mr. YI Nam-ki.

2. Mr. Habib welcomed Mr. Yun and Mr, Yi to the negotiations on behalf of the American negotiating team. He then expressed the appreciation of the American negotiators for the cooperation and understanding which Mr. Ku had consistently displayed and for Mr. Ku's great devotion to achieving a successful outcome of the negotiations. The U.S. negotiators greatly regretted that Mr. Ku would not be present for the signing of the Agreement. Mr. Habib then introduced Mr. Goodwin Shapiro, who was replacing Mr. Robert Lewis as a member of the U.S. negotiating team.

3. Mr. Chang welcomed Mr. Shapiro. Mr. Ku then expressed his personal regret at having to leave the negotiations before they were successfully concluded.

Criminal Jurisdiction

4. Mr. Chang stated that the Korean negotiators wished to review the positions of the two sides regarding the three most important unresolved issues, namely the provisions regarding waiver, and duty certificates, in the Criminal Jurisdiction Article and certain aspects of the Claims Article.

5. Taking up first the use in Paragraph 1(b) of the U.S. draft of the phrase "civil authorities of the Republic of Korea", Mr. Chang made the following statement:

0154

"a. With respect to the phrase 'civil authorities of the Republic of Korea' in the U.S. draft, the U.S. negotiators had previously stated that the position that jurisdiction over the U.S. armed forces by the host government should be limited to the civil authorities of the government was a firm U.S. position in every country in which a SOFA is in force. The U.S. negotiators wanted to have it stated explicitly in the SOFA with the ROK Government. At the 60th session, the U,Ss negotiators had again reiterated that the U.S. negotiators of the Agreements with Japan and the NATO governments had not conceived of the possibility that military authorities of the host country could exercise jurisdiction. Inasmuch as that possibility does exist in the Republic of Korea, the U.S. negotiators wished to make the language of the provision quite clear by having it read 'the civil authorities of the Republic of Korea'.

"b. To accommodate the oft-repeated U.S. concern above, and to meet the Korean requirement, the Korean negotiators had given to the U.S. negotiators an unqualified assurance for the negotiating record that under no circumstances would members of the U.S. armed forces and civilian components be subject to trial by Korean military authorities, in the hope that the U.S. negotiators would agree to the deletion of the word 'civil' from the draft.

"c. The Korean negotiators had further wished at the 60th session to clarify the U.S. position by asking whether the U.S. position was to accept the assurance as an agreed minute and delete the word 'civil' from the text. Although the U.S. side declined to respond to the question on the ground that the question was a hypothetical one, we wish reiterate position that the as-

"surance made for the Joint Summary Record should be sufficient to settle the problem. In other words, we cannot accept the word 'civil', either in the text or in an agreed minute, but are prepared to negotiate to meet the U.S. requirement through assurances in a form other than text or agreed minute. We wonder what still keeps the U.S. negotiators from accepting the Korean assurances which squarely meet the U.S. requirement. If the U.S. negotiators have in mind any other reasons for insisting on the word 'civil' in the text, we have so far no way of knowing them.

"d. The Korean negotiators ask the U.S. negotiators to take into consideration the position of the Korean negotiators and accept it."

6. Turning to the question of duty certificates, Mr. Chang made the following statement:

"a. With respect to the issuance of official duty certificates, the Korean negotiators had proposed at the 52nd session a revised draft which recognized the U.S. military authorities as the authorities to issue a certificate, and had further stated that a certificate issued by the U.S. military authorities would be sufficient evidence in determining the primary jurisdiction over offenses and any objection which might be raised by the Korean authorities should be decided by the Joint Committee.

"b. At the 58th session, the U.S. negotiators had in return proposed as the basis of discussion of the Korean draft the following two understandings:

(1) The certificate will be conclusive

0156

unless modification is agreed upon.

(2) The accused should not be deprived of his entitlement to a prompt and speedy trial as a result of protracted reconsideration of the duty certificate.

With regard to the 2nd understanding, the Korean negotiators had in principle no objection to the U.S. proposal. Accordingly, the Korean negotiators had expressed their willingness to set any number of days to meet the U.S. concern.

"c. Regarding the first understanding, the Korean negotiators had stated that although we believed that the certificate issued by the U.S. military authorities would in most of the cases be honored, in case any objection is raised by the Korean authorities, the problem of validity of a duty certificate should be solved by consultation and agreement between the representatives of both sides at the Joint Committee. We are firmly opposed to any idea which would entertain the possibility that the decision may be made unilaterally by the U.S. military authorities.

"d. The Korean negotiators have carefully studied the precedents presented by the U.S. negotiators at the 60th session. In fact, we would be most willing to comply with international precedents. However, we also believe that any dispute in international society should be amicably settled through agreement between the parties concerned and settlement of any controversy over duty certificates should be no exception.

"e. We request the U.S. negotiators to reconsider the Korean proposal and present their views at the earliest possible date."

0157

7. Turning to the question of waiver of jurisdiction, Mr. Chang made the following statement:

"a. The Korean negotiators wish to review their position on the draft regarding the waiver of primary right to exercise jurisdiction, thereby reminding the U.S. negotiators of outstanding issues and difficulties which confront us in connection with the waiver problem.

"b. According to the U.S. draft, even though we consider it absolutely necessary to try an accused in specific cases, we would be obliged to hand him over to the U.S. authorities and then undergo afterwards necessary procedures to recall the waived case by seeking agreement at the Joint Committee. Furthermore, the U.S. draft does not guarantee any assurance which enables us to obtain successful recall in specific cases.

"c. In the past, the U.S. negotiators had emphasized that it was the intention of the U.S. negotiators to obtain maximum waiver from the Korean authorities. To meet the U.S. concern, the Korean negotiators had reiterated that we would waive as many cases as other countries do under their SOFA's. Nevertheless, we firmly maintain that our position is to retain the principle so that we could waive primary right to the U.S. authorities except when we determine that it is of particular importance to try an accused in the Korean court.

"d. Time and again, we are ready to assure the U.S. negotiators that the Korean authorities will waive as generously as other SOFA countries do; however, we wish to retain discretion on our part as to whether or not to waive. In this connection, we believe that we are asking the U.S. negotiators not any new or unique provisions

0158

"but only universal ones which have been generally accepted by other SOFA's so that we could reserve as a hosting country primary right to exercise jurisdiction not in general but in specific cases under special circumstances.

"e. We ask once again that the U.S. negotiators reconsider our difficulties toward this problem and accept the Korean views."

8. Mr. Habib replied that Mr. Chang had given a clear recapitulation of the views of the Korean negotiators on key issues remaining in the Criminal Jurisdiction Article. He assured the Korean negotiators that their views have received and will continue to receive the full consideration of the U.S. negotiators.

Claims

9. Turning to the Claims Article, Mr. Chang stated that the Korean negotiators had studied the position of the U.S. negotiators carefully and wished to make their own position quite clear. He then made the following statement:

"a. The U.S. negotiators have stated throughout the past discussions of this Article that they preferred the present system of the U.S. Armed Forces Claims Service in Korea to the system proposed by the Korean negotiators, because the formula concept envisaged by the latter is proved to be time-consuming and expensive to administer.

"b. However, on those concerns of the U.S. negotiators regarding the Korean proposal, the Korean negotiators have fully explained that the existing Korean claims system is operated efficiently, equitably, and would overcome the problems envisaged by the U.S. negotiators without any difficulty.

"c. In this regard, the U,S. negotiators indicated that the present U.S. system was operated efficiently, equitably and to the general satisfaction of the claimant concerned, whereas the Korean system had relatively shorter experience than the U.S. Armed Forces Claims Service in Korea and had no legally published standard of awards for various claims. Particularly, the U.S. negotiators pointed out that the lack of legal standards would leave open the possibility of settlement of individual claims on bases not related to any standard.

"d. The Korean negotiators believe that the foregoing U.S. negotiators' concerns are neither called for nor well-founded, and they would like to point out the reasons why they believe so.

"e. The U.S. authorities, in the settlement of claims in Korea as military authorities of a sending state, would not deny the significance of the following views: that the award should be paid in a just and reasonable manner, and that the settlement of claims should not adversely affect the promotion and maintenance of friendly relations between the people of the ROK and the United States.

"f. It is, therefore, believed that, for the settlement of claims, the U.S. authorities would not hesitate in providing just and reasonable procedures as well as maximum convenience for the claimant in Korea.

"g. The claims system proposed by the Korean negotiators, particularly with regard to the procedures for the settlement of the claims arising out of acts or omissions of members or employees of the U.S. armed forces done in the performance of official duty, or out of any other act, omission or occurrence for which the U.S. armed forces are legally responsible, and causing damage to the third parties other than the Government of the ROK, at which the U.S. negotiators expressed a deep con-

0100

"cern, is so provided that all the claimants could enjoy the full protection guaranteed by the Korean laws. The Government of the ROK will be responsible for the settlement of all the claims arising out of the above acts or omissions. And in case the claimant is dissatisfied with the disposition of the Korean Government, he would be able to have recourse to the Korean court so that all the claims arising within the ROK could be settled by the same procedures regardless of whether the loss or damage is caused by the U.S. armed forces or all the other claims normally arising out of acts or omissions of the ROK armed forces and officials of the Korean Government.

"h. Therefore, there is left no room for the claimant to express discontent with the settlement of claims to the Government of the U.S. or the U.S. military authorities in Korea. This procedure will certainly prevent the national emotion of the Korean people from turning to the direction which both the Governments and people do not desire, and will, in fact, contribute to the furtherance of the friendly relations now existing between both sides.

"i. However, if the claims were to be settled by the procedures proposed by the U.S. negotiators, awards would have to be paid only in accordance with the military regulations of the U.S. armed forces, specifically, the AR 25-90 of 1957, "Claims Arising in Foreign Countries". In this procedure, the claimants are not duly protected from the legal point of view. When the claimants are not satisfied with the award decided by the U.S. authorities, all "they could do would be an appeal to the same authorities for reconsideration. And the claimants have no chance for redress through a competent court.

"j. The Korean negotiators also believe that the U.S. negotiators will fully realize the short-comings of the appeal system of the U.S. claims service in which the same persons who initially decided the award consider the same case again.

"k. For the claimant concerned, it would be hard to approve of procedures whereby the loss or damage caused by his own Government should be given a chance to be tried fairly in the court and the similar loss or damage caused by the foreign authorities should not.

"l. The U.S. [illegible] negotiators might be concerned at the possibility that the proposed Korean system would not work as it should, and that the Korean authorities would make unjust and discriminatory decisions. The concern is based on the premise that the Korean system lacks the so-called 'legally published standard'. To the knowledge of the Korean negotiators, the U.S. side has so far failed to present its system of the legally published standard.

"m. However, such a possibility is not existing anywhere in the Korean draft as well as in the existing Korean Claims System as witnessed by some of the U.S. negotiators. In fact, the Korean Government would be in the paying side of an award like the U.S. Government because it has to share a considerable portion of the award. And this, we believe, is a sufficient guarantee to the U.S. Government that illegitimate,

0162

"unreasonable, and inequitable awards will not be paid as well as a firm determination of the Korean Government that the settlement of claims should be made without prejudice by the authorities of the ROK.

"n. Therefore, the Korean negotiators sincerely request the U.S. negotiators to reconsider their position and to proceed with the discussion of the Claims Article based on the Korean draft."

10. Mr. Habib stated that the U.S. negotiators understood the position of the Korean negotiators. The meeting was then adjourned.

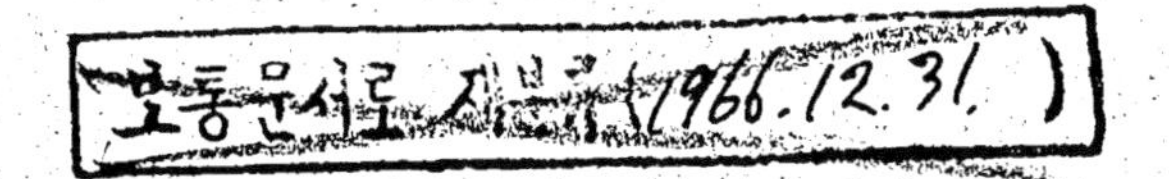

0163

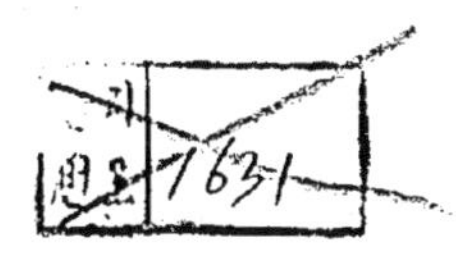

1
3

JOINT SUMMARY RECORD OF THE 66TH SESSION

1. Time and Place: 3:00 - 4:15 P.M. November 24, 1964 at the Foreign Ministry's Conference Room (No.1)

2. Attendants:

ROK Side:

Mr. Chang, Sang Moon	Director European and American Affairs Bureau
Mr. Yoon, Woon Young	Director Prosecutors Bureau Ministry of Justice
Mr. Koo, Choong Whay	Chief, America Section Ministry of Foreign Affairs
Mr. Lee, Nam Ki	Chief America Section Ministry of Foreign Affairs
Col. Kim, Won Kil	Chief Military Affairs Section Ministry of National Defense
Mr. Choo, Moon Ki	Chief Legal Affairs Section Ministry of Justice
Mr. Oh, Jae Hee	Chief Treaty Section Ministry of Foreign Affairs
Mr. Lee, Myung Hi	Prosecutor Prosecutors Section Ministry of Justice
Mr. Lee, Keun Pal (Rapporteur and Interpreter)	3rd Secretary Ministry of Foreign Affairs
Mr. Hwang, Young Jae	3rd Secretary Ministry of Foreign Affairs

U.S. Side:

Mr. Philip C. Habib	Counselor American Embassy
Brig. Gen. Carroll H. Dunn	Deputy Chief of Staff 8th U.S. Army
Col. Howard Smigelow	Deputy Chief of Staff 8th U.S. Army
Capt. John Wayne	Assistant Chief of Staff USN/K

0164

Col. Kenneth C. Crawford	Staff Judge Advocate 8th U.S. Army
Mr. Frank R. LaMacchia	First Secretary American Embassy
Mr. Benjamin A. Fleck (Rapporteur and Press Officer)	First Secretary American Embassy
Mr. Robert A. Kinney	J-5 8th U.S. Army
Mr. Goodwin Shapiro	Second Secretary American Embassy
Maj. Alton H. Harvey	Staff Judge Advocate's Office 8th U.S. Army
Mr. David Y.S. Lee (Interpreter)	Second Secretary American Embassy

1. Mr. Chang opened the meeting by introducing Mr. Yun Un-yong, who has replaced Mr. Yun Tu-sik as Director of the Prosecutors' Bureau, Ministry of Justice. Mr. Chang stated that Mr. Yun Un-yong would play the major role for the Ministry of Justice in the negotiations. Mr. Chang then announced the impending departure of Mr. KU Chung-hoe for an overseas assignment. Remarking that Mr. Ku had participated in the negotiations for a longer period than anyone else on the Korean negotiating team, Mr. Chang stated that his Korean colleagues would sorely miss Mr. Ku's contributions to the negotiations. He then introduced as Mr. Ku's successor on the negotiating team and as Chief of the Foreign Ministry's America Section, Mr. YI Nam-ki.

2. Mr. Habib welcomed Mr. Yun and Mr. Yi to the negotiations on behalf of the American negotiating team. He then expressed the appredíation of the American negotiators for the cooperation and understanding which Mr. Ku had consistently displayed and for Mr. Ku's great devotion to achieving a successful outcome of the negotiatinns. The U.S. negotiators greatly regretted that Mr. Ku would not be present for the signing of the

0165

Agreement. Mr. Habib then introduced Mr. Goodwin Shapiro, who was replacing Mr. Robert Lewis as a member of the U.S. negotiating team.

3. Mr. Chang welcomed Mr. Shapiro. Mr. Ku then expressed his personal regret at having to leave the negotiations before they were successfully concluded.

Criminal Jurisdiction

4. Mr. Chang stated that the Korean negotiators wished to review the positions of the two sides regarding the three most important unresolved issues, namely the provisions regarding waiver, and duty certificates, in the Criminal Jurisdiction Article and certain aspects of the Claims Article.

5. Taking up first the use in Paragraph 1(b) of the U.S. draft of the phrase "civil" authorities of the Republic of Korea", Mr. Chang made the following statement:

"a. With respect to the phrase 'civil authorities of the Republic of Korea' in the U.S. draft, the U.S. negotiators had previously stated that the position that jurisdiction over the U.S. armed forces by the host government should be limited to the civil authorities of the government was a firm U.S. position in every country in which a SOFA is in force. The U.S. negotiators wanted to have it stated explicitly in the SOFA with the ROK Government. At the 60th session, the U.S. negotiators had again reiterated that the U.S. negotiators of the Agreements with Japan and the NATO governments had not conceived of the possibility that military authorities of the host country could exercise jurisdiction. Inasmuch as that possibility does exist in the Republic of Korea, the U.S. negotiators wished to make the language of the provision quite clear by having it read 'the civil authorities of the Republic of Korea'.

0166

"b. To accommodate the oft-repeated U.S. concern above, and to meet the Korean requirement, the Korean negotiators had given to the U.S. negotiators an unqualified assurance for the negotiating record that under no circumstances would members of the U.S. armed forces and civilian components be subject to trial by Korean military authorities, in the hope that the U.S. negotiators would agree to the deletion of the word 'civil' from the draft.

"c. The Korean negotiators had further wished at the 60th session to clarify the U.S. position by asking whether the U.S. position was to accept the assurance as an agreed minute and delete the world 'civil' from the text. Although the U.S. side declined to respond to the question on the ground that the question was a hypothetical one, we wish to reiterate our position that the assurance made for the Joint Summary Record should be sufficient to settle the problem. In other words, we cannot accept the word 'civil', either in the text or in an agreed minute, but are prepared to negotiate to meet the U.S. requirement through assurances in a form other than text or agreed minute. We wonder what still keeps the U.S. negotiators from accepting the Korean assurances which squarely meet the U.S. requirement. If the U.S. negotiators have in mind any other reasons for insisting on the word 'civil' in the text, we have so far no way of knowing them.

"d. The Korean negotiators ask the U.S. negotiators to take into consideration the position of the Korean negotiators and accept it."

6. Turning to the question of duty certificates, Mr. Chang made the following statement:

0167

"a. With respect to the issuance of official duty certificates, the Korean negotiators had proposed at the 52nd session a revised draft which recognized the U.S. military authorities as the authorities to issue a certificate, and had further stated that a certificate issued by the U.S. military authorities would be sufficient evidence in determining the primary jurisdiction over offenses and any objection which might be raised by the Korean authorities should be decided by the Joint Committee.

"b. At the 58th session, the U.S. negotiators had in return proposed as the basis of discussion of the Korean draft the following two understandings:

(1) The certificate will be conclusive unless modification is agreed upon.

(2) The accused should not be deprived of his entitlement to a prompt and speedy trial as a result of protracted reconsideration of the duty certificate.

With regard to the 2nd understanding, the Korean negotiators had in principle no objectinn to the U.S. proposal. Accordingly, the Korean negotiators had expressed their willingness to set any number of days to meet the U.S. concern.

"c. Regarding the first understanding, the Korean negotiators had stated that although we believed that the certificate issued by the U.S. military authorities would in most of the cases be honored, in case any objection is raised by the Korean authorities, the problem of validity of a duty certifiaate should be solved by consultation and agreement between the representatives of both sides at the Joint Committee. We are firmly opposed to any idea which would entertain the possibility that the decision may be made unilaterally by the U.S. military authorities.

0168

"d. The Korean negotiators have carefully studied the precedents presented by the U.S. negotiators at the 60th session. In fact, we would be most willing to comply with international precedents. However, we also believe that any dispute in international society should be amicably settled through agreement between the parties concerned and settlement of any controversy over duty certificates should be no exception.

"e. We request the U.S. negotiators to reconsider the Korean proposal and present their views at the earliest possible date."

7. Turning to the question of waiver of jurisdiction, Mr. Chang made the following statement:

"a. The Korean negotiators wish to review their position on the draft regarding the waiver of primary right to exercise jurisdiction, thereby reminding the U.S. negotiators of outstanding issues and difficulties which confront us in connection with the waiver problem.

"b. According to the U.S. draft, even though we consider it absolutely necessary to try an accused in specific cases, we would be obliged to hand him over to the U.S. authorities and then undergo afterwards necessary procedures to recall the waived case by seeking agreement at the Joint Committee. Furthermore, the U.S. draft does not guarantee any assurance which enables us to obtain successful recall in specific cases.

"c. In the past, the U.S. negotiators had emphasized that it was the intention of the U.S. negotiators to obtain maximum waiver from the Korean authorities. To meet the U.S. concern, the Korean negotiators had reiterated that we would waive as many cases as other countries do under their SOFA's. Nevertheless, we firmly maintain that our position is to retain the principle so that we could waive primary right to the U.S. authorities except when we determine that it is of particular importance to try an accused in the Korean court.

"d. Time and again, we are ready to assure the U.S. negotiators that the Korean authorities will waive as generously as other SOFA countries do; however, we wish to retain discretion on our part as to whether or not to waive. In this connection, we believe that we are asking the U.S. negotiators not any new or unique provisions "but only universal ones which have been generally accepted by other SOFA'so so that we could reserve as a hosting country primary right to exercise jurisdiction not in general but in specific cases under special circumstances.

"e. We ask once again that the U.S. negotiators reconsider our difficulties toward this problem and accept the Korean views."

8. Mr. Habib replied that Mr. Chang had given a clear recapitulation of the views of the Korean negotiators on key issues remaining in the Criminal Jurisdiction Article. He assured the Korean negotiators that their views have received and will continue to receive the full consideration of the U.S. negotiators.

Claims

9. Turning to the Claims Article, Mr. Chang stated that the Korean negotiators had studied the position of the U.S. negotiators carefully and wished to make their own position quite clear. He then made the following statement:

"a. The U.S. negotiators have stated throughout the past discussions of this Article that they preferred the present system of the U.S. Armed Forces Claims Service in Korea to the system proposed by the Korean negotiators, because the formula concept envisaged by the latter is proved to be

0170

time-consuming and expensive to administer.

"b. However, on those concerns of the U.S. negotiators regarding the Korean proposal, the Korean negotiators have fully explained that the existing Korean claims system is operated efficiently, equitably, and would overcome the problems envisaged by the U.S. negotiators without any difficulty.

"c. In this regard, the U.S. negotiators indicated that the present U.S. system was operated efficiently, equitably and to the general satisfaction of the claimant concerned, whereas the Korean system had relatively shorter experience than the U.S. Armed Forces Claims Service in Korea and had no legally published standard of awards for various claims. Particularly, the U.S. negotiators pointed out that the lack of legal standards would leave open the possibility of settlement of individual claims on bases not related to any standard.

"d. The Korean negotiators believe that the foregoing U.S. negotiators' concerns are neither called for nor well-founded, and they would like to point out the reasons why they believe so.

"e. The U.S. authorities, in the settlement of claims in Korea as military authorities of a sending state, would not deny the significance of the following views: that the award should be paid in a just and reasonable manner, and that the settlement of claims should not adversely affect the promotion and maintenance of friendly relations between the people of the ROK and the United States.

0171

"f. It is, therefore, believed that, for the settlement of claims, the U.S. authorities would not hesitate in providing just and reasonable procedures as well as maximum convenience for the claimant in Korea.

"g. The claims system proposed by the Korean negotiators, particularly with regard to the procedures for the settlement of the claims arising out of acts or omissions of members or employees of the U.S. armed forces done in the performance of official duty, or out of any other act, omission or occurrence for which the U.S. armed forces are legally responsible, and causing damage to the third parties other than the Government of the ROK, at which the U.S. negotiators expressed a deep concern, is so provided that all the claimants could enjoy the full protection guaranteed by the Korean laws. The Government of the ROK will be responsible for the settlement of all the claims arising out of the above acts or omissions. And in case the claimant is dissatisfied with the disposition of the Korean Government, he would be able to have recourse to the Korean court so that all the claims arising within the ROK could be settled by the same procedures regardless of whether the loss or damage is caused by the U.S. armed forces or all the other claims normally arising out of acts or omissions of the ROK armed forces and officials of the Korean Government.

"h. Therefore, there is left no room for the claimant to express discontent with the settlement of claims to the Government of the U.S. or the U.S. military authorities in Korea. This procedure will certainly prevent the national emotion of the Korean people from turning

0172

to the direction which both the Governments and people do not desire, and will, in fact, contribute to the furtherance of the friendly relations now existing between both sides.

"i. However, if the claims were to be settled by the procedures proposed by the U.S. negotiators, awards would have to be paid only in accordance with the military regulations of the U.S. armed forces, specifically, the AR 25-90 of 1957, "Claims Arising in Foreign Countries". In this procedure, the claimants are not duly protected from the legal point of view. When the claimants are not satisfied with the award decided by the U.S. authorities, all they could do would be an appeal to the same authorities for reconsideration. And the claimants have no chance for redress through a competent court.

"j. The Korean negotiators also believe that the U.S. negotiators will fully realize the short-comings of the appeal system of the U.S. claims service in which the same persons who initially decided the award consider the same case again!

"k. For the claimant concerned, it would be hard to approve of procedures whereby the loss or damage caused by his own Government should be given a chance to be tried fairly in the court and the similar loss or damage caused by the foreign authorities should not.

"l. The U.S. negotiators might be concerned at the possibility that the proposed Korean system would not work as it should, and that the Korean authorities would make unjust and discriminatory decisions. The concern is based on the premise that the Korean system lacks the so-called 'legally published standard'. To the knowledge of

0173

the Korean negotiators, the U.S. side has so far failed to present its system of the legally published standard.

"m. However, such a possibility is not existing anywhere in the Korean draft as well as in the existing Korean Claims System as witnessed by some of the U.S. negotiators. In fact, the Korean Government would be in the paying side of an award like the U.S. Government because it has to share a considerable portion of the award. And this, we believe, is a sufficient guarantee to the U.S. Government that illegitimate, unreasonable, and inequitable awards will not be paid as well as a firm determination of the Korean Government that the settlement of claims should be made without prejudice by the authorities of the ROK.

"n. Therefore, the Korean negotiators sincerely request the U.S. negotiators to reconsider their position and to proceed with the discussion of the Claims Article based on the Korean draft."

10. Mr. Habib stated that the U.S. negotiators understood the position of the Korean negotiators. The meeting was then adjourned.

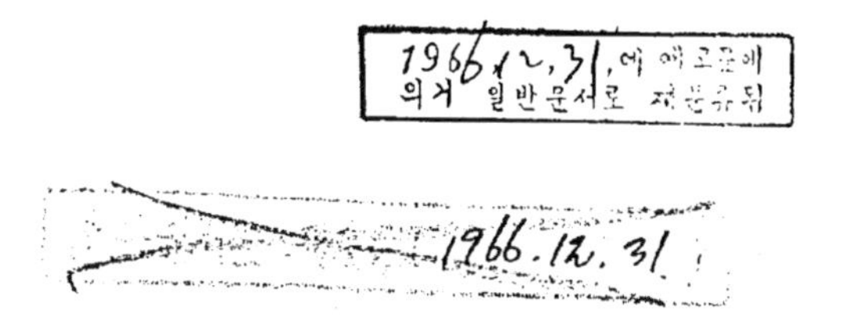

0174

The Authorities of the ROK to exercise Jurisdiction

1. With respect to the phrase "civil authorities of the Republic of Korea" in the U.S. draft, the U.S. negotiators had previously stated that the position ~~of the U.S. negotiators~~ that jurisdiction over the U.S. armed forces by the host government should be limited to the civil authorities of the government was a firm U.S. position in every country in which a SOFA is in force. The U.S. negotiators wanted to have it stated explicitly in the SOFA with the ROK Government. At the 60th session, the U.S. negotiators had again reiterated that the U.S. negotiators of the Agreements with Japan and the NATO governments had not conceived of the possibility that military authorities of the host country could exercise jurisdiction. Inasmuch as that possibility does exist in the Republic of Korea, the U.S. negotiators wished to make the language of the provision quite clear by having it read "the civil authorities of the Republic of Korea."

2. To accommodate the oft-repeated U.S. concern above, and to meet the Korean requirement, the Korean negotiators had given to the U.S. negotiators an unqualified assurance for the negotiating record that under no circumstances would members of the U.S. armed forces and civilian components be subject to trial by Korean military authorities, in the hope that the U.S. negotiators would agree to the deletion of the word "civil" from the draft.

3. The Korean negotiators had further wished at the 60th session to clarify the U.S. position by asking whether the U.S. position was to accept the assurance as an agreed

0175

minute and delete the word "civil" from the text. Although the U.S. side declined to respond to the question on the ground that the question was a hypothetical one, we wish to reiterate our position that the assurance made for the Joint Summary Record should be sufficient to settle the problem. In other words, we cannot accept the word "civil", either in the text or in an agreed minute, but are prepared to negotiate to meet the U.S. requirement through assurances in a form other than text or agreed minute. We wonder what still keeps the U.S. negotiators from accepting the Korean assurances which squarely meet the U.S. requirement. If the U.S. negotiators have in mind any other reasons of insisting on the word "civil" in the text, we have so far no way of knowing them.

The Korean negotiators ask the U.S. negotiators to take into consideration the position of the Korean negotiators and accept it.

0176

Issuance of Official Duty Certificate

1. With respect to the issuance of official duty certificate, the Korean negotiators had proposed at the 52nd session a revised draft which recognized the U.S. military authorities as the authorities to issue a certificate, and had further stated that a certificate issued by the U.S. Military authorities would be sufficient evidence in determining the primary jurisdiction over offenses and any objection which might be raised by the Korean authorities should be decided by the Joint Committee.

2. At the 58th session, the U.S. negotiators had in return proposed as the basis of discussion of the Korean draft the following two understandings:

a. The certificate will be conclusive unless modification is agreed upon.

b. The accused should not be deprived of his entitlement to a prompt and speedy trial as a result of protracted reconsideration of the duty certificate.

With regard to the 2nd understanding, the Korean negotiators had in principle no objection to the U.S. proposal. Accordingly, the Korean negotiators had expressed their willingness to set any number of days to meet the U.S. concern.

3. Regarding the first understanding, the Korean negotiators had stated that although we believed that the certificate issued by the U.S. military authorities would, in most of the cases be honored, in case any objection is raised by the Korean authorities, the problem of validity

0177

of duty certificate should be solved by consultation and agreement between the representatives of both sides at the Joint Committee. We are firmly opposed to any idea which would entertain the possibility that the decision may be made unilaterally by the U.S. military authorities.

4. The Korean negotiators have carefully studied the precedents presented by the U.S. negotiators at the 60th session. In fact, we would be most willing to comply with international precedents. However, we also believe that any dispute in international society should be amicably settled through agreement between the parties concerned and settlement of any controversy over duty certificates should be no exception.

We request the U.S. negotiators to reconsider the Korean proposal and present their views at the earliest possible date.

0178

Waiver of Primary Right to exercise Jurisdiction

1. The Korean negotiators wish to review their position on the draft regarding the waiver of primary right to exercise jurisdiction, thereby reminding the U.S. negotiators of outstanding issues and difficulties which confront us in connection with the waiver problem.

2. According to the U.S. draft, even though we consider it absolutely necessary to try an accused in specific cases, we would be obliged to hand him over to the U.S. authorities and then undergo afterwards necessary procedures to recall the waived case by seeking agreement at the Joint Committee. Furthermore, the U.S. draft does not guarantee any assurance which enables us to obtain successful recall in specific cases.

3. In the past, the U.S. negotiators had emphasized that it was the intention of the U.S. negotiators to obtain maximum waiver from the Korean authorities. To meet the U.S. concern, the Korean negotiators had reiterated that we would waive as many cases as other countries do under their SOFA's. Nevertheless, we firmly maintain that our position is to retain the principle so that we could waive primary right to the U.S. authorities except when we determine that it is of particular importance to try an accused in the Korean court.

4. Time and again, we are ready to assure the U.S. negotiators that the Korean authorities will waive as generously as other SOFA countries do, however, we wish to retain discretion on our part as to whether or not to waive. In this connection, we believe that we are asking the U.S. negotiators not any new or unique ~~languages~~ provisions but only universal ones which have been generally accepted by

0179

other SOFA's so that we could reserve as a hosting country primary right to exercise jurisdiction not in general but in specific cases under special circumstances.

We ask once again that the U.S. negotiators reconsider our difficulties toward this problem and accept the Korean views.

0180

Claims Article

Regarding the Claims Article, the Korean negotiators have studied the position of the U.S. negotiators carefully.

The U.S. negotiators have stated throughout the past discussions on this Article that they preferred the present system of the U.S. armed forces claims service in Korea to the system proposed by the Korean negotiators, because the formula concept envisaged by the latter is proved to be time-consuming and expensive to administer.

However, on those concerns of the U.S. negotiators regarding the Korean proposal, the Korean negotiators have fully explained that the existing Korean claims system is operated efficiently, equitably, and would overcome the problems envisaged by the U.S. negotiators without any ~~such~~ difficulty.

In this regard, the U.S. negotiators indicated that the present U.S. system was operated efficiently, equitably and to the general satisfaction of the claimant concerned, whereas the Korean system had relatively shorter experience than the U.S. armed forced claims service in Korea and had no legally published standard of awards for various claims. Particularly, the U.S. negotiators pointed out that the lack of legal standards would leave open the possibility of settlement of individual claims on basis not related to any standard.

The Korean negotiators believe that the foregoing U.S. negotiators' concerns are neither called for nor well-founded, and they would like to point out the reasons why they believe so.

0181

The U.S. authorities, in the settlement of claims in Korea as military authorities of a sending state, would not deny the significance of the following views; that the award should be paid in a just and reasonable manner, and that the settlement of claims should not adversely affect the promotion and maintenance of friendly relations between the people of the ROK and the U.S.

It is, therefore, believed that, for the settlement of claims, the U.S. authorities would not hesitate in providing just and reasonable procedures as well as maximum convenience for the claimant in Korea.

The claims system proposed by the Korean negotiators, particularly with regard to the procedures for the settlement of the claims arising out of acts or omissions of members or employees of the U.S. armed forces done in the performance of official duty, or out of any other act, omission or occurrence for which the U.S. armed forces are legally responsible, and causing damage to the third parties other than the Government of the ROK, at which the U.S. negotiators expressed a deep concern, is so provided that all the claimant could enjoy the full protection guaranteed by the Korean laws. The Government of the ROK will be responsible for the settlement of all the claims arising out of the above acts or omissions. And in case the claimant is dissatisfied with the disposition of the Korean Government, he would be able to have recourse to the Korean court so that all the claims arising within the ROK could be settled by the same procedures regardless of whether the loss or damage is caused by the U.S. armed forces or all the other claims normally arising out of acts or omissions of the ROK armed forces and officials of the Korean Government.

0182

Therefore, there is left no room for the claimant to express discontent with the settlement of claims to the Government of the U.S. or the U.S. military authorities in Korea. This procedure will certainly prevent the national emotion of the Korean people from turning to the direction which both the Governments and people do not desire, and will, in fact, contribute to the furtherance of the friendly relations now existing between both sides.

However, if the claims were to be settled by the procedures proposed by the U.S. negotiators, award would have to be paid only in accordance with the military regulations of the U.S. armed forces, specifically, the AR 25-90 of 1957, "Claims Arising in Foreign Countries". In this procedure, the claimants are not duly protected from the legal point of view. When the claimants are not satisfied with the award decided by the U.S. authorities, all they could do would be an appeal to the same authorities for reconsideration. And the claimants have no chance for redress through a competent court.

The Korean negotiators also believe that the U.S. negotiators will fully realize the short-coming of the appeal system of the U.S. claims service in which the same persons who initially decided the award consider the same case again.

For the claimant concerned, it would be hard to approve of procedures whereby the loss or damage caused by his own Government should be given a chance to be tried fairly in the court and the similar loss or damage caused by the foreign authorities should not.

0183

The U.S. negotiators might be concerned at the possibility that the proposed Korean system would not work as it should, and that the Korean authorities would make ~~an~~ unjust and discriminatory decisions. The concern is based on the premise that the Korean system lacks the so-called "legally published standard". To the knowledge of the Korean negotiators, the U.S. side has so far failed to present ~~their~~ its system of the legally published standard.

However, such a possibility is not existing anywhere in the Korean draft as well as in the existing Korean Claims system as witnessed by some ~~of the members~~ of the U.S. negotiators. In fact, the Korean Government would be in the paying side of an award like the U.S. Government because it has to share ~~the~~ a considerable portion of the award. And this, we believe, is a sufficient guarantee to the U.S. Government that illegitimate, unreasonable, and inequitable awards will not be paid as well as a firm determination of the Korean Government that the settlement of claims should be made without prejudice by the authorities of the ROK.

Therefore, the Korean negotiators sincerely request the U.S. negotiators to reconsider their position and to proceed with the discussion ~~on~~ of the Claims Article based on the Korean draft.

0184

5. 제67차 회의, 12.16

0185

관리 번호 1654

기 안 용 지

자 체 통 제		기안처	미 주 과 이 근 팔	전화번호	근거서류접수일자
	과장	국장	차관	장관	
관 계 관 서 명					
기 안 년 월 일	1964. 12. 15.	시 행 년월일		보 존 년 한	정 서 기 장
분 류 기 호	외구미 722.2—	전 체 통 제		종결	
경 유 수 신 참 조	건 의			발 신	
제 목	제 67 차 주둔군지위협정 체결 교섭실무자회의에 임할 우리의 입장				

제 67 차 주둔군지위협정 체결 교섭 실무자회의에서 토의될 형사재판관할권에 관하여 1964. 12. 14. 개최된 관계부처 실무자회의에서는 우리측 입장을 별첨과 같이 수립하였읍니다.

유 첨: 제 67 차주둔군지위협정 체결 교섭실무자회의에 임할 우리의 입장. 끝.

~~보통문서로 재분류(1966.12.31.)~~

1966.12.31.에 예고문에 의거 일반문서로 재분류됨.

승인서식 1-1-3 (11-00900-03) (195mm×265mm16절지)

0186

제 67 차 주둔군지위협정 체결 교섭 실무자회의에
임할 우리측 입장

1. 관계부처실무자회의 개최 일자: 1964. 12. 14. 상오 10 시 부터 12 시 까지.

2. 장 소: 외무부 구미국장실

3. 참 석 자:

외무부	구미국장	장 상 문
	미주과장	이 남 기
법무부	검찰과장	여 형 구
	검 사	이 명 희
외무부	미 주 과	김 기 조
	미 주 과	이 근 팔
	미 주 과	황 영 재

4. 토의 내용:

(1) 형사재판관할권의 중요 문제점인 (ㄱ) 미국측의 관할권 행사당국, (ㄴ) 한국측 관할권 행사기관, (ㄷ) 피적용자의 범위, (ㄹ) 공무 집행중 범죄, (ㅁ) 관할권의 포기, (ㅂ) 재판전 피의자의 신병 구금을 중심으로 별첨 내용에 의거 우리측의 종전 입장과 아울러 제 67 차 회의에 임할 입장을 검토하였으며,

(2) 동 석상에서 법무부측으로 부터 차기 회의에서는 미측이 대안을 제시하게 되어 있음으로 미측의 대안 제시를 기다려 그에 대한 우리측 입장을 수립하는 것이 좋겠다는 제의가 있었음으로 차기회의에서는 종전 입장을 계속 주장하기도 하고 문제점에 대한 대안을 포함한 우리측 입장을 계속 검토하기로 하였음.

(3) 12 월 15 일 법무부 검찰과장은 상기와 같은 법무부 입장을 재확인 하였음.

5. 차기 본회의일자: 1964. 12. 16. 하오 3 시. 끝.

유 첨: 형사재판관할권 조항에 대한 검토자료. 끝.

0187

형사재판관할권 조항에 대한 검토자료

1964. 12. 11.

1. 미국측 행사기관

미국: 미국당국

한국: 미국군당국

제1안 미측이 종래 미국의 행사당국을 "미국당국" 으로 주장함에 있어서도 우리측의 우려를 해소하기 위하여 "미국은 한국내에서 재판권을 행사할수 있는 미군사재판소 이외의 어떠한 재판소도 한국에 설치하지 않을 것이다"라는 양해사항을 기록에 남겨도 좋다는 의견을 제시한바 있다.

따라서 미측이 우리주장을 수락하지 않을 경우에는 상기와 같은 미측의 보장을 양해사항 또는 합의의사록으로 규정하고 미측안을 수락한다.

제2안 우리안 대로 "미국군당국"으로 계속 주장한다.

그 근거로서는:

(1) 우리는 주한미군의 지위를 규정하려는 것입으로 한국내에 있어서의 주한미군당국 이외의 여하한 미국의 일반적 기관의 재판권 행사를 인정할수 없다.

(2) 미측은 "미국당국"으로 할 것으로 주장하는 근거로서 장차 제정될 입법을 들고 있으나 그러한 장래의 불확실한 입법은 이유가 될수 없으며 또 그러한 입법이 제정되면 우리는 언제던지 협정의 수정을 위한 교섭을 개시할 용의가 있다.

2. 미적용자의 범위

미국: 미국군대구성원, 군속 및 그들의 가족

한국: 미군법에 복하는 자

제1안 미국안대로 "미국군대구성원, 군속 및 그들의 가족"으로 한다.

0188

문제점 : (1) 미국안대로 수락한다면 미측의 관할권 행사기관을 미국당국으로 해야할 것이다. 그 이유는 민간인 범법자는 미군법재판에는 복할수 없고 다만 헌법상의 모든 권리가 보장되는 미국일반법정의 관할권에 복하게 되어 있기 때문이다.

(2) 각항마다 규정을 검토하여 가족을 추가 삽입해야 할것이다.

3. <u>한국측 행사기관</u>

미국 : 한국민사당국

한국 : 한국당국

<u>제 1안</u> 종래의 우리주장을 계속한다.

즉, "여하한 경우에도 미국군대구성원, 군속 및 그들의 가족(가족을 삽입키로 한다면 모함)을 한국의 군법회의에 회부하지는 않을 것이다." 라는 양해사항을 기록 또는 기타 협정문과 합의의사록외의 형태로 규정한다.

<u>제 2안</u> 우리측이 미측의 행사당국 및 피적용자의 범위를 수락하는 대신 미측에 우리측 주장의 수락을 제의한다.

4. <u>공무집행중 범죄</u>

미국 : 미군당국이 발행한 공무집행중 범죄증명서는 수정이 합의되지 않는한 확정적이다.

한국 : 한국당국이 증명서에 대한 반증을 제시하면 합동위원회에서 양측 합의에 의하여 해결되어야 한다.

<u>제 1안</u> 상기 우리측 입장을 계속 주장하기 위하여 다음과 같이 수정 제안한다.

(1) 공무집행중 범죄 증명서 발급에 관한 우리측 초안중 다음 구절을 삭제한다:

0189

"상기 규정은 여하한 경우에도 형사소송법 제 308 조의 규정을 저해하는 것은 아니다"

(2) 그대신 양측의 공무집행중 범죄의 결정 표준으로 미측의 제안한 공무의 정의를 우리측안 합의의사록중의 공무의 정의와 대체한다.

"공무라 함은 미군대구성원 및 군속이 공무중 행한 모든 행위를 포함하는 것을 의미하는 것이 아니며 개인이 집행하는 공무의 기능으로서 행하여 질 것이 요구되는 행위에만 적용되는 것을 의미한다. 그러므로 어떤자가 특정 공무에 있어서 행할 것이 요구되는 행위로 부터 상당히 이탈된 행위는 통상 그의 공무밖의 행위이다."

제 2 안 미측이 우리안을 수락하는 조건으로 우리도 미측양해사항을 수락한다.

제 3 안 미측이 미측입장을 고집하거나 또는 동일관계 조항에 따른 안을 제시할 경우에는 관할권 포기에 관한 우리측안을 미측이 수락할 것을 전제로 미측안 수락.

5. 관할권의 포기

미국: 한국은 미국이 미군구성원, 군속 및 그들의 가족의 규율과 질서를 유지할 주된 책임이 있음을 인정하고 제 1 차 관할권을 포기한다.

특수한 경우 특수한 사정으로한국당국이 관할권을 행사함이 특히 중대하다고 사려할 때에는 통고 접수 후 15일이내에 합동위원회의 합의를 얻어 포기를 철회한다.

포기의 효과는 모든 목적을 위하여 최종적이며 한국당국 및 국민은 형사소송을 제기할수 없다.

0190

한국: 한국당국은 한국당국이 관할권을 행사함이 특히 중대하다고 결정하는 경우를 제외하고 제1차 관할권을 미국당국에 포기한다.
포기를 위한 상호간 절차는 합동위원회에서 결정한다. 한국당국이 포기한 사건과 한국민이 관련된 공무집행중 범죄사건은 특별한 합의가 없으면 범죄자로 부터 합리적인 거리내에서 재판되어야 한다.

제1안 우리입장을 계속 주장

제2안 공무집행중 범죄에 관한 미측주장 수락과 관련하여 우리측 입장 주장

제3안 그리스 안에 따라 수정 제안

제4안 미측이 독일안에 유사한 초안을 제시할 경우는 우리가 특히 필요한 경우의 재판권을 확보할 것을 강구한다.

6. 재판전 피의자의 구금

미국: 미국당국의 수중에 있을 경우: 모든 재판절차가 끝나고 한국당국의 요청이 있을때까지 미국당국이 구금.
한국당국의 수중에 있을 경우: 즉시 미국당국으로 신병을 이양하고 모든 재판절차가 끝나고 한국당국이 요청할때까지 미국당국이 구금한다.
한국의 안전에 관한 피의자의 구금에 있어서는 쌍방이 합의해야 한다.

한국: 미국당국 수중에 있을 경우: 미측안 수락.
한국당국의 수중에 있을 경우: 피의자의 신병을 한국당국 수중에 둘 정당한 이유와 필요가 있을 경우를 제외하고 미측에 인도하며 요청하면 기소시 한국당국에 구금을 이양해야 한다.
한국의 안전에 관한 피의자의 구금은 한국당국이 한다. 그경우 구금에 관한 쌍방의 합의는 필요치 않다.

0191

제 1안 우리안을 계속 주장

단, 다음 제점을 수정할 것을 고려한다.

(1) 가족을 1항에서 수락할 경우 여기서도 수락해야 할 것인가의 문제.

(2) 한국당국의 수중에 있는 피의자의 신병을 미측에 인도하였을 경우 한국당국에 재인도하는 시기를 미측수중에 있을 경우와 동일하게 하는 문제.

제 2안 한국의 안전에 대한 신병 구금에 관한 미측 주장을 수락한다.

0192

SOFA NEGOTIATION

Agenda for the 67th Session

15:00 December 16, 1964

1. Continuation of Discussions on
   a. Criminal Jurisdiction Article
2. Other Business
3. Agenda and Date of the Next Meeting
4. Press Release

0193

AGREED MINUTE RE PARAGRAPH 3

The Republic of Korea, recognizing that it is the primary responsibility of the United States authorities to maintain good order and discipline where persons subject to United States law are concerned, waives its primary right to exercise jurisdiction under paragraph 3b. In accordance therewith, the United States authorities shall notify the authorities of the Republic of Korea of their intention to exercise jurisdiction in such cases through the Joint Committee. When the authorities of the Republic of Korea, after consultation with United States authorities, are of the opinion that, by reason of special circumstances in a specific case involving an offense against the security of the Republic of Korea, or of forcible rape, or of a malicious killing, the exercise of Korean jurisdiction is of vital importance to the Republic of Korea in that case, they will notify the United States authorities of that opinion within fifteen days after receipt of notification that the United States intends to exercise jurisdiction. The United States shall not have the right to exercise jurisdiction within those fifteen days. If any question arises concerning who is to exercise jurisdiction the United States diplomatic mission will be afforded an opportunity to confer with the proper authorities of the Republic of Korea before a final determination of this matter is made.

Trials of cases in which the authorities of the Republic of Korea waive the primary right to exercise jurisdiction, and trials of cases involving offenses described in para 3(a)(ii) committed against the state or nationals of the Republic of Korea will be held within a reasonable distance from the place where the offenses are alleged to have taken place unless other

CLASSIFIED

0194

arrangements are mutually agreed upon. Representatives of the Republic of Korea may be present at such trials.

In the implementation of the provisions of Article   and this Minute, and to facilitate the expeditious disposal of offenses, arrangements may be made between the authorities of the United States and the Republic of Korea to dispense with notification.

Dec 16, '64
new paragraph

CLASSIFIED

Agreed Minute Re Paragraph 3(a)

2. Where a member of the United States armed forces or civilian component is charged with an offense, a certificate issued by competent authorities of the United States forces stating that the alleged offense, if committed by him, arose out of an act or omission done in the performance of official duty shall be sufficient evidence of the fact for the purpose of determining primary jurisdiction.

In those exceptional cases where the chief prosecutor for the Republic of Korea considers that there is proof contrary to a certificate of official duty, it may be made the subject of review through discussions between appropriate officials of the Government of the Republic of Korea and the diplomatic mission of the United States in Korea.

0196

ARTICLE

Either Government may at any time request the revision of any Article of this Agreement, in which case the two Governments shall enter into negotiations through appropriate channels.

0197

I. Each Party waives all its claims against the other Party for damage to any property owned by it and used by its land, sea or air armed forces, if such damage:

(a) was caused by a member or an employee of the armed forces of the other Party in the performance of his official duties; or

(b) arose from the use of any vehicle, vessel or aircraft owned by the other Party and used by its armed forces, provided either that the vehicle, vessel or aircraft causing the damage was being used for official purposes, or that the damage was caused to property being so used.

Claims by one Party against the other Party for maritime salvage shall bewaived provided that the vessel or cargo salvagged was owned by a Party and being used by its armed forces for official purposes.

2. In the case of damage caused or arising as stated in paragraph I to other property owned by a Party:

(a) each Party waives its claim up to the amount of $I 400 or its equivalent in Korean currency at the rate of exchange provided for in the Agreed Minute to Article__________ at the time the claim is filed.

(b) claims in excess of the amount stated in subparagraph (a) shall be settled by the Party against which the claim made in accordance with its domestic law.

0198

3. For the purpose of parargraphs I and 2 of this Article, the expression "owned by a Party" in the case of a vessel includes a vessel on bare boat charter to that Party or requisitioned by it on bare boat charter terms or seized by it in prize (except to the extent that the risk of loss or liability is borne by some other person than such Party).

4. Each Party waives all its claims against the other Party for injury or death suffered by any member of its armed forces while such mimber was engaged in the performance of his official duties.

5. Claims (Other than contractual claims) arising out of the acts or omissions of members or employees of the United States armed forces done in the performance of official duty, or out of any other act, omission or occurrende for which the United States armed forces are legally responsible, and causing damage in the Republic of Korea to third parties other than the two Governments shall be processed and settled in accordance with the applicable provisions of United States law. The United States Government shall entertain other non-contractual claims against members of the United States armed forces or of the civilian component and may offer an ex gratia payment in such cases and in such amoubt as is determined by the appropriate United States Authroities.

0199

6. (a) A member or employee of the United States armed forces shall not be afforded immunity from the jurisdiction of the civil courts of Korea except: (I) in a matter arising out o of acts or ommissions done in the performance of officiab duty; or (2) in respect to any claim where there has been payment in full satisfaction of the claim.

(b) In the case of any private movable property, excluding that in use by the United States armed forces, which is subject to compulsory execution under Korean law, and is within the facilities and areas in use by the United States armed forces, the United States authorities shall, upon the request of the Korean courts, render all assistance within their power to see that such property is turned over to the Korean authorities.

7. The authorities of the United States and Korea shall cooperate in the procurement of evidence for a fair disposition of claims under this Article.

8. Paragraphs 2 and 5 of this Article shall apply only to claims arising incident to noncombat activities.

9. For the purposes of this Article, each Party shall have the right to determine whether a member or employee of its armed forces was engaged in the performance of official duties and whether property owned by it was being used by its armed forces for official purposes.

IO. For the purposes of this Article, members of the Korean Augmentation to the United States Army (KATUSA) shall be considered as members of the United States armed forces, and

0200

members of the Korean Service Corps (KSC) shall be considered as employees of the armed forces of the Republic of Korea.

II. The provisions of this Article shall not apply to any claims which arose before the entry into force of thisAgreement.

0201

ARTICLE

Health and Sanitation

Consistent with the right of the United States to furnish medical support for its armed forces, civilian component and their dependents, matters of mutual concern pertaining to the control and prevention of diseases and the coordination of other public health, medical, sanitation, and veterinary services shall be resolved by the authorities of the two Governments in the Joint Committee established under Article ________.

0202

ARTICLE

Local Procurement

1. The United States may contract for any supplies or construction work to be furnished or undertaken in the Republic of Korea for purposes of, or authorized by, this Agreement, without restriction as to choice of supplier or person who does the construction work. Such supplies or construction work may, upon agreement between the appropriate authorities of the two Governments, also be procured through the Government of the Republic of Korea.

2. Materials, supplies, equipment and services which are required from local sources for the maintenance of the United States armed forces and the procurement of which may have an adverse effect on the economy of the Republic of Korea shall be procured in coordination with, and, when desirable, through or with the assistance of, the competent authorities of the Republic of Korea.

3. Materials, supplies, equipment and services procured for official purposes in the Republic of Korea by the United States armed forces, including their authorized procurement agencies, or procured for ultimate use by the United States armed forces shall be exempt from the following Korean taxes upon appropriate certification by the United States armed forces:

(a) Commodity tax;

(b) Traffic tax;

(c) Petroleum tax;

(d) Electricity and gas tax;

(e) Business tax.

With respect to any present or future Korean taxes not specifically referred to in this Article which might be found to constitute a significant and readily identifiable part of the gross purchase price of materials, supplies, equipment and services procured by the United States armed forces, or for ultimate use by such forces, the two Governments will agree upon a procedure for granting such exemption or relief therefrom as is consistent with the purpose of this Article.

4. Neither members of the United States armed forces, civilian component, nor their dependents, shall by reason of this Article enjoy any exemption from taxes or similar charges relating to personal purchases of goods and services in the Republic of Korea chargeable under Korean legislation.

5. Except as such disposal may be authorized by the United States and Korean authorities in accordance with mutually agreed conditions, goods purchased in the Republic of Korea exempt from taxes referred to in paragraph 3, shall act be disposed of in the Republic of Korea to persons not entitled to purchase such goods exempt from such tax.

AGREED MINUTE

1. The United States armed forces will furnish the Korean authorities with appropriate information as far in advance as practicable on anticipated major changes in their procurement program in the Republic of Korea.

2. The problem of a satisfactory settlement of difficulties with respect to procurement contracts arising out of differences between Korean and United States economic laws and business practices will be studies by the Joint Committee or other appropriate persons.

3. The procedures for securing exemptions from taxation on purchases of goods for ultimate use by the United States armed forces will be as follows:

(a) Upon appropriate certification by the United States armed forces that materials, supplies and equipment consigned to or destined for such forces, are to be used, or wholly or partially used up, under the supervision of

0204

such forces, exclusively in the execution of contracts for the construction, maintenance or operation of the facilities and areas referred to in Article ______ or for the support of the forces therein, or are ultimately to be incorporated into articles or facilities used by such forces, an authorized representative of such forces shall take delivery of such materials, supplies and equipment directly from manufacturers thereof. In such circumstances the collection of taxes referred to in Article , paragraph 3, shall be held in abeyance.

representative

(b) The receipt of such materials, supplies and equipment in the facilities and areas shall be confirmed by an authorized agent of the United States armed forces to the Korean authorities.

(c) Collection of the taxes on such materials, supplies and equipment shall be held in abeyance until.

(1) The United States armed forces confirm and certify the quantity or degree of consumption of the above referred to materials, supplies and equipment, or

(2) The United States armed forces confirm and certify the amount of the above referred to materials, supplies, and equipment which have been incorporated into articles or facilities used by the United States armed forces.

(d) Materials, supplies, and equipment certified under (c) (1) or (2) shall be exempt from taxes referred to in Article , paragraph 3, insofar as the price thereof is paid out of United States Government appropriations or out of funds contributed by the Government of the Republic of Korea for disbursement by the United States.

0205

ARTICLE ________

SECURITY MEASURES

"The United States and the Republic of Korea will cooperate in taking such steps as may from time to time be necessary to ensure the security of the United States armed forces, the members thereof, the civilian component, the persons who are present in the Republic of Korea pursuant to Article ________, their dependents and their property. The Government of the Republic of Korea agrees to seek such legislation and to take such other action as may be necessary to ensure the adequate security and protection within its territory of installations, equipment, property, records and official information of the United States , of the persons referred to in this paragraph, and their property and, consistent with Article ________, to ensure the punishment of offenders under the applicable laws of the Republic of Korea."

0206

ARTICLE________

TAXATION

I. The United States armed forces shall not be subject to taxes or similar charges on property held, used or transferred by such forces in Korea.

2. Members of the United States armed forces, the civilian component, and their dependents shall not be liable to pay any K Korea on income received as a result of their service with or employment by the United States armed forces, the including the act activities provided for in Article . Persons in Korea solely by reason of being members of the United States armed forces, the civilian component, or their dependents shall not be liable to pay any Korean taxes to the Government of Korea or to any taxing agency in Korea on income derived from sources outside of Korea, nor shall periods during which such persons are in Korea for the purpose of Korean taxation. The provisions of this Article do not exempt such persons from payment of Kotean taxes on income derived from ~~sources of Korean taxes on income~~ sources, other than those sources referred to in the first sentence of this parqgraph, nor do they exempt United States citizens who claim Korean residence ce for United States income tax purposes frompayment of Korean atxes on income.

0207

3. Members of the United States armed forces, the civilian component, and their dependents shall be exempt from taxation in Korea on the holding, use, transfer *inter se*, or transfer by death of movable property, tangible or intangible, the presence of which in Korea is due solely to the temporary presence of these persons in Korea, provided that such exemption shall not apply to property held for the purpose of investment or the conduct of business in Korea or to any intangible property registered in Korea.

0208

ARTICLE

LICENSING OF MOTOR VEHICLES

I. Korea shall accept as valid, without a driving test or fee, the driving permit or license or military driving permit issued by the United States, or political subdivision thereof, to a member of the United States armed forces, the civilian component, and their dependents.

2. Official vehicles of the United States armed forces and the civilian component shall carry distinctive numbered plates or individual markings which will readily identify them.

3. Privately owned vehicles of members of the United States armed forces, the civilian component and their dependents may be licensed or registered, and shall be provided with license plate or other identification as appropriate, by the United States. The authorities of the United States shall take adequate safety measures for, and shall assure the technical supervision of, the vehicles licensed by them and shall, where necessary, and at the request of the Government of the Republic of Korea, furnish the name and address of the owner of a vehicle licensed by them.

0209

ARTICLE

3. The Government of the Republic of Korea will license and register those vehicles privately owned by members of the United States armed forces, the civilian component, or dependents. The names of the owners of such vehicles and such other pertinent information as is required by Korean law to effect the licensing and registration of such vehicles, shall be furnished to the Government of the Republic of Korea by officials of the United States Government through the Joint Committee. Except for the actual cost of the issuance of license plates, members of the United States armed forces, the civilian component, and their dependents shall be exempt from the payment of all fees and charges relating to the licensing, registration, or operation of vehicles in the Republic of Korea and, in accordance with the provisions of Article ____, from the payment of all taxes relating thereto.

0210

관리번호 1657

기 안 용 지

자체통제		기안처	미주과 이근팔	전화번호	근거서류접수일자
	과장	국장	차관	장관	
	17/12		대결		
관계관 서명					
기안년월일	1964. 12. 17.	시행년월일		보존년한	정서 / 기장
분류기호	외구미 722.2	전체통제		종결	
경수참 유신조	대통령, 참조: 비서실장 국무총리, 참조: 비서실장 사본: 법무부장관		발신	장관	
제목	제 67 차 주둔군지위협정 체결 교섭실무자회의 결과 보고				

1964 년 12 월 16 일 하오 4 시 부터 동 5 시 까지 외무부 제 1 회의실에서 개최된 제 67 차 주둔군지위협정 체결 교섭 실무자회의에서 토의된 형사재판관할권 에 관한 내용을 별첨과 같이 보고합니다.

유 첨: 제 67 차 주둔군지위협정 체결 교섭실무자회의 보고서. 끝

~~검토필 후 관리되면 보통문서로 재~~

1964.12.31 에 예고문에 의거 일반문서로 재분류됨

발송 1964.12.18 외무부

승인서식 1-1-3 (11-00900-03) (195mm×265mm16절지)

법무부장관 앞 공한(관리번호 1658호)은 형사재판관할 건에 (64-D) 있음.

0211

외 무 부

외구미 722.2 1964. 12. 18.

수신 법무부장관
참조 검찰국장
제목 제67차 주둔군지위협정 체결 교섭실무자회의 결과 보고

1. 1964. 12. 16일 개최된 제67차 주둔군지위협정 체결 교섭 실무자회의에서 토의된 형사재판관할권에 관한 보고서 사본을 송부하오니 이를 검토하시와 그 수락 여부에 대한 귀견을 회보하여 주시기 바라며 만일 미측제안을 수락할수 없다고 사료하실 경우에는 우리측이 제시할 대안을 작성 송부하여 주시기 바랍니다.

2. 당부로서는 미측이 금번 제시한 포괄적 제안에 대하여 약간의 수정을 가하여 수락하는 방도가 강구될수 있다고 사료하오나 우리측이 미측의 제안을 수락않거나 또는 거리가 먼 대안을 제시할 경우에는 교섭의 조기 타결을 기하기 어려울 것으로 봅니다.

유첨 - 제67차 주둔군지위협정 체결 교섭 실무자 회의 결과 보고서 사본. 끝

외 무 부 장 관 이 동 원

0212

외 무 부

외구미 722.2 1964. 12. 18.

수신 대통령, 국무총리
참조 비서실장
사본 법무부장관
제목 제67차 주둔군지위협정 체결 교섭실무자회의 결과 보고

1964. 12. 16일 하오 4시부터 동 5시까지 외무부 제1회의실에서 개최된 제67차 주둔군지위협정 체결 교섭 실무자회의에서 토의된 형사재판관할권에 관한 내용을 별첨과 같이 보고합니다.

유첨 - 제67차 주둔군지위협정 체결 교섭 실무자회의 보고서. 끝.

첨부문에서 분리되면 보통문서로 재분류

외 무 부 장 관 이 동 원

0213

제 67 차

한 . 미간 주둔군지위협정 체결 교섭
실무자회의 보고서

1. 일시 1964. 12. 16 일 , 하오 4 시부터 동 5 시까지
2. 장소 외무부 제 1 회의실
3. 토의사항

형사재판관할권

가. 미측은 형사재판관할권에 관한 우리측의 종래의 입장을 면밀히 검토한바 있으며 또한 교섭의 조기 타결을 원한다고 전제한다음 형사재판관할권 중 (ㄱ) 제 1 차 관할권의 포기 , (ㄴ) 공무집행중 범죄 , (ㄷ) 재판전 피의자의 신병구금 , (ㄹ) 피의자의 권리등 4 개중요문제에 관하여 미측의 종래의 주장을 수정하여 다음과 같이 포괄적 대안을 제출하고 우리측이 일괄 수락할 것을 촉구하였다 .

(1) 관할권의 포기

미측이 종래의주장을 철회하고 제시한 대안은 다음과 같다 :

" 대한민국은 미국법에 복하는 자에 관하여 질서와 규율을 유지함이 미국당국의 주된 책임임을 인정하여 3 (b) 항의 규정에 의한 관할권을 행사하는 제 1 차적 권리를 포기한다 . 상기한바에 따라 미국당국은 그러한 경우에 관할권을 행사할 의사를 합동위원회를 통하여 대한민국당국에 통고하여야 한다 . 대한민국당국은 미국당국과 협의한 후 대한민국의 안전 , 강간 , 또는 고의적인 살인에 대한 범죄에 관련된 특별한 사건에서는 특수한 사정이라는 이유로 한국이 그사건에 있어서 대한민국을 위하여 특히 중대하다는 의견을 가질때 대한민국당국은 미국이 관할권을

64-3-86

0214

0215

행사할 의도가 있다는 통고의 접수 후 15일 이내에 그의견을 미국당국에 통고한다. 미국은 상기 15일 이내에는 관할권을 행사할 권리를 갖지 못한다. 만약에 어느 편이 관할권을 행사할 것인가에 관하여 의문이 제기 된다면 미국외교사절은 본건에 관한 최종적 결정이 이루워지기 전에 대한민국의 관계당국 과 협의할 기회가 부여된다.

"대한민국이 관할권을 행사할 제 1 차적 권리를 포기하는 사건의 재판과 제 3 (a) (ii) 항에 규정된 범죄(공무집행중 범죄)로서 대한민국 또는 대한민국 국민에 대하여 범하여 진 범죄에 관련된 사건의 재판은 별도의 조치가 상호 합의되지 않는한 범죄가 행하여 졌다는 장소로 부터 적당한 거리 내에서 행하여 진다. 대한 민국의 대표는 그러한 재판에 입회할수 있다.

"___조 및 본합의의사록의 규정을 시행하며 또한 범죄의 신속한 처리를 촉진하기 위하여 미국 및 대한민국 당국간에 통고로서 ~~없이~~ 처리하기 위한 조치를 할수 있다."

(2) 공무집행중 범죄

(가) 미측은 제 58 차 회의에서 미측이 제안한바 있는 공무집행중 범죄에 관한 2개의 양해 사항을 한국측이 수락할것을 조건으로 다음과 같은 수정안을 제시하였다.

"미국군대 구성원 또는 군속이 범죄의 혐의를 받았을 때 (is charged with an offense)그 자가 범하였다면 혐의된 범죄가 공무집행중에 행한 작위 또는 부작위에

0216

64-3-87

0217

기인한 것임을 진술한 미국군대의 권한 있는 당국이 발행한 증명서는 제1차 관할권을 결정하기 위한 사실의 충분한 증거가 된다.

"대한민국의 검찰청장은 공무집행증명서에 대한 반증이 있다고 사료하는 예외적인 경우에는 공무집행증명서는 대한민국 정부의 관계관과 주한미국외교사절간의 협의를 통한 재심의 대상이 될수있다."

(나) 그런데 미측이 제58차 회의에서 제시한 2개의 양해사항은 다음과 같다.

(ㄱ) 미군당국이 발행한 공무집행증명서는 미측이 수정하지 않는한 구속력을 갖는다.

(ㄴ) 공무집행증명서에 대한 재심의 지연으로 피의자의 신속한 재판을 받을 권리가 박탈되어서는 아니된다.

(3) <u>피의자의 재판전 구금</u>

미측은 우리측이 제52차회의에서 제의한바 "한국의 안전에 관한 피의자의 신병은 한국당국이 구금한다"는 제안을 미측이 수락하는 대신 우리측이 다음과 같은 사항을 수락할 것을 요구하였다.

(가) 신병 구금에 관한 다음과 같은 미측초안 (요지)

(ㄱ) 피의자의 신병이 미측 수중에 있을 때에는 모든 재판절차가 끝나고 한국당국이 신병의 인도를 요청할 때까지 미측이 구금한다.

(ㄴ) 피의자의 신병이 한국당국 수중에 있을 때에는 한국당국은 피의자의 신병을

0218

64-3-7/8

0219

즉시 미국당국에 인도해야 하며 모든 재판절차가 끝나고 한국당국이 신병의 인도를 요청할때까지 미국당국이 신병을 구금한다.

(ㄷ) 미국당국은 한국당국의 요청이 있으면 한국당국이 피의자에 대한 수사 또는 재판을 할수 있게 한다.

(ㄹ) 한국당국은 미국당국이 군인 군속 또는 가족의 신병을 구금함에 있어 조력을 요청하는 경우 호의적 고려를 한다.

(나) 대한민국의 안전에 대한 피의자의 신병 구금에 관한 미측의 다음과 같은 2개의 양해사항.

(ㄱ) 한국측의 신병 구금 사정의 적당여부에 대하여 한·미양국간의 상호 합의가 있어야 한다.

(ㄴ) 한국의 구금시설은 미국수준으로 보아 적당하여야 한다.

(4) 피의자의 권리

한국의 재판권에 복하게 되는 미군관계 피의자의 기본적 인권보장은 미국회와 미국민의 비상한 관심사임으로 미측이 합의의사록에서 제안한 피의자의 모든 권리를 한국측이 수락하여야 한다.

나. 우리측은 미측이 교섭의 조속한 타결을 위하여 형사재판관할권의 중요문제에 관하여 광범위한 포괄적인 제안을 한 성의에 대하여 감사하는 한편 미측 제안이 상금 한국측의 주장과는 상당한 거리가 있음을 지적하고, 관계부처와 더불어 검토한후 다음 기회에 우리태도를 밝히기로 하고 폐회하였다.

다. 차기회의일자: 1964년 12월23일 하오 3시. 끝

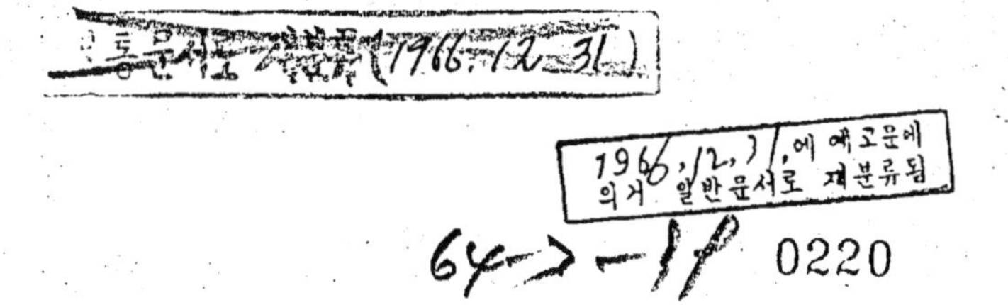

14-3-35(4)　　미국문 111-2(4)

0221

STATUS OF FORCES NEGOTIATIONS: 67th Meeting

SUBJECT: Criminal Jurisdiction

PLACE: Ministry of Foreign Affairs

DATE: December 16, 1964

PARTICIPANTS:

Republic of Korea	United States
CHANG Sang-mun	Philip C. Habib
~~YI~~ LEE Nam-ki	Brig. General Carroll H. Dunn, USA
YUN Un-yong	Captain John Wayne, USN
O Chae-hi	Colonel Kenneth C. Crawford, USA
YI Myong-hi	Frank R. LaMacchia
HWANG Yong-chae	Benjamin A. Fleck
KIM ~~Ki-jocho~~ (Kee, Joe)	Robert A. Kinney
YI Kun-pal (Interpreter)	Goodwin Shapiro
PARK, WON Chul	Major Alton Harvey, USA
	David Y.C. Lee (Interpreter)

3/12

0222

CONFIDENTIAL

1. Mr. Chang opened the meeting by introducing Mr. KIM ~~Chi-cho~~ KEE JOE, of the America Section, Ministry of Foreign Affairs, a newly-appointed member of the Korean negotiating team. Mr. Habib welcomed Mr. Kim to the negotiations on behalf of the American negotiators.

Criminal Jurisdiction

2. Taking up the Criminal Jurisdiction Article, Mr. Habib said the U.S. negotiators wished to resume the presentation of their views. A review of the negotiating record showed that the views of both sides had been explored in great depth. Both sides realize that this article is the key to the entire Agreement. The U.S. negotiators believe that considerable progress has been made in reconciling the views of the two negotiating teams. In some respects, the U.S. negotiators have already made a number of substantial concessions to the Korean position. At this meeting, the U.S. negotiators would table a comprehensive package proposal designed to provide solutions to the four major outstanding issues in this article: waiver of jurisdiction, duty certificates, pre-trial custody, and trial safeguards. Resolution of these issues would leave a number of additional points to be clarified but these four issues are the key elements in the article. U.S. willingness to agree to each of the four positions set forth in the package is contingent on the agreement of the Korean negotiators to accept all four positions.

0223

3. Mr. Habib stated that the U.S. negotiators were prepared to table significant modifications of the U.S. positions on the waiver and duty certificate issues, which were designed to be responsive to views previously expressed by the Korean negotiators, consistent with essential U.S. requirements. The U.S. negotiators had previously tabled modified positions on the pre-trial custody and trial safeguards issues. They believed that some agreement in principle had been reached on the latter two issues.

4. Mr. Habib then tabled the following revision of the Agreed Minute Re Paragraph 3, U.S. draft:

> "The Republic of Korea, recognizing that it is the primary responsibility of the United States authorities to maintain good order and discipline where persons subject to United States law are concerned, waives its primary right to exercise jurisdiction under paragraph 3(b). In accordance therewith, the United States authorities shall notify the authorities of the Republic of Korea of their intention to exercise jurisdiction in such cases through the Joint Committee. When the authorities of the Republic of Korea, after consultation with United States authorities, are of the opinion that, by reason of special circumstances in a specific case involving an offense against the security of the Republic of Korea, or of forcible rape, or xx of a malicious killing, the exercise of Korean jurisdiction is of vital importance to the Republic of Korea in that case, they will notify the United States authorities of that opinion within fifteen days after receipt of notification that the United States intends to

0224

"exercise jurisdiction. The United States shall not have the right to exercise jurisdiction within those fifteen days. If any question arises concerning who is to exercise jurisdiction the United States diplomatic mission will be afforded an opportunity to confer with the proper authorities of the Republic of Korea before a final determination of this matter is made.

"Trials of cases in which the authorities of the Republic of Korea waive the primary right to exercise jurisdiction, and trials of cases involving offenses described in Paragraph 3(a)(ii) committed against the state or nationals of the Republic of Korea will be held within a reasonable distance from the place where the offenses are alleged to have taken place unless other arrangements are mutually agreed upon. Representatives of the Republic of Korea may be present at such trials.

"In the implementation of the provisions of Article ___ and this Minute, and to facilitate the expeditious disposal of offenses, arrangements may be made between the authorities of the United States and the Republic of Korea to dispense with notification."

5. Mr. Habib explained that the Agreed Minute just tabled would combine an automatic waiver with a right of recall by the Korean authorities under the circumstances specified in the Minute. When the Korean authorities , after consultation with ▬ United States authorities, decided that, due to special circumstances in a particular case involving the security of the Republic of Korea, a forcible rape, or a malicious killing, the exercise of Korean jurisdiction was of vital importance, they would so notify the United States authorities. If any question should arise concerning the exercise of jurisdiction, the United States diplomatic mission would be afforded the opportunity to confer with authorities of the Republic of Korea before a final determination was made. This formula, Mr. Habib emphasized, recognizes the right of the [Government of the] Republic of Korea to determine when under the specified circumstances a waiver may be recalled.

6. Mr. Habib recalled that the Korean negotiators have always stated that the exercise of Korean jurisdiction was contemplated only in those cases [which were deemed to be] of particular importance. The formula proposed by the U.S. negotiators provides for this and includes those serious crimes committed against either the Government of the Republic of Korea

or Korean individuals. In those cases, the ROK Government would determine whether or not the waiver should be recalled, although the right of U.S. authorities to confer on such recall is provided. Mr. Habib called the attention of the Korean negotiators to the fact that the second paragraph of the tabled Agreed Minute is a new addition to the U.S. draft. This provision was added in order to incorporate the position set forth in the third paragraph of the Agreed Minute Re Paragraph 3(c) of the Korean draft. The U.S. negotiators view these provisions as desirable and are pleased to be able to accede to the wishes of the Government of the Republic of Korea by incorporating them in the U.S. draft.

7. Mr. Habib recalled that at the 52nd negotiating meeting, the Korean negotiators had tabled a proposed Agreed Minute to Paragraph 3 (a)(ii) pertaining to duty certificates. As understood by the U.S. negotiators, the major objection of the Korean negotiators to Agreed Minute #2 Re Paragraph 3(a) of the U.S. draft was its provision that the duty certificate issued by a commanding officer would be conclusive. The U.S. negotiators continued to believe that the duty certificate must be controlling but they were now prepared to make a major concession by tabling a revised Agreed Minute #2 Re Paragraph 3(a) which they believe embodies certain essential principles previously tabled by the Korean negotiators.

8. Mr. Habib then tabled the following revised Agreed Minute #2 Re Paragraph 3(a

> "2. Where a member of the United States armed forces or civilian component is charged with an offense, a certificate issued by competent authorities of the United States forces stating that the alleged offense, if committed by him, arose out of an act or omission done in the performance of official duty shall be sufficient evidence of the fact for the purpose of determining primary jurisdiction.
>
> " In those exceptional cases where the chief prosecutor for the Republic of Korea considers that there is proof contrary to a certificate of official duty, it may be made the subject of review through discussions between appropriate officials of the Government of the Republic of Korea and the diplomatic mission of the United States in Korea."

0226

9. Mr. Habib recalled that the Korean draft defined the duty certificate as "sufficient evidence" rather than as being conclusive. The Korean draft also had contained a distinction regarding the issuing authority. The revised U.S. Agreed Minute would provide that the duty certificate will be issued by "competent authorities of the United States" rather than by the Staff Judge Advocate. This change is deemed necessary because many major units of the U.S. forces do not have a Staff Judge Advocate assigned to them, even though such units may always request any legal advice from their superior headquarters. Another modification in the revised Agreed Minute relates to the body to whom the ROK Chief Prosecutor would refer if he determined that there was proof contrary to the duty certificate. Under the terms of the revision, the question would be reviewed by the appropriate authorities of the Republic of Korea and the United States diplomatic mission rather than by the Joint Committee. The U.S. negotiators regard this as a better system since it will result in reaching a final determination more quickly.

10. Regarding the duty certificate itself, Mr. Habib continued, the U.S. negotiators continue to hold strong views. Both sides recognize the fact that the accused should not be deprived of his entitlement to a prompt and speedy trial as a result of a prolonged review by officials of the two governments. The U.S. negotiators also believe that the duty certificate must be controlling. Therefore, if agreement is not reached within a specified time on a specific case, the duty certificate would be conclusive for that case but discussions could continue concerning the propriety of issuing a duty certificate under similar circumstances in future cases. The U.S. revised Agreed Minute would provide the ROK Chief Prosecutor the right to question the duty certificate. It would provide the means for discussing the matter and the possibility of modifying the certificate. However, unless modified, the duty certificate would be controlling. This is fully consistent with practice and precedents elsewhere.

11. Mr. Habib stated that the U.S. negotiators were offering the

0227

foregoing amendments to important provisions of the Article with the understanding that they were part of a package which also contained additional proposals which he would now explain.

12. First, Mr. Habib continued, the U.S. negotiators continued to deem necessary subparagraph 5 (c) of the U.S. draft, pertaining to pre-trial custody. The U.S. negotiators would agree to the adoption of subparagraph 5(e) proposed by the Korean negotiators (which would provide for ROK custody in security cases) if the Korean negotiators would agree to the inclusion in the Joint Agreed Summary of the understanding proposed at the 58th meeting, i.e.:

a. Mutual agreement [must be reached] as to the circumstances in which custody is appropriate in security cases; and

b. Confinement facilities must be adequate by U.S. standards.

13. Secondly, Mr. Habib stated, it is essential to U.S. needs that the trial safeguards be enumerated in the SOFA. Therefore, the enumeration of trial safeguards contained in Paragraph 9 and the related Agreed Minutes must be accepted. This subject had already been discussed at length and in detail and the U.S. negotiators did not believe further discussion was necessary.

14. Mr. Habib stated that the U.S. negotiators believe that the Korean negotiators are well aware of the special importance that the United States Government attaches to the custody provisions and the fair trial guarantees. The U.S. negotiators, like the Korean negotiators, must be able to justify the provisions of the Agreement before their legislature and the Korean negotiators surely realize the great importance which the U.S. Congress places on guarantees of a fair trial.

15. Mr. Habib pointed out that the package proposal also included deletion of the provisions of the U.S. draft relating to the combat zone (Agreed Minute No. 1 Re Paragraph 1(b)) and to the primary right of jurisdiction in those cases in which a ROK

0228

court-martial would be appropriate if a Korean serviceman were the accused (Agreed Minute No. 1 Re Paragraph 3(a)). In recognition of the dislike for these provisions previously expressed by the Korean negotiators, the U.S. negotiators had already agreed to their deletion.

16. Mr. Habib stated that the U.S. negotiators presented this comprehensive package proposal with the objective of achieving an early, successful conclusion to the negotiations. They had made major concessions on the issues of waiver of jurisdiction and duty certificates, subject to Korean acceptance of the U.S. positions on custody and trial safeguards. The U.S. negotiators hoped that the Korean negotiators and the authorities of the ROK Government, in considering the U.S. proposals, would keep in mind that these proposals represent the carefully formulated views of the U.S. Government and reflect the desire on the part of U.S. Government authorities to be as responsive as possible to ROK views, consistent with essential U.S. requirements. Other questions remain to be settled in this Article but the U.S. negotiators believe that they can be settled expeditiously if agreement is reached on the four major issues. The U.S. negotiators, therefore, asked the ROK negotiators to give these proposals the most careful consideration.

17. Mr. Chang replied that the Korean negotiators appreciated the intensive and comprehensive package proposal made by the U.S. negotiators. They recognized that the proposal was made by the U.S. negotiators with a view to expediting the negotiations. Although the U.S. negotiators had said that the proposals regarding waiver and duty certificates constituted significant modifications of the U.S. position, a considerable gap still remained between the U.S. and Korean positions on those subjects. The Korean negotiators would study the U.S. proposals and comment on them at a subsequent meeting.

18. It was agreed to hold the next meeting on December 23 at 3:00 p.m.

0229

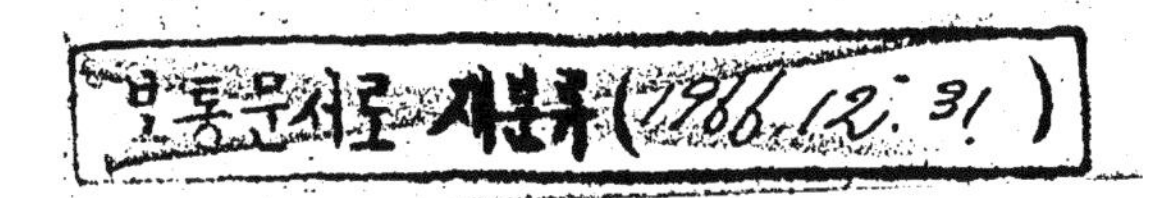

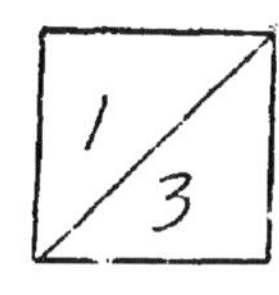

JOINT SUMMARY RECORD OF THE 67TH SESSION

1. Time and Place: 4:00 - 5:00 P.M. December 16, 1964 at the Foreign Ministry's Conference Room (No.1)

2. Attendants:

ROK Side:

Mr. Chang, Sang Moon	Director European and American Affairs Bureau
Mr. Yoon, Woon Young	Director Prosecutors Bureau Ministry of Justice
Mr. Lee, Nam Ki	Chief America Section Ministry of Foreign Affairs
Mr. Oh, Jae Hee	Chief Treaty Section Ministry of Foreign Affairs
Mr. Lee, Myung Hi	Prosecutor Prosecutors Section Ministry of Justice
Mr. Kim, Kee Joe	3rd Secretary Ministry of Foreign Affairs
Mr. Lee, Keun Pal (Rapporteur and Interpreter)	3rd Secretary Ministry of Foreign Affairs
Mr. Hwang, Young Jae	3rd Secretary Ministry of Foreign Affairs
Mr. Park, Won Chul	3rd Secretary Ministry of Foreign Affairs

U.S. Side:

Mr. Philip C. Habib	Counselor American Embassy
Brig. Gen. Carroll H. Dunn	Deputy Chief of Staff 8th U.S. Army
Capt. John Wayne	Assistant Chief of Staff USN/K. [illegible]

0230

Col. Kenneth C. Crawford	Staff Judge Advocate 8th U.S. Army
Mr. Frank R. LaMacchia	First Secretary American Embassy
Mr. Benjamin A. Fleck (Rapporteur and Press Officer)	First Secretary American Embassy
Mr. Robert A. Kinney	J-5 8th U.S. Army
Mr. Goodwin Shapiro	Second Secretary American Embassy
Maj. Alton H. Harvey	Staff Judge Advocate's Office 8th U.S. Army
Mr. David Y.S. Lee (Interpreter)	Second Secretary American Embassy

1. Mr. Chang opened the meeting by introducing Mr. KIM Kee Joe, of the America Section, Ministry of Foreign Affairs, a newly-appointed member of the Korean negotiating team. Mr. Habib welcomed Mr. Kim to the negotiations on behalf of the American negotiators.

Criminal Jurisdiction

2. Taking up the Criminal Jurisdiction Article, Mr. Habib said the U.S. negotiators wished to resume the presentation of their views. A review of the negotiating record showed that the views of both sides had been explored in great depth. Both sides realize that this article is the key to the entire Agreement. The U.S. negotiators believe that considerable progress has been made in reconciling the views of the two negotiating teams. In some respects, the U.S. negotiators have already made a number of substantial concessions to the Korean position. At this meeting, the U.S. negotiators would table a comprehensive package proposal designed to provide solutions to the four major outstanding

issues in this artocle: waiver of jurisdiction, duty certificates, pre-trial custody, and trial safeguards. Resolution of these issues would leave a number of additional points to be clarified but these four issues are the key elements in the article. U.S. willingness to agree to each of the four positions set forth in the package is contingent on the agreement of the Korean negotiators to accept all four positions.

waiver

3. Mr. Habib stated that the U.S. negotiators were prepared to table significant modifications of the U.S. positions on the waiver and duty certificate issues, which were designed to be responsive to views previously expressed by the Korean negotiators, consistent with essential U.S. requirements. The U.S. negotiators had previously tabled modified positions on the pre-trial custody and trial safeguards issues. They believed that some agreement in principle had been reached on the latter two issues.

4. Mr. Habib then tabled the following revision of the Agreed Minute Re Paragraph 3, U.S. draft:

> "The Republic of Korea, recognizing that it is the primary responsibility of the United States authorities to maintain good order and discipline where persons subject to United States law are concerned, waives its primary right to exercise jurisdiction under paragraph 3(b). In accordance therewith, the United States authorities shall notify the authorities of the Republic of Korea of their intention to exercise jurisdiction in such cases through the Joint Committee. When the authorities of the Republic of Korea, after consultation with United States authorities, are of the opinion that, by reason of special circumstances in a specific case involving an offense against the security of the Republic of Korea, or of forcible rape, or of a malicious killing, the exercise of Korean jurisdiction is of vital importance to the Republic of Korea in that case, they will notify the United States authorities of that opinion within fifteen days after receipt of notification that the United States intends to exercise jurisdiction. The United States shall not have the right to exercise jurisdiction within those fifteen days. If any question arises concerning who is to

0232

exercise jurisdiction the United States diplomatic mission will be afforded an opportunity to confer with the proper authorities of the Republic of Korea before a final determination of this matter is made.

"Trials of cases in which the authorities of the Republic of Korea waive the primary right to exercise jurisdiction, and trials of cases involving offenses described in Paragraph 3(a) (ii) committed against the state or nationals of the Republic of Korea will be held within a reasonable distance from the place where the offenses are alleged to have taken place unless other arrangements are mutually agreed upon. Representatives of the Republic of Korea may be present at such trials.

"In the implementation of the provisions of Article ______ and this Minute, and to facilitate the expeditious disposal of offenses, arrangements may be made between the authorities of the United States and the Republic of Korea to dispense with notification."

5. Mr. Habib explained that the Agreed Minute just tabled would combine an automatic waiver with a right of recall by the Korean authorities under the circumstances specified in the Minute. When the Korean authorities, after consultation with United States authorities, decided that, due to special circumstances in a particular case involving the security of the Republic of Korea, a forcible rape, or a malicious killing, the exercise of Korean jurisdiction was of vital importance, they would so notify the United States authorities. If any question should arise concerning the exercise of jurisdiction, the United States diplomatic mission would be afforded the opportunity to confer with authorities of the Republic of Korea before a final determination was made. This formula, Mr. Habib emphasized, recognizes the right of the Government of the Republic of Korea to determine when under the specified circumstances a waiver may be recalled.

6. Mr. Habib recalled that the Korean negotiators have always stated that the exercise of Korean jurisdiction was contemplated only in those cases which were deemed to be

0233

of particular importance. The formula proposed by the U.S. negotiators provides for this and includes those serious crimes committed against either the Government of the Republic of Korea or Korean individuals. In those cases, the ROK Government would determine whether or not the waiver should be recalled, although the right of U.S. authorities to confer on such recall is provided. Mr. Habib called the attention of the Korean negotiators to the fact that the second paragraph of the tabled Agreed Minute is a new addition to the U.S. draft. This provision was added in order to incorporate the position set forth in the third paragraph of the Agreed Minute Re Paragraph 3(c) of the Korean draft. The U.S. negotiators view these provisions as desirable and are pleased to be able to accede to the wishes of the Government of the Republic of Korea by incorporating them in the U.S. draft.

7. Mr. Habib recalled that at the 52nd negotiating meeting, the Korean negotiators had tabled a proposed Agreed Minute to Paragraph 3(a) (ii) pertaining to duty certificates. As understood by the U.S. negotiators, the major objection of the Korean negotiators to Agreed Minute #2 Re Paragraph 3(a) of the U.S. draft was its provision that the duty certificate issued by a commanding officer would be conclusive. The U.S. negotiators continued to believe that the duty certificate must be controlling but they were now prepared to make a major concession by tabling a revised Agreed Minute #2 Re Paragraph 3(a) which they believe embodies certain essential principles previously tabled by the Korean negotiators.

Official Duty

8. Mr. Habib then tabled the following revised Agreed Minute #2 Re Paragraph 3(a):

0234

"2. Where a member of the United States armed forces or civilian component is charged with an offense, a certificate issued by competent authorities of the United States forces stating that the alleged offense, if committed by him, arose out of an act or omission done in the performance of official duty shall be sufficient evidence of the fact for the purpose of determining primary jurisdiction.

"In those exceptional cases where the chief prosecutor for the Republic of Korea considers that there is proof contrary to a certificate of official duty, it may be made the subject of review through discussions between appropriate officials of the Government of the Republic of Korea and the diplomatic mission of the United States in Korea."

9. Mr. Habib recalled that the Korean draft defined the duty certificate as "sufficient evidence" rather than as being conclusive. The Korean draft also had contained a distinction regarding the issuing authority. The revised U.S. Agreed Minute would provide that the duty certificate will be issued by "competent authorities of the United States" rather than by the Staff Judge Advocate. This change is deemed necessary because many major units of the U.S. forces do not have a Staff Judge Advocate assigned to them, even though such units may always request any legal advice from their superior headquarters. Another modification in the revised Agreed Minute relates to the body to whom the ROK Chief Prosecutor would refer if he determined that there was proof contrary to the duty certificate. Under the terms of the revision, the question would be reviewed by the appropriate authorities of the Republic of Korea and the United States diplomatic mission rather than by the Joint Committee. The U.S. negotiators regard this as a better system since it will result in reaching a final determination more quickly.

0235

10. Regarding the duty certificate itself, Mr. Habib continued, the U.S. negotiators continue to hold strong views. Both sides recognize the fact that the accused should not be deprived of his entitlement to a prompt and speedy trial as a result of a prolonged review by officials of the two governments. The U.S. negotiators believe also that the duty certificate must be controlling. Therefore, if agreement is not reached within a specified time on a specific case, the duty certificate would be conclusive for that case but discussions could continue concerning the propriety of issuing a duty certificate under similar circumstances in future cases. The U.S. revised Agreed Minute would provide the ROK Chief Prosecutor the right to question the duty certificate. It would provide the means for discussing the matter and the possibility of modifying the certificate. However, unless modified, the duty certificate would be controlling. This is fully consistent with practice and precedents elsewhere.

11. Mr. Habib stated that the U.S. negotiators were offering the foregoing amendments to important provisions of the Article with the understanding that they were part of a package which also contained additional proposals which he would now explain.

Custody

12. First, Mr. Habib continued, the U.S. negotiators continued to deem necessary sub-paragraph 5(c) of the U.S. draft, pertaining to pre-trial custody. The U.S. negotiators would agree to the adoption of sub-paragraph 5(e) proposed by the Korean negotiators (which would provide for ROK custody in security cases) if the Korean negotiators would agree to the inclusion in the Joint Agreed Summary of the understanding proposed at the 58th meeting, i.e.:

0236

a. Mutual agreement must be reached as to the circumstances in which custody is appropriate in security cases; and

b. Confinement facilities must be adequate by U.S. standards.

13. Secondly, Mr. Habib stated, it is essential to U.S. needs that the trial safeguards be enumerated in the SOFA. Therefore, the enmeration of trial safeguards contained in Paragraph 9 and the related Agreed Minutes must be accepted. This subject had already been discussed at length and in detail and the U.S. negotiators did not believe further discussion was necessary.

14. Mr. Habib stated that the U.S. negotiators believe that the Korean negotiators are well aware of the special importance that the United States Government attaches to the custody provisions and the fair trial guarantees. The U.S. negotiators, like the Korean negotiators, must be able to justify the provisions of the Agreement before their legislature and the Korean negotiators surely realize the great importance which the U.S. Congress places on guarantees of a fair trial.

15. Mr. Habib pointed out that the package proposal also included deletion of the provisions of the U.S. draft relating to the combat zone (Agreed Minute No.1 Re Paragraph 1(b)) and to the primary right of jurisdiction in those cases in which a ROK court-martial would be appropriate if a Korean serviceman were the accused (Agreed Minute No. 1 Re Paragraph 3(a)). In recognition of the dislike for these provisions previously expressed by the Korean negotiators, the U.S. negotiators had already agreed to their deletion.

0237

16. Mr. Habib stated that the U.S. negotiators presented this comprehensive package proposal with the objective of achieving an early, successful conclusion to the negotiations. They had made major concessions on the issues of waiver of jurisdiction and duty certificates, subject to Korean acceptance of the U.S. positions on custody and trial safeguards. The U.S. negotiators hoped that the Korean negotiators and the authorities of the ROK Government, in considering the U.S. propôsals, would keep in mind that these proposals represent the carefully formulated views of the U.S. Government and reflect the desire on the part of U.S. Government authorities to be as responsive as possible to ROK views, consistent with essential U.S. requirements. Other questions remain to be settled in this Article but the U.S. negotiators believe that they can be settled expeditiously if agreement is reached on the four major issues. The U.S. negotiators, therefore, asked the ROK negotiators to give these proposals the most careful consideration.

17. Mr. Chang replied that the Korean negotiators appreciated the intensive and comprehensive package proposal made by the U.S. negotiators. They recognized that the proposal was made by the U.S. negotiators with a view to expediting the negotiations. Although the U.S. negotiators had said that the proposals regarding waiver and duty certificates constituted significant modifications of the U.S. position, a considerable gap still remained between the U.S. and Korean positions on those subjects. The Korean negotiators would study the U.S. proposals and comment on them at a subsequent meeting.

18. It was agreed to hold the next meeting on December 23 at 3:00 p.m.

1966,12,31,에 예고문에 의거 일반문서로 재분류됨

보통문서로 재분류(1966.12.31)

0238

6. 제68차 회의, 12.23

0239

SOFA NEGOTIATION

Agenda for the 68th Session

15:00 December 23, 1964

1. Continuation of Discussions on:

   a. Labor Procurement Article

2. Other Business

3. Agenda and Date of the Next Meeting

4. Press Release

0240

Dec 23, '64

15 December 1964

Revised US Draft of Labor Article

(The underlined parts are modifications authorized by State-Defense in Dec 1964)

1. In this Article the expression:

(a) "employer" refers to the United States Armed Forces (including nonappropriated fund activities) and the persons referred to in the first paragraph of Article______.

(b) "employee" refers to any civilian (other than a member of the civilian component) employed by an employer, except (1) a member of the Korean Service Corps and (2) a domestic employed by an individual member of the United States Armed Forces, civilian component or dependent thereof.

2. Employers may recruit, employ and administer their personnel. Recruitment services of the Government of the Republic of Korea will be utilized insofar as is practicable. In case employers accomplish direct recruitment of employees, employers will provide available relevant information as may be required for labor administration to the Office of Labor Affairs of the Republic of Korea.

3. To the extent not inconsistent with the provisions of this article or the military requirements of the United States Armed Forces, the conditions of employment, compensation, and labor-management practices established by the United States Armed Forces for their employees will conform with the labor laws, customs and practices of the Republic of Korea.

4. (a) An employee shall have the same right to strike as an employee in a comparable position in the employment of the Armed Forces of the Republic of Korea. Such an employee may voluntarily organize and join a union or other employee group whose objectives are not inimical to the

0241

interests of the United States. Membership or nonmembership in such groups shall not be a cause for discharge or nonemployment.

(b) Employers will maintain procedures designed to assure the just and timely resolution of employee grievances.

5. (a) Should the Republic of Korea adopt measures allocating labor, the United States Armed Forces shall be accorded employment privileges no less favorable than those enjoyed by the armed forces of the Republic of Korea.

(b) In the event of a national emergency, employees who have acquired skills essential to the mission of the United States Armed Forces shall be exempt from Republic of Korea military service or other compulsory service. The United States armed forces shall furnish to the Republic of Korea lists of those employees deemed essential.

6. Members of the civilian component shall not be subject to Korean laws or regulations with respect to their terms and conditions of employment.

AGREED MINUTES

1. The Republic of Korea will make available, at designated induction points, qualified personnel for Korean Service Corps units in numbers sufficent to meet the requirements of United States Armed Forces. The employment of a domestic by an individual member of the United States Armed Forces, civilian component or dependent thereof shall be governed by applicable Korean law and in addition by wage scales and control measures promulgated by the United States Armed Forces.

2. The undertaking of the United States Government to conform to Korean labor laws, customs, and practices, does not imply any waiver by the United

0242

States Government of its immunities under international law. The United States Government may terminate employment at any time the continuation of such employment is inconsistent with the military requirements of the United States Armed Forces.

3. Employers will withhold from the pay of their employees, and pay over to the Government of the Republic of Korea withholdings required by the income tax legislation of the Republic of Korea.

4. It is understood that the Government of the Republic of Korea shall be reimbursed for direct costs incurred in providing assistance requested pursuant to paragraph 2.

5. With regard to any dispute between employers and any recognized employee organization or employees which cannot be settled through the use of existing procedures of the United States Armed Forces, settlement shall be accomplished as provided below. During such disputes neither employee organizations nor employees shall engage in any practices disruptive of normal work requirements:

(a) The dispute shall be referred to the Office of Labor Affairs, Ministry of Health and Social Affairs, Republic of Korea, for conciliation.

(b) In the event that the dispute is not settled by the procedure described in (a) above, the matter may be referred to the Joint Committee, which may refer the matter to the Labor Sub-Committee or specially designated Committee, for further fact-finding, review and conciliation efforts.

(c) In the event that the dispute is not settled by the procedures outlined above, the Joint Committee will resolve the dispute. The decisions

0243

of the Joint Committee shall be binding.

(d) Failure of any recognized employee organization or employee to abide by the decision of the Joint Committee on any dispute, or engaging in practices disruptive of normal work requirements during settlement procedures, shall be considered just cause for the withdrawal of recognition of that organization and the discharge of that employee.

0244

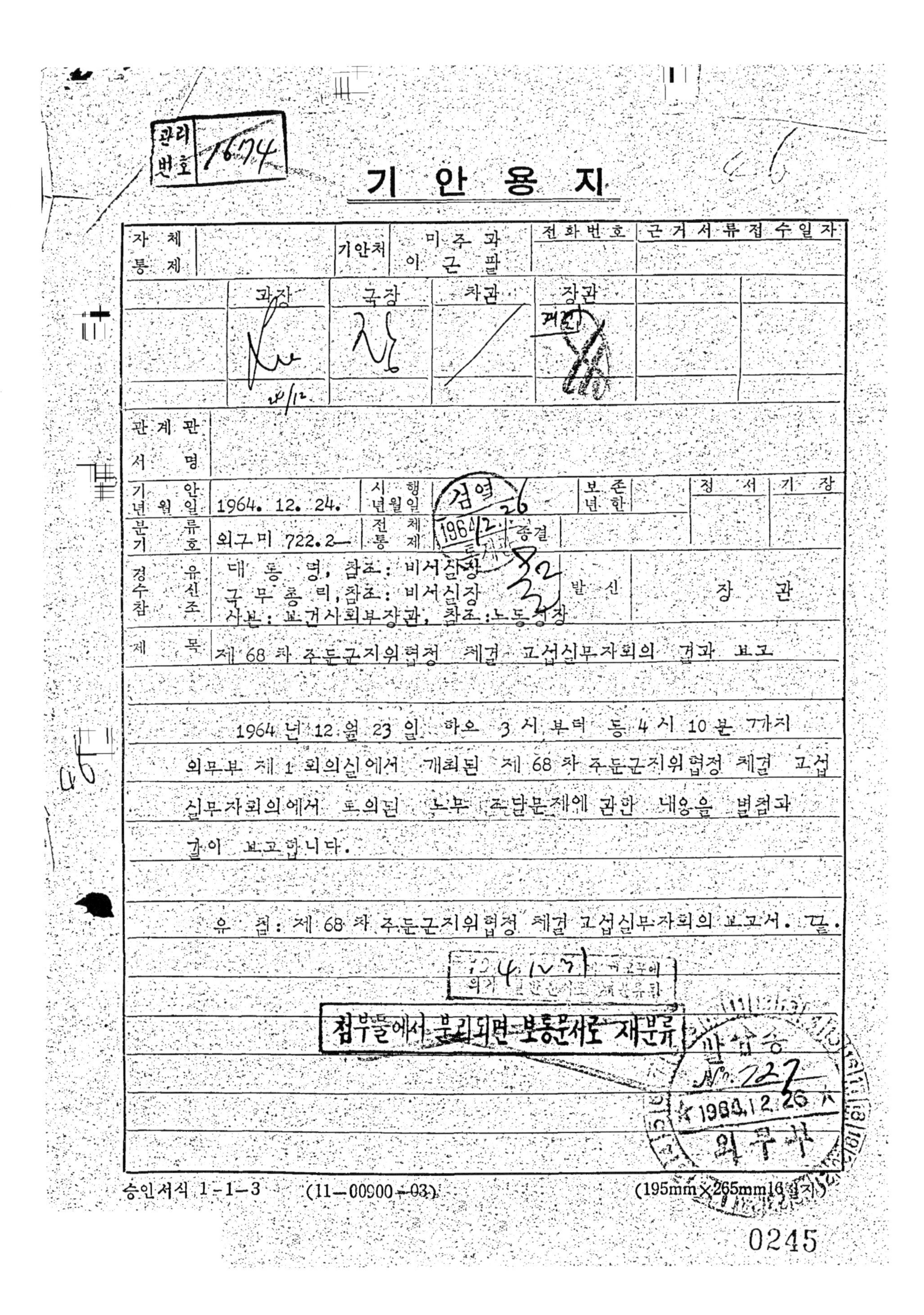

관리번호 1674

기 안 용 지

자체 통제		기안처	미주과 이근팔	전화번호	근거서류접수일자
	과장	국장	차관	장관	
관계관 서명					
기안 년월일	1964. 12. 24.	시행 년월일		보존 년한	정서 기장
분류 기호	외구미 722.2	전체 통제	1964.12.26 종결		
경유 수신 참조	대통령, 참조: 비서실장 국무총리, 참조: 비서실장 사본: 보건사회부장관, 참조: 노동청장		발신	장관	
제목	제 68 차 주둔군지위협정 체결 교섭실무자회의 결과 보고				

1964 년 12 월 23 일 하오 3 시부터 동 4 시 10 분 까지 외무부 제 1 회의실에서 개최된 제 68 차 주둔군지위협정 체결 교섭실무자회의에서 토의된 노무 조달문제에 관한 내용을 별첨과 같이 보고합니다.

유 첨: 제 68 차 주둔군지위협정 체결 교섭실무자회의 보고서. 끝.

첨부물에서 분리되면 보통문서로 재분류

발송 No. 227 1964.12.26 외무부

승인서식 1-1-3 (11-00900-03) (195mm×265mm16절지)

0245

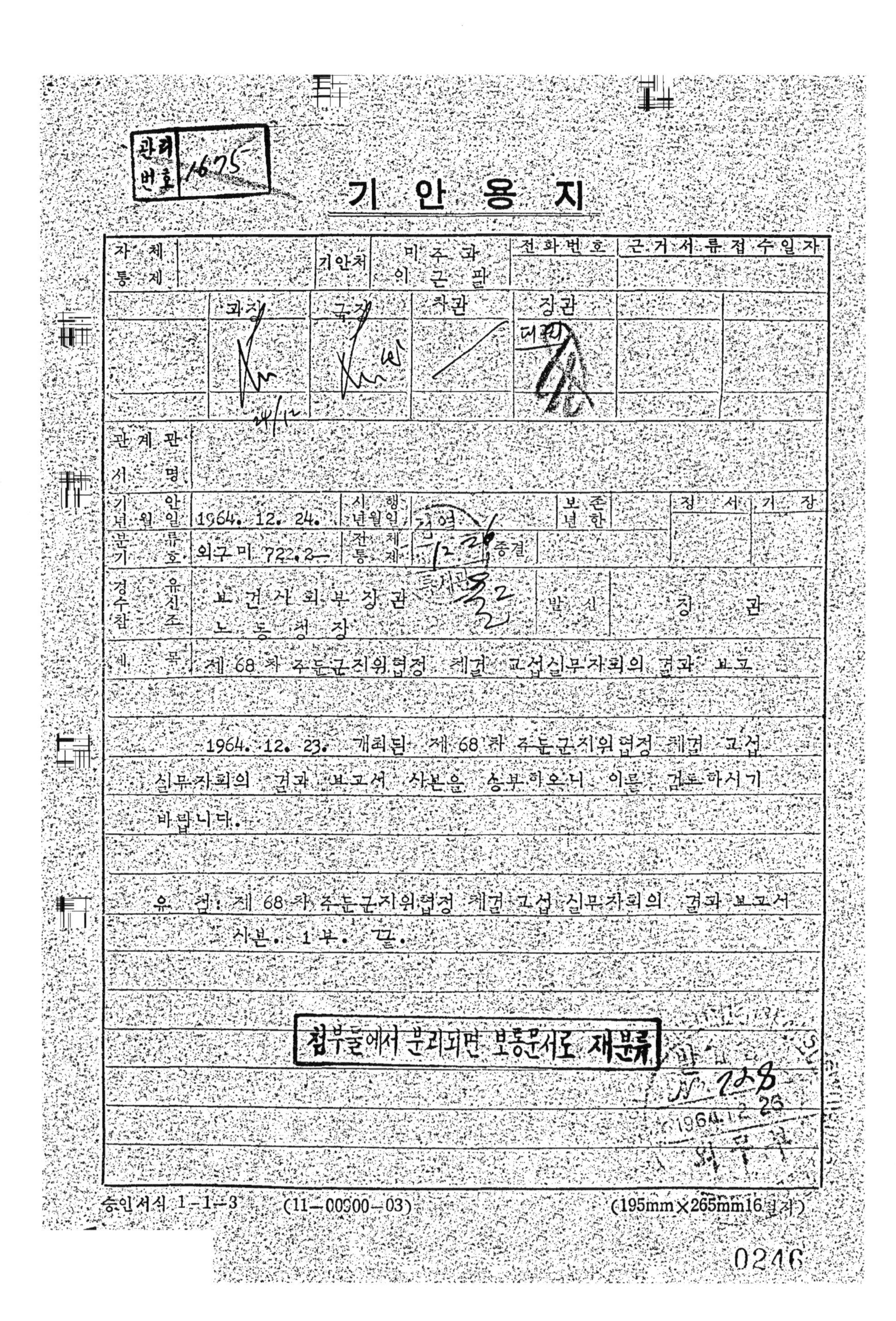

관리번호 1675

기 안 용 지

자체통제		기안처	미주과 이근팔	전화번호	근거서류접수일자
	과장	국장	차관	장관	
관계관 서명					
기안년월일	1964. 12. 24.	시행년월일		보존년한	정서 기장
분류기호	외구미 722.2	전체통제	종결		
경수참 유신조	보건사회부장관 노동청장			발신	장관
제목	제 68 차 주둔군지위협정 체결 교섭실무자회의 결과 보고				

1964. 12. 23. 개최된 제 68 차 주둔군지위협정 체결 교섭 실무자회의 결과 보고서 사본을 송부하오니 이를 검토하시기 바랍니다.

유 첨: 제 68 차 주둔군지위협정 체결 교섭 실무자회의 결과 보고서 사본. 1부. 끝.

첨부물에서 분리되면 보통문서로 재분류

발송 1964. 12. 26 외무부

승인서식 1-1-3 (11-00900-03) (195mm×265mm16절지)

0246

외 무 부

외구미 722.2 1964. 12. 28.

수신 보건사회부장관
참조 노동청장
제목 제68차 주둔군지위협정 체결 고섭 실무자회의 결과보고

1964.12.23 개최된 제68차 주둔군지위협정 체결 고섭 실무자회의 결과보고서 사본을 송부하오니 이를 검토하시기 바랍니다.

유첨 - 제68차 주둔군지위협정 체결 고섭 실무자회의 결과 보고서 사본 1부. 끝

첨부물에서 분리되면 보통문서로 재분류

외무부장관 이 동 원

0247

외 무 부

외구미 722.2 1964. 12. 28.

수신 대통령, 국무총리

참조 비서실장

사본 보건사회부장관

제목 제68차 주둔군지위협정 체결 교섭 실무자회의 결과 보고

1964. 12. 23일 하오 3시부터 동 4시 10분까지 외무부 제1회의실에서 개최된 제68차 주둔군지위협정 체결 교섭 실무자회의에서 토의된 노무조달문제에 관한 내용을 별첨과 같이 보고합니다.

유첨 - 제68차 주둔군지위협정 체결교섭 실무자회의 보고서. 끝

첨부물에서 분리되면 보통문서로 재분류

외 무 부 장 관 이 동 원

0248

제 68 차

한 • 미간 주둔군지위협정 체결 교섭 실무자회의

보 고 서

1. 일시 1964. 12. 23 일
2. 장소 외무부 제 1 회의실
3. 토의사항

노무조달

(가) 미측은 제 65 차회의에서 미군노무자의 모집, 고용조건과 노 • 사간의 분쟁해결절차에 관한 우리측 제안에 대하여 다음과 같이 미측 주장을 수정 제안하였다:

(1) 미군관계 고용주는 노무자를 모집, 고용관리할수 있다. 한국정부의 노무자 모집기관은 가능한한 이용한다. 고용주가 노무자를 직접 고용하였을때에는 관계정보를 한국노동청에 제공한다.

(2) 노무조달 규정과 미군의 군사상 필요성에 위배되지 않는 한도내에서 미군은 고용조건, 보상 및 노무관리에 관하여 한국의 법령 및 관행을 준수할 것이다.

(3) 미국정부가 한국법과 관행을 준수할 것이라 함은 미국정부가 국제법에 의하여 향유하는 면제특권을 포기하는 것을 의미하는 것은 아니다. 미국정부는 고용관계의 계속이 미군의 군사상의 필요성에 위배될시에는 언제던지 해고할수 있다.

(4) 미군의 기존절차에 의하여 해결할수 없는 노 • 사간의 분쟁은 다음과 같은 절차에 의하여 해결한다. 분쟁기간중 노동단체 또는 노무자는 정상적 작업수요를 방해하는 행위를 할수없다.

0249

(가) 분쟁은 조정을 위하여 한국노동청에 회부되어야 한다.

(나) 분쟁이 상기절차에서 해결되지 않을 경우에는 합동위원회에 회부될수 있으며 합동위원회는 시신의 조사, 재심 및 조정을 위하여 노동분과위원회 또는 특별위원회에 회부할수 있다.

(다) 상기 절차에서도 해결되지 않은 경우에는 합동위원회가 분쟁을 해결하며 합동위원회의 결정은 구속력을 갖는다.

(라) 합동위원회의 결정에 복종하지 않거나 또는 분쟁조정기간중 정상적 작업수요를 방해하는 행위를 하는 것은 노동조합에 대한 인가의 취소 및 노무자에 대한 해고의 정당한 이유가 된다.

(나) 우리측은 미측의 제안에 대하여 이를 검토한후 다음 회의에서 우리측 태도를 밝히기로 하고 다음과 같이 논평하였다.

(1) 우리측은 미측의 금번 제안이 종래의 주장과 별다른 차이점이 없다고 사료하며,

(2) 다만 미군이 "기본적 노무관리의 필요성이라는 어구대신 "군사상의 필요성"에 위배되지 않는 한도내에서 한국법과 관행을 준수할 것이라고 한것 만이 하나의 중요한 수정이라고 보지만 "군사상의 필요성"이라는 어구의 뜻이 애매하고 광범위하다.

(3) 미측의 분쟁해결절차중 분쟁기간중 정상적 작업의 수요를 방해하는 행위를 한수 없다 함은 노무자의 권리를 박탈하는 것임으로 부당하며 일정한 기간을 설정할 필요가 있다.

0250

제 68 차

한.미 간 주둔군지위협정 체결 교섭실무자회의

보 고 서

1. 일 시: 1964 년 12 월 23 일 하오 3 시 부터 동 4 시 10 분 까지.

2. 장 소: 외무부 제 1 회의실

3. 토의사항:

노무 조달

(가) 미측은 제 65 차회의에서 미군노무자의 모집, 고용조건과 노.사 간의 분쟁해결절차에 관한 우리측 제안에 대하여 다음과 같이 미측 주장을 수정 제안하였다:

(1) 미군관계 고용주는 노무자를 모집, 고용 관리할 수 있다. 한국정부의 노무자 모집기관은 가능한 한 이용한다. 고용주가 노무자를 직접 고용하였을 때에는 관계정보를 한국 노동청에 제공한다.

(2) 노무 조달 규정과 미군의 군사상 필요성에 위배되지 않는 한도에서 미군은 고용조건, 보상, 및 노무관리에 관하여 한국의 법령 및 관행을 준수할 것이다.

(3) 미국정부가 한국법과 관행을 준수할 것이라 함은 미국정부가 국제법에 의하여 향유하는 면제특권을 포기하는 것을 의미하는 것은 아니다. 미국정부는 고용관계의 계속이 미군의 군사상의 필요성에 위배될 시 에는 언제든지 해고할 수 있다.

(4) 미군의 기존 절차에 의하여 해결할 수 없는 노.사간의 분쟁은 다음과 같은 절차에 의하여 해결한다. 분쟁기간중 노동단체 또는 노무자는 정상적 작업 수으를 방해하는 행위를 할 수 없다.

(가) 분쟁은 조정을 위하여 한국 노동청에 회부되어야 한다.

(나) 분쟁이 상기 절차에서 해결되지 않을 경우에는 합동위원회에 회부될 수 있으며 합동위원회는 사실의 조사, 재심 및 조정을 위하여 노동분과위원회 또는 특별위원회에 회부할 수 있다.

0251

64-3-150

14-3-36 (2)　　미주과 III-1(2)

0252

(다) 상기 절차에서도 해결되지 않을 경우에는 합동위원회가 분쟁을 해결하며 합동위원회의 결정은 구속력을 갖는다.

(라) 합동위원회의 결정에 복종하지 않거나 또는 분쟁 조정 기간중 정상적 작업수오를 방해하는 행위를 하는 것은 노동조합에 대한 인가의 취소 및 노무자에 대한 해고의 정당한 이유가 된다.

(나) 우리측은 미측의 제안에 대하여 이를 검토한 후 다음 회의에서 우리측 태도를 밝히기로 하고 다음과 같이 논평하였다.

(1) 우리측은 미측의 금번 제안이 종래의 주장과 별다른 차의점이 없다고 사료하며,

(2) 다만 미군이 "기본적 노무관리의 필요성이라는 어구 대신 "군사상의 필요성"에 위배되지 않는 한도 내에서 한국법과 관행을 준수할 거이라고 한 것 만이 하나의 중요한 수정이라고 보지 만 "군사상의 필요성"이라는 어구의 뜻이 애매하고 광범위하다.

(3) 미측의 분쟁해결절차중 분쟁 기간중 정상적 작업의 수으를 방해하는 행위를 할 수 없다함은 노무자의 권리를 박탈하는 것임으로 부당하며 일정한 기간을 설정할 필요가 있다.

(4) 우리측이 만약 미측 제안을 수락한다면 현재 미군 노무자가 향유하고 있는 권리까지도 박탈하는 결과가 될 것이며 우리가 교섭을 하는 목적이 노무자의 권리를 보호하고 그 지위를 향상 하려는데 있는 것이지 결코 현재 행사하고 있는 권리를 약화 할 수는 없는 것이다.

4. 차기 회의 일자: 양측 실무자가 차후 결정키로 함. 끝

1966.12.31.에 예고문에 의거 일반문서로 재분류됨

보통문서로 재분류(1966.12.31.)

0253

64-3-1이 6

0254

(4) 우리측이 만약 미측 제안을 수락한다면 현재 미군노무자가 향유하고 있는 권리까지도 박탈하는 결과가 될것이며 우리가 교섭을 하는 목적이 노무자의 권리를 보호하고 그 지위를 향상하려는데 있는 것이지 결코 현재 향사하고 있는 권리를 약화할수는 없는 것이다.

4. 차기회의일자 : 양측 실무자가 추후 결정키로 함. 끝

보통문서로 재분류(1966.12.31.)

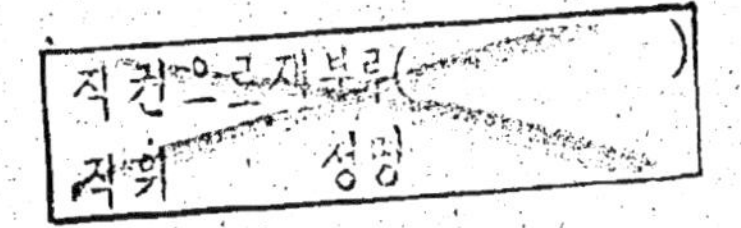

1966.12.31.에 예고문에 의거 일반문서로 재분류됨

0255

CONFIDENTIAL

STATUS OF FORCES NEGOTIATIONS: 68th Meeting

SUBJECT: Labor

PLACE: Ministry of Foreign Affairs

DATE: December 23, 1964

PARTICIPANTS:

Republic of Korea

CHANG Sang-mun
LEE YI Nam-ki
O Chae-hi
HUH Sung Joon <KIM Kee Joe
HWANG Yong-chae
Major YI Kae-hun, ROKA
YI Kun-pal (Interpreter)
Park, Won Chul

United States

Philip C. Habib
Brig. General Carroll H. Dunn, USA
Captain John Wyne, USN
Colonel Kenneth C. Crawford, USA
Frank R. LaMacchia
Benjamin A. Fleck
Robert A. Kinney
Goodwin Shapiro
Major Alton Harvey, USA
David Y.C. Lee (Interpreter)

Ogden Reed (Observer)

0256

1. The discussion was begun by Mr. Habib, who stated that since the Labor Article was last discussed (at the 65th negotiating meeting), the U.S. authorities had carefully reviewed the status of this article, including the views expressed by the Korean negotiators at the formal and informal negotiating sessions during the past ten months. The U.S. negotiators were now prepared to table significant modifications of the U.S. draft, which were designed to be responsive to the views of the Korean authorities to the maximum extent consistent with the essential requirements of the U.S. armed forces in carrying out their important defense mission in Korea. For the convenience of the negotiators, the U.S. negotiators were tabling a fresh draft of the entire article, in which the modifications being proposed at this meeting were underlined. The U.S. negotiators hoped that early agreement could be reached on the article on the basis of the modified U.S. positions now being tabled. Mr. Habib then tabled the revised U.S. draft and said he would explain the modifications.

2. With regard to Paragraph 2, Mr. Habib explained, the U.S. negotiators propose revision of the first sentence, dividing it into two separate sentences. The first sentence of the revision is a simple and direct statement that the U.S. armed forces, as the employers of over 33,000 Korean personnel, may recruit, employ, and administer such personnel. The new second sentence had been included in response to Korean desires and explicitly states that the recruitment services of the Government of the Republic of Korea will be utilized insofar as is practicable. The third sentence in the revised paragraph was included earlier at the request of the ROK authorities. The U.S. negotiators believe that this revised Paragraph 2 fully takes into account the views of the ROK authorities, as expressed at both formal and informal negotiating meetings, and therefore should be acceptable to the Korean negotiators.

3. With regard to Paragraph 3, Mr. Habib siad the U.S. negotiators were proposing a modification of this paragraph in response to the objections expressed by the Korean negotiators at the 65th meeting to the phrase "the

basic management needs" in the earlier U.S. draft. This phrase was said to be too broad and ambiguous and therefore it has been replaced by the words "the military requirements". The U.S. armed forces, which are in Korea pursuant to the U.S.-ROK Mutual Defense Treaty of November 17, 1954, are here to assist in the defense of the Republic of Korea. The U.S. armed forces have tried to be good employers to their Korean employees and expect to continue to conform generally to ROK labor laws and practices. Under the present conditions of armistice, the U.S. armed forces must be prepared to meet any military contingencies, including developments which are unforeseeable. The U.S. negotiators believe that the ROK authorities, including the National Assembly, recognize the realities of the military situation in Korea and will be prepared, therefore, to agree that the words "the military requirements" are necessary in this context in Paragraph 3.

4. Mr. Habib recalled that the ROK negotiators had expressed a strong desire to append an Agreed Minute to the Labor Article which would establish procedures for the settlement of labor disputes which cannot be settled internally by the U.S. armed forces. In response to this desire, the modified U.S. draft contained a new Agreed Minute 5, along the lines proposed by the Korean negotiators at the 65th negotiating meeting. This new Agreed Minute would provide for a three-stage procedure for settling any labor dispute which cannot be settled internally by the U.S. armed forces. The first step would be to refer the dispute to the ROK Office of Labor Affairs, Ministry of Health and Social Affairs, for conciliation. If the dispute cannot be settled through the conciliation efforts of the Office of Labor Affairs, the Minute would provide that the dispute may then be referred to the Joint Committee. At that time, the Joint Committee might refer the matter to a labor sub-committee or to a specially designated committee for further fact-finding, review, and conciliation efforts. If the dispute cannot be settled by the procedures outlined above, the

0258

proposed Agreed Minute provides that the Joint Committee will resolve the dispute and its decisions shall be binding. The U.S. Government believes that the ROK and U.S. authorities should be able to resolve any labor dispute through these procedures.

5. Mr. Habib pointed out that if the disputes machinery is to be effective, every settlement must be adhered to. Therefore, the proposed Agreed Minute stipplates that neither an employee organization nor employees shall engage in any practice disruptive of normal work requirements while the settlement procedures are in progress. This is a normal characteristic of conciliation procedures. The U.S. negotiators believed that agreement had already been reached that the decisions of the Joint Committee must be binding. Therefore, failure of any recognized employee organization or employee to abide by decisions of the Joint Committee in the settlement of disputes should be considered to be just cause for withdrawal of recognition of that employee organization and/or the discharge of that employee. It is the firm view of the U.S. Government, Mr. Habib continued, that the Korean employees of the U.S. armed forces, like the American civilian employees of those forces and the civilian employees of the ROK armed forces, are a vital factor in the defense of the Republic of Korea. In this regard, such employees are considered to be in a comparable position to the civilian employees of the ROK armed forces and the American civilian employees of the U.S. armed forces. It is the intention of the U.S. armed forces to do everything possible to promote and maintain good employer-employee relations with their Korean employees and, in cooperation with the ROK Government, as provided in Agreed Minute 5, to resolve labor disputes which cannot be settled internally.

6. Mr. Habib pointed out that the revised U.S. draft also contained a revised Agreed Minute #2. The first sentence of the Minute, identical with that in the previous version, would make clear that the undertaking of the U.S. armed forces to conform to Korean labor laws, customs, and practices does not imply any waiver of the immunities of the U.S. Government under international law. ROK Govern-

0259

ment authorities have indicated agreement with this principle. The second sentence would stipulate that the U.S. Government may terminate employment at any time that the continuation of such employment is inconsistent with the military requirements of the U.S. armed forces. As the U.S. negotiators had previously explained, the military requirements of the U.S. armed forces make it necessary for them to have this authority in order to insure that essential defense and security requirements can be met.

7. Mr. Habib concluded his presentation of the revised U.S. draft by saying that the U.S. negotiators believed the Korean negotiators would find the revisions generally responsive to their views and consistent with joint U.S.-ROK defense requirements. The U.S. negotiators believed that the revised U.S. draft of the Labor Article would aid materially in maintaining and enhancing the effective employer-employee relations which currently exist between the U.S. armed forces and their Korean employees. The U.S. negotiators had tabled this draft with the full understanding that the U.S. armed forces highly value their Korean employees and the existing relationship with them. The U.S. armed forces believed that they had established a good reputation as an employer and were determined to continue their efforts to promote the well-being and training of those employees.

8. Mr. Chang replied that the Korean negotiators would comment in detail on the revised U.S. draft at a subsequent meeting. However, he wished to make some preliminary comments. The U.S. negotiators had said that their revised draft contained significant modifications. The Korean negotiators recognized this to be the case with respect to the substitution of "military requirements" for "basic management needs". However, the Korean negotiators expressed the view that the addition of a new sentence to Agreed Minute 2 would be unnecessary duplication of the revised Paragraph 3, and that the U.S. negotiators had retreated to a rigid position in the application of the phrase "military requirements." With regard to Agreed Minute #5, the revised draft appeared to be not significantly different from the views expressed by the U.S. negotiators at the 65th meeting.

0260

CONFIDENTIAL

9. Mr. Chang stated that even the phrase "military requirements" was still ambiguous and too broad. The Korean negotiators would like to have it defined or explained. Mr. Habib replied that "military requirements" were those requirements which contributed to the accomplishment of the military mission of the U.S. armed forces. The interpretation of the phrase in individual cases would be up to the Joint Committee, which therefore would have a very important role to play in this regard. Mr. Chang replied that the Korean negotiators believed interpretation of the phrase should not be left to the Joint Committee. The phrase should be defined before reaching agreement on this article.

10. Mr. Habib replied that if a specific case arose, presumably it would be referred to the Joint Committee. Basically, the U.S. armed forces are in Korea to fulfill certain defense and security requirements. Whatever actions they perform should be consistent with those requirements. The same rule should apply to the Korean employees of those forces. Paragraph 3 of the U.S. draft states "to the extent not inconsistent with ..... the military requirements".

11. Mr. Chang replied that the Korean negotiators viewed the revision of Paragraph 3 as the only major change proposed by the U.S. negotiators. However, the phrase "military requirements" was ambiguous. If this revised draft were agreed to, the Korean employees of the U.S. armed forces would be denied rights which they now enjoy. The purpose of the labor article is to safeguard their rights. Therefore, the Korean negotiators called on the U.S. negotiators to take into consideration the rights which the Korean employees presently enjoyed and the comments of the Korean negotiators.

0261

12. Mr. Habib replied that the U.S. negotiators doubted very much that this language would deny the rights of the Korean employees. This was not the intent nor did the language have this meaning. The remarks of the Korean negotiators called into question the sincerity of the U.S. negotiators with regard to the other portions of the article. This paragraph had been carefully drafted with the military mission of the U.S. armed forces in mind. The Korean negotiators were raising unjustified questions and finding differences where they did not exist.

13. Mr. Chang replied that the Korean negotiators did not mean to question the sincerity of the U.S. negotiators. The introduction of the phrase "military requirements" was the major modification proposed by the U.S. negotiators. If the Korean negotiators accepted the U.S. revised draft, the privileges presently enjoyed by the Korean employees of the U.S. armed forces would be diminished.

14. When asked to explain how the privileges would be diminished, Mr. Chang replied that subparagraph (d) of Agreed Minute #5 would eliminate the right of the employees to strike. Mr. Habib replied that the provisions of subparagraph (d) were normal procedures which were provided for in ROK labor laws. Mr. Chang said that the ROK law provided that disruptive practices were not allowed for a specific number of days. However, argument concerning a labor dispute could drag on and on in the Joint Committee.

15. Mr. Reed stated that it was his understanding that the ROK law provided that during mediation and arbitration procedures, there was no right to strike, even after the 20-day and 30-day cooling-off periods. Mr. Chang replied that if conciliation failed, the right to strike after a certain number of days existed. Mr. Reed pointed out that the concept ofa limited period was not contained in the U.S. draft. Article 7, Chapter 2 of the ROK Labor Disputes Act provides that there shall be no disruptive action unless mediation or arbitration efforts fail. The procedures proposed by the U.S. negotiators were intended to lead to the settlement of disputes. The U.S. negotiators did not believe that any strike would be justified if these

0262

procedures were followed.

16. Mr. Chang replied that the Korean negotiators would study the U.S. proposals. The meeting was then adjourned with the understanding that the Korean negotiators would call the next meeting.

0263

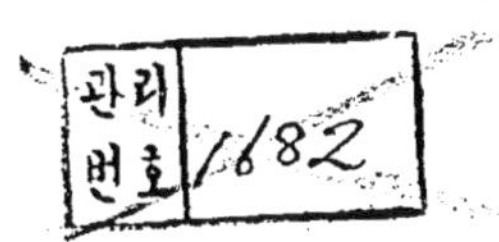

JOINT SUMMARY RECORD OF THE 68TH SESSION

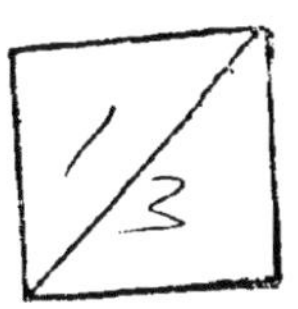

1. Time and Place: 3:00-4:10 P.M. December 23, 1964 at the Foreign Ministry's Conference Room (No.1)

2. Attendants:

ROK Side:

Mr. Chang, Sang Moon	Director European and American Affairs Bureau
Mr. Hu, Sung Joon	Director Labor Administration Bureau Office of Labor Affairs
Mr. Lee, Nam Ki	Chief America Section Ministry of Foreign Affairs
Mr. Oh, Jae Hee	Chief Treaty Section Ministry of Foreign Affairs
Maj. Lee, Kye Hoon	Military Affairs Section Ministry of National Defense
Mr. Kim, Kee Joe	3rd Secretary Ministry of Foreign Affairs
Mr. Lee, Keun Pal (Rapporteur and Interpreter)	3rd Secretary Ministry of Foreign Affairs
Mr. Hwang, Young Jae	3rd Secretary Ministry of Foreign Affairs
Mr. Park, Won Chul	3rd Secretary Ministry of Foreign Affairs

U.S. Side:

Mr. Philip C. Habib	Counselor American Embassy
Brig. Gen. Carroll H. Dunn	Deputy Chief of Staff 8th U.S. Army
Capt. John Wayne	Assistant Chief of Staff USN/K
Col. Kenneth C. Crawford	Staff Judge Advocate 8th U.S. Army

0264

Mr. Frank R. LaMacchia	First Secretary American Embassy
Mr. Benjamin A. Fleck (Rapporteur and Press Officer)	First Secretary American Embassy
Mr. Robert A. Kinney	J-5 8th U.S. Army
Mr. Goodwin Shapiro	Second Secretary American Embassy
Maj. Alton H. Harvey	Staff Judge Advocate's Office 8th U.S. Army
Mr. David Y.S. Lee (Interpreter)	Second Secretary American Embassy

Labor Article

1. The discussion was beguh by Mr. Habib, who stated that since the Labor Article was last discussed (at the 65th negotiating meeting), the U.S. authorities had carefully reviewed the status of this article, including the views expressed by the Korean negotiators at the formal and informal negotiating sessions during the past ten months. The U.S. negotiators were now prepared to table significant modifications of the U.S. draft, which were designed to be responsive to the views of the Korean authorities to the maximum extent consistent with the essential requirements of the U.S. armed forces in carrying out their important defense mission in Korea. For the convenience of the negotiators, the U.S. negotiators were tabling a fresh draft of the entire article, in which the modifications being proposed at this meeting were underlined. The U.S. negotiators hoped that early agreement could be reached on the article on the basis of the modified U.S. positions now being tabled. Mr. Habib then tabled the revised U.S. draft and said he would explain the modifications.

0265

2. With regard to Paragraph 2, Mr. Habib explained, the U.S. negotiators propose revision of the first sentence, dividing it into two separate sentences. The first sentence of the revision is a simple and direct statement that the U.S. armed forces, as the employers of over 33,000 Korean personnel, may recruit, employ, and administer such personnel. The new second sentence had been included in response to Korean desires and explicitly states that the recruitment services of the Government of the Republic of Korea will be utilized insofar as is practicable. The third sentence in the revised paragraph was included earlier at the request of the ROK authorities. The U.S. negotiators believe that this revised Paragraph 2 fully takes into account the views of the ROK authorities, as expressed at both formal and informal negotiating meetings, and therefore should be acceptable to the Korean negotiators.

3. With regard to Paragraph 3, Mr. Habib said the U.S. negotiators were proposing a modification of this paragraph in response to the objections expressed by the Korean negotiators at the 65th meeting to the phrase "the basic management needs" in the earlier U.S. draft. This phrase was said to be too broad and ambiguous and therefore it has been replaced by the words "the military requirements". The U.S. armed forces, which are in Korea pursuant to the U.S.-ROK Mutual Defense Treaty of November 17, 1954, are here to assist in the defense of the Republic of Korea. The U.S. armed forces have tried to be good employers to their Korean employees and expect to continue to conform generally to ROK labor laws and practices. Under the present conditions

0266

of armistice, the U.S. armed forces must be prepared to meet any military contingencies, including developments which are unforeseeable. The U.S. negotiators believe that the ROK authorities, including the National Assembly, recognize the realities of the military situation in Korea and will be prepared, therefore, to agree that the words "the military requirements" are necessary in this context in Paragraph 3.

4. Mr. Habib recalled that the ROK negotiators had expressed a strong desire to append an Agreed Minute to the Labor Article which would establish procedures for the settlement of labor disputes which cannot be settled internally by the U.S. armed forces. In response to this desire, the modified U.S. draft contained a new Agreed Minute 5, along the lines proposed by the Korean negotiators at the 65th negotiating meeting. This new Agreed Minute would provide for a three-stage procedure for settling any labor dispute which cannot be settled internally by the U.S. armed forces. The first step would be to refer the dispute to the ROK Office of Labor Affairs, Ministry of Health and Social Affairs, for conciliation. If the dispute cannot be settled through the conciliation efforts of the Office of Labor Affairs, the Minute would provide that the dispute may then be referred to the Joint Committee. At that time, the Joint Committee might refer the matter to a labor sub-committee or to a specially designated committee for further fact-finding, review, and conciliation efforts. If the dispute cannot be settled by the procedures outlined above, the proposed Agreed Minute provides that the Joint Committee will resolve the dispute and its decisions shall be binding. The U.S. Government believes that the ROK and U.S. authorities should be able to

0267

resolve any labor dispute through these procedures.

5. Mr. Habib pointed out that if the disputes machinary is to be effective, every settlement must be adhered to. Therefore, the proposed Agreed Minute stipulates that neither an employee organization nor employees shall engage in any practice disruptive of normal work requirements while the settlement procedures are in progress. This is a normal characteristic of conciliation procedures. The U.S. negotiators believed that agreement had already been reached that the decisions of the Joint Committee must be binding. Therefore, failure of any recognized employee organization or employee to abide by decisions of the Joint Committee in the settlement of disputes should be considered to be just cause for withdrawal of recognition of that employee organization and/or the discharge of that employee. It is the firm view of the U.S. Government, Mr. Habib continued, that the Korean employees of the U.S. armed forces, like the American civilian employees of those forces and the civilian employees of the ROK armed forces, are a vital factor in the defense of the Republic of Korea. In this regard, such employees are considered to be in a comparable position to the civilian employees of the ROK armed forces and the American civilian employees of the U.S. armed forces. It is the intention of the U.S. armed forces to do everything possible to promote and maintain good employer-employee relations with their Korean employees and, in cooperation with the ROK Government, as provided in Agreed Minute 5, to resolve labor disputes which cannot be settled internally.

6. Mr. Habib pointed out that the revised U.S. draft also contained a revised Agreed Minute #2. The first sentence of the Minute, identical with that in the previous version,

0268

would make clear that the undertaking of the U.S. armed forces to conform to Korean labor laws, customs, and practices does not imply and waiver of the immunities of the U.S. Government under international law. ROK Government authorities have indicated agreement with this principle. The second sentence would stipulate that the U.S. Government may terminate employment at any time that the continuation of such employment is inconsistent with the military requirements of the U.S. armed forces. As the U.S. negotiators had previously explained, the military requirements of the U.S. armed forces make it necessary for them to have this authority in order to insure that essential defense and security requirements can be met.

7. Mr. Habib concluded his presentation of the revised U.S. draft by saying that the U.S. negotiators believed the Korean negotiators would find the revisions generally responsive to their views and consistent with joint U.S.-ROK defense requirements. The U.S. negotiators believed that the revised U.S. draft of the Labor Article would aid materially in maintaining and enhancing the effective employer-employee relations which currently exist between the U.S. armed forces and their Korean employees. The U.S. negotiators had tabled this draft with the full understanding that the U.S. armed forces highly value their Korean employees and the existing relationship with them. The U.S. armed forces believed that they had established a good reputation as an employer and were determined to continue their efforts to promote the well-being and training of those employees.

0269

8. Mr. Chang replied that the Korean negotiators would comment in detail on the revised U.S. draft at a subsequent meeting. However, he wished to make some preliminary comments. The U.S. negotiators had said that their revised draft contained significant modifications. The Korean negotiators recognized this to be the case with respect to the substitution of "military requirements" for "basic management needs". However, the Korean negotiators expressed their view that the addition of a new sentence to Agreed Minute 2/would be unnecessary duplication of the revised Paragraph 3, and that the U.S. negotiators had retreated to a rigid position in the application of the phrase "military requirements". With regard to Agreed Minute #5, the revised draft appeared to be not significantly different from the views expressed by the U.S. negotiators at the 65th meeting.

9. Mr. Chang stated that even the phrase "military requirements" was still ambiguous and too broad. The Korean negotiators would like to have it defined or explained. Mr. Habib replied that "military requirements" were those requirements which contributed to the accomplishment of the military mission of the U.S. armed forces. The interpretation of the phrase in individual cases would be up to the Joint Committee, which therefore would have a very important role to play in this regard. Mr. Chang replied that the Korean negotiators believed interpretation of the phrase should not be left to the Joint Committee. The phrase should be defined before reaching agreement on this Article.

10. Mr. Habib replied that if a specific case arose, presumably it would be referred to the Joint Committee.

0270

Basically, the U.S. armed forces are in Korea to fulfill certain defense and security requirements. Whatever actions they perform should be consistent with those requirements. The same rule should apply to the Korean employees of those forces. Paragraph 3 of the U.S. draft states "to the extent not inconsistent with ... the military requirements."

11. Mr. Chang replied that the Korean negotiators viewed the revision of Paragraph 3 as the only major change proposed by the U.S. negotiators. However, the phrase "military requirements" was ambiguous. If this revised draft were agreed to, the Korean employees of the U.S. armed forces would be denied rights which they now enjoy. The purpose of the labor article is to safeguard their rights. Therefore, the Korean negotiators called on the U.S. negotiators to take into consideration the rights which the Korean employees presently enjoyed and the comments of the Korean negotiators.

12. Mr. Habib replied that the U.S. negotiators doubted very much that this language would deny the rights of the Korean employees. This was not the intent nor did the language have this meaning. The remarks of the Korean negotiators called into question the sincerity of the U.S. negotiators with regard to the other portions of the article. This paragraph had been carefully drafted with the military mission of the U.S. armed forces in mind. The Korean negotiators were raising unjustified questions and finding differences where they did not exist.

13. Mr. Chang replied that the Korean negotiators did not mean to question the sincerity of the U.S. negotiators. The introduction of the phrase "military requirements"

0271

was the major modification proposed by the U.S. negotiators. If the Korean negotiators accepted the U.S. revised draft the privileges presently enjoyed by the Korean employees of the U.S. armed forces would be diminished.

14. When asked to explain how the privileges would be diminished, Mr. Chang replied that subparagraph (d) of Agreed Minute #5 would eliminate the right of the employees to strike. Mr. Habib replied that the provisions of sub-paragraph (d) were normal procedures which were provided for in ROK labor laws. Mr. Chang said that the ROK law provided that disruptive practices were not allowed for a specific number of days. However, argument concerning a labor dispute could drag on and on in the Joint Committee.

15. Mr. Reed stated that it was his understanding that the ROK law provided that during mediation and arbitration procedures, there was no right to strike, even after the 20-day and 30-day cooling-off periods. Mr. Chang replied that if conciliation failed, the right to strike after a certain number of days existed. Mr. Reed pointed out that the concept of a limited period was not contained in the U.S. draft. Article 7, Chapter 2 of the ROK Labor Disputes Act provides that there shall be no disruptive action unless mediation or arbitration efforts fail. The procedures proposed by the U.S. negotiators were intended to lead to the settlement of disputes. The U.S. negotiators did not believe that any strike would be justified if these procedures were followed.

16. Mr. Chang replied that the Korean negotiators would study the U.S. proposals. The meeting was then adjourned with the understanding that the Korean negotiators would call the next meeting.

외교사실 년표 작성 자료

(주둔군지위협정 체결교섭회의)

64. 1. 9.	제 38 차	미주둔군지위협정체결을 위한 한미 실무자교섭회의 개최
64. 1. 17.	제 39 차	"
64. 1. 24.	제 40 차	"
64. 2. 6.	제 41 차	"
64. 2. 14.	제 42 차	"
64. 2. 20.	제 43 차	"
64. 2. 28.	제 44 차	"
64. 3. 6.	제 45 차	"
64. 3. 13.	제 46 차	"
64. 3. 20.	제 47 차	"
64. 4. 3.	제 48 차	"
64. 4. 10.	제 49 차	"
64. 4. 23.	제 50 차	"
64. 5. 5.	제 51 차	"
64. 5. 20.	제 52 차	"
64. 5. 28.	제 53 차	"
64. 6. 9.	제 54 차	"
64. 6. 19.	제 55 차	"
64. 6. 26.	제 56 차	"
64. 7. 8.	제 57 차	"
64. 7. 16.	제 58 차	"
64. 7. 28.	제 59 차	"
64. 8. 7.	제 60 차	"
64. 8. 14.	제 61 차	"
64. 8. 28.	제 62 차	"
64. 9. 11.	제 63 차	"
64. 10. 16.	제 64 차	"
64. 10. 23.	제 65 차	"
64. 11. 24.	제 66 차	"

0273

64. 12. 16. 제 67 회 "

64. 12. 23. 제 68 회 "

0274

외교문서 비밀해제: 주한미군지위협정(SOFA) 9
주한미군지위협정(SOFA) 서명 및 발효 9

초판인쇄 2024년 03월 15일
초판발행 2024년 03월 15일

지은이 한국학술정보(주)
펴낸이 채종준
펴낸곳 한국학술정보(주)
주 소 경기도 파주시 회동길 230(문발동)
전 화 031-908-3181(대표)
팩 스 031-908-3189
홈페이지 http://ebook.kstudy.com
E-mail 출판사업부 publish@kstudy.com
등 록 제일산-115호(2000. 6. 19)

ISBN 979-11-7217-020-2 94340
979-11-7217-011-0 94340 (set)

책에 대한 더 나은 생각, 끊임없는 고민, 독자를 생각하는 마음으로 보다 좋은 책을 만들어갑니다.